Noir Urbanisms

Publications in partnership with
the Shelby Cullom Davis Center at Princeton University

Noir Urbanisms

Dystopic Images of the Modern City

EDITED BY
Gyan Prakash

PRINCETON UNIVERSITY PRESS   Princeton and Oxford

Copyright © 2010 by Princeton University Press

Published by Princeton University Press, 41 William Street, Princeton, New Jersey 08540

In the United Kingdom: Princeton University Press, 6 Oxford Street, Woodstock, Oxfordshire OX20 1TW

press.princeton.edu

Library of Congress Cataloging-in-Publication Data

Noir urbanisms : dystopic images of the modern city / edited by Gyan Prakash.

  p. cm.

  Includes bibliographical references and index.

  ISBN 978-0-691-14643-0 (hardback : alk. paper) — ISBN 978-0-691-14644-7 (pbk. : alk. paper)

1. Film noir—History and criticism. 2. Cities and towns in motion pictures. 3. City and town life in motion pictures. I. Prakash, Gyan.

  PN1995.9.F54N68 2010

  791.43'655—dc22   2010002331

British Library Cataloging-in-Publication Data is available

This book has been composed in Minion with Myriad display

Printed on acid-free paper. ∞

Printed in the United States of America

10 9 8 7 6 5 4 3 2 1

Contents

■

Noir Urbanisms

Introduction

∎

Imaging the Modern City, Darkly

GYAN PRAKASH

As the world becomes increasingly urban, dire predictions of an impending crisis have reached a feverish pitch. Alarming statistics on the huge and unsustainable gap between the rates of urbanization and economic growth in the global South is seen to spell disaster. The unprecedented agglomeration of the poor produces the specter of an unremittingly bleak "planet of slums."[1] Monstrous megacities do not promise the pleasures of urbanity but the misery and strife of the Hobbesian jungle. The medieval maxim that the city air makes you free appears quaint in view of the visions of an approaching urban anarchy. Urbanists write about fortified "privatopias" erected by the privileged to wall themselves off from the imagined resentment and violence of the multitude. Instead of freedom, the unprecedented urbanization of poverty seems to promise only division and conflict. The image of the modern city as a distinct and bounded entity lies shattered as market-led globalization and media saturation dissolve boundaries between town and countryside, center and periphery.[2] From the ruins of the old ideal of the city as a space of urban citizens there emerges, sphinx-like, a "Generic City" of urban consumers.[3]

As important as it is to assess the substance of these readings of contemporary trends in urbanization, it is equally necessary to examine their dark form as a mode of urban representation. This form is not new. Since the turn of the twentieth century, dystopic images have figured prominently in literary, cinematic, and sociological representations of the modern city. In these portrayals, the city often appears as dark, insurgent (or forced into total obedience), dysfunctional (or forced into machine-like functioning), engulfed in ecological and social crises, seduced by capitalist consumption, paralyzed by crime, wars, class, gender, and racial conflicts, and subjected to excessive technological and technocratic control. What characterizes such representations is not just their bleak mood but also their mode of interpretation, which ratchets up a critical reading of specific historical conditions to diagnose crisis and catastrophe.

This volume returns to the history of dark representations of the city in order to explore them as forms of urban criticism. There exists, of course, a sophisticated body of scholarship on the dystopic imagination as a distinct literary form. Unlike utopian texts, which transport us to an imaginary future that indicts the present, the dystopic imagination places us directly in a terrifying world to alert us of the danger that the future holds if we do not recognize its symptoms in the present.[4] In this sense, a utopian desire animates dystopic texts. While recognizing the critical potential of the dystopic imagination, this volume examines it as a form of urban representation; the modern city, after all, appears to be an instantiation of a dystopic form of society.

The approach is global because such is the history of modernity. For this reason, we do not limit our consideration to the classic image of urban dystopia, which emerged as a specific literary and cinematic construct in the West. Nor do we offer a taxonomical classification of urban dystopia, for that would confer a global status to a provincial cultural and historical phenomenon. Thus, while analyzing urban dystopia as a particular form, the collection treats the term metaphorically to expand the historical and geographical range of dark criticisms of the city. Moving from Germany to Mexico to Japan to India to South Africa and China, the contributors read urban representations historically and explore their strengths and limits as critiques.

The essays are united by their focus on representations of the city and move from considering the images of the city to the imagined city, from urban imaginations to urban imaginaries. This is not because they are unaware of the specific intellectual histories associated with these terms; rather, it is because they recognize that modernity is inseparable from image production and circulation. Photography, cinema, print, and advertising have trained our senses to experience modern life through images. Even if we do not always realize it, visuality is integral to our knowledge and practice. It is thus that the image of the city imperceptibly becomes the imagined space in which we live. Visuality saturates the symbols, values, and desires that make up urban society as an imaginary institution.

The title of the volume registers cinema's prominent role in inserting visuality in the experience of modern life. Of course, film noir is a specific form. But because of the wide circulation of its classic uses of light and dark spaces, the term "noir" has acquired a wider and a more varied meaning. While film scholars use the term to identify specific cinematic techniques, the practitioners in other disciplines deploy it metaphorically to refer to a grim, dystopic reality. Keeping in mind the specific genealogy of noir, the volume also places it in a broader interdisciplinary register. This is in line with our approach to both recognize the pivotal role of the production and circulation of media representations in modernity and to scrutinize the historical reach and meanings of their dark, visual significations. The contributors ask: What pictures of urban society do these representations bring into view? What do they express and conceal? How were these images produced and circulated, and what were their meanings?

Modernism and Urban Dystopia

Modernism was a uniquely metropolitan phenomenon. Emerging from the tumultuous changes of the twentieth century, modernism represented the high-culture expressions of the city. As writers, poets, artists, architects, and filmmakers breathed the air of rapidly changing and growing cities, they were exhilarated by the new urban experience. For poets and novelists, the street appeared as the magical stage for the enactment of modern life. They found the chaotic energy of the traffic and the maelstrom of the crowd awe-inspiring. Writers and filmmakers alike were fascinated by the clockwork-like rhythm of daily life as thousands of workers and office-goers entered and exited their workspaces at regular hours. As technology reshaped the cityscape, the spirit of architects and designers soared. Harnessing the awesome power of science and technology, they planned utopias of perfectly designed and synchronized housing, streets, traffic, and artifacts of daily life.

But a shadow always hung over the modernist halo. Inequity and oppression punctuated the drama of freedom on the street. The experience of immersion in the crowd produced feelings of estrangement and atomization, and the gathering of the multitude could easily become part of the spectacle of mass society that capitalism staged. The rhythm of daily urban life might suggest a symphony, but it also spelled the boredom of routinization. The awesome promise of technology and planned futures was also terrifying. One way in which modernism expressed this terror was through the image of urban dystopia. Its dark visions of mass society forged by capitalism and technology, however, did not necessarily mean a forthright rejection of the modern metropolis but a critique of the betrayal of its utopian promise. The dystopic form functioned as a critical discourse that embraced urban modernity rather than reject it.

Eric Weitz writes: "Weimar was Berlin, Berlin Weimar."[5] The experience of urban modernity was global, but it was in Weimar Germany where it was felt with particular intensity. Appropriately, then, Anton Kaes opens the section on the urban dystopias of modernism with an examination of Fritz Lang's 1927 film *Metropolis*. Lang's film has been the subject of much scholarly study, and its apocalyptic images of bleakness and destruction have never ceased to inspire science fiction and dystopic films. Kaes returns to the film to read in it the biblical imagery of the destruction of the Tower of Babel in the Book of Genesis and the extinction of the city of Babylon in the Book of Revelation. He argues that the biblical reference served to suggest that only the apocalyptic destruction of the dystopic city held the promise of a new beginning. This dystopia was the Machine City, the utopia of technology ratcheted up several notches to extinguish human agency altogether. Lang achieves this representation by ingeniously bringing together the city, the machine, and the technological apparatus of cinema. His dystopic city is a purely cinematic creation, accomplished with dissolves, fades, high camera angles, sharp cuts, and shots of moving pistons, streaks of light, and mechanical parts superimposed over the image of the cityscape.

Embodying the power of technology that it critiques, *Metropolis* is caught between being enthralled and frightened by the machinic big city. Thus, Kaes points out, the last image of the destruction of the largest building, called the "New Tower of Babel" in *Metropolis*, ends by repeating the inscription from the beginning of the scene: "Great is the world and its Creator! And great is Man!" When the film ends with the apocalyptic destruction of the city and the start of a new future, we have been warned of what modernity could become. But the biblical imagery of the apocalypse locates the source of destruction not in human actions or historical forces but in the malfunction of the machine. The dystopic form does not completely reject technology, only its excessive and dehumanizing development into the Machine City.

James Donald points to another impulse in modernism's dystopic moment by examining its encounter with the sounds of the city and its machines in early twentieth-century Europe. Reading the modernist writers' responses to the "hell of modern urban noise," he finds the utopian-dystopian binarism too constricting. The dystopic strain in their response to the noise of factory sirens and electric streetcars did not signify an opposition to utopia but an acknowledgment of the impossibility of perfection. With such an approach, Donald interprets the dystopic elements in modernist writings on urban noise as attempts to train the senses to the new experiences of the modern city. This training was a process of translation that sought solutions posed by unfamiliar sounds. It involved gaining a sociological and aesthetic understanding of emerging sounds of the Machine Age. It entailed coming to grips with the new sensory experience of hearing the working of machines, the babel of immigrant tongues in the city, the hiss of the radio, the mechanically reproduced sound of the gramophone, and jazz. In the modernists' dystopian response to the shock and stimuli of the modern city, Donald hears a note of "affective diagnosis," a lesson in coming to terms with what Emily Thompson calls the "soundscape of modernity."[6]

With Rubén Gallo's essay, we turn to modernism's international career in Mexico. Modernist cultural production through cameras, typewriters, radios, and print had made its appearance in Mexico after the armed conflicts of the early twentieth century. A utopian desire to transform society through technology took hold of Mexican artists.[7] They believed that technological modernism would propel the country into the future, shaking off the burden of its premodern past. Gallo writes about the debris of Mexican urban architectural utopia as it collapses into a dystopia in the 1960s. The dystopia he examines is not the one that the modernists imagined but the ruins of their utopian plans in Mexico City.

Gallo begins with Rem Koolhaas's typically provocative proposal for Paris: raze ("liberate") an entire district of the city and make it available to an urban planner willing to conceive projects for the emptied space. What Paris promptly rejected, Mexico City had already experienced. Through its history, large parts of the city had been regularly razed and turned into a tabula rasa available for new architecture. Gallo focuses on the case of the modernist housing complex of Tlatelolco in Mexico City. The architect was Mario Pani, who had been trained in Paris, where Le Corbusier's idea of *la ville radieuse* made a deep impression on him. On his return to Mexico City, he won several government projects for working-class housing in which he implemented Le Corbusier's ideas. The biggest project was the Tlatelolco housing complex, consisting of fifteen thousand apartments, contained in several superblocks and spread over several thousand meters of a decaying neighborhood. Two years after its completion in 1966, it became the site of a tragic massacre of students who had gathered to protest undemocratic rule. In 1985, a powerful earthquake leveled many of the buildings. Gallo argues that the ruins of Tlatelolco serve as the memory of utopian dreams returning as dystopic nightmares. The megalomania of modernist architecture is revealed as the site of political oppression and disaster. Like the urban dystopia in *Metropolis*, the relics of modernist architecture in Mexico City point to the utopian promise gone out of control.

What emerges clearly from these three accounts of the experiences with technological urban modernity is that dystopic representations afforded varying critiques. The crucial variable seems to have been the room that they left open for human intervention. *Metropolis*, produced with the technological apparatus of cinema, offered a critique of the Machine City while retaining a utopian belief in technology and leaving no room for human agency. If the modernist writers, about whom Donald writes, responded to the "hellish noise" of the modern city by coming to terms with it, by training their senses, this was because they did not confer autonomous power to the machine; they placed themselves in the dystopic soundscape and learned to make a place for the sound of the machine in their sensory experience. Gallo, too, demonstrates that it was the tragic massacre of protesting students that brought the technological utopia of Tlatelolco down to earth. When the earthquake turned it into rubble, people saw in the natural catastrophe a just end to the authoritarian fantasies of architectural modernism. Fittingly, it is in Mexico City that we see the dystopic debris of technological modernism that once expressed Europe's global hegemony.

The Aesthetics of the Dark City

Writing about cinema, Walter Benjamin stated: "Our bars and city streets, our offices and furnished rooms, our railroad stations and our factories seemed to close relentlessly around us. Then came film and exploded this prison-world with the dynamite of the split-second, so that now we can set off calmly on journeys of adventure among its far-flung debris."[8] He pointed out that with such techniques as close-ups, enlargement, slow motion, and editing, cinema rearranged the cityscape and brought to light "entirely new structures of matter" and "unknown aspects within them."[9] This recomposed representation of the urban experience by film was related to cultural transformations in perception in the modern city, "changes that are experienced on the scale of private existence by each passerby in big-city traffic."[10] In this sense, cinema, according to Benjamin, was not restricted to images on-screen in the darkened theater but formed part of the larger apparatus of perception in the modern city.[11]

As films like Walter Ruttmann's *Berlin: Symphony of a Great City* (1927) and Dziga Vertov's *Man with a Movie Camera* (1929) deployed this perceptual apparatus, they also gave expression to a sense of the urban uncanny,[12] a feeling that the urban order of reason, transparency, and technology contained within it the seeds of discontinuity, instability, disorder, and chaos. *Metropolis* expressed this uncanny in a dystopic form. Since then, different narrative and aesthetic genres of films, such as sci-fi and film noir, have developed to offer dark representations of urban space. The essays in this section analyze the cinema of darkness as the "archive of the city," to use Ranjani Mazumdar's evocative term.[13] How do we locate these films? What are the social imaginaries contained in their aesthetics of darkness?

Mark Shiel opens this section with an essay on the geographical underpinnings of film noir, the Hollywood crime dramas of the 1940s and 1950s. Using a black-and-white visual style inspired by German expressionism, noir offered a distinct aesthetic representation of changing postwar American cities. With its signature use of lighting to not only define space but also inflect it with psychological character and motivations, film noir projected a mood of urban anxiety and nihilism. It represented the city with images of deserted streets, crumbling neighborhoods, shadowy spaces and glittering skylines, petty criminals, elliptically speaking hard-boiled detectives, and characters with ambiguous sexual and moral motivations.

Historians and film studies scholars suggest that the noir style expressed the unsettling experience of postwar capitalist restructuring of urban life. The old city appeared irretrievably changed with the growing presence of African Americans. Feeling besieged, the whites fled to the suburbs, intensifying the dispersal of the population. Capitalist modernization and the rise of big corporations rendered social relations more opaque. Emerging in this context, film noir expressed nostalgia for the vanishing city and fear of the emergent urban forms.[14] Shiel accepts this interpretation but wishes to read the genre as more than a representation of generic American urban modernity. Rather than treat film noir as the expression of an iconic urban darkness, Shiel reads it in relation to its specific geography. Analyzing films produced in the decade from 1940 to 1950, he concludes that the number of films set in small towns and in the Midwest and the Northeast declined, whereas the proportion set in big cities and in the Southwest and California increased. More specifically, New York gave way to Los Angeles. A rightward drift in politics and anti-union actions by the Hollywood studio moguls, Shiel argues, enabled the emergence of the LA noir: there was a "real dystopian analogue" to the dystopia of the reel. The "the hidden meaning" of the dark city on-screen was the offscreen noir picture of the rightward capitalist restructuring of American urban life, Los Angeles, and Hollywood.

With William Tsutsui's essay, we turn from the dystopic city of postwar film noir to the fictional destruction of Tokyo in Japanese films, television series, and animation after World War II. The attention turns from the low-key, black-and-white visual style to the aesthetics of horror and science fiction. Like film noir, however, Japanese doom culture does not refer to an actual city but offers iconic sci-fi representations of an urban dystopia. We see Tokyo destroyed again and again on-screen by giant tidal waves, fires, floods, volcanoes, alien invasions, giant monsters, robots, toxic pollution, and nuclear explosion. Of course, destruction is not alien to Tokyo's history. During its five-and-a-half centuries of existence, fires, firebombing, and earthquakes have repeatedly destroyed the city.

Scholars and writers have interpreted Japan's doom culture in relation to the experience of the atomic annihilation of Hiroshima and Nagasaki that looms large in Japanese memory. The prime example, of course, is Godzilla, the 164-foot radioactive monster reptile that rises from the Tokyo bay to destroy the city in the 1954 Japanese film *Gojira*. But Godzilla was not all. Tsutsui points to the appearance of several other monsters on cinema and television screens, wreaking havoc on the city. The fear of a nuclear cataclysm is plain to see in these fantasies of urban annihilation. While acknowledging the gloomy influences of these memories and fears, Tsutsui argues that a note of millenarian hope and optimism pervades doom culture. Rather than relentless pessimism and nihilism, the depictions of urban ruins and mushroom clouds rising over Tokyo contain within them the pop millenarianism of Japan's postwar sci-fi dreamers. By expressing nostalgia for Japan's wartime destruction, these visions of doom broke taboos and fantasized about a new future. Thus, much like *Metropolis*, a new beginning follows destruction in several monster films. The city spontaneously regenerates after destruction, ready for the movie cameras to roll again and the next monster to once again go on a rampage. In the end, then, the sci-fi aesthetic offers a certain critical mood, a utopian desire that animates images of urban annihilation.

We turn from sci-fi images of urban dystopia to neorealism in Li Zhang's essay on the aesthetics of cinematic representation of postsocialist urban transition in China. She argues that the classic forms of dystopic representations familiar to the West—noir and sci-fi—are rarely invoked in China. Because of the Maoist state's control over culture and media, Western forms of dystopic images were never widely circulated. Thus, when the Sixth-Generation Chinese filmmakers emerged in the 1990s, they developed as an independent cinema movement and fashioned a distinct critical form. The Sixth-Generation has been called an urban generation because it has focused on the urban experience. While drawing on the noir style, this cinema mounts its criticism of China's urban transition under market economy by pulling the lives and struggles of the "insignificant" people into the frame. While films of the New Documentary movement present bleak and melancholic images of urban dislocation, dispossession, and abandonment, a fictional film like *Suzhou River* presents Shanghai as a gloomy and decaying industrial wasteland.

With an anthropologist's feel for changing urban conditions, Zhang shows how the melancholia of the independent cinema expresses the experience of loss and disorientation. The city of these films marks a distance from both the socialist utopia of the Maoist era and the glittering images of wealth and economic success in postsocialist China. Zhang calls the critical force of the Sixth-Generation cinema "post-ideological." By this she does not mean that it is beyond ideology but that it advocates neither socialism nor capitalism. Yet, developing in the shadow of socialism, this cinema expresses the predicaments of the postsocialist world. The filmmakers adopt the point of view of urban migrants and the "insignificant" people to represent a critique of China's plunge into market utopia.

Ranjani Mazumdar closes this section with an essay on what she calls the Urban Fringe of Bombay cinema. As the largest film industry in the world, Bombay cinema has been known for its melodrama. Mazumdar focuses on three recent films that consciously break from the prevalent form to paint a landscape of urban dystopia. She argues that at the core of these films lies the city of Mumbai as it copes with urban violence while undergoing tumultuous transformation under market-driven globalization. During the 1950s, Hindi cinema's crime melodramas often drew on film noir to represent the urban experience of inequality, dislocation, and disillusionment. In her earlier work, Mazumdar analyzed the figure of the urban vigilante in the Hindi cinema of the 1970s and described the images of the "panoramic interior" and the "gangster city" with which filmmakers grappled with the city under globalization.[15] She identifies the Urban Fringe as a "non-genealogical" form that emerges at the beginning of this century in the wake of a series of contemporary transformations linked to globalization.

Nishikant Kamat's *Dombivli Fast*, Homi Adjania's *Being Cyrus*, and Anurag Kashyap's *No Smoking*, says Mazumdar, are films that have emerged on the periphery of the dominant film industry. These films are experimental, innovative, and driven by certain tendencies in international cinema. With an analysis of the formal codes deployed by these films, Mazumdar shows how the Urban Fringe offers images of friction, collision, and the grotesque to paint a dystopic imagination unavailable through the vision of Bombay's popular melodramas. Thus, *Dombivli Fast* offers us the violence that simmers under the machine-like daily life in the city. *Being Cyrus* turns the urban interior inside out, showing a grotesque private world as a mirror of the publicly visible city. In Kashyap's Kafkaesque *No Smoking*, the city appears as an instantiation of an oppressive order of surveillance, rationality, and governmentality. For Mazumdar, the crisis of the human emerges as the overall thematic arc in the three films. This theme turns the cinematic city of Mumbai into a twisted, nightmarish landscape where the human struggles for survival.

The essays in this section extend the meaning of urban dystopia to include in it other depictions of darkness. This underscores the historical specificity and meaning of cinematic conventions as forms of urban representations. Thus, Shiel resists reading film noir as the expression of a generic American urban bleakness and identifies the offscreen rightward restructuring of capitalism and the studio system in the rise of LA noir. Tsutsui's counterintuitive interpretation that postwar Japanese doom culture articulates the utopian desire of sci-fi dreamers reminds us of the particular historical meanings of *Godzilla* and other monster films in Japan. Zhang notes the remoteness of the classic conventions of urban dystopia in Chinese films about the contemporary experience of the city. The Sixth-Generation filmmakers in China draw on

noir images, but they also adopt neorealist and documentary styles to critique the shining image of the city of neoliberal capitalism. In Mumbai too,
Mazumdar shows, it is not the classic dystopic form but images of collision,
friction, and the grotesque that represent the urban experience. While drawing from international styles, these portraits in the Urban Fringe cinema draw
their meanings by breaking from the codes of melodrama. In short, the essays
collectively show that while cinema functions as a global language, particular
historical situations have fashioned specific aesthetic devices to offer critical
visions of the city.

Imaging Urban Crisis

Crisis signifies a turning point, the irruption of a moment of stress, vola-
tility, and disintegration. What is particular about the experience of urban
crisis under modernity is its expression in images. Marx wrote insightfully
about commodity fetishism, but it was Walter Benjamin who developed this
insight into the idea of the phantasmagoria as an allegory of modernity, viewing commodity culture as "a projection—not a reflection—of the economy"
and understanding "the centrality, the constitutive force, of the image within
modernity."[16] If modern urban society is to be apprehended through its image life, then it is appropriate that contributors turn to representations of the
experience of urban crisis.

David R. Ambaras offers an account of the critical representation of
Tokyo's urban experience as it grew rapidly during the 1920s and 1930s to
become the showpiece of Japan's imperial and cosmopolitan modernity. Dramatic urban growth and changing urban forms were accompanied by a proliferation in the city's representation in geographical gazettes, urban plans,
social surveys, professional bulletins, general-interest books and magazines,
popular guides, movies, photographs, art, and the popular press. Drawing on
James Donald's argument that the city exists in the traffic between the urban
fabric, representation, and imagination,[17] Ambaras sketches the experience of
Tokyo as a place of anxiety and insecurity, of fear and horror, not progress.
This experience was rooted in the "topographies of distress" that the daily
press and popular magazines produced by sensationalizing dark and transgressive spaces and figures. Seizing on a spate of suspicious infant deaths in
the poor neighborhood of Iwanosaka, the popular press fashioned and circulated dystopic images of everyday urban life in the slum.

With the historian's instinct for context, Ambaras locates the media's
dark portraits of Iwanosaka against the background of the economic depression. But he does not read off the context of socioeconomic turmoil in the

texts of cultural representations. Instead, Ambaras reconstructs the history of image production, tracing connections between the media portraits of Iwanosaka and the representation of slums as monstrous, living hells by classic Western texts and Japanese writings on working-class life. The infant deaths crystallized these connections, resulting in the representation of Iwanosaka as a space of miserable tenements, sinister alleyways, beggars, prostitutes, and criminals. Fear, insecurity, and violence stalked the slum. This was not the experience of those who lived in Iwanosaka, but the representation of middle-class authors and readers who understood the neighborhood through these sensational and shocking images. Nevertheless, the Iwanosaka images, and the *fait divers* more broadly, exerted an anxious influence because, in view of the endemic economic crisis, the petty bourgeois readers could see in them the possibility of their own social collapse or descent into deviance. Thus, the portrait of the slum as the embodiment of urban horror emerged as a critique of urban conditions.

The dystopic image of the slum also figures prominently in contemporary pictures of urban crisis in cities of the global South. Jennifer Robinson subjects these representations to a trenchant critique to reveal their limitations. She points out that current urban writings suggest that dystopia is not a faraway, fictional place, in the future. Rather, it is already here, in Third World cities. Robinson acknowledges that Mike Davis's contemporary classic, *Planet of Slums*,[18] which envisions the urban future in light of the world's poorest regions, offers a biting critique of the disastrous effects of neoliberal capitalist globalization. However, it is also a perspective from the metropolitan West, alerting its inhabitants to what is coming their way from somewhere else. That somewhere else, she suggests, is typically Africa, a living dystopia of grinding poverty, exploitation, disorder, and violence. Unlike Rem Koolhaas, who sees the potential for innovative urban design in the chaos of Lagos, Davis views African cities as maps of a Dickensian hell that threaten to overrun the planet.

As against this disabling image of the "planet of slums," Robinson turns to the fiction of the South African writer Ivan Vladislavić to identify critical and enabling representations of Johannesburg's post-apartheid transition. Vladislavić's novel, *The Restless Supermarket*, concerns Hillbrow, a high-rise, low-income white neighborhood that experienced a change in its racial composition, first through the 1980s and then with the end of apartheid. Unlike the dystopic writings of the current urbanists, Vladislavić does not offer either a singular image of the city or the perspective of an outside narrator. He does not present the transition as a change from apartheid dystopia to post-apartheid utopia. Moving between the viewpoints of old and new residents, white and black, order and disorder, and real and fantastic spaces, Vladislavić offers a complex, multivalent picture of Hillbrow's changeover, as well as a series of possible futures. We are not immobilized by the fearsome image of a dystopia with no exit.

Ravi Sundaram's essay brings the volume to a close with an account of the image of an urban breakdown in Delhi. He also begins with a critique of Mike Davis's apocalyptic scenario of urbanism in the periphery, pointing out that this is an image that urban planners and the old, reformist elites have adopted with a sense of melancholic resignation in the face of turbulent urban change. Classic modernist allegories of urban crisis, imaged in portraits of infrastructural decline and factories enveloped in ghostly silence, are of little use in the face of a heady mix of exploding urbanization and growing media sensorium. Dystopian sci-fi landscapes of conflicts between machines and humankind, darkness and light, are too outmoded and static for the experience of proliferation, implosion, and informality that characterize the urbanism of the global South.

Sundaram offers a reading of an unhinged, wild urbanism that emerged in Delhi during the 1980s and the 1990s. Under proliferating squatter settlements, illegal markets, and informal work, the dreams of modernist planners and bureaucratic elites unraveled. Gripped with a sense of urban crisis, the elites periodically unleash the force of law, bringing to light a vast, unauthorized city, characterized by Sundaram as a pirate city. Enmeshed in the urban sensorium of cassettes, mobile telephony, video and digital technologies, print, and television, this city is so deeply entangled in the pragmatic and viral media life that the classic dualisms of public-private, plan-counterplan, and order-chaos cannot capture its kinetic movement and elusiveness. It is this dynamic media city of informality, proliferation, speed, piracy, and commodity that appears in the sensational image of an out-of-control, delirious urban order, creating an endless loop between the material and the imaginary. Sundaram argues that in the face of this constellation that folds into itself the experience of urban crisis, the classic dystopic critique falls short.

The location of Sundaram's analysis at the level of the experience of the media city highlights this section's shared concern with the imaging of urban crisis. Treating critiques of urbanism at this level permits the contributors to interrogate the image-truth of the slum and the delirious urban order. This allows them to read what these images both disclosed and concealed. Thus, we learn from Ambaras that the while the projection of the slum as the iconic image of Tokyo's modernity undercut the narrative of progress, it also served as an elitist representation that expressed the fear of crime and immorality that they saw lurking in the poor neighborhood. Robinson and Sundaram also subject "the planet of slums" to a critical reading, but they do so by mounting counterimages of other urban experiences, thereby achieving a "profane illumination" of the representation of urban crisis.

What emerges clearly from this interdisciplinary exploration extending from Weimar urbanism to the media city of contemporary Delhi, from modernist architecture in Mexico City and film noir in Los Angeles to post-apartheid Johannesburg, from the slum images and sci-fi doom culture in Tokyo to dystopic landscapes of Chinese and Bombay cinema, is an uncanny alchemy between dark representations and the urban experience. Significantly, this uncanny alchemy is registered in the realm of images composed by photography, art, cinema, and architecture, for it is here that, as James Donald suggests,[19] the familiar turns unfamiliar, the city of planning and order gives way to the unsettling influence of dark mysteries and memories. As the contributors analyze the work of this urban alchemy in specific historical and global contexts, they reveal different shades and meanings of the uncanny. We learn that the opening that dystopic images provide for human agency inflects their critical meaning. Equally relevant is their aesthetics, developed in particular historical and formal situations, which offer portraits ranging from urban anxiety and nihilism to utopian desire, from scenes of dislocation and dispossession to "warped spaces" in which the urban uncanny appears as the nightmarish crisis of the human.[20] Finally, this volume shows that images of urban crisis, to return to the theme we began with, function as urban allegories that express the fear of the "unintended city,"[21] the city of slums and media sensorium. The cities of darkness, it turns out, reveal as much as they hide.

Notes

Thanks are due to David Ambaras and Ravi Sundaram for their comments on an earlier draft of this essay. I am also grateful to the two anonymous reviewers for their criticisms and suggestions.

1 Mike Davis, *Planet of Slums* (New York: Verso, 2006).

2 For a historical examination of the classic image of the modern city, see Gyan Prakash, introduction to Gyan Prakash and Kevin Kruse, eds., *The Spaces of the Modern City: Imaginaries, Politics, and Everyday Life* (Princeton: Princeton University Press, 2008), 1–18.

3 For "Generic City," see Rem Koolhaas, "The Generic City," in *S,M,L,XL* (New York: Monacelli Press, 1998), 1248–64. Frederic Jameson offers an insightful reading of Koolhaas's urbanism in "Future City," *New Left Review* 21 (May–June 2003): 65–79.

4 For careful and insightful recent interpretations of dystopia as a form, see Tom Moylan, *Scraps of the Untainted Sky* (Boulder, CO: Westview Press, 2000); and Raffaella Baccolini and Tom Moylan, eds., *Dark Horizons: Science Fiction and the Dystopian Imagination* (New York: Routledge, 2003).

5 Eric Weitz, *Weimar Germany: Promise and Tragedy* (Princeton: Princeton University Press, 2007), 41. On the cultural matrix of Weimar urban modernity, see Janet Ward, *Weimar Surfaces: Urban Visual Culture in 1920s Germany* (Berkeley: University of California Press, 2001).

6 Emily Thompson, *The Soundscape of Modernity: Architectural Acoustics and the Culture of Listening in America, 1900–1933* (Cambridge, MA: MIT Press, 2002).

7 Rubén Gallo's *Mexican Modernity: The Avant-Garde and the Technological Revolution* (Cambridge, MA: MIT Press, 2005) offers a splendid account of the dreams and repressions of Mexican modernism.

8 Walter Benjamin, "The Work of Art in the Age of Its Reproductibility," in *Walter Benjamin: Selected Writings*, ed. Michael Jennings (Cambridge, MA: Belknap Press of Harvard University Press, 2002), 3:117.

9 Ibid.

10 Ibid., 3:132.

11 In recent years, film and cultural studies scholars have paid focused attention to the affinities between cinema and the modern city that Benjamin theorized. See, for example, David B. Clarke, ed., *The Cinematic City* (New York: Routledge, 1997); James Donald, "Light in Dark Spaces: Cinema and City," in his *Imagining the Modern City* (Minneapolis: University of Minnesota Press, 1999), 63–94; and the two important edited collections by Mark Shiel and Tony Fitzmaurice, *Cinema and the City* (Oxford: Blackwell, 2001) and *Screening the City* (New York: Verso, 2003).

12 Donald, *Imagining the Modern City*, 82–84; see also Carsten Strathausen, "Uncanny Spaces: The City in Rutmann and Vertov," in Shiel and Fitzmaurice, *Screening the City*, 15–40.

13 Ranjani Mazumdar, *Bombay Cinema: An Archive of the City* (Minneapolis: University of Minnesota Press, 2007).

14 Edward Dimenberg, *Film Noir and the Spaces of Modernity* (Cambridge, MA: Harvard University Press, 2004), 7. The literature on film noir is vast, but see Kelly Oliver and Benigno Trigo, *Noir Anxiety* (Minneapolis: University of Minnesota Press, 2003); Eric Avila, *Popular Culture in the Age of White Flight: Fear and Fantasy in Suburban Los Angeles* (Berkeley: University of California Press, 2004); and Sheri Chinen Biesen, *Blackout: World War II and the Origins of Film Noir* (Baltimore: Johns Hopkins University Press, 2005).

15 Mazumdar, *Bombay Cinema*.

16 Derek Gregory, *Geographical Imaginations* (Cambridge, MA: Blackwell, 1994), 233.

17 Donald, *Imagining the Modern City*, 10.

18 Davis, *Planet of Slums*.

19 Donald, *Imagining the Modern City*, 69–73.

20 I refer here to Anthony Vidler's concept of spatial warping, which emerges in the traffic between art, film, media, and architecture. See his *Warped Space* (Cambridge, MA: MIT Press, 2001).

21 Jai Sen, "The Unintended City," *Seminar* 200 (April 1976): 38–47.

Modernism and Urban Dystopia

Chapter 1 ∎

The Phantasm of the Apocalypse

Metropolis and Weimar Modernity

ANTON KAES

Men have to destroy if they want to create anew.
—Joseph Goebbels, *Michael* (1928)

The fascination with urban dystopia and destruction has a long tradition dating back to the Book of Genesis (in which the Tower of Babel is destroyed) and the Book of Revelation (in which the city of Babylon is annihilated). Fritz Lang's *Metropolis*, which opened in Berlin in January 1927, draws its apocalyptic imagery from both the Book of Genesis and the Book of Revelation. Configuring dystopia in biblical terms, Lang offered a blueprint for the religious subtext of most science fiction films today. Following *Metropolis*, these films use apocalyptic motifs to dramatize modernity's nefarious consequences. Only complete devastation and erasure of the old assures, as in the Book of Revelation, a new utopia. Most apocalyptic films, including *Metropolis*, try to "restart" the program that crashed: the catastrophe is usually followed by a brief glimpse of a new beginning, one that holds the promise of an alternative to dystopia.

In both its secular-anarchist and messianic variations, apocalyptic thinking is fundamentally anti-historical. The end does not come as a predictable consequence of historical forces or personal actions but as rupture, shock, and unexpected intervention—a traumatic event that can only be explained after the fact. However, since cataclysms tend to destroy observers along with measuring instruments, apocalypse is less an event to be reported than an event to be *imagined*. For two thousand years, the phantasm of an impending apocalypse has inspired prophets, painters, poets, and, for the past hundred years, ever more filmmakers. As a medium that permits the hyperrealistic representation of fully fantasized scenarios, film has proven especially fertile ground for imagining urban destruction. Itself a product of the technological era, film has always shown a strange ambivalence toward technology: it depends on it (both the film camera and the projection apparatus are highly complex machines), but it invariably condemns it. Film's structural affinity with fast-moving, shock-prone city life has produced movies that both glorify the urban project and vilify its dystopian nature.

As *Metropolis* suggests (again following biblical tradition), big cities are sites of decadence and hubris, of volatile masses and revolutionary potential. They are also, as Paul Virilio comments in *City of Panic*,[1] naturally vulnerable and inviting targets for destruction. An *Urtext* for noir visions of the city, *Metropolis* provides an early instance of the ambivalent thrill of seeing the built environment destroyed by means of the latest technology. The modern medium of film seems intent on critiquing and even demolishing the technological modernity it depicts.

The City as Machine

From the start *Metropolis* establishes a nexus between urban space, mechanical movement, and the technical apparatus of moving pictures.[2] Lang uses compositional principles of abstract film to convey the dynamics of the big city and to literalize its precise and unflagging automatism. Low-angle panoramic shots of a cityscape are superimposed on close-ups of three pistons moving up and down. Their shafts and triangular tops invert the shape of the city's pyramidal skyscrapers and underscore on the purely cinematic level the sublime affinity between sleek buildings and metallic machines. The rhythmic, vertical movement of the pistons animates the tall structures. Suddenly three horizontal streaks of light shoot across the image, adding another, emphatically nonrepresentational layer to the composition and reminding the viewer that this film does not depict some visible reality but a constructed, strictly filmic artifact.

No human agency is visible; the mechanical parts move by themselves. Nor do we know what these machines produce. By mapping machines upon the cityscape, the first few seconds of the film graphically illustrate the city's clock-like exactness and tireless energy. But precisely because the montage equates the city with a perfectly functioning assemblage of interlocking cogwheels, it also hints at catastrophic consequences, were even the smallest part to malfunction. Pressure and precision are further emphasized by a sudden cut to a huge ten-hour clock that synchronizes movement and marks the commencement of a new ten-hour shift. The sounding of a siren, shown by a vertical burst of white steam, signals the beginning of the film's narrative, which presents various reactions to the tyranny of machines.

Lang's film stages the argument of Oswald Spengler's widely discussed book *Der Untergang des Abendlandes* (*The Decline of the West*): that the downfall of the Western world, which culminated in the apocalyptic self-destruction of World War I, was a result of the supremacy of the machine and the technological spirit. Tellingly, Spengler concludes the second and final volume of his magisterial book with a chapter simply titled "The Machine." (Volume 2 of *The Decline of the West* was published in 1922, just two years before Thea von Harbou finished the script for *Metropolis*.) In a sweeping march through world history from the Assyrians to the present, Spengler traces the emergence of a modern, mechanical worldview to its logical end: a technological war that resulted in millions of casualties caused by machine guns, mortar shells, and poison gas. For Spengler, the War's global destruction was the outcome of an inexorable world-historical process linked to the rise of instrumental rationality. In a more nuanced reaction to the mechanical age, Lang emphasizes not only the destructive potential of the machine but also, in the tradition of Italian Futurism, its beauty and energy. *Metropolis's* ambivalence toward modernity and technology may explain why it has never ceased to enthrall viewers and critics. When asked about *Metropolis* in the 1960s, Lang responded that it was the machines that interested him, not the story's fairy-tale ending.[3]

The film is indeed engrossed by the aura of machines: it animates them and gives them both human and divine form (as in Rotwang's android Maria and the fuming god Moloch, respectively). It is no surprise that the inventor plays a central role in *Metropolis*. Rotwang is modeled after a Faustian mad scientist who mingles the latest technology with black magic. For Spengler it was exactly "Faustian man" who had become "the slave of his creation"[4] after scientific progress began subjugating the factory worker. "Both become slaves, and not masters, of the machine, which now for the first time develops its devilish and occult power."[5] *Metropolis's* famed Moloch scene translates Spengler's nexus of destructive technology and ancient religion into powerful images.

The scene begins with Freder, the industrialist's privileged son, coming upon the machine hall for the first time. An extreme long shot dwarfs him, dressed in white, within the gigantic space. Turbines swirl overhead and black-clad workers stand in front of panels, moving their bodies rhythmically from left to right, servicing identical machines. Their motions are mechanical and abstracted, carrying echoes of the *Triadic Ballet*, a Bauhaus dance piece choreographed by Oskar Schlemmer in 1922.

Freder witnesses an industrial accident, which Lang stages as a gigantic bomb explosion: the force of the blast lifts one worker into the air; others are thrown down from high above. Freder runs toward them but is hurled back, blinded by the flash of light and intense smoke. In shock, he begins to hallucinate: the machine hall changes into an Orientalist-biblical scenario, in which he sees battalions of workers sacrificed to the ancient god Moloch; workers that resist are dragged up the stairs and thrown into a huge gaping hole. Lang boldly translates the Old Testament's Moloch myth into a comment about technology's inhuman demands. The reference to the gigantic machine as man-devouring Moloch also recalls World War I, when soldiers were seen as human fodder for the Moloch of war.

It bears noting that the group of half-naked, uniformly shaven men who fight against their fate in Freder's hallucination is followed by black-clad worker battalions, who echo the film's first scene. There they marched in lockstep from one shift to the next; here they move like robots to their willing extinction. The film emphasizes the terrifying automatism with which the workers accept their destiny. As Freder's hands reach out to this vision, it blurs and undulates, giving way to a scene of workers carrying their dead or wounded comrades down the stairs. In the background we see new workers taking the place of those who had become victims of the explosion—industrial work knows no pause for mourning. Nevertheless the camera cuts to Freder and briefly introduces a dimension of grief and remembrance. In a beautifully composed shot we see Freder far in the background watching, his hand clutched over his heart, as a procession of silhouetted workers passes by. They carry men on stretchers who were killed or maimed by the explosion. Freder rushes forward to intervene but it is too late.

This scene stages Freder's first traumatic shock as he enters the veritable war zone of industrial production. We see urban dystopia through his eyes—as a novice he is shell-shocked by the unpreventable explosion and his own near-death. In response to his son's fiery retelling of this traumatic experience, his father responds coldly: "Accidents happen." If the city is a giant machine (with workers as expendable parts just like the soldiers on the front), losses and disasters are no reason for despair. The dystopian dimension of the futurist mega-city could not be expressed more clearly.

The Tower of Babel

The screenplay for *Metropolis* by Lang's wife, Thea von Harbou, was completed in June 1924; the shooting lasted from May 1925 to July 1926, and the film opened on January 10, 1927. These dates situate Lang's film as a transitional work, spanning two distinct artistic movements that articulated differing attitudes toward the city: on the one hand, the Expressionist movement whose painters, poets, and dramatists created apocalyptic images of urban destruction; on the other, New Objectivity, which reevaluated technology, the machine, and the big city in positive terms. As the political turmoil of

World War I receded and influence of the United States grew, it became fashionable to embrace a new "American" modernity. *Metropolis* can be seen as a battleground on which these two contentious German reactions to urban modernity—rejection and imitation—clashed.

Metropolis evokes both the fascination of the city and the irresistible thrill of destroying it. To express this ambivalence, Lang enlists the biblical Tower of Babel as the oldest model for urban destruction fantasies and embeds the legend into its narrative as a film within a film. This three-minute sequence encapsulates in allegorical shorthand the entirety of the two-and-a-half-hour film—a visual synopsis of the conception, building, and destruction of a metropolis. From Babylon to New York, the big city has always served as a screen upon which the collective imagination could project images of devastation. More than any other city, Babylon has been an emblem for imagining the erasure of cities: from the Book of Revelation to Alfred Döblin's big-city novel of 1928, *Berlin Alexanderplatz*, which figures Berlin as a decadent, Babylonian dystopia. American movies have frequently staged the imaginary obliteration of New York, and one might even see the attack on New York's Twin Towers on September 11, 2001, as a perverse fulfillment of the destruction fantasies already present in popular memory.[6] The terrorists wished to assault the epitome of modernity and thus challenge the hubris of unbridled Western progress.

In *Metropolis*, the Tower of Babel legend is presented as part of a secret meeting of workers in a space far below the futurist world of the city. An earlier intertitle refers to old Christian catacombs. The film suggests that Metropolis, the prototypical modern mega-city, rests on the remnants of past centuries; its mythical past lies at its core and is inevitably part of the present. The film's vertical organization—the city's leaders living in luxury high above and mob-like masses in misery far below—translates modernity's radical loss of community into spatial terms. The world below the city is dark, womb-like, as if carved out of the soil, a site where mythical, occult, and premodern—but also revolutionary—forces flourish. The clandestine assembly hall is shown as a space of regression as well as revolt, a space that not coincidentally resembles an early working-class cinema.

The legend is set off from the rest of the film by rays of light streaking from all four corners of the screen—as if Lang wanted to put the film within a film in quotation marks. The last scene shows the tower in ruins. Not unlike seventeenth-century tragedy about which Walter Benjamin wrote around the same time, the film's allegory carries a didactic moral, in this case both for the working class (Do not revolt!) and for their masters (Do not exploit!). The heart, Maria claims, must mediate between the head and the hand if a functioning community is to be achieved. The workers look skeptical and are soon manipulated into a revolt. The orgy of self-destruction that follows Maria's sermon unequivocally (and ironically) demonstrates that they did not learn their lesson.

What, then, is the function of the Tower of Babel sequence? Since biblical times the Tower of Babel has served as the archetype for bold and defiant projects that challenge the natural order and exceed human scale. Oscillating between myth and fact, between architectural fantasy and archaeological reality, the Tower of Babel is the oldest visionary building, but also the newest: its audacious verticality continues to inform modern reincarnations in ever more daring skyscrapers. Not surprisingly, the tallest building in *Metropolis* is called the "New Tower of Babel." It is also not surprising that some commentators associated the destruction of the Twin Towers with the destruction of the Tower of Babel and that Daniel Libeskind, in his statement for the proposed Freedom Tower for the new World Trade Center, placed himself in a tradition of visionary architects who considered the skyscraper the "spiritual peak" of the city.[7]

The Tower of Babel legend goes back to the first book of the Old Testament. Genesis 11:1–9 tells of the descendants of Noah who decided to build a city "to make a name for themselves" and erect a tower whose top was to reach heaven. But, according to Genesis, the Lord frowned upon this hubris and confounded their languages so that they could no longer understand each other and thus could not finish the tower. "Therefore it is called Babel," Genesis states, "for there the Lord made the language of all the world babble. And from there the Lord scattered them over all the earth." This biblical legend—itself a retrospective and polemical commentary from a later Christian perspective—has engendered a rich pictorial and exegetical tradition, ranging from Pieter Bruegel's 1563 painting to Vladimir Tatlin's proposed four-hundred-meter constructivist tower in 1919 ("Monument to the Third International") and Jacques Derrida's ruminations about translation in *Des Tours de Babel*. Centered on humankind's aspiration to transcend earthly limits, it ultimately declares the impossibility of fulfilling this desire. The Tower of Babel speaks to undeterred progress and secular modernity halted by divine intervention. In spatial terms, the story is about a vertical scale that exceeds human measure. Dutch painters of the sixteenth century were fascinated by the Tower of Babel as a symbol of human labor and depicted it in ever-new variations. The best known is of course Bruegel's painting, which Fritz Lang had most certainly seen in the original in the Wiener Kunsthistorisches Museum. Bruegel's *Tower of Babel* combines features of the Roman coliseum and the Mesopotamian ziggurat temple (a building consisting of rectangular brick terraces of diminishing size) in a fantastical image that simultaneously shows the tower's construction and decay.

For the Babel scene Lang hired more than a thousand unemployed workers as extras whose shaved hair and identical clothing demonstrated the massive power that they could yield if they only had a leader. The film shows an oppressed and anonymous mass suddenly becoming an uncontrollable mob that destroys, in a single self-destructive moment, all that it had labored to build. The penultimate image of this scene is especially poignant: a sea of raised fists, filmed from a low angle to emphasize their destructive force, obscures the tower that lies in ruins. The last image, however, reinscribes the architectural aspirations by repeating the message from the beginning of the scene: "Great is the world and its Creator! And great is Man!" It is left ambiguous whether this self-assertion ("great is Man") is meant as an ironic spin on a dystopian architecture that has betrayed and negated its utopian potential.

"Death Descends on the City"

Following one of the most dazzling sequences in the film—the lascivious dance of Maria's mechanical double—Freder is shown reading a large-format book. A sudden and unmotivated close-up reveals its title: *Die Offenbarung Sankt Johannis* (*The Revelation of St. John*); it also states the book's publisher (Avalun) and place of publication (Hellerau). The precision of the information given in this insert shot is noteworthy because such a book was indeed published by Avalun Press in Dresden-Hellerau in 1923. This glimpse of documentary evidence in the middle of a highly stylized science fiction film anchors the futurist vision in its historical moment, when it was possible to buy a precious illustrated reprint of the apocalypse in a limited edition. The reference to the Book of Revelation also frames Freder's hallucination within the biblical tradition and places his private crisis in a larger theological framework. Furthermore, it illustrates the Book of Revelation's first paragraph: "Blessed is the one who reads aloud the words of the prophecy, and blessed are those who hear and who keep what is written in it; for the time is near." By intrusively pointing to the biblical apocalypse as a source, Lang also provides a key to understanding the way his narrative is structured: as a palimpsest on the Book of Revelation. He overwrites the biblical apocalypse for the modern period and interprets the dystopian city of the future through the lens of an ancient text.[8]

The sequence in question begins when Freder mistakes the robot Maria for the woman with whom he has fallen in love. Unaware of Maria's double when he discovers her in the arms of his widowed father, Freder experiences a psychological shock that Lang illustrates through a barrage of special effects— we see white circles going in and out of focus, stars exploding like bombs, and dizzyingly rotating images that offer brief glimpses of a skull playing flute on a bone, the mad visage of inventor Rotwang, the stern gaze of the father, and the multiply iterated faces of Maria. Freder loses the ground under his feet and begins a free fall through what seem to be several rings of hell, until the screen goes dark. Like so many young protagonists in the cinema of the 1920s, he ends up in a sick bed, recovering from his shock and in need of care. At the same time, Rotwang presents the female robot as a dancer to a gathering of upper-class men. The robot's dance reduces them to nothing but leering eyes, to one voracious act of collective looking. The film literalizes their being "all eyes" by cutting to a montage of a dozen eyes in extreme close-up. The dance is Rotwang's proof that the machine double cannot be distinguished from its human original. Although Freder only knows about this dance through an invitation accidentally left on his bedside table, the film editing makes him part of the show through crosscutting. In his delirium, as one of the intertitles declares, he imagines the apocalypse—an increasingly frantic mix of semi-nude dancing, reaction shots, quotes from the Book of Revelation, and an animated medieval tableau of Death and the Seven Deadly Sins.

The Book of Revelation, also known as the Apocalypse of St. John, is the last canonical book of the New Testament. Full of hallucinatory images of decadence and doom, the book describes the end of the world in terrifying detail. Peace is restored only after God's final victory over Satan at Armageddon and his violent judgment on non-believers. The controversial text was written by St. John of Patmos in the first century after Christ, during the reign of Nero and the heightened persecution of Christians. The film refers indirectly to this story by having Maria and the workers meet for worship in catacombs deep under the city, like the early Christians.

Lang quotes his biblical sources selectively, using them as stylized set pieces—not unlike the early cinema of attractions in which visual pleasure exceeded narrative economy. The depiction of the lasciviously dancing cyborg (Maria's machine double), rising up on a stone beast with seven heads, triggers in Freder associations with the Whore of Babylon, which in the apocalypse signified pre-Christian, pagan Rome. In *Metropolis*, the Whore of Babylon becomes a femme fatale stripper whose erotic dance causes men to lose their composure. A title card declares the meaning of this show of urban decadence and depravity in biblical terms: "Verily, I say unto you, the days spoken of in the Apocalypse are nigh!"—a reference to the Book of Revelation, which elaborates: "Fallen! Fallen is Babylon the Great! It has become a dwelling place of demons, a haunt of every foul spirit, a haunt of every foul and hateful bird; for all the nations have drunk the wine of her impure passions. . . . Alas, alas, for the great city that was clothed in fine linen, purple and scarlet, bedecked with gold, with jewels, and with pearls! In one hour all this wealth has been laid waste."[9]

Punctuated by reaction shots of an increasingly agitated Freder, the frenzied montage also includes a long shot of Death as a skeleton and statues of the Seven Deadly Sins—a shot repeated from an earlier scene in the film. The soundtrack changes from jazzy dance music to the thirteenth-century Latin hymn *Dies Irae, Dies Illa, Solvet Saeclum in favilla*, whose text describes the wrath, terror, and despair of judgment day. Brought to life by Freder's hallucination, Death and the Seven Deadly Sins step down from their pedestal and jerkily move toward the camera. The scenario stages depictions of the Dance of Death that emerged in the late Middle Ages after the plague decimated a third of Europe's population. Innumerable woodcuts and illustrations recorded and remembered this event for centuries. In the so-called *Dresden Dance of Death*, a relief from 1543, a skeleton is shown playing the flute and carrying a scythe, symbolizing the act of harvesting the soul from the body. The film cuts from the skeleton with scythe to the industrial cityscape of skyscrapers and smokestacks, and then to a quick reaction shot of Freder holding his ears to keep out a siren's blast signaling the beginning of the workers' shift. As if in response to the inhumanity of the city, the film cuts from the smokestacks back to the Grim Reaper, now alone, approaching the camera (as well as Freder and us, the audience). He holds the scythe high, intent on mowing down anything in front of him. A cut back to Freder reveals his terrified expression; his body and arms are frantically reaching forward as if to warn us before the intertitle announces: "Death descends upon the city [Der Tod ist über der Stadt] . . . !" The skeleton keeps moving forward and in a third and final mowing motion produces a huge scratch across the image that seems to erase Freder and with him the film's material base, the very emulsion on the celluloid. An avant-garde technique that foregrounds the materiality of film, the radical abrasion suggests that the apocalyptic scenario threatens not just the city but also the viewer and even the very medium of film.

This sequence establishes, strictly on the formal level, a nexus between the biblical apocalypse, the medieval dance of death, and the dystopian modern city. Soon after this scene, the workers attack the machines and the city breaks down. As in myriad subsequent science fiction films, an inordinate amount of film time is spent displaying images of crumbling walls, exploding machines, flickering lights, bursting pipes, and rising water. As Susan Sontag points out in "The Imagination of Disaster," there is a strange appeal and aesthetic pleasure in watching disaster and destruction: "In films it is by means of images and sounds, not words that have to be translated by the imagination, that one can participate in the fantasy of living through one's own death and more, the death of cities, the destruction of humanity itself."[10]

The final scene of *Metropolis* gestures toward the beginning of a new order *after* the destruction—a redemptive glimpse of a city reborn. Von Harbou's novel is quite explicit about the dialectics of destruction and regeneration. Freder confronts his father:

> Father, don't you understand? Your city is being destroyed! Your machines have come to life, they're rampaging through the city! They're tearing Metropolis to pieces! . . . Why do you allow Death to lay his hand upon the city which is your own?[11]

The father answers: "The city must fall, Freder, so that you may build it up once more."[12] Had he planned all along for the workers to destroy their city in order to "force guilt upon the people" and enable his son to redeem them? This invocation of apocalypse, regeneration, and redemption mimicked the inflationary use of these messianic concepts in the recent war: the world had to be destroyed in order to be rebuilt from the ground up.

In a high angle shot the film's finale shows an orderly mass of workers slowly filling the frame. The workers shuffle forward in formation. They come to a halt and stand in a triangle before the cathedral, silent witnesses to the publicly staged reconciliation between proletariat and management. Disillusioned and purged of revolutionary ardor, the mass of workers unknowingly forms what later in the same year Siegfried Kracauer would call a "mass ornament," possibly in reaction to *Metropolis*.[13] It is the technical apparatus of the camera that not only makes this formation visible but in fact produces it. The workers have become part of a giant spectacle created by the very act of filming. Benjamin once noted that the masses encounter themselves in these spectacles.[14]

The "disciplined mass" at the end of the film acts as a silent audience (mimicking the position of the film's spectators) that watches the resolution of both the private and public narratives: the love story between the industrialist's son and the worker's daughter ends with an embrace and a kiss, while the struggle between management and labor is resolved, after some hesitation and prodding, with a handshake. This deliberate fairy-tale ending is symptomatic. It points to the shared dream, just a few years after the double trauma of military defeat and crushed revolution, of a regenerated and reunified modern nation based on discipline and social peace. With the handshake the nation is resurrected: under the same leader, but with a pacified working class, which has learned the lesson of the Tower of Babel after all. It is expected that once the revolutionary mob violence was squelched the city would function again, like the machine whose interlocking parts we saw superimposed over the cityscape at the beginning of the film. In *Metropolis* the evocation of the apocalypse happens in a fever dream, bringing into representation what is normally hidden and repressed: the dark and secret fear of "death descending on the city."

There are more than a hundred films today in which Lang's *Metropolis* is referenced, adapted, or spoofed. The film epitomizes to this day the awe-inspiring sublimity of urban modernity as well as instrumental rationality's high price. It shows that the skyscrapers cover up an unbridgeable class division, an irrational reliance on machines, alienated and exploitative work, and a division between body and soul. It also shows that workers (like soldiers ten years prior) are dispensable, and in effect about to be replaced by robots. Machines are the workers of the future, the inventor Rotwang proudly announces when unveiling his android. *Metropolis* further demonstrates that opposition against the inhuman conditions created by modernity's instrumental reason will itself have apocalyptic consequences. Proletarian revolt is shown as possible but unwise, ineffective and even terrifying. Because the gigantic urban machine envelops everything and everyone, resistance seems nothing more than a temporary malfunction.

Approximately nine months after *Metropolis* opened, another city film premiered, Walter Ruttmann's celebrated documentary *Berlin, die Sinfonie der Großstadt* (Berlin—Symphony of a Big City). Does this film provide an alternative to the dystopian urban view of *Metropolis*? Opening on September 23, 1927, *Berlin Symphony* depicts a day in the life of the city of Berlin from morning to midnight, replete with location shooting and snapshots of people, animals, and cars in perpetual motion. This documentary of urban life in 1927 is made in the realistic style of New Objectivity and thus stands in opposition to the highly stylized, "expressionist" design of *Metropolis*. And yet, upon closer inspection, both films share an attitude toward the big city that is critical of the mechanization of urban life and the inevitable meltdowns it produces—in *Metropolis* hyperbolically staged as apocalypse, in *Berlin Symphony* presented as stimulus overload and suicide. Like *Metropolis*, *Berlin Symphony* emphasizes the machine-like routine that makes a city work—every movement is calculated in one gigantic circulation of traffic, money, and people. Human will is given over to machines—from automobiles and factory work to images of mechanical dolls.

In one often-quoted scene in *Berlin Symphony* the camera is mounted on a roller-coaster car and rapidly rises and falls with it. At the Lunapark, a popular Berlin fairground in the 1920s, the roller-coaster ride whizzed by painted backgrounds of New York and provided the experience of accelerated speed and urban danger.[15] It also dramatized the willing submission of thrill seekers to a technology over which they had no control—once seated, the machine takes over. As the pace picks up, one-word newspaper headlines are interjected: crisis, murder, stock market, marriage, and, finally, money. Money is a word rhythmically repeated six times to underscore the principle of circulation and exchange that structures the urban environment as well as the film itself. However, the orderly circulation seems headed for a crisis, and the film performs the imminent breakdown through point-of-view shots of passengers on the roller coaster. With them we plunge down and race up and around a curve, all with rapid speed that blurs everything in sight; the increasingly abstract image ultimately turns into a rotating spiral graphic that spins vertiginously downward. A quick shot of an expensive necklace in a store window and a destitute old woman standing in front it, begging. Suddenly a storm stirs up leaves, pedestrians are swept along, and a woman runs across the street to reach a bridge over a river. As she stares at the choppy water, swirling like a vortex, we catch a glimpse of her wide-open eyes and frightened face in a close-up, reminiscent of Sergei Eisenstein's *Battleship Potemkin*, which played in Berlin in 1926. Cut to the frenetic roller coaster descending downward. Suddenly a splash in the water. A long shot shows pedestrians pointing to the river, which has swallowed her body. The woman's suicidal jump from the bridge is not explained psychologically (we do not know who the woman is) but follows structurally: the increasingly frantic editing cries out for an end. This scene is remarkable because it is the only segment in the documentary that is ostensibly staged. Ruttmann was willing to sacrifice the film's claim to authenticity to make the point that the complexity and tempo of urban life produce breakdowns and acts of self-destruction. The shock of this private revolt against life itself is further emphasized by harsh editing: a fashion show follows the suicide, as if nothing had happened. The viewer is made to believe that the individual's crisis is part of anonymous urban life, without any impact or consequence. This scene echoes *Metropolis*, which also insists that the individual does not count: after the explosion has killed numerous workers, the machine does not stop, life goes on, the dead workers are simply replaced.

More modern than *Metropolis*, Ruttmann's *Berlin Symphony* is no longer based on the biblical paradigm of apocalyptic destruction and utopian beginning but on the concept of circulation and the eternal return of the same daily routine. But in the end both films refrain from advocating a structural change of the underlying conditions; they show that resistance has no bearing on an overpowering and uncontrollable system that functions like the abstract machines in *Metropolis* or the roller coaster in *Berlin Symphony*. Both films share a dark view of the modern city as a place of repressed panic. Seen in this way, both *Metropolis* and *Berlin Symphony* prefigure American film noir, in which devastation and death lurk under the surface, ready to rip apart the city's slick façade at any moment. In their critique of modernity, these films articulate a fear that the urban environment may generate its own apocalyptic end.

Notes

1 Paul Virilio, *City of Panic*, trans. Julie Rose (New York: Berg, 2007). The original French version of 2003, *Ville Panique*, had the subtitle "Ailleurs commence ici,"

which was dropped in the English publication. See also *Panik Stadt*, ed. Ulrich Conrads (Berlin: Vieweg, 1979).

2 My analysis is based on the 2004 restored edition of *Metropolis*, available on DVD with English intertitles from Kino International. In summer 2008, approximately thirty minutes of the famously missing footage, believed lost for almost eighty years, were found in the Museo del Cine in Buenos Aires. According to first reports, this full-length version, which is not yet available, offers new scenes that flesh out subplots and minor characters; it also provides more footage of apocalyptic deluge and destruction. Portions of the following analysis follow my longer reading of *Metropolis* in Anton Kaes, *Shell Shock Cinema: Weimar Culture and the Wounds of War* (Princeton: Princeton University Press, 2009), 167–210.

3 Peter Bogdanovich, *Fritz Lang in America* (New York: Praeger, 1967), 124.

4 Oswald Spengler, *The Decline of the West*, vol. 2, trans. Charles Francis Atkinson (New York: Knopf, 1926), 504.

5 Ibid.

6 The Hollywood action picture *Die Hard* (1988) prefigured the use of planes to topple the Twin Towers, while the leveling of big cities is common fare in such movies as *Armageddon* (1998), *Independence Day* (1996), and *Collateral Damage* (2002), among many others.

7 See http://architecture.about.com/library/bl-libeskind-statement.htm. In the wake of the catastrophe of World War I, Bruno Taut suggested the building of an inspirational sky-scraping tower. See *Die Stadtkrone* (Jena: E. Diederichs, 1919). On the myth of the Tower of Babel, see Ulrike B. Wegener, *Die Faszination des Maßlosen: Der Turmbau zu Babel von Pieter Bruegel bis Athanasius Kircher* (Hildesheim: Olms, 1995); and Moritz Wullen and Günther Schauerte, eds., *Babylon: Mythos* (Berlin: Staatliche Museen, 2008).

8 On the concept of the apocalypse, see Klaus Vondung, *The Apocalypse in Germany*, trans. Stephen D. Ricks (Columbia: University of Missouri Press, 2000); and Jürgen Brokoff, *Die Apokalypse in der Weimarer Republik* (Munich: Fink, 2001).

9 Revelation 18:2–3, 18:16–17, in *New Oxford Annotated Bible* (New York: Oxford University Press, 2007). In Alfred Döblin's city novel, *Berlin Alexanderplatz*, which he began writing in 1927, the "Whore of Babylon" is invoked six times.

10 Susan Sontag, "The Imagination of Disaster," in *Against Interpretation and Other Essays* (New York: Farrar, Straus & Giroux, 1986), 212.

11 Quoted in Michael Minden and Holger Bachmann, eds., *Fritz Lang's* Metropolis: *Cinematic Visions of Technology and Fear* (Rochester, NY: Camden House, 2000), 67.

12 Ibid., 68.

13 See Siegfried Kracauer's essay "The Mass Ornament," which appeared in the *Frankfurter Zeitung* on June 9 and 10, 1927: "The structure of the mass ornament reflects that of the entire contemporary situation. Since the principle of the *capitalist production process* does not arise purely out of nature, it must destroy the natural organisms that it regards either as a means or as resistance. Community and personality perish when what is demanded is calculability." Siegfried Kracauer, *The Mass Ornament: Weimar Essays*, ed. and trans. Thomas Y. Levin (Cambridge, MA: Harvard University Press, 1995), 78.

14 Walter Benjamin, "The Work of Art in the Age of Its Technological Reproducibility," in Walter Benjamin, *Selected Writings, 1938–40*, ed. Howard Eiland and

Michael W. Jennings, trans. Edmund Jephcott et al. (Cambridge, MA: Harvard University Press, 2003), 4:282: "In great ceremonial processions, giant rallies, and mass sporting events, and in war, all of which are now fed into the camera, the masses come face to face with themselves. . . . In general, mass movements are more clearly apprehended by the camera than by the eye. A bird's-eye view best captures assemblies of hundreds of thousands. . . . This is to say that mass movements, including war, are a form of human behavior especially suited to the camera."

15 See Janet Ward, *Weimar Surfaces: Urban Visual Culture in 1920s Germany* (Berkeley: University of California Press, 2001), 161–63. See also Sabine Hake, "Urban Spectacle in Walter Ruttmann's Berlin: Symphony of the Big City," in *Dancing on the Volcano: Essays on the Culture of the Weimar Republic*, ed. Thomas W. Kniesche and Stephen Brockmann (Columbia, SC: CamdenHouse, 1994), 127–42; Anton Kaes, "Leaving Home: Film, Migration, and the Urban Experience," *New German Critique*, no. 74 (Spring–Summer 1998): 179–92.

Chapter 2

■

Sounds Like Hell

Beyond Dystopian Noise

JAMES DONALD

*Thousands of people in Britain and around the world are dying prematurely
from heart disease triggered by long-term exposure to excessive noise,
according to research by the World Health Organisation. Coronary heart
disease caused 101,000 deaths in the UK in 2006, and the study suggests that
3,030 of these are caused by chronic noise exposure, including to daytime
traffic.*

—*Guardian* online, August 23, 2007

For the philosopher Arthur Schopenhauer, in 1844, hell was the sound of
whips cracking in the Nuremberg streets.

> [T]he truly infernal cracking of whips in the narrow resounding
> streets of a town must be denounced as the most unwarrantable and
> disgraceful of all noises. It deprives life of all peace and sensibility.
> Nothing gives me so clear a grasp of the stupidity and thoughtless-
> ness of mankind as the tolerance of the cracking of whips. This sud-
> den, sharp crack which paralyses the brain, destroys all meditation,
> and murders thought, must cause pain to any one who has anything
> like an idea in his head. Hence every crack must disturb a hundred
> people applying their minds to some activity, however trivial it may
> be; while it disjoints and renders painful the meditations of the
> thinker; just like the executioner's axe when it severs the head from
> the body. . . . Hammering, the barking of dogs, and the screaming of
> children are abominable; but it is *only* the cracking of a whip that is
> the true murderer of thought. Its object is to destroy every favour-
> able moment that one now and then may have for reflection.[1]

The remorseless intrusion of noise is how Schopenhauer experienced, quite viscerally, the selfishness of his fellow-citizens, the irrationality of nineteenth-century social arrangements, and so, one might say, the dystopian aspect of modern urban life. That prompts an intriguing counterfactual question. If hell is the noise of other people, what then would an urban utopia sound like? According to Schopenhauer's logic—if that is the right term for a diatribe so far over the top—utopia might mean a perfectly ordered society that conjures forth the perfectly rational, perfectly fulfilled, perfectly uninterrupted citizen. The sound of utopia would then be, presumably, the sound of silence, or some quietly harmonious music soothing the sensibility and engendering reflective thought. In which case, it becomes clear that utopian schemes for a perfect society may be, in reality, no more than a fantasy disavowal of the presence of others. Dystopia is not the opposite of utopia. It is hardly a plan to produce the irrational person. Rather, imagined dystopian cities are a projection of the inherent irrationality of interpersonal relations onto urban space. They are a forlorn acknowledgment of the impossibility of the perfect city—and, quite possibly, its undesirability.

Raucous Hells

Schopenhauer's phobia and its concomitant ideal of utopian silence reappear in the beginnings of organized movements for noise abatement at the beginning of the twentieth century. "Culture is evolution towards silence!" proclaimed the cultural philosopher and social critic Theodor Lessing in his polemical 1908 book *Der Lärm: Eine Kampfschrift gegen die Geräusche unseres Lebens* (Noise: A Tirade against the Sounds of Our Life).[2] This teleology was born of an explicitly dystopian response to modern urban sounds. Noise pollution was both sign and vehicle of cultural degeneration; it vulgarized life and, more particularly, it stupefied alienated white-collar workers in the "raucous hells of the big cities." This was an abiding passion, even an obsession, for Lessing. Nearly two decades later, in his 1926 article "The Blue-Black Rose," he was still bewailing the noisiness of German cities: "I hate the cries of the street merchants and newspaper vendors. I hate the ringing of the church bells, I hate the senseless noise of the factory sirens, but what I hate most are the stinking autos."[3] For Lessing, as for Schopenhauer, the sounds of the city and its machines represented something worse than an intrusion into a citizen's right to privacy. Noise destroyed the silence necessary for inner reflection, for thought, and thus for self-development and artistic or intellectual creation. In 1908 he had declared, "A refined and educated man will always be distinguished by his silence and by his hostility towards a noisy and ill-disciplined way of life."[4] Driven to even greater distraction in defeated, postwar Germany, Lessing now fantasized about desperate measures: "Banish the 'symbols of culture' from the thoroughly wired landscape, filled with advertisements and smokestacks; perhaps one site will remain holy and unspoiled. I've decided to steal a pocketwatch at some point—with the hope of being arrested. In prison I will at least have peace from the rug beating, the piano playing, the car horns, the gramophones, and the telephones."[5]

Lessing was no mere armchair critic, railing against the evils of noise.[6] He was also an active campaigner who, in 1908, the same year that he published his polemic against noise, founded the Deutscher Lärmschutzverband in Hanover. Over the next couple of years, branches of this Association for Protection against Noise were set up in a number of German cities and in Vienna. Membership was not large—in October 1910, Vienna was the sixth-largest branch with thirty-five members—and it was pretty much restricted to the liberal and professional middle classes: doctors, engineers, writers, artists, and intellectuals. The association set up a journal with a remarkably bombastic and, one can only hope, self-ironizing title: *Der Antirüpel, das recht auf Stille: Monatsblätter zum Kampf gegen Lärm, Roheit und Unkultur in deutschen Wirtschafts-, Handels- und Verkehrsleben* (The Anti-rowdy, the Right to Silence: Monthly Journal for the Campaign against Noise, Brutality, and Lack of Culture in German Economy, Trade, and Traffic). Although it received some good press, this particular movement did not attract sufficiently broad support to be sustainable, and it folded in 1911. By that time, however, Lessing had established himself as the leading anti-noise campaigner in German-speaking Europe. In 1911, for example, he gave a couple of well-received lectures in Vienna, in which he backed up his argument about the evils of excessive noise by using brass instruments, baby rattles, and bells (and quite possibly whistles). "Being quick to learn," noted one wry observer, "the audience thanked the lecturer not by clapping their hands but by waving handkerchiefs."[7]

In a way, the most enduring achievement of early campaigns like Lessing's lay less in the spread of their polemics than in their ability to translate urban noise from a dystopian symptom into a problem, with at least the potential for technical and political solutions. Here is an empirical example of how one of Lessing's supporters, a Viennese dramaturge who went on to become director of the Viennese Imperial Court Theatre, heard and conceptualized the sounds of the early twentieth-century European city. On an apparently quiet summer evening in 1907, in the supposedly quiet Hietzing district of Vienna, Alfred Freiherr von Berger undertook an experiment. Quite simply, he decided to catalogue the sounds actually discernible in that evening's "quiet." Berger heard:

Three bands, one very close, one further away, one very far away; two barking dogs, one in a low register, the other in a high one; a whimpering dog; the rattling of a vehicle; bells chiming; two automobiles buzzing and hooting; the twittering of many sparrows; two pianos, a lady singing; a microphone alternately giving off an orchestra piece and an English song, the cry of a peacock, the roaring of the wild animals in the Schönbrunn far away; the whistles of at least three factories from various distances; the wailing roar of an electric streetcar; a train of the city railroad—its wheels rattling and brakes screeching; the whistling and puffing of the switchers on the Western railroad; the metallic bang of the bumpers; the wind rustling through the trees; a parrot; the vile shouting of a driver urging on the horses of his cart; a scythe being sharpened; trumpet signals from barracks; carpets and furniture being beaten; a passer-by whistling; the neighbour's garden being watered by a hissing jet of water; a barrel-organ; the bells and the muffled rolling of the steam street car.[8]

Although Berger may share Schopenhauer's earlier antipathy to urban noise, here at least his approach to the problem is more scientific and aesthetic than emotional and ethical. He seems almost to prefigure John Cage's revolutionary rethinking of sound and silence in his *4'33".* "What the city dweller calls silence is a mixture of all sorts of sounds he has become used to," observed Berger in 1909. "He does not hear them any more and therefore to him, they represent silence."[9] As for Cage, then, the difference between silence and sound is not so much acoustic as a question of *attention.*[10] Whereas Schopenhauer hears, unwillingly, and rants, Berger at least decides to listen in an attempt to identify the source of the problem and to specify the problem in a way that allows for its amelioration. As a result, he hears quite differently.

Of course, the sounds Berger heard in 1907 Vienna had changed significantly from those that assailed Schopenhauer in Nuremberg in 1844. Some of the differences may be ascribed to the rate of expansion in the great European capitals, in terms of land, population density, and economic activity. Between 1850 and the time Berger was writing, Vienna grew in area from 55.4 square kilometers to 275.9 square kilometers, largely by incorporating existing suburbs (in 1850), dismantling its old fortifications, from 1857 on, to create space for development, and then adding the rural periphery beyond the old ramparts (in 1890–92) and districts across the Danube (in 1904). At the same time, its population multiplied nearly fivefold from 431,000 to just over two million. The sheer growth in housing, places of work, and traffic was enough to usher in a busier, noisier soundscape. The speed of the expansion required a hectic rate of construction, and noise levels were exacerbated by the design of the buildings and the materials used. Paved roads, increasingly dense and multistoried residential buildings and business premises, and public buildings and factories created, as the Viennese urban historian Peter Payer puts it, "street canyons, which became deeper and deeper the closer one moved toward the city center. Sound reflected and rebounded from their stone walls."[11]

The most consistent object of complaints submitted to the Viennese branch of Lessing's anti-noise campaign—as Berger's catalogue suggests—was undoubtedly the increasing volume (both senses intended) of traffic and new forms of transportation. The construction of the Ringstraße toward the end of the nineteenth century was a concrete acknowledgment that the city was being redesigned around the movement of traffic, as well as a certain monumental politics of the spectacle. Between 1870 and 1913, the amount of street space in Vienna given over to traffic expanded from 2.7 million square meters to 15.7 million. In 1900, 4,686 hired carriages were registered. Horse-drawn streetcars were introduced in 1865, to be followed by steam-powered models in the 1880s and by electrification around the turn of the century. Many of the inner-city streets were already cobbled, and some of the intensity of traffic noise at around the time Berger made his experiment was associated with the slowness of the Viennese authorities to introduce sound-reducing surfaces. Tarmac had been available at least since 1870, but whereas 30 percent of Paris streets (nearly 2,750,000 square meters) had been covered with "soundless" surfaces by 1900, the equivalent for Vienna was just 2.2 percent (174,300 square meters). The city railroad to which Berger refers was being completed at around this time, to a design by Otto Wagner. Although automobiles were by no means common, they too were making an impact. In 1914, 3,858 cars and 748 motorcycles were registered in the city. (There was also a vogue for bicycles in the 1890s that saw around seventy thousand active cyclists in Vienna in 1900.) In short, as the decades went by, there were more people, those people moved around more, and, in doing so, they made more noise. Between 1870 and 1910, as another sign of the times, the average Viennese went from using public transport twenty times per year to making 131 trips. And, encouraged in part by electric street lighting, this increased activity ate into what had previously been the tranquil hours of night. Streetcars began to run until 10 P.M. in the winter and 10.30 P.M. in the summer.

Apart from the noise of people, animals, factories (now, and again quite late in comparison with other European cities, beginning to be zoned separately from residential districts), and transport, Berger's inventory includes the sounds of public music. The traditional pleasures/irritants of bands and barrel-organ-grinders (a frequent bone of contention) were now joined and exacerbated by the seepage of domestic musical activities. He notes the Viennese vogue for pianos and the beginnings of mechanical media (the gramophone, or what he refers to as "a microphone").

For the purposes of his experiment, Berger treats this variety of sounds as a fact of modern life. Rather than describing the sound *of* his garden, therefore, he attempts to catalogue the sounds heard *in* his garden. As he does so, sound ceases to be heard as the integral acoustic dimension of place. Instead, it is conceived as discrete auditory signals being emitted by identifiable sources. Berger's taxonomic approach thus presages a move beyond description to the measurement of sound, which did not become possible technically until the 1920s, and the management of noise as part of a twentieth-century biopolitics.

Lessing's campaign against the hell of modern urban noise was not without its critics, who opposed it for being anti-modern, over-precious, and/or self-serving. Some went so far as to assert that the noise of the modern city, even if not exactly utopian, was at least a stimulant rather than a narcotic. Here is Edmund Wengraf, writing in *Die Zeit* in 1911: "Let us be frank: City dwellers like we are actually cannot live without this street noise. It is the mental stimulation of our days and the lullaby of our nights. It is part of the environment that we cannot do without because we have become used to it."[12] Even in the difficult postwar Berlin of the 1920s, some of Lessing's contemporaries heard in the jarring symphony of the modern city a distinctively new energy that should not just be tolerated but might be put to work in a modernist ethic of self-creation. Here, in a response to a newspaper questionnaire in 1926 rather than to Lessing's polemics, is the novelist Alfred Döblin, author of *Berlin Alexanderplatz*: "The city as a whole has an intensely inspiring, energizing power; this commotion of the streets, shops and vehicles provides the heat I must have in order to work, at all times. It is the fuel that makes my motor run."[13] Setting Wengraf and Döblin against Lessing and his supporters might suggest an argument that even if early twentieth-century cities cannot be neatly compartmentalized into utopias or dystopias, then at least it may be possible to distinguish between utopian and dystopian perspectives on the modern city, roughly along the lines of pro-modernists versus anti-modernists. That would, at least, acknowledge that cities embody the benefits, as well as the costs, of strangers sharing space in close proximity. To think purely in terms of the dystopian-utopian binarism still represents a rush to judgment, however, one that slides too quickly over the prior question of whether, and how, the experience of the modern city was changing at a sensory (and thus preconscious) level.

It is in this sense that Berger's way of hearing can properly be described as *aesthetic*. It is concerned with "perception through the senses" as a preliminary to any judgment about the worth of that experience. Furthermore, the aesthetic relation to the world implicit in Berger's new way of hearing was a precondition for the possibility of the new biopolitics because that politics worked on, and at the level of, the senses. It was the emerging regime of perception, provoked by the increasing complexity, objectification, and mechanization of modern urban life, that was, as Walter Benjamin put it, subjecting "the human sensorium to a complex kind of training."[14]

Trained Hearing

Nowhere is the nature of this "training" conveyed more brilliantly than at the beginning of Robert Musil's *The Man without Qualities*. Writing in the 1920s but conjuring up Vienna in the final days before the Great War changed everything, Musil establishes, right at the start of the novel, the growing disconnection of languages of description from the texture of everyday sensory experience—or, rather, the way that the former became a source of "training" for the latter. Musil's opening paragraph thus, daringly, offers a parodic meteorological account of the global weather patterns affecting the weather in Vienna on a particular day, and then pulls the rug from this highfalutin scientific discourse with a simple summary: "It was a fine day in August 1913."

Musil then switches from the weather to the sounds and noise of Vienna on that day, and from a scientific discourse to an aesthetic one. His visual imagery recalls contemporary experiments in abstract and rhythmic filmmaking by Walter Ruttmann, Hans Richter, or Viking Eggling. Blocks of light and shade are crosscut by lines in motion—speeding automobiles in Musil's case—while the movement of pedestrians, negotiating their way through the city's streets, creates more fluid, fractal patterns. The way Musil *hears* the city is more ambivalent and less assertively modernist. His "wiry texture" of sound shares the jagged angularity and dynamism of the visual images. But the way in which he then anchors this particular soundscape to Vienna seems to hark back to the more traditional aesthetic that assumed sound to be a dimension of place.

> Automobiles shot out of deep, narrow streets into the shallows of bright squares. Dark clusters of pedestrians formed cloudlike strings. Where more powerful lines of speed cut across their casual haste they clotted up, then trickled on faster and, after a few oscillations, resumed their steady rhythm. Hundreds of noises wove themselves into a wiry texture of sound with barbs protruding here and there, smart edges running along it and subsiding again, with clear notes splintering off and dissipating. By this noise alone, whose special quality cannot be captured in words, a man returning after years of absence would have been able to tell with his eyes shut that he was back in the Imperial Capital and Royal City of Vienna. Opening his

> eyes, he would know the place by the rhythm of movement in the streets long before he caught any characteristic detail. It would not matter even if he only imagined he could do this.[15]

Had this imagined exile returned ten years later, when Musil was writing, would the sound of the city still have identified it so immediately and unchangingly as Vienna and nowhere else? And would our exile, with eyes shut or wide open, have listened to the city in the same way? It is doubtful. He would now have found himself in Red Vienna, struggling to re-create itself in the straitened aftermath of war and revolution, rather than in Imperial and Royal Vienna in its final spasms of self-deluding pomp. So the purr and jangle of ostentatious wealth and the brassy *folies de grandeur* of autocratic power would to a large degree have been silenced. More striking would have been the noisy business of building a livable social-democratic city, and the sounds of a city opening up to more demotic, international, and commercial forms of culture and communication. Vienna's particular political makeup, its demographic changes, the speed of its economic recovery, the particular emphasis on building workers' housing and constructing a social infrastructure, the continuing, exponential growth in public and private transport, and the emergence of new media technologies and leisure venues—all these factors, and others, would have combined to produce a distinctive mix that would have made the city still sound different from Berlin, Paris, or London. Equally, however, new sounds associated with social changes were increasingly common to all the cities, and so their soundscapes were inevitably becoming more and more similar. This helps explain why the idea of sound as the acoustic genius of place was being superseded by the idea of noise as an intrusive and wiry-textured aspect of the urban environment, which needed to be measured, managed, and controlled.

This new style of listening becomes dominant as Musil switches the emphasis of his narration from the uniqueness of Vienna's historical soundscape to its modern typicality.

> So let us not place any particular value on the city's name. Like all big cities it was made up of irregularity, change, forward spurts, failures to keep step, collisions of objects and interests, punctuated by unfathomable silences; made up of pathways and untrodden ways, of one great rhythmic beat as well as the chronic discord and mutual displacement of its contending rhythms. All in all, it was like a boiling bubble inside a pot made of the durable stuff of buildings, laws, regulations, and historical traditions.[16]

It is worth noting here that the way in which Musil imagines a changing Vienna is neither utopian nor simply dystopian but critical and sociological.

His metaphors still operate within the paradigm set out in Georg Simmel's 1903 essay "The Metropolis and Mental Life." Not only had this prefigured Musil's theme of the loss of *qualities* (or the individual, subjective characteristics that Simmel termed "personality"); it had also offered an explanation for the phenomenon. "The individual," wrote Simmel, "has become a mere cog in an enormous organisation of things and powers which tear from his hands all progress, spirituality, and value in order to transform them from their subjective form into the form of a purely objective life." What Simmel calls the "overwhelming fullness of crystallised and impersonal spirit" is identical to Musil's "durable stuff of buildings, laws, regulations, and historical traditions."[17] The difference between the two accounts lies in the novelist's ability to convey what the implosion of "personality" actually felt like by presenting an almost synaesthesic conflation of the social with the sensory—with vision and movement, but also with hearing and sound. Modernity in Vienna was experienced as cacophony and syncopation: *the chronic discord and mutual displacement of its contending rhythms.* And again, this observation cannot be reduced to a rejection of the emerging modern Vienna as a dystopia. More interestingly, it suggests how the increasing complexity and objectification of urban culture was reshaping aesthetic and subjective human experience.

The Machine Age

My thinking about the soundscape of Machine Age Europe in light of Benjamin's "complex training" of the human sensorium, rather than in terms of Lessing's dystopianism, owes much to Emily Thompson's enlightening book *The Soundscape of Modernity: Architectural Acoustics and the Culture of Listening in America, 1900–1933*. Thompson defines a "soundscape" as "an auditory or aural landscape."

> Like a landscape, a soundscape is simultaneously a physical environment and a way of perceiving that environment; it is both a world and a culture constructed to make sense of that world. The physical aspects of a soundscape consist not only of the sounds themselves, the waves of acoustical energy permeating the atmosphere in which people live, but also the material objects that create, and sometimes destroy, those sounds. A soundscape's cultural aspects incorporate scientific and aesthetic ways of listening, a listener's relationship to their environment, and the social circumstances that dictate who gets to hear what.[18]

As an architectural historian, Thompson is interested in the new relationship between built space and the management of sound, and especially in the architectural manipulation of materials and techniques in the attempt to mitigate the damage—physical, psychological, social, and industrial—caused by excessive sound. The subtlety of her definition, however, lies in her emphasis on the fact that new ways of hearing are not just the result of new sounds hitting the ear but of the "complex training" provided by the *culture constructed to make sense of* the changing sensory environment.

That is why the evidence of novels, and other cultural forms, is especially relevant to understanding historical soundscapes. Not only do they make it possible to track changes in perceptual styles. In their day, they also had a pedagogic function, modeling as well describing emerging ways of hearing. They were part of the sense-making culture of sound. Take, as an example of this pedagogic process, the treatment of Machine Age soundscapes and listening styles in Ilya Ehernburg's documentary novel *The Life of the Automobile* (1929). Here is his description of the Citroën car factory outside Paris.

> The Citroën works had twenty-five thousand employees. Once, they had spoken different languages. Now they kept silent. A close look revealed that these people came from different places. There were Parisians and Arabs, Russians and Bretons, Provençals and Chinese, Spaniards and Poles, Africans and Annamites. The Pole had once tilled the soil, the Italian had grazed sheep, and the Don Cossack had faithfully served the Tsar. Now they were all at the same conveyor belt. They never spoke to one another. They were gradually forgetting human words, words as warm and rough as sheepskin or clods of freshly plowed earth.
>
> They listened to the voices of the machines. Each had its own racket. The giant drop-hammers boomed. The milling machines screamed. The boring-machines squealed. The presses banged. The grinding-lathes groaned. The pulleys sighed. And the iron chain hissed venomously.
>
> The roar of the machines deafened the Provençals and the Chinese. Their eyes became glassy and vacant. They forgot everything in the world: the color of the sky and the name of their native village. They kept on tightening nuts. The automobile had to be noiseless. Engineers sat and thought. How could they build a mute engine? These valves had to be silenced. The buyer was so nervous! The men along the belt had no nerves. They only had hands: to tighten a nut, to fasten a wheel.[19]

What are the lessons to be learned about listening from this passage? The first, overriding impression is, of course, that of the brutal, deafening machinery of mass production not just silencing the human voice but actually crushing the human spirit. This is conventional enough. It is a dystopian style of listening traceable back, through Lessing, at least as far as Schopenhauer. But that ethical denunciation is now nuanced by an awareness of the more recent discourse of noise abatement. In Ehrenburg's satire, noise reduction matters to Citroën, if only because fussy bourgeois consumers want quieter cars. It is a telling barb, even though by the late 1920s, and even if largely for reasons of enlightened self-interest, manufacturers were sponsoring research by designers into ways of mitigating the effects of excessive noise on workers. (Damaging their health had a negative impact on their productivity.) Implicit in the passage, then, are other discourses about hearing: the technological discourse of acousticians who were developing electro-acoustical instruments to measure and quantify sound, with a view to mitigating its side effects, a medical discourse that sought means of curing and preventing noise-induced diseases, and architectural discourses about soundproofing and the acoustic design of buildings. Also present, in this multilayered style of hearing, is what might be called a proto-globalization discourse. Ehrenburg observes how capitalist production prompts the flow of economic migrants to metropolitan centers of industry. This has two consequences for the Machine Age soundscape. First, the metropolis becomes increasingly like a modern, multi-tongued Babel—even if the various voices of the workers on the assembly line are rendered mute by the sound of the machines. Second, as a result of this flow of people, language, as well as sound, becomes increasingly dissociated from any particular place.

In an earlier passage, near the beginning of *The Life of the Automobile*, Ehrenburg addresses another sonic dimension of the Machine Age: not the cacophony of industrial production but the commodification of mechanically reproduced sound and its cultural consequences. In writing a portrait of the first man to be killed in a car accident in France—another of modernity's lethal side effects—Ehrenburg suggests how the Citroën workers' linguistic displacement is mirrored by the creation, within the metropolis, of a new kind of virtual multilingualism. This is brought into being by the accessibility, and apparent immediacy, of the world through technologies like cinema and radio.

Then a new serpent moved into his home. It hissed sweetly. It was the radio. Bernard's days still had an appearance of well-being. But at night he went crazy. He wore warm slippers with pompoms. But he wasn't sitting at his fireplace; no, he was whizzing through the world. His lips moved suspiciously. He was looking for waves. Here was Barcelona. . . . Here was Karlsruhe. . . . The German word "bitte." Bach. Spaniards. A charleston. The winner of the race at Oxford. The Royal Dutch rates. An Italian lesson: forte, morte, cannelloni. The victory of the Conservatives in Sweden. The bells of the Kremlin: The *Internationale*. Another charleston. The world moohed, bleated, meowed.[20]

The radio stations set up across Europe in the early 1920s were indeed cosmopolitan in their content, in just the way that Ehrenburg describes. But they were also cosmopolitan in another sense. They brought into being a new audience, a new community, that was at least potentially universal: widely scattered across cities and nations, wearing slippers with pompoms or not, but linked together in time "with a simultaneity that made physical travel seem antediluvian by comparison."[21] Paradoxically, this experience of hearing the world in your living room did not lead to more extensive or less constrained communication. Instead, it taught people that where they happened to live was not the world but one place in an increasingly complicated and mysterious world. The complex training of radio listening accelerated the atomization and aesthetics of defensive self-creation, diagnosed a couple of decades earlier by Simmel.

The virtuality of radio "presence" thus added an uncanny dimension to the objectification of modern life, a sense of placelessness, as everyday experience was increasingly mediated through sounds and stories carried electronically through the air. This was a strange and confused, yet not wholly dystopian, new world; an immaterial yet compelling soundscape, populated by mechanically reproduced voices and sounds that changed the very nature of subjective being. This mediated dimension of sound was nicely captured at the time by a song written in 1928 Berlin. In "Es liegt in der Luft" (There's Something in the Air), the lyricist Marcellus Schiffer and the composer Mischa Spoliansky first observe how the technologies of telephone, radio, and cinema not only add to the noise of the city but at the same time *informationalize* culture. They turn the symbolic into something like electricity, into signals as well as signs.

> There's something in the air called objectivity (*Sachlichkeit*),
> There's something in the air like electricity.

Then they go on to conjure up the disconcerting and unprecedented barrage of sounds and images being carried by those signals.

> What has come over the air these days?
> Oh, the air has fallen for a brand new craze.
> Through the air are swiftly blown
> Pictures, radio, telephone.
> Through the air the whole lot flies,

Till the air simply can't believe its eyes.
Planes and airships, think of that!
There's the air, just hear it humming!
Trunk calls, Trios in B flat
In the gaps that are left a picture's coming.[22]

The point of the song is that the mediated soundscape does not just produce a new regime of sensory perception but teaches a new relationship to distance and time and therefore new subjective dispositions. "As society becomes progressively aestheticized," writes Michael North in *Reading 1922*, "as audiences begin to consume imaginative and symbolic materials as they had previously consumed material goods, then everyday life acquires *an inherently ironic distance from itself.*"[23]

This was the internal distance and self-alienation that Proust for one had sheeted home to new communication technologies. In *The Guermantes Way*, published in 1920 and 1921, the narrator, Marcel, is thrown by his first telephone conversation with his beloved grandmother, as the "tiny" and "abstract" sound of her voice, divorced from her face and her physical presence, is translated into pure signal.

> It is she, it is her voice that is speaking, that is there. But how far away it is! . . .
>
> Many were the times, as I listened thus without seeing her who spoke to me from so far away, when it seemed to me that the voice was crying to me from the depths out of which one does not rise again . . . for always until then, every time that my grandmother had talked to me, I had been accustomed to follow what she said on the open score of her face, in which the eyes figured so largely; but her voice itself I was hearing that afternoon for the first time.

For Marcel the uncanny experience of hearing this disembodied voice acts as an intimation of mortality, accentuating as it does the finitude of the body.

> "Granny!" I cried to her, "Granny!" and I longed to kiss her, but I had beside me only the voice, a phantom as impalpable as the one that would perhaps come back to visit me when my grandmother was dead. "Speak to me!" But then, suddenly, I ceased to hear the voice, and was left even more alone. . . . It seemed to me as though it was already a beloved ghost that I had allowed to lose herself in the ghostly world, and, standing alone before the instrument, I went on vainly repeating: "Granny! Granny!" as Orpheus, left alone, repeats the name of his dead wife.[24]

Although the mediation and virtualization of human relationships are thus seen to hollow out experience and perhaps deprive the individual of "qualities" or "personality," this loss also inculcates a new, distinctively modern sensitivity to the presence of death in life. In more comic mode, in *Ulysses*, Leopold Bloom ponders the possibility of using the gramophone to triumph over time and keep an audible record of the departed: "Have a gramophone in every grave or keep it in the house. After dinner on a Sunday. Put on poor old greatgrandfather. Kraahraark! Hellohellohello amawfullyglad kraark awfullygladaseeagain hellohello amawf krpthsth. Remind you of the voice like the photograph reminds you of the face. Otherwise you couldn't remember the face after fifteen years, say."[25] The accounts of modern sound quoted thus far, drawn from a variety of evidential genres, confirm that the noise of cities, of machines, and of commodified, mechanically reproduced sound had informed a changing external reality. They constitute the aural dimension of Simmel's "crystallised spirit," Musil's "durable stuff," or simply Spolianksy and Schiffer's "objectivity." That is only half the story, however. They are not just evidence of changing sounds in the physical environment. As Emily Thompson suggests, they were also part of a cultural framework for "processing" sound that produced another, less obvious new reality. This was a subjectivity that was no longer conceivable in terms of individual qualities but one now mediated through mass-produced sounds and technologies, which were dislocating, or subverting, the familiar coordinates of space and time. This learned estrangement of the senses appears to have been experienced less as dystopian than as a disturbing existential rhythm—a rhythm that was sometimes stultifying, often febrile, and, on occasion, ecstatic. This was the tempo of modern life, a tempo to be learned, managed, improvised around, and, with any luck, enjoyed.

Modern Music

This was the modern tempo that Robert Musil heard in the "chronic discord and mutual displacement" of the modern city's "contending rhythms." It is also the tempo that many of his contemporaries heard in, and as, *jazz*. The move from noise to sound to music is an important one because it suggests a way beyond the overly melodramatic contrast between utopian and dystopian perspectives. A utopian perspective says *either* that the ideal, and therefore impossible, city should embody perfectly rational, perfectly conflict-free relations between human beings, *or*, equally implausible, that an actually existing city might represent social relations that are as good as they can be imagined. A dystopian view sees, and hears, the frictions, discomforts, and aggravations of the shared space and overlapping lives of all-too-human fellow-citizens as a soul-destroying torment. The third way that emerges here holds back on either endorsement or denunciation, proposing instead that it may be possible to shape a self, and to conduct a life, by making creative and pragmatic use of the physical, sensory, and symbolic materials provided by the urban environment. It suggests how we might live reasonably well in the far-from-perfect, but not impossible, city.

This dialectic is again visible in the take-up and uses of jazz in the 1920s. Its detractors heard jazz as the hellish cacophony of modern urbanity and modern machinery, a racket that reduced humans to robots but also, at the same time, unleashed a savage impulse that could, in a drumbeat, make civilization regress to barbarism and the jungle. At the utopian end of the spectrum, enthusiasts like the musician Paul Stefan celebrated the modernity of jazz and embraced its rejuvenating energy. In an editorial for the avant-garde music journal *Anbruch* in 1925 he wrote: "For us, jazz means: a rebellion of the people's dulled instincts against a music without rhythm. A reflection of the times: chaos, machines, noise, the highest peak of intensity. The triumph of irony, of frivolity, the wrath of those who want to preserve good times. The overcoming of Biedermeyer hypocrisy."[26] In a more measured view, jazz provided a soundtrack for modern mass society that articulated its Zeitgeist. "The rhythm of our time is jazz," the composer Kurt Weill accepted. "The Americanization of our whole external life, which is happening slowly but surely, finds its most peculiar outcome here. Unlike art music, dance music does not reflect the sense of towering personalities who stand above time, but rather reflects the instinct of the masses."[27] In the early 1920s, jazz was thus heard in Europe more as the sound of a potentially daemonic, but always modern, and specifically American, energy than as a vehicle of African American self-expression. It was cosmopolitan in the sense that whatever anxieties, desires, and fantasies European audiences were projecting onto black American culture, and however they were using the music to fashion a self-image and a public face, jazz became part of the modern Babel. In 1924, while working as a dishwasher in Le Grand Duc, Langston Hughes captured the beat of this cultural and linguistic mongrelization in his poem "Jazz Band in a Parisian Cabaret."

> Play that thing,
> Jazz band!
> Play it for the lords and ladies,
> For the dukes and counts,
> For the whores and gigolos,
> For the American millionaires,

And the school teachers
Out for a spree.
Play it,
Jazz band!
You know that tune
That laughs and cries at the same time.
You know it.
    May I?
    Mais oui.
    Mein Gott!
    Parece una rumba.
Play, jazz band!
You've got seven languages to speak in
And then some,
Even if you do come from Georgia.
    Can I come home wid yuh, sweetie?
Sure.[28]

Babel as failed utopia or dystopian cosmopolitanism provides the organizing image, as well as the title, for another novel, published in 1922, that evokes cities and music to address Simmel's theme, that is, how modern self-creation is both driven and constrained by the dynamic between the standardization of the external world and the atomization of subjective life. The author, John Cournos, was a Russian-born Jewish American who shuttled back and forth between New York and London and took an active role in the prewar bohemian avant-garde in England.[29] Like *The Man without Qualities*, *Babel* looks back from a postwar perspective, and with a postwar sensibility, to London in 1913. In doing so, Cournos provides an object lesson in presenting a phenomenology of modernity projected through the lens of a modernist sensibility. Here, again, can be found imagery of the demonic energy of the modern city and the ambivalent responses it provoked. This is the protagonist and narrator, Gombarov, on Broadway in New York.

Myriads of lights, twinkling, glimmering, revolving, quivering, performing "stunts" in plenty. Vulgar some of them, yet very wonderful.
"Perfectly diabolic, don't you think?" asked Winifred.
He laughed and answered enigmatically:
"What would be the glory of God without Satan?"[30]

Cournos also uses jazz, in quite conventional cultural and sociological terms, as a metaphor for the double-edged impact of American-led modernization. Listening to a jazz band on a Cunarder taking him back to New York, Gombarov interprets the music as symptom of both primitivism and cosmopolitanism.

That was strange: the spectacle of civilized society, well-groomed men and exquisite, refined-ankled, delicately turned women, responding to the most primitive essences in the arts: tribal music and steps and movements richly symbolic of sex. . . . And odd it was, that the Congo should be conquering America, and that in her turn, America should be conquering Europe. This new music would soon be heard from San Francisco to Moscow.[31]

Psychologically, jazz is taken to express, quite directly, the dissonance of modern subjectivity: "His head on the pillow, his body curled up under the sheets, his numbed brain began to thaw and release all manner of thoughts, harsh, jangling, full of contrariety, like the tunes of the band he had heard on the evening of his arrival. His mind was in a state of jazz, was jazz."[32] A different kind of modern music is invoked in Cournos's most striking soundscape. When Gombarov first arrives in London and boards a bus at Victoria Station, he is struck by the distinctiveness of the city's sounds. In contrast to the wiry texture and angular abstraction of Musil's Viennese soundscape, Cournos creates something more like a post-Impressionist tone poem.

Having left Westminster Cathedral behind, the red 'bus almost noiselessly glided on, cunningly brushing past other red 'buses, with a gondola-like grace which was incredible; at times no more than a hair's breadth separated them. And there was no sudden, sharp, shrieking noises of taxi-horns and overhead trains as in New York; but there was a trembling and a rumbling in the air, steady and constant, the even breathing of modern life over vast spaces. All the noises were swallowed up and became as one noise, vibrant like that of a ship's turbine, incessantly throbbing, reduced to normal pulsation, diffuse mellowness of a tone painting, in which conflicting colours take their place without quarrelling with one another, and none shrieking. This, Gombarov had time to observe before reaching the end of his journey, had its counterpart in the physical contours of the streets, which were curiously free from sharp abutting angles so characteristic of the streets of the New World.[33]

Sitting on the top deck of the bus, the modern interplay of objective and subjective life is made conscious to Gombarov as he notices the international entertainments advertised along the Charing Cross Road. It is here that he invokes the metaphor of "ultra-modern music"—not jazz but, presumably, the music of Schönberg and the Second Viennese School.

The soul of old England was left behind in Trafalgar Square; the 'bus rolled on through one of the corridors of the new England. Up Charing Cross Road, past a cinema house, announcing "The Grim

Avenger: A Thrilling Romance of Three Continents," past the Hippodrome, blazing with lights; past the buildings of new flats, utterly banal but for the curve of the old street; past a music hall, flaunting across its front the pirouetting figure of a Russian toe dancer on a coloured screen, while underneath, flashing for the world to see, letters of bright light proclaiming other attractions: a Cockney Comedian, a Spanish Tango Turn, a Swedish Acrobat Troupe, American Clog Dancers, an Argentine "Stunt" Artist, Naughty Fifi the French Comic Chanteuse, and Mimi, her Eccentric Accompanist, and so on, and so on: "How amazingly international!" mused Gombarov, and laughed to himself, as the after-thought struck him: "And here am I, a Russo-American Jew, looking on!"

Was this chaos or unity? It was chaos, and had a unity after a fashion. It was the unity of a many-tuned medley, each tune of which maintained its entity, losing it only at the moment of embracing another tune; at best, it was the unity of ultra-modern music, shaped out of discords, beaten but not molten into a harmony.[34]

The opposition between unity and chaos reprises not just the question of whether the European metropolis was utopia or dystopia but also the challenge of how it might be possible to live with the inevitably ambivalent answer. By listening to the city as well as looking at it, John Cournos probably gets it about right. It was dystopian, insofar as the shocks and stimuli experienced every day by the citizens of London, Berlin, Vienna, and Paris were being ratcheted up to a new intensity and new technologies and cultural forms were producing a specifically modern, and uncanny, hollowing-out of experience and loss of personal qualities. And yet, it was utopian "after a fashion," an "ultra-modern" fashion that can be glimpsed in the vogue for jazz as another facet of Benjamin's "complex training" of the human sensorium.

This ambivalence, which is also a working-through and a sentimental education, recurs in another, final, novel of the period. There is undoubtedly more dystopia than utopia in David Vogel's portrait of Vienna in his Hebrew-language novel *Married Love*, published in 1928. At one moment, Vogel offers an expressionist sketch that captures the sensory overload and sheer *strangeness* of the city of electric night.

After deciding to go to the Opernkeller they got up and left the café.

It was about half past ten. The noise in the streets was already growing weaker, as if there were holes gaping in it. The asphalt stretched out before them, swelling and gleaming with a nocturnal glitter. The passers-by were reflected in it as in a distorting mirror, squat and dwarf-like or exaggeratedly long and thin. Rays of an orange coloured light issued from the luxurious cafés, a glaring, arrogant light, so bright that when you entered it your eyes shrank and blinked momentarily in pain. The revolving doors disgorged people from one side and swallowed them from the other, like some strange machine. In their garish uniforms the doormen bowed ceremoniously, making sweeping gestures with their arms as if they were opening great doors in the air. Fragments of jazz, foxtrots and tangos came reeling from all directions, flying around you like invisible bats and leaving you slightly stunned, your arms and legs throbbing in time to the tunes. In the middle of all this the solitary policeman idly patrolling the street looked superfluous, pitiful and forlorn.

Again, this is not just a representation of the dystopian modern city but a lesson in how to survive, at least, the city, however painfully. Vogel's iconography prefigures the bleak, anomic city of film noir and thus also the didactic science fiction dystopias of *Alphaville*, *Blade Runner*, and *Sin City*. The later generic appropriations of the imagery are less important, though, than its *presentness*. There is a beauty to this dystopian moment, the beauty of modernity that Baudelaire saw in "the ephemeral, the fugitive, the contingent." Yet Vogel presents an ethics as well as an aesthetics, in the form of an affective diagnosis of the moment in this particular, contingent space. The gloss by the novel's hero, Gurdweill, recognizes that this moment-place reflects less the nature of urbanism as such than the projection of existential and historical anxieties onto the city.

People rush to places of amusement and dancing and bawdiness not always out of any real appetite for pleasure, but more often in the need to escape. Most of these people are unhappy, sick of their lives, unable to stand themselves. . . . Burdened by daily cares, boredom, or simply fear, an obscure fear of which they are not even aware—a fear which unconsciously robs them of their peace of mind, drives them relentlessly on, and prevents them from looking directly and courageously at the commotion in their souls and all around them. The rootlessness grew even worse after the war, until it sometimes seems that all these people are actually sorry they survived.[35]

Elsewhere, Vogel strikes a different note as he captures the other half of Baudelaire's modern beauty, that is, the eternal and the immutable to be found in the evanescent, which also sustain a new form of utopianism and a new way of being. The impact of externalized culture, especially information technologies and mediated communication, caused, or at least accelerated, the modern sense of placelessness and even homelessness. In these circumstances, utopianism ceased to be the fantasy of a perfect future. Modern citizens learned to experience it instead as a kind of objectless nostalgia. This is what Vogel captures in his description of the landscape and soundscape of Vienna at dusk.

> In the mild spring air a pure, gentle stillness seemed to drop from the darkening sky. The deserted streets looked as if they had just been swept. The city was sinking into sleep in the orange glow of the streetlamps. From time to time, at increasing intervals, a tram split the silence like a nightmarish awakening. A distant train emitted a long, muffled hoot. And for a moment the imagination was captured by long journeys through the soundlessly breathing night, strange cities populated by millions of human beings.[36]

What, finally, was the lesson about living with modernity that all these campaigners, philosophers, and novelists learned from the unignorable, hellish, and energizing sounds of the city and passed on to their fellow-citizens? One aspect was the need to transcend the reassuring binary of dystopia and utopia, with its implicit narrative of fall and redemption. Dystopian jeremiads against the noise of the modern city at least helped set the ground rules by reminding modern citizens that silence would not be an option. Utopianism figures only as evasive covering of one's ears, at best, or yearning for the silence of the death-drive, at worst. The emerging, more pragmatic alternative, sketched here, appears to have been a disenchanted ethical disposition: the acknowledgment that, in practice, modern self-formation is possible only through sensory adaptation to modern life and in the imperfect normality of everyday life.

This is a lesson that Schopenhauer would have hated. Mixing Baudelaire with Nietzsche, it seems to be a lesson about how to experience oneself, *hic et nunc*, in the difficult city and the fugitive present, as being also infinite and eternal. It is the lesson of Langston Hughes's jazz band: Enjoy your dystopia, sweetie! Sure.

Notes

The research on which this essay is based has been supported by ARC Discovery Grant DP0664990. The essay develops themes and arguments previously addressed in "A Complex Kind of Training: Cities, Technologies and Sound in Jazz-Age Europe," in *Talking and Listening in the Age of Modernity: Essays on the History of Sound*, ed. Joy Damousi and Desley Deacon (Canberra: ANU E Press, 2007).

1 Arthur Schopenhauer, "On Noise," http://www.mgilleland.com/asonnoise.htm (accessed February 27, 2008).

2 Cited in Peter Payer, "The Age of Noise: Early Reactions in Vienna, 1870–1914," *Journal of Urban History* 33, no. 5 (July 2007): 781. I have taken many of my empirical Viennese examples from this fascinating article. I am grateful to David Ambaras for bringing it to my attention.

3 Theodor Lessing, "Die blauschwarze Rose," in *"Ich warf eine Flaschenpost ins Eismeer der Deschichte": Essays und feuilletons, 1923–1933* (Darmstadt, 1986), 400, trans. and cited in Hans Ulrich Grumprecht, *In 1926: Living at the Edge of Time* (Cambridge, MA: Harvard University Press, 1997), 28. Translation modified.

4 Payer, "The Age of Noise," 781.

5 Grumprecht, *In 1926*, 231. Translation modified. There is a terrible irony about what Lessing wishes for here. Having been hounded out of his job at the Technical Institute of Hanover in 1926 by right-wing, anti-Semitic students for lampooning Hindenburg's presidency in a series of newspaper articles, Lessing was assassinated in exile in Marienbad by Czechoslovakian Nazis in 1933.

6 This account of the Deutscher Lärmschutzverband draws on Payer, "The Age of Noise," 781–83.

7 See ibid., 783.

8 Alfred Freiherr von Berger, *Autobiographische Schriften*, vol. 3, *Reden und Aufsätze* (Deutch-Öster, 1913), 314–15; Payer, "The Age of Noise," 773–74.

9 Payer, "The Age of Noise," 778.

10 Cage learned that there is no such thing as silence, in the sense of a total absence of sound, when he visited an anechoic chamber at Harvard University in 1951 in order to hear silence. Instead of "nothing," he heard two sounds, one high and one low. These were, apparently, his nervous system and the circulation of his blood. As a result, Cage rethought silence as the absence of *intended* sounds, or the turning off of the hearer's awareness. "Silence is not acoustic, it is a change of mind. A turning around." See John Cage, "Experimental Music," in *Silence* (Middletown, CT: Wesleyan University Press, 1961), esp. 14.

11 Payer, "The Age of Noise," 775.

12 Ibid., 783.

13 Döblin quoted in Peter Hall, *Cities in Civilization: Culture, Innovation, and Urban Order* (London: Phoenix Giants, 1998), 243.

14 Walter Benjamin, *Charles Baudelaire: A Lyric Poet in the Era of High Capitalism*, trans. Harry Zohn (London: New Left Books, 1973), 132.

15 Robert Musil, *The Man without Qualities*, trans. Sophie Wilkins (New York: Alfred A. Knopf, 1995), 3.

16 Ibid., 4.

17 "The individual has become a mere cog in an enormous organisation of things and powers which tear from his hands all progress, spirituality, and value in order to transform them from their subjective form into the form of a purely objective life. It needs merely to be pointed out that the metropolis is the genuine arena of this culture which outgrows all personal life. Here in buildings and educational institutions, in the wonders and comforts of space-conquering technology, in the formations of community life, and in the visible institutions of the state, is offered such an overwhelming fullness of crystallised and impersonal spirit that the personality, so to speak, cannot maintain itself under its impact." David Frisby and Mike Featherstone, eds., *Simmel on Culture* (London: Sage, 1988), 184.

18 Emily Thompson, *The Soundscape of Modernity: Architectural Acoustics and the Culture of Listening in America, 1900–1933* (Cambridge, MA: MIT Press, 1988), 1–2.

19 Ilya Ehrenburg, *The Life of the Automobile*, trans. Joachim Neugroschel (1929; New York: Urizen Books, 1976), 22–23.

20 Ibid., 2.

21 Michael North, *Reading 1922: A Return to the Scene of the Modern* (New York: Oxford University Press, 1999), 15–16.

22 Translated and cited in John Willett, *The New Sobriety: Art and Politics in the Weimar Period, 1917–33* (London: Thames & Hudson, 1982), 111.

23 North, *Reading 1922*, 208; emphasis added.

24 Marcel Proust, *Remembrance of Things Past*, vol. 2, trans. C. K. Scott Moncrieff and Terence Kilmartin (London: Chatto & Windus, 1968), 135, 137.

25 For an insightful discussion of both the Proust and Joyce examples, see Sara Danius, *The Senses of Modernism: Technology, Perception and Aesthetics* (Ithaca: Cornell University Press, 2002), 182.

26 Quoted in Claire Taylor-Jay, *The Artist-Operas of Pfitzner, Krenek and Hindemith: Politics and the Ideology of the Artist* (Aldershot: Ashgate, 2004), 100.

27 Kurt Weill, *Der Deutsche Rundfunk* 4 (March 14, 1926): 732–33, cited in Anton Kaes, Martin Jay, and Edward Dimendberg, eds., *The Weimar Republic Sourcebook* (Berkeley: University of California Press, 1995), 597.

28 Quoted in Brent Hayes Edwards, *The Practice of Diaspora: Literature, Translation and the Rise of Black Internationalism* (Cambridge, MA: Harvard University Press, 2003), 63.

29 See Peter Brooker, *Bohemia in London: The Social Scene of Early Modernism* (Basingstoke: Palgrave Macmillan, 2007).

30 John Cournos, *Babel* (London: Heinemann, 1923), 307.

31 Ibid.

32 Ibid., 321.

33 Ibid., 70.

34 Ibid., 73–74.

35 David Vogel, *Married Life*, trans. Dalya Bilu (1929–30; New York: Grove Press, 1988), 74–75.

36 Ibid., 29–30.

Chapter 3

■

Tlatelolco

Mexico City's Urban Dystopia

RUBÉN GALLO

A few years ago, in a catalogue for an exhibition on utopias, critic Frédéric Rouvillois mused on the relationship between utopias and totalitarianism in the twentieth century. Why is it, he wondered, that so many projects for a complete overhaul of society—from the Russian Revolution to German National Socialism—that began as utopian dreams ended up producing history's worst nightmares? It appears, he writes, "as if utopia were nothing more than the premonition of totalitarianism and totalitarianism the tragic execution of the utopian dream."[1] As recent history demonstrates, there does seem to be a close link between utopias, dystopias, and totalitarian governments.

In Mexico, the Revolution of 1910–20 was followed by a bright era of optimism and utopian dreams. In a case that has many parallels to the early history of the Soviet Union, the new "revolutionary" government attempted to overhaul all aspects of Mexican society: from education to architecture, and from farming to urban planning. Many of these ambitious projects resulted in disastrous nightmares that continue to haunt the country like the specters of a distant era.

One of the most poignant case studies is the housing complex of Nonoalco-Tlatelolco, a monumental project designed to introduce the most modern—and utopian—urban planning concepts into Mexico City. Tlatelolco was the brainchild of architect Mario Pani and the Mexican president at the time, Gustavo Díaz Ordaz, who would go down in history as a man with a totalitarian governing style whose administration was marred by unprecedented police brutality, violence, and repression. The utopian dream of Tlatelolco soon degenerated into one of the worst dystopic nightmares in Mexico City's urban fabric. Could this unraveling be explained by Rouvillois's theory about the connection between utopias and totalitarianism?

Utopias and Urbanism

In 1991 Rem Koolhaas, the enfant terrible of architecture, proposed a hair-raising project: taking an entire district of Paris, the industrial area behind the Grand Arche de la Défense that had become an eyesore and a postmodern ruin of sorts, and demolishing every building that was older than twenty-five years. The process was to be repeated every five years until the entire site had been—in Koolhaas's words—"laundered," "liberated," and made available to an urban planner willing to conceive of new uses for the thousands of meters of empty space.[2]

Koolhaas's project never got off the ground, but it did send shivers up the spine of more than one preservationist. His was an act of provocation, an architectural crime against what the French have codified into law as the "le patrimoine," a cultural heritage to be preserved, maintained, restored, and defended against the vandal impulses of mischievous architects. It is significant that Koolhaas chose to propose this project in Paris, the one city in the world that has preserved an aura of historical authenticity. Curiously, this proposal—which seems so outrageous in the context of the French capital—is a perfect description for the history of urbanism in Mexico City since the fifteenth century: entire areas of the city are periodically "laundered" and "liberated" to make room for a new generation of urban planners and their projects for modernizing and improving the urban fabric.

Much to the horror of conservative planners and preservationists, Mexico City has been caught in an apparently endless cycle of demolition and rebuilding. In the 1520s the Spanish conquistadores razed the Aztec city of Tenochtitlán to build a new European capital: the canals that inspired travelers to describe the capital as a "Venice of the new world" were filled and transformed into streets and avenues. In the seventeenth and eighteenth centuries, dozens of buildings in the city center were razed to make room for grand palaces and churches, decorated in the heavy baroque style that would become typical of New World architecture, to better represent the power and riches of the capital of New Spain, a metropolis that had become the crown jewel of the Spanish Empire. In the nineteenth century, architects rebelled against the dominant baroque style, which they criticized as outmoded and mired in the past, and opted for the sober lines of neoclassical architecture: their proposals led to the redesign of the façades of a good number of baroque churches and palaces in central Mexico City. Baroque ornament gave way to straight lines and triangular frontispieces. The same process continued in the twentieth century: around the turn of the last century there was more demolition to make room for Art Nouveau residential areas like Colonia Roma; in the 1920s an entire neighborhood, Colonia Condesa, became a laboratory for experimenting with functionalism and modern construction techniques; and in the 1940s and 1950s, large sections of the city were bulldozed to make room for vast modernist housing projects, including Tlatelolco, the subject of this essay.

But this dialectic of demolition and rebuilding, of "liberation" and "laundering," has been decried by Mexican historians as an urban planning disaster and a dystopic nightmare. Consider, for instance, the harsh assessment offered by historian Guillermo Tovar de Teresa in his *City of Palaces: Chronicle of a Lost Heritage*, one of the classic texts on the urban transformations undergone by Mexico City: "We Mexicans suffer from an illness, a rage, a desire for self-destruction, to cancel and erase ourselves, to leave no trace of our past, or the way of life in which we believed and to which we devoted ourselves. . . . We Mexicans still believe that it is necessary to destroy the past to make way for the present. More than just a bad habit, this is a serious problem of national identity."[3]

Paris and Mexico City represent two extremes of urban planning: one is a city frozen in time, the other, an ever-changing construction site. But which is the utopia and which the dystopia?

Grand Ensembles

The decades of the 1950s and 1960s were a period when the city's most influential urban planners hailed the Corbusierian model of the modern city as the most desirable plan for the Mexican capital. The resulting projects marked a turning point in the dialectic of laundering and liberation that shaped the capital's history. Between 1950 and 1968, Mexico City underwent the most radical transformation in its history: a postwar economic boom, combined with mass migration from the countryside to the city, resulted in a population explosion that took the city's population from about three million in 1950 to almost seven million in 1970. To cope with this exponential growth, architects and urban planners embarked on an ambitious project to redesign the capital, building ring roads, expressways, and even a subway system. The two architects who were most closely involved in planning the new city were Luis Barragán and Mario Pani.

The work of Barragán is well-known outside Mexico. Most histories of modern architecture—including Kenneth Frampton's—usually present him as the lone representative of this tendency in Mexico.[4] The work of Pani, on the other hand, is virtually unknown outside Mexico and has received scant attention by architectural historians or critics (with the exception of Edward Burian, who devoted a chapter to Pani's work in his *Modernity and the Architecture of Mexico*).[5]

Barragán and Pani designed new neighborhoods that expanded Mexico City's metropolitan area by many miles to the north and the south: Barragán designed the suburbs of Pedregal (to the south) and Ciudad Satélite (to the north); Pani collaborated on the design of the vast college campus known as Ciudad Universitaria on the southern edge of the city. Between the two of them, they carved a significant portion of the modern-day capital. Barragán would go down in history as the creator of an original Mexican modern architectural style, while Pani would be remembered chiefly for his controversial housing projects, including Tlatelolco.

Pani was born in 1911, the son of a diplomat, and during the 1930s he studied at the École des Beaux Arts in Paris, where he discovered the work of Le Corbusier. As he told Graciela de Garay in an interview, he became fascinated by urban planning and after his return to Mexico spent many years lobbying the Mexican government to transform the capital into a radiant city.[6]

Pani benefited from his family's political connections, and in the late 1940s he secured a government commission to build the first Corbusierian housing complex in Mexico City. City officials had planned to build several hundred small houses for workers, but Pani convinced them that such an idea was out of sync with modern urbanism. He argued that the city should build housing units modeled on Le Corbusier's ideas and eventually won approval to build the Multifamiliar Miguel Alemán, completed in 1949, a massive project containing over one thousand apartments distributed among twelve buildings. As Louise Noelle Merles has pointed out, "the term *multifamiliares* was coined for this type of multifamily housing in Mexico, which also featured the separation of the pedestrian and the automobile in the superblock."[7]

A year after the Multifamiliar Alemán was completed, Pani embarked on a second, even more ambitious project: Multifamiliar Presidente Juárez, another housing complex completed in 1952. By 1960 the young architect was already at work on a third housing complex, this time more massive, more ambitious, and more monumental than either of the two projects he had done before. Pani set out to build a complex designed to house one hundred thousand inhabitants in fifteen thousand apartments distributed over dozens of buildings in an area occupying several thousand square kilometers in Tlatelolco, a decaying industrial neighborhood in northern Mexico City.

The area was poor and bleak, and Pani proposed treating it as a tabula rasa—to use Koolhaas's terminology—on which a complex of modernist apartment towers would be built. It is almost identical to the project Koolhaas presented for Paris, and Pani even made the same argument as the Dutch architect—that the neighborhood was in ruins, that it lacked any historical buildings that merited preservation, and that the best strategy to regenerate such an urban area was to raze it. Pani carefully calculated the expected flux of thousands of families that had been living in premodern housing in adjacent neighborhoods and drew a series of graphs showing their orderly flow into Tlatelolco.

The Tlatelolco site measured almost two kilometers from east to west and five hundred meters from north to south. It was a vast area of one million square meters, which Pani divided into three superblocks, to be filled with apartment towers ranging in height from four to twenty-two stories.

In an interview, Pani described his vision for Tlatelolco as follows: "We still need to regenerate over half of Mexico City, which is full of awful neighborhoods. The one advantage is that most of these neighborhoods are so awful that they are just waiting to be regenerated, to be torn down and rebuilt properly."[8] Pani's ambitious building projects illustrate the influence Le Corbusier's urbanism had in Mexico. As Frampton has written, "the typical Corbusian solution to high-density housing . . . was to be copied with disastrous consequences in a great deal of subsequent urban development, and the alienating environment created in many of the postwar grands ensembles clearly owes much to the influence of this model."[9]

Pani saw Tlatelolco as simply the beginning of a massive urban project lending to the demolition of vast areas of Mexico City. Koolhaas once characterized Le Corbusier's Plan Voisin to rebuild Paris as "megalomania" (Jane Jacobs gives a similar characterization in her *Death and Life of Great American Cities*), but when compared to Pani, the French architect, who only got to build one, relatively modest, *unité d'habitation* in Marseilles, appears like a humble planer.[10] In an interview given in 1990, shortly before his death, Mario Pani lamented that he only got to construct one Tlatelolco. He told an interviewer: "We wanted to continue with more projects, to expel all those who were living in poor neighborhoods, we wanted to build more and more housing complexes. I was planning on building five or six Tlatelolcos, with an extension of over 3 million square meters, two million square meters of gardens, and a capacity for 66,000 families."[11]

Had Pani gotten his way, he would have unleashed a thousand Tlatelolcos on Mexico City. Like Shakespeare's Caliban, who dreamed of propagating himself in the form of "a thousand Calibans," Pani dreamed of spreading his legacy throughout the capital in the form of thousands and thousands of dwelling units, a sort of Calibannian modernism gone wild.

Traumatic Returns

As Pani prepared to launch his most ambitious housing project, an unexpected discovery threatened to derail his project. Tlatelolco was the site of an ancient pre-Columbian city, and archaeologists opposed his plan on the grounds that the construction would destroy the historical artifacts that might lie buried below ground. There was also a more formidable obstacle for the construction of his Mexican *unité d'habitation*: the grounds included the ruins of an Aztec pyramid that had been razed by the Spaniards in the sixteenth century as part of their design to transform the capital into a European city.

Pani must have been mortified: an Aztec ruin did not fit into his vision of a *ville radieuse*, and even the lax Mexican authorities would not allow such an important monument to be razed—not for a second time—in the name of architectural modernism. What had been repressed by the Spaniards, the Aztec city with its pyramidal structures, suddenly reemerged with a vengeance and threatened Pani's ambitious plans to modernize Mexico's urban fabric.

In many ways, the pyramid is the structural opposite of the housing block that Pani designed for Tlatelolco. The block represented modernity; the pyramid the country's ancient past. The block was linked to Corbusierian urbanism; the pyramid to archaeological excavation. Pani's blocks were to rise upward, lifting their inhabitants' hopes toward the sky in a utopian gesture. The pyramid, in contrast, was located in a sunken pit and its remains pointed toward the entrails of the earth—an apt metaphor for the sinking feeling Pani must have experienced when he learned of the archaeological restrictions. Housing blocks represented the triumph of order and rational principles over living spaces; the pyramid, in contrast, was an alarming reminder of Octavio Paz's claim that the irrational forces associated with the Aztecs—ritual murder and human sacrifice—persisted in twentieth-century Mexico.[12] Pani dreamed of erecting buildings on the exact same site in which archaeologists wanted to dig down into the ground to uncover the ancient city of Tlatelolco.

Modernism as Racial Trope

Pani was a master of public relations and he found a way to turn the bothersome pyramid to his advantage. He was not allowed to raze the pyramid, but he was allowed to build around it, and thus dozens of housing blocks rose around the shell of a pyramid. Pani even found a way to modernize the pyramid—or, rather, to create a modernist reinterpretation of the ancient Aztec structure: the tallest building he designed for Tlatelolco was a pyramid but one that was planned according to modernist principles to rise in all its geometric splendor over the Aztec ruin.

But the Aztec pyramid was not the only element from the past that would return to haunt Pani's modernist vision. Next to the pyramid there was the sixteenth-century church and convent of Santiago Tlatelolco. In the end the architect incorporated both church and pyramid into the Corbusierian com-

Figure 3.1. Detail of the Nonoalco-Tlatelolco housing complex. From Manuel Larrosa, *Mario Pani: Arquitecto de su época* (Mexico City: UNAM, 1985). Courtesy of Ms. Márgara Pani.

plex, placing them in the midst of a large plaza surrounded by modernist towers.

In a public relations coup, city officials promoted this strange amalgam of Aztec pyramid, Spanish convent, and modernist planned city as the "Plaza of the Three Cultures," a name inspired by a staple of post-Revolutionary ideology promoted by the ruling party: the theory that modern Mexico was a new mestizo culture born out of the encounter of two previous civilizations: the Aztecs and the Spaniards.

This mythological reworking of the plaza deserves some comment. On the one hand, the plaza of the three cultures refers to three historical periods: there was the Aztec empire, followed by the Spanish viceroyalty, which eventually gave way to an independent Mexico. Following this logic, the pyramid is a remnant of Aztec architecture, the church a vestige of Spanish construction, and the modernist complex an example of modern Mexican planning. But in official rhetoric the "three cultures" are often linked to ethnicity (Indian, European, and mestizo), and it was this aspect that planners chose to emphasize in the plaque that can still be seen today in Tlatelolco's Plaza of the Three Cultures: "On August 13, 1521, after being heroically defended by Cuauhtémoc,

Tlatelolco fell to Hernán Cortés. It was neither victory nor defeat, but the painful birth of the mixed-blood country that is Mexico today."

The history of Mexico, so official mythology proclaims, is the history of three races: the country was first inhabited by the Aztecs; after the arrival of the Spanish conquistadores the two races combined to create a third race, the modern Mexicans, a mixed-blood people born, painfully as the sign reminds us, of the clash between the two earlier groups. The plaza of the three cultures is also the plaza of the three races, and each of the disparate buildings emerges as a racial trope: the pyramid represents the Aztec race; the church the Spaniards; and—in a truly surprising twist—Pani's housing blocks emerge as the symbol of the mixed-blood inhabitants of modern Mexico. In Pani's project, modernism no longer represents the purity of forms but the impurity and intermingling of blood, and Le Corbusier turned into an apostle of racial mixing.

A pyramid, a church, and a modernist housing complex. In his plans for the *ville radieuse* Le Corbusier sought to separate living, working, and leisure areas. Pani's Mexican version of the *ville radieuse* takes the plan further: each of the three buildings in the Plaza of the Three Cultures fulfills radically different functions: the colonial church is still used for the celebration of mass; until recently one of the modernist towers served as a passport office; and the pyramid—at least according to Octavio Paz's reading, which will be discussed below—continues to be used for human sacrifices.

The Pyramid

In 1968, two years after the last structure in Pani's complex had been completed, Tlatelolco became the stage of the bloodiest event in twentieth-century Mexican history. On October 2, a group of several thousand students assembled on the Plaza of the Three Cultures for a protest rally against the city government's repressive policies. In the previous months there had been several clashes between police and students throughout the city, the army had briefly occupied the main campus of the National University of Mexico, and dozens of young men and women had been arrested and imprisoned.[13]

Inspired by the events of May 1968 in Paris, Mexican students had staged several peaceful marches and protests against what they saw as the government's increasingly undemocratic tendencies. The president, Gustavo Díaz Ordaz, had ordered the police and the army to fight back. He feared a local replay of the massive strikes and demonstrations that had paralyzed Paris and, above all, he was terrified that the students and their protests would jeopardize the Olympic Games, which were scheduled to open on October 12.

Hundreds of protesters and sympathizers assembled peacefully in the Plaza of the Three Cultures, where student leaders gave speeches and read statements. Suddenly, the army surrounded Tlatelolco, and tanks and helicopters moved in on the square and opened fire on the students. All entrances to the housing complex were shut, and the students were trapped inside Tlatelolco, "as in a mousetrap," as one of them later recalled. About three hundred students were killed and over one thousand were arrested.

The Tlatelolco massacre shattered the vision of the Institutional Revolutionary Party (PRI) as a benevolent institution that had maintained peace and order and that, while not entirely democratic, had saved Mexico from the repressive regimes—from juntas to military dictatorships—that had plagued so many Latin American countries since the 1930s.

In one of the most eloquent texts on the Tlatelolco events, Octavio Paz argues that the massacre brought about a peculiar Mexican version of the return of the repressed. In his view, what had been repressed and now returned to haunt the country was the Aztec practice of human sacrifice, a ritual that had been staged atop the pyramids before the Conquest. The pyramid, argued Paz, represented a powerful archetype with a visible continuity from Aztec times to the twentieth century: it was a stage for human sacrifice but also a metaphor for the almost unlimited power exercised by Mexican rulers, from Aztec emperors to twentieth-century presidents. In Mexico, power has always been concentrated at the top of the pyramid, in the figure of an all-mighty ruler, and exerted, authoritatively, over a vast population occupying the base of the pyramid.

In "Posdata," an essay published in response to the Tlatelolco massacre, Paz writes:

> Mexico's geography has a pyramidal shape, as if there were a secret but perceptible connection between natural space and symbolic geometry, between the latter and what I have called our invisible history. Archaic archetype of the universe, geometric metaphor of the cosmos, the pre-Columbian pyramid culminates in a magnetic space: the platform for sacrifices. . . . The pyramid, petrified time, locus of divine sacrifice, is also the image of the Aztec nation and its mission: to guarantee the continuity of the sun cult, the source of life, through the sacrifice of war prisoners. . . . The pyramid is the world and the world is Mexico-Tenochtitlan: a deification of the Aztec nation through its identification with the atavistic image of the cosmos: the pyramid. For the heirs of Aztec power [modern Mexicans], the connection between religious ritual and acts of political domination has disappeared, but the unconscious model of power remains the same: the pyramid and human sacrifice.[14]

There is another reason why Paz might have attuned to the dialectic between Tlatelolco and the pyramid: after his return to Mexico City in the 1970s he lived in a building designed by Mario Pani—an extremely elegant modernist structure on the corner of Río Guadalquivir and Paseo de la Reforma, Mexico City's main thoroughfare, that was also the country's first condominium. Perhaps Paz feared that the modernist block he called home would also be upturned by the emergence of an atavistic pyramid.

Modernist Reverse Panopticons

Paz found a symbolic relation between the massacre and the pyramid; I'd like to make a bolder argument and suggest that there was a clear connection between Pani's modernist planning and the student massacre.

As critics from Michel Foucault to Guy Debord have argued, architecture is a means of exercising control, and nowhere is this more evident than in modernist housing complexes, especially the type of Corbusierian projects favored by Mario Pani.[15]

The Tlatelolco complex was designed to control the living environment, leisure activities, and even the movements of its inhabitants. The complex featured only a few access points, with gates that could be closed in a few seconds, preventing anyone from entering or exiting. Elsewhere, fortified walls prevented unauthorized access to the complex. Pani hailed the walls around the complex as elements that guaranteed the safety of the inhabitants and forced residents and visitors to enter and exit the buildings in an orderly fashion, using only designated accesses. It was precisely this architecture of control that allowed the army to trap the students inside the complex. If the rally had taken place in downtown Mexico City, a lively—and chaotic—urban space filled with streets, alleys, subway tunnels, and passageways, the students could have dispersed in a few minutes.

Once the students arrived at the Plaza of the Three Cultures, the site became a reverse panopticon: in the panopticon the guard stands at a central point from which he can survey the entire prison population. In the reverse panopticon, there is a central position that can be observed from every point in the structure. A panopticon can be surveyed by a single individual—the prison guard—while the reverse panopticon allows a multiplicity of vantage points from which to survey a central space. In Tlatelolco, the plaza could be seen from hundreds of vantage points throughout the complex, and this allowed soldiers to position themselves on rooftops and balconies. The protesters became easy targets since they could be seen, observed, and targeted from every building in the complex. Army snipers climbed atop the modernist blocks and had an unobstructed view of the students, who were trapped in the plaza as if in a mousetrap. "Visibility," as Foucault writes of the panopticon, "is a trap."[16]

La noche de Tlatelolco, Elena Poniatowska's compilation of testimonies about the student massacre, includes several accounts emphasizing how quickly the plaza became a trap.

> I told everyone that the Plaza of the 3 cultures was a trap, I told them so. ¡There's no way out! It's so obvious. I told them there would be no way to escape, that we would all be boxed in, penned in like animals. I told them so many times. . . .[17]
>
> . . . We could hear heavy rifle fire and the chatter of machine guns. From that moment on, the Plaza de las Tres Culturas was an inferno.[18]

The notion of the modernist housing complex as a dystopian trap has been exploited by several films staged in Tlatelolco, especially *Rojo Amanecer* (Red Dawn [1986–89]) and *Temporada de patos* (Duck Season [2005]).[19] These films are indirect representations of the massacre, and though they are certainly accounts of dystopian living, they present a very different picture of urban nightmares from that found in the other films studied by the authors included in this volume.

Rojo Amanecer was initially censored by the Mexican government and was not released until 1989, two years after its completion. Produced by Jorge Fons, this film featured several well-known television, theater, and film actors including María Rojo, Demian Bichir, and Bruno Bichir.[20]

Fons faced a great challenge: creating a moving image of a tragedy that had never been seen before. The general public understood the magnitude of the events and knew that many students had been killed, but there had been extremely few images of the massacre. Fons also knew that the Tlatelolco events were still a taboo subject in Mexican politics—in fact, the government archives were not fully opened until the late 1990s, and it was not until 2007 that a museum was opened at Tlatelolco to commemorate the events of October 2.

Fons knew that he was touching on a politically explosive subject, and he decided to shoot the film in secret: he did not take his crew or the actors to Tlatelolco. Instead, he filmed all the scenes indoors, in what was supposed to be a middle-class apartment in the housing complex of Tlatelolco. All the events—the student rally, the army shooting, and the ensuing massacre—only enter the apartment as background noise.

The choice of setting the film indoors allowed Fons to avoid clashes with the housing complex's administrators or the police, and it also led him to write an extremely compelling story.

The film tells the story of a lower-middle-class working family living in one of the slabs of the Tlatelolco housing complex. The father is a bureaucrat who works for the city government; the mother is a housewife. They live with the mother's aging father, a retired army officer who fought in the Revolution. They have a teenage daughter, a little boy, and two university-aged sons who have joined the student movement.

The film opens with several scenes depicting a happy family: parents, children, and the grandfather have breakfast together, but then they begin to argue about the student movement. The two sons are ardent believers in the power of peaceful demonstration, while their parents disapprove and insist on the dangers of confronting the government.

A massive student rally is scheduled to take place in the Plaza of the Three Cultures, downstairs from the family's apartment. The army begins firing on the students, and the characters watch the massacre from their apartment—or, rather, they hear it. Most of the representation of the violence is acoustic rather than visual.

The rest of the film maintains this strategy: we are never shown images of the killing, and the most we get to see are the shocked expressions of the family members who witness the violence. We never see images, but we do hear the sounds of machine-guns, screams, crowds running, and sniper shots. This acoustic representation of the massacre lasts for almost a third of the film.

Fons chose a form of representation that is ultimately more eloquent and more dramatic than a purely visual one. The film introduces a curious experiment with diegetic and extra-diegetic images: the characters have access to the sights on the plaza while we, the viewers, do not. While the characters can suture the sounds of machine-guns and rifles to the sights they have seen through the window, viewers are partially blind—or rather, the violence takes place in the viewer's blind spot.

In the end, *Rojo Amanecer* achieves the same effect sought by Poniatowska's *Massacre in Mexico*: to re-create the chaos, uncertainty, and confusion of the events as they were unfolding. She achieved this by creating a collage of disparate voices. Fons did the same event by giving us a reconstruction of the sounds of the killing, stripped of their visual component. Both Fons and Poniatowska emphasize the transformation of Tlatelolco into a trap: Poniatowska by gathering testimonies of students caught inside the complex; Fons by setting the film inside an apartment where the protagonists are literally trapped. In both cases, the Corbusierian *unité d'habitation* becomes the dystopian site of police surveillance.

Asked about the 1968 massacre in an interview, Pani blamed the students. In words that are eerily reminiscent of President Díaz Ordaz's justification for the massacre, he attributed the tragedy to a "worldwide upsurge of leftist tendencies conspiring against governments. . . . In Mexico, since it was a few days before the Olympic Games, the students picked the time and place in order to create the biggest possible scandal. And that it was: a great scandal. And it has given Tlatelolco the reputation of a place where people are killed."[21] Pani conceived Tlatelolco as a monument to planned living. In the popular imagination, it will always be remembered as the site of the 1968 student massacre.

Urban Dystopias

Tlatelolco began as a utopian project, but after 1968 it became the darkest symbol of Mexico's dystopian failures. For almost twenty years the housing complex was associated not with urban reform, with Corbusierian plans, or with Mario Pani but with the tragic massacre of October 2, 1968.

That would change, although not for the better, seventeen years later. On September 19, 1985, just before 8 A.M., Mexico City was shaken by the most powerful earthquake in recent memory, measured at 8.1 on the Richter scale. It lasted less than 120 seconds, but in that short time dozens of office buildings and apartment complexes collapsed, and the official death toll was put at four thousand, though many believe it might have been as high as thirty thousand.

The earthquake leveled many of Pani's buildings: several blocks of the Multifamiliar Juárez collapsed (see figure 3.2), as did one of the tallest apartment towers in Tlatelolco, the Edificio Nuevo León.

In Tlatelolco the high occupational density of the housing blocks translated into a terrifying number of casualties. Investigations launched after the earthquake revealed that the buildings in Tlatelolco had collapsed, in part, due to faulty building techniques. The construction company, it seems, had increased its profits by using inferior materials instead of higher-quality ones for the construction of the housing blocks. The foundations were not as solid as they needed to be, and in some cases fewer columns than were required were used to support the buildings. The use of pilotis, which Le Corbusier had promoted, proved to be a poor choice for an earthquake-prone urban area like Mexico City.

Investigators exposed a web of corruption that reached from city officials to contractors and perhaps even to Pani himself. Asked about his responsibility in the collapse of the Tlatelolco towers, Pani offered the following response.

I remember when one of the towers fell in the 1985 earthquake. It was discovered that the structural reinforcements were made of

Figure 3.2. Bob Schalwijk, Unidad Juárez housing project after the 1985 earthquake, Mexico City. Courtesy of Bob Schalwijk.

aggregate and of metal structures that were not even bound correctly to the main concrete structure. There had been an oversight, and I supposed some of it is my fault, since I should have overseen the workers and made sure they reinforced the building properly.[22]

The collapse of Pani's buildings is symptomatic of the fate of modernism in Mexico City. Le Corbusier's plan for the *ville radieuse* was imported to great fanfare, touted as the solution to many of the country's ills and as a harbinger of social progress. But in the end the country's endemic problems—from corruption to mismanagement—left its grand ambitions in ruins, like the housing blocks after the earthquake, reduced to a dystopian nightmare.

Lieux de Mémoire

Tlatelolco is a perfect example of what Pierre Nora has called "lieux de mémoire," places in which a country's cultural memory has been inscribed. As opposed to monuments designed by governments, where the link between object and memory comes from an institutional directive, *lieux de mémoire* emerge spontaneously from the people's identification of a site with an event. Think, for instance, of the difference between the numerous historical monuments in Washington, D.C., and the improvised memorials, set up on the walls of New York City firehouses, to those who perished in the World Trade Center attacks.[23]

In the minds of most inhabitants of Mexico City, Tlatelolco is linked to several of the most traumatic events of twentieth-century history: the razing of entire neighborhoods in the name of a utopian city of the future; the 1968 student massacre; the transformation of the housing complex into a totalitarian reverse panopticon; and the collapse of buildings, along with the nation's dream of a utopian modernity, during the 1985 earthquake.

Figures 3.3. Pedro Reyes, *Jardín vertical* (2002–8). Courtesy of the artist.

Figure 3.4. Pedro Reyes, *Jardín vertical* (2002–8). Detail. Courtesy of the artist.

In the end, the pyramid proved to be more resistant to earthquakes and other catastrophes than the superblock. The Aztec ruin is still there, and so is Pani's modernist pyramid, though it has been abandoned since 1985, when it was badly damaged during the earthquake. Since then, the ruined modernist pyramid casts an eerie shadow over Mexico City, reminding inhabitants of the hundreds of victims who perished in the housing complex.

At one point the city government proposed relocating the police head-quarters to the pyramid, but Tlatelolco's residents vehemently opposed the project. Perhaps after reading Octavio Paz's theory of the pyramid archetype they were disinclined to place the Mexico City police force at the apex of a structure that had been read as an archetype of domination, oppression, and totalitarianism.

In 2002 the artist and architect Pedro Reyes proposed a utopian project to reclaim the abandoned modernist ruin: transforming the spectral pyramid into a "vertical garden" that could bring back life into the site of so much urban destruction. Reyes's project calls for removing the façade of the current building to expose the open floors, which would then be planted and turned into green gardens. A verdant skyscraper!

Reyes's project turns on its head one of Pani's main justifications for building blocks: his invocation of the Corbusierian principle that towers allow architects to maximize the green areas around the buildings. In Tlatelolco, for instance, Pani reserved over 50 percent of the land for gardens. But after the collapse of the Nuevo León building in the 1985 earthquake, green spaces acquired a dark connotation: these new lawns are phantasmatic spaces, haunted by the specter of buildings that once stood there but have since collapsed, burying their inhabitants in the rubble.

There were once towers in Tlatelolco's gardens. Reyes inverts this proposition by proposing to place gardens in the tower. His proposal is a powerful metaphor of the relationship between collapsed buildings and gardens in Tlatelolco.

If we consider Reyes's project in light of Paz's theory of the archetype, the result is encouraging: the top of the pyramid is no longer occupied by a despotic ruler or by practitioners of human sacrifice but by a void: nothing occupies the top levels. The pyramid has been decapitated or, as Rem Koolhaas might say, "lobotomized."

Conclusion

As a *lieu de mémoire*, Tlatelolco points to two of the most traumatic events in recent Mexican history: the 1968 student massacre and the 1985 earthquake. As a modernist ruin, it represents the catastrophic failure of Pani's utopian plans for transforming Mexico City into an orderly, planned city.

Mexico City is one of the liveliest urban areas anywhere in the world. In most working-class neighborhoods, the streets are packed with the most unlikely collection of pedestrians: street vendors, *ambulantes*, gray-suited bureaucrats rushing back to the office, housewives shopping for meat and vegetables, children—including homeless ones—and even the occasional starry-eyed tourist. The streets are a constant source of entertainment for both passersby and residents, who spend hours peeking out windows or standing by their doorways.

As Jane Jacobs has argued in *The Death and Life of Great American Cities*, it is precisely this kind of street life that many twentieth-century urban planners, from Le Corbusier to Mumford, sought to destroy. Residents and strollers might enjoy the chaotic jumble of social classes and people from all walks of life orchestrated on city streets, but modern planners tend to label these neighborhoods as urban blight that needs to be replaced by a more orderly plan. "Under the surface," Jacobs writes, "these accomplishments prove even poorer than their poor pretenses. They seldom aid the city areas around them, as in theory they are supposed to. These amputated areas typically develop galloping gangrene. To house people in this planned fashion, price tags are fastened on the population, and each sorted-out chunk of price-tagged populace lives in growing suspicion and tension against the surrounding city."[24] This is an accurate description of the fate of working-class neighborhoods in Tlatelolco.

Yet the result of the vast majority of such urban interventions has been a complete disaster. As the case study of Tlatelolco illustrates, lively neighborhoods with an active street life were replaced by cold, planned complexes in which the streets are dead. In contrast to the rest of Mexico City, which is characterized by constant chaos, Tlatelolco, since its inauguration, has been a gloomy, melancholic housing complex. Even before the specters of the massacre and the earthquake installed themselves in this part of town, Tlatelolco has a sad, depressed atmosphere that clashes sharply with Pani's promotion of an ideal city of the future in which residents would live in orderly happiness, surrounded by green areas and gardens.

In *All That Is Solid Melts into Air*, Marshal Berman makes a passionate argument for the street—the unplanned city street—as a stage for the chance encounters and unexpected juxtapositions that have been the source of so much modernist literature. The urban boulevard, Berman writes, "bring[s] explosive material and human forces together."[25] City streets form the stage on which political activism, love, and even avant-garde literature perform the daily rituals of modernity. And it is precisely this lively, explosive, generative power of the city street that gets killed in Corbusierian projects of the type promoted by Pani.

In Mexico City, writers from Artemio del Valle Arizpe to Salvador Novo and Carlos Monsiváis have celebrated the vibrant life of city streets in neighborhoods as diverse as the Centro, Santa María la Ribera, and Coyoacán. No writers, however, have sung the glories of the alleys and passageways inside the Tlatelolco housing complex. As this chapter has argued, there is a vast literature on Tlatelolco that includes Poniatowska's two books and numerous films. These works, however, do not celebrate Pani's complex; they highlight the traumatic history associated with this *lieu de mémoire* and direct attention to the thousands of dead bodies buried under one of the city's most infamous urban disasters.

In contrast to these chronicles of dystopic nightmares, works like Pedro Reyes's *Parque Vertical* propose a homeopathic solution to the urban problems plaguing Tlatelolco: instead of repeating Pani's strategy of bulldozing and rebuilding, this playful project suggests strategies for turning modernist ruins into useful spaces and thus turning dystopian nightmares back into utopian dreams.

Notes

1 Frédéric Rouvillois, "Utopia and Totalitarianism," in *Utopia: The Search for the Ideal Society in the Western World* (New York: New York Public Library, 2000), 316.

2 Rem Koolhaas, "Tabula Rasa Revisited," in *S,M,L,XL* (New York: Monacelli Press, 1995), 1105.

3 Guillermo Tovar de Teresa, *La ciudad de los palacios: Crónica de un patrimonio perdido* (Mexico City: Vuelta, 1992), 13–14.

4 Kenneth Frampton, *Modern Architecture: A Critical History* (London: Thames & Hudson, 1980), 318–19.

5 Louise Noelle Merles, "The Architecture and Urbanism of Mario Pani: Creativity and Compromise," in *Modernity and the Architecture of Mexico*, ed. Edward Burian (Austin: University of Texas Press, 1997), 177–89.

6 Graciela de Garay, *Mario Pani: Historia oral de la Ciudad de México* (Mexico City: CONACULTA, 2000), 1, 74–76.

7 Merles, "The Architecture and Urbanism of Mario Pani," 180.

8 Garay, *Mario Pani*, 83–84.

9 Frampton, *Modern Architecture*, 182.

10 "No matter how vulgarized or clumsy the design, how dreary and useless the open space, how dull the close-up view, an imitation of Le Corbusier shouts 'Look what I made!' Like a great, visible ego it tells of someone's achievement." Jane Jacobs, *The Death and Life of Great American Cities* (New York: Vintage, 1992), 23.

11 Garay, *Mario Pani*, 87–88.

12 Paz made this argument in *Posdata*, published after the 1968 student massacre. See Octavio Paz, *El laberinto de la soledad*, ed. Enrico Mario Santí (Madrid: Cátedra, 1993), 363–415.

13 For an overview of the Tlatelolco events and the response by Mexican intellectuals, see Julia Preston and Samuel Dillon, *Opening Mexico: The Making of a Democracy* (New York: Farrar, Straus & Giroux, 2004), 63–94.

14 Paz, *El laberinto de la soledad*, 395.

15 Michel Foucault, *Discipline and Punish: Birth of the Prison* (New York: Random House, 1975).

16 Ibid., 20.

17 Elena Poniatowska, *Massacre in Mexico* (New York: Viking, 1975), 224. Translation modified.

18 Ibid., 203.

19 Jorge Fons, dir. *Rojo amanecer*, Mexico City, 1989. Fernando Eimbcke, dir., *Temporada de patos*, Mexico City, 2005.

20 On *Rojo Amanecer*, see José Homero, "Rojo amanecer," *Dicine: Revista de diffusion e investigación cinematográficas* 39 (May 1991): 11–12; Luciano Castillo, "Rojo amanecer," *Cine cubano* 132 (1991): 24; Peter Besas, "Rojo amanecer," *Variety* 341 (November 12, 1990): 65; and Rafael Medina de la Serna, "Rojo amanecer," *Dicine* 37 (November 1990): 20–21.

21 Garay, *Mario Pani*, 88.

22 Ibid., 80–81.

23 Pierre Nora, ed., *Les lieux de mémoire*, 3 vols. (Paris: Gallimard, 1984–86).

24 Jacobs, *The Death and Life of Great American Cities*, 4.

25 Marshal Berman, *All That Is Solid Melts into Air* (New York: Penguin, 1982), 165.

The Aesthetics of the Dark City

Chapter 4

■

A Regional Geography of Film Noir

Urban Dystopias On- and Offscreen

MARK SHIEL

Hollywood and Los Angeles after World War II

In the heyday of film noir, from the mid-1940s to the mid-1950s, the utopian aspirations that had driven the foundation and meteoric rise of the Hollywood studio system since World War I suddenly seemed fragile and liable to collapse. For the American Right, which had never much liked Hollywood on moral and political grounds, it came to appear as a Communist command post on American soil; for workers, it was a desperately insecure and often hostile place in which to try to make a living; and for the Hollywood moguls it was a dream they once had that was now threatened by industrial unrest, government regulation, and new technologies such as television.

In a lengthy and spirited defense of the Hollywood film industry from its critics published in the *New York Times* on April 9, 1950, Dore Schary, then head of production at MGM, contended that many Americans viewed Hollywood as a "modern Babylon," full of "white Rolls Royces," "blonde secretaries," and "houses full of bear rugs littered with unclad women."[1] Americans loved Hollywood for its visions of stars on the silver screen but they understood the real place barely at all and viewed its inhabitants with mistrust.

> This combination of interest and repulsion inspires attack from every angle. We are accused of being a reactionary town, interested only in a buck; of being enormously extravagant, and of being Communist-controlled. We are attacked for not using the screen to say something and we are accused of being propagandists and of filling the screen with "messages." We are viewed as a town tortured by labor strife, and we are told that *of course* there is no labor problem in Hollywood because we have corrupted and suborned the labor leaders. We are called insular, cut off from and oblivious of the world, and we are regarded as a transient community which has never developed any roots.[2]

The apparent encircling of Hollywood by hostile voices stood in contrast to what seemed to be the continuing and unstoppable rise to greatness of Los Angeles, the city in which Hollywood was based but with which its relationship had always been ambivalent. Like Hollywood, Los Angeles emerged strongly from World War II, but unlike Hollywood, it seemed to progress onward and upward for the following twenty years as a result of prioritized investment by the federal government that had begun under the New Deal and continued with the expansion of the city's vibrant defense, aircraft, and automobile industries, as well as its maritime trade. In 1940, Los Angeles was the fifth most populous city in the United States with 1.5 million people, behind Detroit, Philadelphia, Chicago, and New York, the latter with a population of 7.4 million.[3] By 1950, Los Angeles was fourth most populous. By 1960, when the city had a population of 2.5 million, it was third, exceeded only by Chicago and New York, although physically it was much larger than both (twice the land mass of Chicago and one and a half times that of New York). And when one considered the population of Los Angeles as a sprawling five-county region, comprising Los Angeles, Riverside, Ventura, San Bernardino, and Orange counties, it had a total population of 7.75 million, putting it in competition with the Big Apple itself. For the majority white population at least, the postwar era was one of economic boom and relative political stability, characterized by Mike Davis as an "Endless Summer" in which the city consolidated its public image as a conservative, affluent, sunny, healthy, and reliable bastion of a certain kind of American comfort, increasingly enhanced by abundant domestic goods, shopping malls, freeways, television, and Disneyland.[4]

Interpretations of Film Noir to Date

However, film noirs from *Double Indemnity* (Billy Wilder, 1944), *Detour* (Edgar G. Ulmer, 1945), and *The Big Sleep* (Howard Hawks, 1946) to *Criss Cross* (Robert Siodmak, 1949), *Kiss Me Deadly* (Robert Aldrich, 1955), and *Plunder Road* (Hubert Cornfield, 1957) undercut the ascent of Los Angeles. In tune with the gathering crisis of the Hollywood studio system, they presented Los Angeles as a disjointed network of nondescript commercial streetscapes, pretty but morally corrupt suburbs, and an increasingly dilapidated downtown as urban jungle. These were couched in the terms of what Paul Schrader has famously called "an uneasy, exhilarating combination of realism and expressionism" in visual style and by means of stories that emphasized betrayal, mental breakdown, or inevitable doom and were frequently recounted through the use of flashbacks accompanied by introspective and maudlin voiceovers.[5] This combination of distinctive approaches to mise-en-scène, filmic style, and narrative in film noir has contributed to the genre's enduring popular appeal and to the rich critical literature that surrounds it. J. P. Telotte has interpreted film noir in terms of a crisis in the classical codes and conventions of representation and narrative favored by the Hollywood studio system.[6] Frank Krutnik has related it to a crisis of patriarchal society in the United States caused by World War II, the mass mobilization for which had the effect of breaking down the traditional distinction between women as homemakers and men as breadwinners.[7] And James Naremore has explained it in terms of the influence on Hollywood cinema of a variety of popular, scientific, and philosophical discourses from realist crime fiction to psychoanalysis and French existentialism.[8] Studies such as these have shed important light on the genre. However, they have engaged very little with the local geography of film noirs, whether set in Los Angeles, New York, or other cities. Rather, they have tended to theorize the genre in terms of a generic American urban modernity. This is evident in the titles of many books on film noir which, notwithstanding their critical insights in other respects, tend to elevate its representation of a certain kind of urban landscape and experience to a quasi-mythical status—titles such as *Voices in the Dark, In a Lonely Street, More Than Night, Somewhere in the Night, Dark City, Shades of Noir, Street with No Name, Black & White & Noir,* and *Noir Anxiety*.[9] These draw attention to the metaphoric power of "noir" and related terms such as "night" and "dark," emphasizing foreboding, menace, and danger and, by implication, thinking about noir in terms of universal moral crisis and a generalizable visual opacity. Although many of these books acknowledge the importance of certain kinds of urban space to noir, they often do so through reference to an iconic but undifferentiated "street."

Moral crisis, visual opacity, and the street *are* tremendously important to noir, and noir does offer fascinating routes into the study of modernity, film style, gender, and the politics of Hollywood cinema. However, in the existing literature there is a curious contrast between the relative lack of attention given to the specific and real cities, neighborhoods, and streets used in film noirs and what is sometimes an obsessive tendency in literature on film noir to enumerate, categorize, and classify the details of film noirs along all sorts of other lines, such as by director, by production designer, by cinematographer, by studio, by star, or by narrative structure. This tendency to generalize about the modern American city in noir seems to have at least two origins. First, the earliest theorizations of noir were presented by French critics such as Nino Frank, Raymond Borde, and Etienne Chaumeton in the late 1940s and 1950s but these critics, being at a great distance physically and culturally, were not necessarily alive to the differences between American cities.[10] In

Borde and Chaumeton's now canonical *Panorama du film noir* (1955), little is done to speak to the specificity of American cities other than to acknowledge their modernity and toughness in general. Borde and Chaumeton refer to New York as a setting of film noir five times, to Los Angeles twice, Chicago once, and San Francisco four times—though in one of the San Francisco references they are mistaken (*Somewhere in the Night* is not set in San Francisco but in Los Angeles) and they never differentiate between the boroughs, districts, or neighborhoods of any given city, between the cinematic image of one city and another, or between the representation of a city from one film or film director to the next. Second, the prevalence of a generic characterization of dystopian urban modernity in film noir must surely be a function of the prominence of psychoanalytically oriented theory and criticism, which has long taken a special interest in noir because of its relatively antagonistic gender politics, because of the frequent intra-diegetic presence of psychoanalysis and psychoanalysts as a plot feature, and because of the efforts of noir filmmakers to use anti-illusionistic visual devices such as dream sequences and flashbacks to articulate neuroses and psychoses. From E. Ann Kaplan's *Women in Film Noir* (1978) to Mary Ann Doane's *Femmes Fatales* (1991) and Helen Hanson's *Hollywood Heroines* (2008), this kind of scholarship has approached film noir as a litmus test of the gender politics of Hollywood cinema as a whole but also a genre in which, for many, female characters displayed a complexity and an autonomy often otherwise lacking in Hollywood films.[11] By elaborating on distinctions between domestic and public space, the space of mise-en-scène and the interior space of the mind, and the respective spaces occupied by the viewer of a film, its characters on-screen, and the camera mediating their relationship, this work has demonstrated that cinematic space is deeply gendered.[12] But, in doing so, it has inevitably paid less attention to the site-specific spatial configuration of particular cities in film noirs.

Some recent scholarship has begun to shed a more precise light on the ways in which film noir engaged with the localities of Los Angeles and their architectural and social complexities. Edward Dimendberg has sought to explore the genre in terms of a gradual prevalence of "centrifugal" (dispersing) over "centripetal" (centralizing) forces in the social and physical shaping of the mid-twentieth-century American city and its representation in film noir, although Dimendberg does not explicitly identify either tendency with one or another specific city.[13] Eric Avila has interpreted the negative representation of Los Angeles in film noir as an expression of a growing distrust of urban environments by the white middle-class audiences to whom the films were primarily addressed, prompted especially by the racialization of the inner city and leading to the response known as "white flight."[14]

The Prominence of Los Angeles in Film Noir

My interest in this essay, therefore, lies in going further in the directions laid out by recent work by elaborating on the geographically specific relationship between Los Angeles and film noir. I aim to do this by analyzing the particular places film noirs most frequently use as settings and what patterns (if any) are evident in the use of settings in film noirs over time. In particular, because of film noir's special association with representations of the urban environment, I am interested in determining to what extent film noirs are set in particular named cities, which cities predominate as settings, and why. Such issues cannot be explored without considering a very large number of film noirs, across which patterns can be detected.

A filmography of all the major and minor examples of the genre, which I have compiled by surveying the most important critical literature for the purposes of this analysis, suggests that a total of 518 film noirs were produced in the United States between 1940 and 1959.[15] Analysis of this filmography confirms certain facts about film noir and its geography, which have been commented on before.[16] As figure 4.1 indicates, the genre peaked twice with fifty-eight films being released in 1947 and fifty-nine films in 1950. Throughout its history the settings of film noirs were predominantly American. Non-U.S. settings did feature—for example, in English gothic noirs such as *Rebecca* (Alfred Hitchcock, 1940) and in noirs concerning Americans abroad such as *Gilda* (Charles Vidor, 1946)—but such settings became slightly less prevalent in the 1950s. As figure 4.2 demonstrates, the vast majority of film noirs set in the United States featured urban settings, no doubt reflecting the significant increase in urbanization that characterized the nation during and after World War II. Having collapsed temporarily during the Depression, the average annual growth in the proportion of the total U.S. population living in cities nearly doubled from 0.7 percent in the 1930s to 1.3 percent in the 1940s and 1.7 percent in the 1950s, a rate higher than at any time since the turn of the twentieth century, while the proportion of the total population living in cities increased from 56.7 percent in 1940 to 64.3 percent in 1950 and 69.9 percent at the beginning of the following decade.[17] At the same time, however, as figure 4.2 indicates, a significant proportion of film noirs in most years also involved small-town or rural settings. This was especially the case, for example, in *The Lady from Shanghai* (Orson Welles, 1947), *They Live by Night* (Nicholas Ray, 1948), and *On Dangerous Ground* (Nicholas Ray, 1952), whose narratives, in a manner typical of many film noirs, involved movement between cities or between urban, small-town, and rural environments.

Analysis of the filmography also reveals features of the geography of film noir that have not been noted before. One hundred and ten films appear to have included New York City settings, and 114 were partly or wholly set in Los Angeles; San Francisco was featured in 36 films, Chicago in 12, and New Orleans in 9. Washington, D.C., was a setting in four films, Miami and Las Vegas in three, Detroit, Kansas City, Philadelphia, and Reno in two each, San Diego, Portland, Atlanta, Raleigh, Boston, Pittsburgh, and Atlantic City in one apiece. However, these simple numbers, which suggest a genre that was geographically widespread, conceal an important trend. The proportion of film noirs with settings in the American South, Midwest, and Northwest was al-

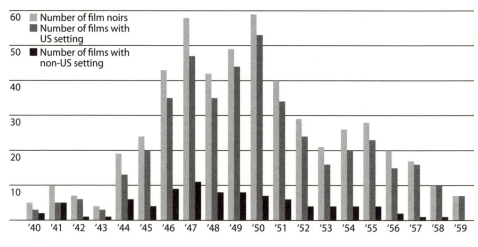

Figure 4.1. Number of American film noirs, 1940–59, and number with U.S. and non-U.S. settings.

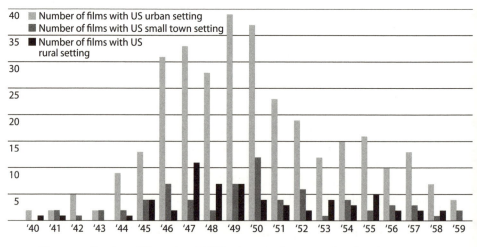

Figure 4.2. Number of film noirs with U.S. urban, small-town, and rural settings.

ways fairly low: for example, in 1947, which saw the release of fifty-eight films, those regions were represented in three, two, and four films, respectively; in 1950, which saw the release of fifty-nine films, they appeared in three, three, and eight films, respectively.[18] But settings in those regions were heavily outweighed in film noirs by settings in the Northeast and Southwest: the former occurred in seventeen films in 1947 and thirteen in 1950, while the latter featured in fourteen and nineteen films, respectively. These years were not exceptions but part of a larger trend. As figures 4.3 and 4.4 suggest, the proportion of film noirs with settings in the Northeast declined from 1940 to

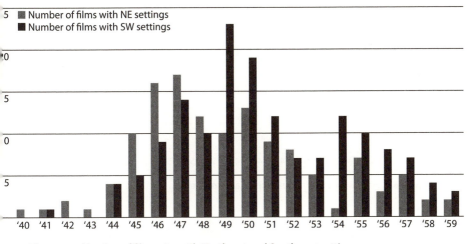

Figure 4.3. Number of film noirs with Northeast and Southwest settings.

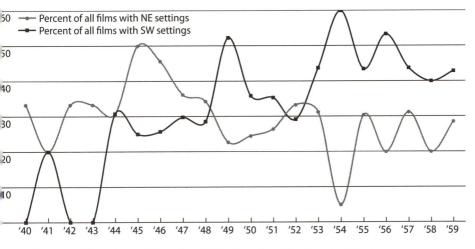

Figure 4.4. Percentage of film noirs with Northeast and Southwest settings.

1959 while the proportion set in the Southwest increased. Figure 4.5 clearly shows that the trend was also toward a greater prominence of settings in California.

These trends are in keeping with the historical reality of what Kirkpatrick Sale has called "the Cowboy Conquest," which saw the postwar American

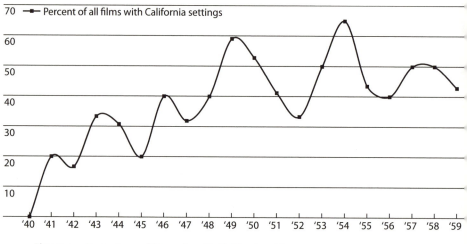

Figure 4.5. Percentage of film noirs with California settings.

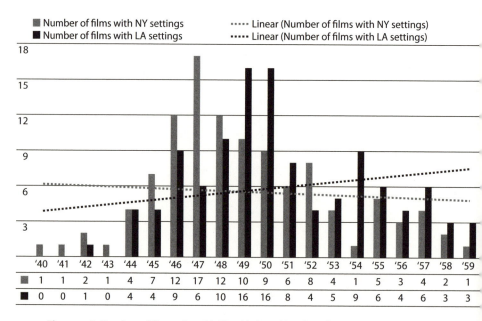

	'40	'41	'42	'43	'44	'45	'46	'47	'48	'49	'50	'51	'52	'53	'54	'55	'56	'57	'58	'59
	1	1	2	1	4	7	12	17	12	10	9	6	8	4	1	5	3	4	2	1
	0	0	1	0	4	4	9	6	10	16	16	8	4	5	9	6	4	6	3	3

Figure 4.6. Number of film noirs with New York and Los Angeles settings.

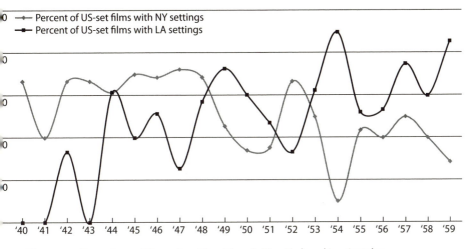

Figure 4.7. Percentage of film noirs with settings in New York and Los Angeles.

West gain a new demographic, economic, and political importance at the expense of other regions of the United States, especially the Midwest and Northeast.[19] Population growth in the West outstripped that of all other parts of the nation by at least 100 percent in every year from the Depression through the 1960s, and the proportion of the total population living in the West grew by nearly 50 percent from 10.5 percent in 1940 to 13 percent in 1950 and 15.6 percent in 1960.[20] This was in contrast to a decline in the share of the national population of all other regions, especially the Northeast, which had been home to approximately 28 percent of the national population throughout the first four decades of the twentieth century but whose share declined by nearly 9 percent from 1940 to 1960.[21] Finally, not only were New York and Los Angeles by far the most numerically prevalent geographically specific settings in film noir but, as figures 4.6 and 4.7 suggest, there was a significant pattern to their distribution. In every year from 1940 to 1948, New York was the more prevalent setting, with the exception of 1944 when it and Los Angeles were equally numerous. In those years, New York featured in approximately one-quarter to one-third of all films while Los Angeles featured in very few films until 1944 and then became gradually more prominent until 1949. In that and every subsequent year, with the exception of 1952 in which New York made a brief comeback, Los Angeles was the more prevalent setting, featuring in at least a quarter and sometimes almost a half of all film noirs from the end of the 1940s through the whole of the following decade. Indeed, the shift is reasonably dramatic and its timing—taking place in 1949—is worth examining in greater detail. It is both emblematic and indicative of a wider range of fundamental new realities at that time not only in cinema but in society, culture, politics, and economics. These new realities were particularly indebted to, and particularly visible in, Los Angeles.

The Decline of New York and the Rise of Los Angeles

In the mise-en-scène of film noirs this geographical shift may be illustrated by noting the overbearing, high-density environment of Manhattan that tends to dominate New York–based films such as *I Wake Up Screaming* (H. Bruce Humberstone, 1941), *Laura* (Otto Preminger, 1944), *The Lost Weekend* (Billy Wilder, 1945), *Scarlet Street* (Fritz Lang, 1945), and *Force of Evil* (Abraham Polonsky, 1948). This may be contrasted with the relatively suburban and automobilized noir that is frequently the hallmark of Los Angeles–based films from *He Walked by Night* (Alfred L. Werker, 1948) and *Criss Cross* to *The Blue Gardenia* (Fritz Lang, 1953), *Kiss Me Deadly*, and *Plunder Road*. Certainly, the contrast relies on degrees of difference rather than an absolute opposition. A significant number of the most celebrated film noir representations of Los Angeles predate the shift to which I am pointing, and much of the action in those takes place in built-up downtown environments—as is the case, for example, in parts of *Double Indemnity* (Billy Wilder, 1944) and *Murder My Sweet* (Edward Dmytryk, 1944). New York continued to be an important setting in film noirs of the 1950s such as *Fourteen Hours* (Henry Hathaway, 1951) and *Edge of the City* (Martin Ritt, 1957). Nonetheless, the significant increase in the prevalence and prominence of LA as a setting in film noir coincides with the genre's gradual evolution at the end of the 1940s and through the following decade away from expressionism and sympathetic portrayals of mentally imbalanced antiheroes and their crimes into the more reactionary form known as the "police procedural" film. In that form, chiaroscuro gave way to high-key lighting and the intricate plotting of murder was neutralized by a new interest in the processes of investigation and apprehension of criminals by law enforcement agencies.[22] This evolution was stylistic, narratological, and epistemological, and, I would suggest, it was to a great extent a function of the relative decline of New York and rise of Los Angeles as real cities and as cinematic settings in the decade and a half after World War II. I have argued elsewhere that New York was *the* American city setting par excellence in American cinema from the first emergence of motion pictures at the end of the nineteenth century until the 1960s when Los Angeles achieved a new prominence as a cinematic setting at New York's expense just as it did in demographic terms, as well as in economics, politics, and culture.[23] But it is in film noir that we first witness the coming dramatic ascent of Los Angeles to not only national but global importance that marked the late twentieth century.

Theorists of postwar American urbanization on a macrogeographical level, such as David Perry and Alfred Watkins, have argued that cities do not coexist in a neutral way but compete with each other for resources and manpower in order to grow and that they constantly have to develop their social and economic systems in order to get or stay ahead of their competitors.[24] Through a process of "uneven interregional development," the 1940s and 1950s saw the United States make a decisive transition from an industrial economy epitomized by New York to a new form of post-industrial "capital accumulation" epitomized by Los Angeles which, like other "Sunbelt" cities such as Houston and Phoenix, "was able to assume the mantle of growth leadership."[25] Or, to put it another way, the growth of one city, which is usually driven by some form of utopian aspiration, necessitates the checking or inversion of utopian aspirations somewhere else. One city's utopia requires another's dystopia. By 1940 Los Angeles was emerging as a major metropolis with a growing industrial base, in the words of a *Los Angeles Times* columnist in January 1940: "World leader in motion picture production; first in America in aircraft manufacture; leads America in secondary automobile manufacture and oil refining; ranks second in tire manufacture and fourth in furniture and women's clothing."[26] After the challenges of the Depression, New York received less of a boost from the wartime economy than either Los Angeles or Chicago, and from 1945 to the mid-1950s saw its industrial employment fall in absolute and relative terms.[27] Chicago's economic performance was very sluggish throughout the postwar period largely because of its failure to attract new technologies, while most major cities in the Northeast and Midwest—including New York, Chicago, and Boston—lost population in net terms in the fifteen years after World War II.

New York's response to Los Angeles's rise was not a passive one, and its civic and business leaders made strenuous efforts to lift the city's economy. As early as 1940, Edwin Schallert reported in the *New York Times*, in a story titled "Why New York Will Not Get Hollywood," that New York City mayor Fiorello LaGuardia had raised hopes of "a wholesale migration of the fabulous motion-picture colony of Hollywood from the West to the East Coast of America."[28] Schallert dismissed as a "phantasm" the idea that the Hollywood moguls would ever seriously consider relocating the industry away from Southern California.[29] For evidence, he pointed to the by-then highly developed infrastructure of the motion picture industry in the region, its well-established pool of skilled labor, its relatively affordable land, and the deep personal roots put down there by its employees. In reality, he insisted, the last effort by any major studio to seriously invest in East Coast production had been made by

First National Pictures in 1923–24 and had ended after an unsuccessful year of operations in which a lot of money had been spent on the facility for little return. However, Schallert nonetheless acknowledged that, from the point of the view of the industry's bosses, a possible departure from Southern California was "an idea that is worth dallying with just for expediency's sake."[30] It was rumored that Hollywood moguls were dissatisfied with relatively high corporate taxes in California and "the high cost of maintaining executive forces at both ends of the continent."[31]

But the more important reason for rumors of a move was said to be the threat of socialism in California, which had been supposedly manifested in the 1934 gubernatorial campaign of the famous muckraker Upton Sinclair known as EPIC (End Poverty in California). During that campaign, Schallert alleged, "the film nabobs [i.e., the Hollywood moguls] themselves made use of the migration mirage to put the quietus on any wild new political theories. They said that if the California votes were favorable to the disturbing candidate, the movies had no other course but to move to another part of the country."[32] Despite the fact that Sinclair achieved by far the highest popular vote in primaries held in August of that year, the majority of the Hollywood film industry's managerial class, including Louis B. Mayer and Joseph M. Schenck, made public statements and raised funds to campaign against him and, in the case of MGM, produced newsreels designed to stoke up conservative fears that immigration and radical ideas would overwhelm the state if Sinclair were elected.[33] Although Sinclair was ultimately defeated, the radicalism he represented extended beyond him in the form of widespread labor unrest that swept the West Coast from the longshoreman's strike, which shut down all of California's ports and led to a four-day general strike in San Francisco and Oakland in the summer of 1934, to the major strike that crippled the Hollywood studios from April 30 to June 7, 1937.[34]

Rumors that the film industry might relocate away from Los Angeles and California appeared to have vanished during World War II, but the industry's sense of fragility reemerged with the return of labor unrest in 1944 and two further major strikes that shut down many studios in 1945 and 1946–47. These were complicated after 1946 by a decline in the box office for Hollywood films occasioned by suburbanization, the rise of television, and the federal government's breaking of the Hollywood studios' monopoly of movie theater ownership.[35] In this context, suggestions of a resurgence of New York as a film-producing center resurfaced from time to time. A 1947 *New York Times* story announced that Mayor William O'Dwyer was attempting to facilitate Manhattan investors and real estate companies by persuading at least one Hollywood major to relocate to the island, offering a 100,000-square-foot converted building on a seventeen-acre site and promising a skilled workforce, low industrial unrest, and a minimum of red tape.[36] In 1950, when United Artists found itself in deep financial crisis and was forced to shut its Beverly Hills office and transfer management to New York, Edwin Schallert returned to his previous subject in expressing the concern that "Elimination of [United Artists'] West Coast offices and executive staff is causing an increasing stir in Hollywood because no one is yet sure of just what it portends."[37]

New York, therefore, remained important to the motion picture industry. It was home to many of the parent companies of the Hollywood studios, it was the center of American film distribution, and it was a tremendously important source of financing for the film industry. Indeed, Ed Sullivan, then a columnist for the *New York Daily News*, reported in 1947 that Wall Street financiers had approximately $600 million tied up in loans to the studios and independent producers.[38] New York continued to play an important role as a display window for Hollywood's cutting-edge products: for example, Cinemascope technology was first installed and shown to the public amid great fanfare in September 1953 at the Roxy Theater on Broadway, the largest movie palace in the world. In the absence of feature film production, New York also emerged as the center of documentary and experimental film in the United States.[39]

But there is no evidence that the Hollywood studio moguls ever took seriously the idea of moving the industry back to the East from whence it had come. Rather, as Neal Gabler has convincingly demonstrated, the Hollywood movie studios continued to constitute for them "an empire of their own" that they, as Jewish entrepreneurs and mostly immigrants or second-generation immigrants, had invented as a business alternative and a cultural alternative to the entrenched industrial and financial interests of East Coast WASP elites.[40] The emergence of television and other such threats caused real panic among many Hollywood studio executives, but the industry soon reached out to incorporate it, and Los Angeles increasingly took the lead in television production that New York had held in the 1940s as the new medium moved from live broadcasts to a diet mostly of recorded shows in the following decade.[41] Indeed, as if to add insult to injury, at least one report in the *New York Times* suggested that Los Angeles might also be emerging as New York's chief rival in theater because it "is thickly populated with actors, directors, designers, producers, composers, playwrights, and technicians who hail directly from the New York theater but who are now located in California."[42]

The relationship between Los Angeles and the other side of the nation was intensified after World War II by the rapid expansion of infrastructure, including interstate highways and railroads. But the real transport novelty of the day, one associated with levels of luxury and convenience only movie stars and other notables could afford, was air travel. The growth of scheduled passenger and cargo air services between the East and West coasts encouraged a new interconnectedness between them as well as a new rivalry. American Airlines began using "[r]emodelled Douglas DC-4s" in 1944 to ship newspapers, magazines, food, and clothing from east to west and "[f]lowers, sportswear, and movie films" from west to east.[43] In February 1946, a daily nonstop service with TWA was initiated from Burbank to New York with the first eastbound flight carrying "thirty-five motion picture stars, producers, and writers," piloted by Howard Hughes.[44] In August 1947, the *New York Times* announced its expansion into the Los Angeles newspaper market with the first copies being specially delivered to "Mayor Fletcher Bowron and Los Angeles civic and business leaders and Hollywood motion picture executives."[45]

Los Angeles Comes into Its Own

The rise of transcontinental air travel was as yet relatively elitist, but it was an indication nonetheless of the growing automobility of Americans and of Californians, in particular, who were the most automobilized Americans of all. Writing in 1946, the historian of California Carey McWilliams estimated that "in 1945 two out of every three people in the state had been born in some other state or nation."[46] Indeed, he argued that what he called "Broadway to Hollywood migration" associated with motion pictures was one of the most important factors contributing to this unique demographic.[47] A small but significant group of film noirs narrativize journeys between New York and the Los Angeles region, beginning in the late 1940s with *Detour, Nobody Lives Forever* (Jean Negulesco, 1946), *They Won't Believe Me* (Irving Pichel, 1947), and *The Man I Love* (Raoul Walsh, 1947) and continuing in the next decade with *The Damned Don't Cry* (Vincent Sherman, 1950), *The Big Bluff* (W. Lee Wilder, 1955), and *The Harder They Fall* (Mark Robson, 1956).

All of these recount the story of a migration from east to west that begins with promise but ends in disillusion, and all support their narrative with a visual contrast between New York and Los Angeles. While many film noirs were shot on location in New York, in most of these films New York is presented in a shorthand manner, equated with Manhattan in establishing shots of its skyline, painted studio backdrops, or occasional sequences of action on streets re-created in a studio or with the aid of rear projection. Emphasizing the verticality of skyscrapers, these are usually brief and concentrated in the earliest parts of the film, providing a visual and narratological pretext against which the rest unfolds. *Nobody Lives Forever*, for example, opens with long shots of the Manhattan skyline in sunshine accompanied by the chirpy voiceover of ex-con man and war veteran Nick Blake (John Garfield), who explains his lifelong love of New York but also his desire to make a clean break after the war by making for California, "a great spot, clear away from everything!" Arriving by train at Los Angeles Union Passenger Terminal in company with the bankrupt nightclub singer Gladys Halvorsen (Geraldine Fitzgerald), he finds the city to be a bright and breezy place of opportunity. Filmed on location, the Los Angeles Plaza is bustling with street life, the Sunset Strip is alive with the music of big bands at the club Mocambo, the beaches are full of bathers, and the picturesque gardens of the Mission San Juan Capistrano are a short drive down the coast to the south. Nick is determined to match his romantic and leisurely new surroundings with a new law-abiding lifestyle, but he soon slides back into the criminal underworld through encounters with other ex-crooks who have also made the journey west. This leads to a showdown with the rival fraudster Doc in a dirty, light industrial landscape of oil derricks, piers, and timber and corrugated metal huts (perhaps San Pedro or Playa del Rey) where the likable elderly crook Pop loses his life, to Nick's dismay.

Much of this pattern and iconography is repeated in subsequent films. In *The Man I Love*, lonely nightclub singer Petey Brown (Ida Lupino) quits her job at the 39 Club in New York to visit her family in Long Beach at Christmas where she struggles to prevent the descent of her brother into a life of crime while romancing a piano player with whom she drinks at the Bamboo Club and takes moonlight walks on a nearby ocean pier. In *They Won't Believe Me*, the action begins with a murder trial in Los Angeles from which a flashback immediately recalls Nick's basement restaurant on 52nd Street in New York where the man on trial, Laurence Ballantyne (Robert Young), has a rendezvous with his lover before his domineering wife removes him from temptation by insisting they move to Beverly Hills and then the Mojave desert. When the young son of Ethel Whitehead (Joan Crawford) is killed by a truck in *The Damned Don't Cry*, she flees her husband and small-town home for New York where she becomes entangled with racketeers and is relocated to "Desert Springs," a casino town filmed on location in Palm Springs, which is full of modernist bungalows typical of postwar Southern California, and where her flirtation with the mob's "West Coast" boss Nick Prenta leads a rival to shoot them both. In *The Big Bluff*, the terminally ill Manhattan heiress Mrs. Bancroft (Martha Vickers) is ordered by her doctor to move to Los Angeles for her health, where she declines tours of the Huntington Library and Griffith Park in favor of the Sunset Strip, and where she lives in a large Spanish-style mansion with whitewashed walls and painted wooden beams while a playboy whom she marries tries to hasten her death by replacing her pills with duds. In *The Harder They Fall*, sportswriter Eddie Willis (Humphrey Bogart) begins a nationwide tour to promote an up-and-coming boxer whose ruthless manager has connections to the mob by flying with American

Airlines to Los Angeles, where they visit Hollywood's Knickerbocker Hotel and the Beverly Hilton and watch a television news report about downtown's Skid Row.

In all of these films the high-rise and high-density urbanism of New York appears relatively jaded, the root of some restriction or dissatisfaction felt by the protagonist, while settings in Los Angeles and nearby locales are presented, at least initially, for their novelty and optimistic connotations. The names of specific real places are foregrounded in numerous lines of dialogue and other intra-diegetic cues such as street signs and newspaper headlines, as are a variety of characteristic exterior settings. As such, these films contributed to the increasing prominence of Los Angeles and its region in film noir and in postwar American cinema in general. This was especially the case in movies that used location filming, a practice already tremendously important to early Los Angeles film noirs such as *This Gun for Hire* (Frank Tuttle, 1942) and *Double Indemnity* (Billy Wilder, 1944). While *The Man I Love* is distinctive because it was evidently shot entirely in the studio, and *The Harder They Fall* because it includes extensive location filming, most films employed a mixture of the two in which the use of real locations became more and more commonplace after World War II.

This was true of Los Angeles film noir in general. The cast and crew of *The Street with No Name* (William Keighley, 1948) was reported to have spent sixty-two of its sixty-five-day shooting schedule on location, filming partly in Washington, D.C., but mostly in Los Angeles, San Pedro, and Santa Ana, California.[48] The shooting schedule for *Pitfall* (André De Toth, 1948) was reported to have "called for 40 separate locations within the Los Angeles city limits. Director André De Toth decided it was a good idea to shoot the scenes right at home, where they were intended to be."[49] The *New York Times* attributed the success of *He Walked by Night* to the "'on location' filming procedures followed, which not only contributed more than a modicum of striking realism and authority, but also kept the budget to modest proportions."[50] The *Los Angeles Times* reviewer of Robert Siodmak's 1949 thriller enthused that "Angelenos will get a special kick out of 'Criss Cross' because much of it was filmed in the city's highways and byways, but the moviegoer in Chicago, Ill. or Hoboken, NJ, will not sit through it unmoved, I'm betting."[51] And in January of that year in the *Daily News*, Dan Smith noted that "The LA City Hall, Union Passenger Terminal, Bunker Hill, and Angel's Flight are all becoming stars or at least featured players in motion pictures."[52] This was evidence that "producers appear to feel that if they get one or all of these elements into a picture, they have definitely stamped their film with a Los Angeles flavor."[53]

Thus by the end of the 1940s Los Angeles had achieved greater and greater prominence because it (and no other city) was the real city on Hollywood's doorstep. Indeed, Los Angeles once again became a cinematic subject in its own right in a way it had not been since the silent slapstick comedies of Buster Keaton, Harold Lloyd, and Charlie Chaplin. Most of those films had included extensive location shooting around Los Angeles but, subsequently, remarkably few Hollywood films made much use of the city as a setting even though they were mostly actually shot there. This was the case especially with the large number of films about the movie business that emerged from the late 1920s through World War II, including King Vidor's *Show People* (1928), George Cukor's *A Star Is Born* (1937), and Delmer Daves's *Hollywood Canteen* (1944), which were set in *Hollywood* more than in *Los Angeles*, and most of which barely acknowledged that there was a larger city outside the walls of the studio lot within which much (and in some cases all) of their action took place. Reports of new developments in Hollywood cinema in the late 1940s frequently highlighted the increasing turn to location filming, which characterized not only film noir but the western, the historical epic, and other genres. A lengthy front-page article in the *Wall Street Journal* in August 1947, for example, portrayed an "exodus from Hollywood" in favor of location filming; the change was ascribed to a variety of motivations including the increasing ease and availability of "fast air travel" for casts and crews, a desire to save money by shooting in real locations where material and labor costs would make them more expensive to re-create in the studio, and "public demand for more authentic pictures, stemming partly from the war."[54] Such reports frequently referred to the fact that postwar film audiences seemed to be more questioning and demanding of the films they watched and valued location shooting, in particular, for its realism and moral truth at a time when a significant portion of Hollywood's audience was made up of war veterans and their families, when the profile of documentary filmmaking had been enhanced by its role in informing the public about the war and its horrors, and when a creative lead in international cinema was being taken by the Italian neorealists from Roberto Rossellini's *Rome Open City* (1945) to Vittorio de Sica's *Umberto D* (1952).

The United States had not been directly affected by the dystopian specter of war that destroyed cities physically, economically, and socially in Europe and in Japan and determined the cinematic representation of cities in those places for years to come. But such destruction entailed a dystopian inversion of the city *as a mental category* that *was* influential in the cinematic representation of American cities at secondhand. Speaking to the *Los Angeles Times* in 1946, Edgar G. Ulmer, the director of *Detour*, the earliest film noir to map the relationship between Los Angeles and New York in detail, explained the new disposition of this cinema in terms of its interest in "life as it exists in this world."[55] In retrospect, we might say that this interest was hardly surprising for a filmmaker who was not only an expatriate born in Czechoslovakia and trained in Vienna and Berlin but the co-director with Robert Siodmak and Fred Zinnemann of one of Weimar Germany's most important realist films, *Mennschen am sonntag* (People on Sunday, 1930), a temporally and spatially concentrated portrait of the lives of Berliners on a typical summertime weekend filmed entirely on location.[56] But Ulmer's interest in "life as it exists in this world" *was* then a novelty for Hollywood cinema and in *Detour* (1945) took shape in the story of Al, a poorly paid piano player who is classically trained but works at the unimpressive Break O'Dawn club in a New York that is always shrouded in darkness and fog. He is in love with Sue, a singer who aspires to move to Hollywood to break into the movies. When she leaves town, the transcontinental distance of Al's phone calls to her from New York is underlined by Ulmer's intercutting of close-ups of their respective faces with shots of a telephone exchange and telephone lines running across the country. When Al strikes out to follow Sue to Los Angeles so that he can marry her, a map filmed in extreme close-up traces Al's journey on foot and by hitchhiking from New York through Pittsburgh, Chicago, and Oklahoma. But a bizarre series of twists of fate ensues in which Haskell, a man who offers Al a ride somewhere in Arizona, turns out, to Al's surprise, to be a gangster who seems to live on the road but who dies during the night of mysterious causes leaving Al in the frame for his murder. Assuming Haskell's identity and retaining his car, Al, in turn, gives a ride to a manic and disheveled blonde who turns out to be Haskell's girlfriend, Vera, a malevolent schemer who threatens to report Al to the police. With Vera in tow, Al arrives in Los Angeles exhausted and under a huge cloud. His voiceover explains, "A few hours later we were in Hollywood. I recognized places Sue had written about. It struck me that far from being at the end of the trip there was a greater distance between Sue and me than when I started out."[57] Not only does it seem that Sue has not made it big in Hollywood and may be unemployed, but Al cannot go back to New York for fear of being arrested. Al's arrival in Los Angeles entails a spatial and temporal rupture with a previous way of life and the shattering of his utopian dream of romance and professional success.

Hollywood as Urban Dystopia for Organized Labor

As such, Ulmer's film provides a deeply pessimistic recapitulation of the westward route taken in the 1930s along Route 66 and other major arteries to Southern California by so many thousands of real impoverished migrant workers, such as those documented in Dorothea Lange and Paul Taylor's photo-journalistic study *American Exodus* (1939) and by their imaginary counterparts in literature and film, including John Steinbeck's Joad family in *The Grapes of Wrath* (1939). But in rebuffing the myth of Hollywood as Mecca, in expressing a profound disillusion with westward migration and a fatalistic sense of the impossibility of return, *Detour* speaks quite specifically to a new post–World War II dispensation. In 1946, Siegfried Kracauer observed this new dispensation in the rise of what he called "terror films" in American cinema, a term he used to describe many films we now call film noirs including *Shadow of a Doubt* (1943), *Spellbound* (1945), *Somewhere in the Night* (1946), and *The Lost Weekend*. According to Kracauer, the salient new feature of these films is that "Apprehension is accumulated; threatening allusions and dreadful possibilities evoke a world in which everybody is afraid of everybody else, and no one knows when or where the ultimate and inevitable horror will arrive."[58] Ulmer's interview for the *Los Angeles Times* took place just after he had completed location shooting of his next film noir, *Strange Woman* (1946), but the context for it was a discussion of the continuing threat to Hollywood as the center of American motion pictures and of the possibility of the industry's move back east. Ulmer explained that for him Hollywood was a better place to make movies because it offered the necessary skilled workforce, a favorable climate, and technical facilities, but its one weakness was its tendency toward "strike conditions."[59] This statement casts his narrative of unsuccessful musicians in Hollywood in *Detour* in a subversive light vis-à-vis the Hollywood film industry of the day. If film producers and studio executives in the late 1940s feared the possible collapse of the studio system, the real dystopia of Hollywood cinema was lived by its out-of-work and exploited workers who lived in a climate of fear that echoed all too closely that described by Kracauer.

As unsuccessful musicians in Hollywood, Al and Sue in *Detour* are emblematic of the reality underscored by the commentator Anthony Dawson in 1947 that behind "the picture of opulence [of Hollywood cinema] . . . stretches a vast sea of men and women of all crafts and abilities striving and pressing for more constant employment in an industry which can use only a fraction of them even at capacity production."[60] Hollywood's ever-present surplus of labor was at the root of the peculiar insecurity of its job market and was acutely felt by workers, especially given the recent memory of the Depression. In 1942, the *New York Times* described "motion picture extra players," for example, as "Hollywood's worst sociological problem," explaining that film extras " 'cling desperately to their chance to starve to death.' "[61] Of seven thousand extras in the business only fifteen hundred were thought to find more than ten days' work per year, and of six thousand members of the Screen Actors Guild, no more than three hundred and fifty were employed on any given day.[62] In 1948, one report calculated average unemployment among skilled workers in the film unions at 31.95 percent, while those who could find work were typically required to work a minimum of fifty-four or sixty hours per week.[63] The two major strikes that rocked the industry in 1945 and 1946–47 lasted ten months and thirteen months, respectively, effectively shutting down production and leading to extensive street fighting between picketers, strike breakers, and police. These effected a further dystopian inversion of Hollywood cinema by undercutting the utopianism that characterized most of its films on the level of form and content and by interfering with the freedom to make movies, which had been the essence of Hollywood for the moguls since the 1910s. As Eric Johnston, president of the Motion Picture Producers' Association of America, chief representative of the studio moguls, declared in 1946, "Utopia is production!"[64]

The key to the dramatic rise of Los Angeles and other Sunbelt cities in the postwar era was not only their identification of and innovation in new types of economic activity but the successful implantation of a new model of citizenship that was promoted by its advocates as a broadening of the benefits of capitalism to embrace the working class but that seemed to many the enforcement of a new political quiescence.[65] The historical record reveals that a remarkably straight line can be drawn between the determination of the Hollywood moguls to ensure the continuing profitability of their industry above all else and the consolidation of a new rightist dispensation in American politics and society in the 1950s whose legacy remains with us today in many respects but whose origins may be traced to the Great Depression of the 1930s.

In the middle of that decade, the Hollywood moguls contracted the Chicago mafia to keep striking to a minimum by taking over the largest labor union in the industry, the International Alliance of Theatrical and Stage Employees (IATSE), and threatening radicals with blacklisting and physical intimidation. In the words of Father George H. Dunne, Jesuit priest and mediator in the Hollywood strike of 1946–47, this demonstrated that the moguls "preferred to co-operate with gangsters rather than face the necessity of engaging in sincere collective bargaining with honest democratic trade unions."[66] In this context, the anti-Communist rhetoric that became increasingly common currency throughout the United States after World War II achieved relatively early public prominence and an unusual intensity in Hollywood. This was evident when management at Walt Disney Productions responded to a strike by animators in July 1941 by sending a telegram to Washington, D.C., demanding that Congress act in support of "patriotic Americans" against "[a]gents of Communism."[67] It was demonstrated again in 1941 when MGM mogul Joseph Schenck and corrupt IATSE leaders with whom he was associated sought to defend themselves against charges of fraud and tax evasion in part by arguing that their efforts to control Hollywood labor unions were motivated by a desire to eliminate Communist infiltration. Then it accelerated exponentially in 1945–47 when studio management argued that the new wave of labor unrest was not the result of legitimate workers' grievances but of agitation by a minority of hard-liners represented by the Conference of Studio Unions (CSU) whose leader, Herb Sorrell, they falsely alleged was a Communist.[68]

Throughout the era, the Hollywood moguls and IATSE labor leaders in their pay used anti-Communist discourse to suppress the demands of workers and, in doing so, benefited from the fact that, as Ingrid Scobie has put it, "California led all other states in anti-subversive activity" both before and after World War II.[69] This entailed encouraging investigations, locally at first, by the Fact-Finding Committee on Un-American Activities of the California State Senate (known as the Tenney Committee for its chair, Republican senator Jack B. Tenney) and then, nationally, by U.S. congressional committees such as the House Labor Committee and the House Un-American Activities Committee. This strategy in turn was a decisive influence on the formulation of the 1948 Taft-Hartley Act, which broke the power of militant labor in the United States as a whole and enforced a new vision of the worker as a shareholder in capitalism, which became a pillar of the postwar *Pax Americana* and the later rise of neoliberalism.

The Hollywood moguls' successful policy of divide and rule pitted one group of workers against another in an industry where the surplus of labor guaranteed there would always be a sufficient number of "scabs" to take jobs vacated by strikers. In this respect, it typified Los Angeles's long history of hostility to labor unions and its tradition of open shop labor relations, which distinguished it from older industrial cities in the East and was one of the reasons the pioneers of the Hollywood film industry in the 1910s were drawn to Los Angeles in the first place.[70] Moreover, militant labor organization was made more difficult by the physical nature of the city, which was at odds with the conditions that had fostered mass demonstrations in other cities at earlier moments in history. The relative decentralization and suburban locations of the film studios in and around Los Angeles, some in Hollywood but others in Burbank, Studio City, and Culver City, together with the significant distance between all of these and downtown Los Angeles, made organizing pickets and amassing strikers in large numbers a greater challenge. The distinctive lack of a pedestrian culture, which typified most parts of the region, and the absence of large public spaces amenable to protesting crowds that were not already overwhelmed by automobiles made symbolic shows of strength by workers seem an anachronistic impossibility.

One of the ways in which the police, civic authorities, and the largely anti-union *Los Angeles Times* responded to the strikes was by condemning the CSU, which they portrayed as a small minority of hard-line Communist or Communist-inspired agitators despite the fact that its membership accounted for up to twelve thousand of the film industry's total of thirty thousand workers.[71] These groups also condemned the strikes because of their interference with freedom of movement in the streets and on sidewalks, and they encouraged the studios to use the law to keep people and traffic in motion. This was especially the case at and around the imposing and often ornate gates of the movie studios themselves, which became the key sites of contestation. Hitherto these had been destinations for movie fans and tourists, and markers of the exclusivity of the lifestyles of the stars beyond which the general public could not pass. But during the strikes they became microcosmic fixed points in a struggle for control of public space.

In March 1945 the *Los Angeles Times* reported, "One of the largest crowds was at Warner Bros studios, where several thousand people milled around. Burbank police patrolled the highway, keeping the throng from blocking roads."[72] That August, the Los Angeles Police Commission complained that, in contravention of picketing laws, "picket lines [in Hollywood] were so large that patrons could not get into theaters and that pedestrians were forced to step off the sidewalk."[73] In October 1945, violence arose at Warner Bros. when individuals attempted to break the picket line by driving through it in automobiles.[74] Burbank City Council instituted new bylaws to make a distinction between "peaceful picketing" and "mass picketing," where the latter phrase was used to describe any group of strikers blocking a thoroughfare, especially the gates of the studio itself, so as to prevent normal use.[75] And Burbank police were forced to call in support from the nearby police departments of Glendale and Los Angeles, as well as the Los Angeles County Sheriff's office, to support their efforts at crowd control.

As the strikes intensified and spread to other locations, so did the contestation of the built environment. The *Los Angeles Times* reported on a three-way clash between IATSE workers, CSU strikers, and police in Hollywood: "Featuring flailing nightsticks and fists and flying feet, Hollywood's grimmest mob scene yesterday was staged—without benefit of film cameras—at the gates of Paramount Studios as non-striking workers braved the gauntlet of massed 'peaceful' picketing which has hampered production for several days."[76] Flashpoints emerged at MGM studios in Culver City, Republic Pictures in Studio City, and Twentieth Century Fox studios on Pico Boulevard in Westwood. Tension increased again when ten to twenty thousand Lockheed workers and thousands more from railroad and shipyard unions and the United Auto Workers were said to be ready to join the pickets.[77] And on November 15, 1946, over seven hundred strikers were arrested outside Columbia Pictures at the corner of Sunset Boulevard and Gower Street in Hollywood in "what veteran police officers declared was the largest ever mass arrest made in California."[78]

While the Hollywood strikes arose out of material issues and injustices, viewed as conflicts over the use of public space, they appear now in an ironic light given what we know about the tendency of Los Angeles to grow in an exceptionally dispersed manner, highly reliant on private automobile transport and dominated by extensive suburban subdivisions and commercial strip development. These were already in evidence and would accelerate significantly in later years. As early as 1930, Los Angeles had the highest percentage of single-family dwellings in the nation at 93.9 percent compared to that of New York (52.8 percent) and Chicago (52 percent).[79] By 1949, there was one car for every 3.9 persons in Los Angeles, compared to one car for every 7.1 persons in Chicago, and one for every 12 in New York City, while the respective population densities for the three cities in 1950 were, respectively, 10,399, 17,409, and 26,046 persons per square mile.[80] As Dana Cuff has argued, the "dispersion" that characterized the planning and architecture of Los Angeles in the late 1940s was driven by a powerful but politically conservative coalition of private real estate developers, citizens groups, civic bodies, and industrial corporations, supported by the police and the courts. These sought to promote a conception of urban space in which private property rights reigned supreme, epitomized by large communities of peaceful suburban single-family homes from which non-whites, the poor, and political radicals were excluded. Debates and clashes between private and public interests informed the growth of all American cities, but they were nowhere more intense than in Los Angeles.[81]

In the heyday of film noir, therefore, not only did Los Angeles gain ground on New York and other older cities, but it was able to do so, in large part, because of an unmistakable rightward reorganization both of cinema and of the physical and social character of the city. Film noirs from *Detour* and *Nobody Lives Forever* to *The Big Bluff* and *The Harder They Fall* articulated the disillusioned leftist or left-liberal sentiments of filmmakers forced to articulate their ideas in a veiled way.[82] But the dystopian imaginary of film noir needs to be understood more fully in terms of macrogeographical developments after World War II, which were its real dystopian analogue. Hollywood in the late 1940s became ground zero in a new post-industrial political economy, a template for a larger restructuring of labor and everyday life that continues to reverberate in American society and throughout the neoliberal world today. This restructuring is a hidden meaning in film noirs that literally relate Los Angeles to older cities and ways of life, but it is also evident in the displacement of the center of gravity of film noir from New York to Los Angeles in the postwar era as a whole.

Notes

1 Dore Schary, "Exploring the Hollywood Myth," *New York Times*, April 9, 1950, p. 14.
2 Ibid.

3 See Campbell Gibson, *Population of the 100 Largest Cities and Other Urban Places in the United States, 1790–1990* (Washington, DC: U.S. Bureau of the Census, 1998), especially table 18, "Population of the 100 Largest Urban Places," http://www.census.gov/population/www/documentation/twps0027.html; see also *Counting California*, California Digital Library, University of California, 2005, http://countingcalifornia.cdlib.org/.

4 Mike Davis, *City of Quartz: Excavating the Future in Los Angeles* (New York: Vintage, 1992), 67.

5 Paul Schrader, "Notes on *Film Noir*," in *Film Genre Reader*, ed. Barry Keith Grant (Austin: University of Texas Press, 1986), 167–82, 174.

6 J. P. Telotte, *Voices in the Dark: The Narrative Patterns of Film Noir* (Urbana: University of Illinois Press, 1989).

7 Frank Krutnik, *In a Lonely Street: Film Noir, Genre, Masculinity* (London: Routledge, 1991).

8 James Naremore, *More Than Night: Film Noir in Its Contexts* (Berkeley: University of California Press, 1998).

9 Telotte, *Voices in the Dark*; Krutnik, *In a Lonely Street*; Naremore, *More Than Night*; Nicholas Christopher, *Somewhere in the Night: Film Noir and the American City* (Berkeley, CA: Shoemaker and Hoard, 2006); Spencer Selby, *Dark City: The Film Noir* (Jefferson, NC: McFarland, 1997); Joan Copjec, ed., *Shades of Noir* (New York: Verso, 1993); Andrew Dickos, *Street with No Name: A History of the Classic American Film Noir* (Lexington: University of Kentucky Press, 2002); Paula Rabinowitz, *Black & White & Noir* (New York: Columbia University Press, 2002); Kelly Oliver and Benigno Trigo, *Noir Anxiety* (Minneapolis: University of Minnesota Press, 2002).

10 Nino Frank, "Un nouveau genre 'policier': L'aventure criminelle," *L'Écran français* 61 (August 1946): 8–9, 14; Raymond Borde and Etienne Chaumeton, *Panorama of Film Noir, 1941–1953*, trans. Paul Hammond (San Francisco: City Lights, 2002).

11 E. Ann Kaplan, *Women in Film Noir* (London: BFI, 1978); Mary Ann Doane, *Femmes Fatales: Feminism, Film Theory, and Psychoanalysis* (New York: Routledge, 1991); Helen Hanson, *Hollywood Heroines: Women in Film Noir and the Female Gothic Film* (London: I. B. Tauris, 2008).

12 An exceptionally nuanced, close analysis of these distinctions is provided by Laura Mulvey in her study of Alfred Hitchcock's *Notorious* (1946) in "Pandora: Topographies of the Mask and Curiosity," in *Sexuality and Space*, ed. Beatriz Colomina (Princeton: Princeton University Press, 1992), 53–72.

13 Edward Dimendberg, *Film Noir and the Spaces of Modernity* (Cambridge, MA: Harvard University Press, 2004).

14 Eric Avila, *Popular Culture in the Age of White Flight: Fear and Fantasy in Suburban Los Angeles* (Berkeley: University of California Press, 2004), 65–105.

15 I have compiled the filmography from the following sources: Michael L. Stephens, *Film Noir: A Comprehensive, Illustrated Reference to Movies, Terms, and Persons* (Jefferson, NC: McFarland, 1995); Selby, *Dark City*; Michael F. Keaney, *Film Noir: 745 Films of the Classic Era, 1940–1959* (Jefferson, NC: McFarland, 2003); Arthur Lyons, *Death on the Cheap: The Lost B Movies of Film Noir* (Cambridge, MA: Da Capo Press, 2000); Alain Silver and Elizabeth Ward, *Film Noir: An Encyclopedic Reference to the American Style* (Woodstock, NY: Overlook Press, 1979); and

the American Film Institute Catalog of Feature Films, 1893–1971, http://www.afi
.com/members/catalog/. Unlike the widest definitions of film noir, such as that
by Keaney, I have chosen not to include in my analysis noir westerns such as
Yellow Sky (William Wellman, 1948), noir serials such as *The Shadow* (James W.
Horne, 1940), or films of non-U.S. origin. I have identified the most important
settings on a film-by-film basis by reference to the films themselves, by reference to production reports and contemporary film reviews, and by using the AFI
catalog. I have tabulated these settings chronologically, by date of the film's first
U.S. release, and geographically, by differentiating between U.S. and non-U.S.
settings, urban, small-town, and rural settings, specific cities by name, and major
U.S. regions from the eastern seaboard to California.

16 Naturally, there are some methodological limits to the geographical specificity
of the analysis. It allows me to identify the key settings in each film but, where a
film is set in more than one place, it does not allow me to identify the amount or
proportion of time spent in each place, nor the dramatic significance of the place
relative to others in any given film; it does not allow me to specify whether a setting is re-created in the studio or shot on location (nor, if shot on location, *where*
on location); and it does not allow me to indicate the degree to which a setting is
specifically identified in a film through visual cues, captions, dialogue, or other
intra- or extra-diegetic information, although in my tabulation I have specifically
included a category for films set in cities that are not named at all—for example,
John Huston's *The Asphalt Jungle* (1950). However, these limits do not hamper the
interpretation I provide in this essay.

17 Table Aa22-35, "Selected Population Characteristics—Median Age, Sex Ratio, Annual Growth Rate, and Number, by Race, Urban Residence, and Nativity, 1790–
2000," *Historical Statistics of the United States,* Millennial Edition Online, ed.
Susan B. Carter, Scott Sigmund Gartner, Michael R. Haines, Alan L. Olmstead,
Richard Sutch, and Gavin Wright (New York: Cambridge University Press, 2006),
http://hsus.cambridge.org/HSUSWeb/table/showtablepdf.do?id=Aa22-35.

18 In 1950 there was a spike in representations of the American Northwest because
in that year seven films were set, in whole or in part, in San Francisco. These were
*Born to Be Bad, D.O.A., The Man Who Cheated Himself, No Man of Her Own,
Once a Thief, Shakedown,* and *Woman on the Run.*

19 Kirkpatrick Sale, *Power Shift: The Rise of the Southern Rim and Its Challenge to
the Eastern Establishment* (New York: Vintage, 1976), 207–71.

20 Figure 1.7, "Population Distribution by Region, 1900–2000," U.S. Census Bureau,
Demographic Trends in the Twentieth Century, Census 2000 Special Reports, November 2002, p. 19, http://www.census.gov/prod/2002pubs/censr-4.pdf.

21 Ibid. Indeed, the decline in the share of national U.S. population held by the
Northeast has continued, standing at 19 percent in the 2000 census. This shift
is noted by the U.S. Census Bureau as one of the most significant demographic
changes of the second half of the twentieth century.

22 This evolution in film noir is described by Krutnik in terms of a shift of emphasis at the end of the 1940s from "private eye films" and the "criminal-adventure
thriller" to the "semi-documentary," "police-procedural," and "rogue cop" thriller.
See Krutnik, *In a Lonely Street,* 92–164, 191–93, 202–8. See also Robert Reiner,
"Keystone to Kojak: The Hollywood Cop," in *Cinema, Politics, and Society in*

America, ed. Philip Davies and Brian Neve (Manchester: University of Manchester Press, 1981), 195–220; and Christopher P. Wilson, *Cop Knowledge: Police Power and Cultural Narrative in Twentieth-Century America* (Chicago: University of Chicago Press, 2000), 57–93.

23 I have developed this thesis in relation to American cinema of the 1960s and 1970s in "A Nostalgia for Modernity: New York, Los Angeles, and American Cinema in the 1970s," in *Screening the City*, ed. Mark Shiel and Tony Fitzmaurice (New York: Verso, 2003), 160–79.

24 David C. Perry and Alfred J. Watkins, "Regional Change and the Impact of Uneven Urban Development," in *The Rise of the Sunbelt Cities*, ed. Perry and Watkins (Beverly Hills, CA: Sage, 1977), 19–54.

25 Ibid., 23, 49.

26 "Billion Dollar Industry," *Los Angeles Times*, January 2, 1940, p. C7.

27 Janet Abu-Lughod, *New York, Chicago, Los Angeles: America's Global Cities* (Minneapolis: University of Minnesota Press, 1999), 192, 233, 245.

28 Edwin Schallert, "Why New York Will Not Get Hollywood," *Los Angeles Times*, March 3, 1940, p. H4.

29 Ibid.

30 Ibid.

31 Ibid.

32 Ibid.

33 Donald L. Singer, "Upton Sinclair and the California Gubernatorial Campaign of 1934," in *A Southern California Anthology: Selections from the Annual and Quarterly Publications of the Historical Society of Southern California, 1883–1983*, ed. Doyce B. Nunis Jr. (Los Angeles: Historical Society of Southern California, 1984), 351–78. For a contemporary report on Sinclair's campaign success, see "Sinclair Piles Up Commanding Lead in California Vote," *New York Times*, August 29, 1934, pp. 1–2.

34 On contemporary labor activism among longshoremen and agricultural workers in California, see Anne Loftis, *Witnesses to the Struggle: Imaging the 1930s California Labor Movement* (Reno: University of Nevada Press, 1998).

35 During the war, Hollywood, Los Angeles, and Southern California experienced a different sense of fragility when they seemed to be under threat of possible attack by Japanese forces. For a contemporary account, see "Lights Dimmed by Hollywood," *New York Times*, July 19, 1942, p. XX7.

36 "Offers Reported to Attract Films to New York," *New York Times*, October 2, 1947, p. 2; see also "City Would Lure Movie Industry," *New York Times*, July 10, 1947, p. 23; and Bosley Crowther, "Hollywood versus New York," *New York Times* magazine, August 3, 1947, pp. 10, 17–18.

37 Edwin Schallert, "United Artists Corp. Shuts Office Here," *Los Angeles Times*, February 25, 1950, p. 2.

38 Ed Sullivan, *New York Daily News*, November 26, 1947, quoted in Janet Wasko, *Movies and Money: Financing the American Film Industry* (Norwood, NJ: Ablex Publishing, 1982), 110.

39 Flora Rheta Schreiber, "New York: A Cinema Capital," *Quarterly of Film, Radio, and Television* 7.3 (Spring 1953): 264–73.

40 Neal Gabler, *An Empire of Their Own: How the Jews Invented Hollywood* (New York: Crown Publishers, 1988).

41 For an early indication of the studios' nervousness about the advent of television, see "What's Ahead for Hollywood?" *Los Angeles Times*, January 2, 1940, p. E3. On the relationship between New York, Los Angeles, and television, see "Hollywood Outdistanced by East," *New York Times*, June 13, 1948, p. XX20; Aline Mosby, "'You Are There': NY TV Show, Moves to Coast," *Los Angeles Times*, February 23, 1955, p. 24; Cecil Smith, "East, West Coasts Changing Places?" *Los Angeles Times*, October 14, 1959, p. A10.

42 "Hollywood a Theater Hub? Broadway Producer Says Recent Events on Coast Indicate Such a Transformation May Be in the Making," *New York Times*, December 14, 1947, p. X4.

43 "Air Freight Liners Mark Fifth Year: Apparel Is the Biggest Item—Planeloads of Flowers Leave the West Nightly," *New York Times*, October 17, 1949, p. 39.

44 "Film Notables Hop to New York," *Los Angeles Times*, February 15, 1946, p. 14; see also "New Air Service Opens: Coast-to-Coast Trips through Chicago Started by United," *New York Times*, July 15, 1946, p. 47.

45 "Los Angeles Gets *Times* in Morning: First of Regular Air Freight Deliveries Reaches West Coast by Breakfast Time," *New York Times*, August 16, 1947, p. 26. In congratulating the *New York Times* on this new initiative, Bowron was quick to compare his city with New York, declaring "it shows that Los Angeles and New York, the two truly great cities of the nation, are just neighbors after all."

46 Carey McWilliams, "Culture and Society in Southern California," *Annals of the American Academy of Political Science* 248, Labor Relations and the Public (November 1946): 209–13, 209.

47 Ibid.

48 "'Street' Cuts Studio Use to Three Days," *Los Angeles Times*, May 23, 1948, p. C2.

49 Ibid.

50 "The Screen in Review," *New York Times*, February 7, 1949, p. 15.

51 Philip K. Scheuer, "Drama of Violence Thrilling," *Los Angeles Times*, January 20, 1949, p. 21.

52 Dan Smith, *Daily News*, January 20, 1949, clipping file for *The Pitfall* (1948), Academy of Motion Picture Arts and Sciences.

53 Ibid.

54 Joseph W. Taylor, "Mobile Movie Men: Hollywood Film Makers Hit the Road to Give Pictures 'Real' Settings," *Wall Street Journal*, August 8, 1947, pp. 1, 4. See also Philip K. Scheuer, "Army Trains Huston in Location Shooting," *Los Angeles Times*, June 29, 1947, p. C1; and Fred Stanley, "Hollywood Goes Afield," *New York Times*, May 12, 1946, p. 47.

55 Philip K. Scheuer, "Hollywood Clings to Lead as Film-Production Center: Labor Unrest Puts Position in Jeopardy," *Los Angeles Times*, December 15, 1946, pp. B1, B3, quote on p. B1.

56 Like Ulmer, two other directors of film noirs concerned with journeys from New York to Los Angeles were also originally from Central or Eastern Europe: that is, Jean Negulesco, director of *Nobody Lives Forever*, and W. Lee Wilder, brother of Billy Wilder and director of *The Big Bluff*.

57 *Detour* was produced on a budget of $30,000 and was shot over one week in June 1945. While much of its action took place in New York and Los Angeles interiors and was filmed in the studio, it used location filming for its Arizona sequences and rear projections of second unit photography of actual street scenes for its Los

Angeles exteriors. Ulmer, like many of his contemporaries, liked location filming because it was relatively affordable. In relation to his film *Strange Woman* (1946), Ulmer explained that "we can figure on New York primarily as a location, and not as a studio setup" but that New York will continue to be used because "it costs more to duplicate nature on a sound stage than to shoot it in the raw!" Scheuer, "Hollywood Clings to Lead," p. B3.

58 Siegfried Kracauer, "Hollywood's Terror Films: Do They Reflect an American State of Mind?" *New German Critique*, no. 89, Film and Exile (Spring–Summer 2003): 105–11, 106; reprinted from *Commentary* 2 (1946): 132–36.

59 Scheuer, "Hollywood Clings to Lead," p. B1. See also Taylor, "Mobile Movie Men," 4, where it is alleged that industrial unrest in the Hollywood studios in the late 1940s encouraged location filming by pushing up the cost of labor by carpenters, painters, and other workers essential to the creation of studio sets.

60 Anthony A. P. Dawson, "Hollywood's Labor Troubles," *Industrial and Labor Relations Review* 1.4 (July 1948): 638–47, 640.

61 Thomas F. Brady, "Communique from the West Coast," *New York Times*, March 1, 1942, p. X3.

62 Ibid.; Dawson, "Hollywood's Labor Troubles," 641.

63 Dawson, "Hollywood's Labor Troubles," 643; and Mike Nielsen and Gene Mailes, *Hollywood's Other Blacklist: Union Struggles in the Studio System* (London: British Film Institute, 1995), 51.

64 Johnston made this statement in an address to the 1946 annual convention of the largest union in the Hollywood film industry, the International Alliance of Theatrical and Stage Employees. Quoted in Nielsen and Mailes, *Hollywood's Other Blacklist*, 143.

65 Perry and Watkins, "Regional Change and the Impact of Uneven Urban Development," 39–40; see also David C. Perry and Alfred J. Watkins, "People, Profit, and the Rise of the Sunbelt Cities," in *The Rise of the Sunbelt Cities*, ed. Perry and Watkins, 277–306.

66 Fr. George H. Dunne, *Hollywood Labor Dispute: A Study in Immorality* (Los Angeles: Conference Publishing, 1950), 19.

67 "Disney Strike Tangle Told: Communists and Labor Board Scored in Wire Sent to Washington," *Los Angeles Times*, July 15, 1941, p. A2.

68 "Sorrell Swears He Has Never Been Communist—Hollywood Unionist Asserts Party Card Was 'Planted' Against Him, Hinting Forgery," *Los Angeles Times*, March 4, 1948, p. 2; "Red Card Signed by Sorrell, FBI Reports to House Group," *Los Angeles Times*, March 13, 1948, p. 2. The matter of Sorrell's supposed communism was raised repeatedly by his critics from 1946 through 1948 on the basis of what was alleged to be a 1937 Communist Party membership card signed in his name, although the authenticity of the card was thoroughly disputed and official attempts to prove his membership proved fruitless.

69 Ingrid Winther Scobie, "Jack B. Tenney and the 'Parasitic Menace': Anti-Communist Legislation in California, 1940–1949," *Pacific Historical Review* 43.2 (May 1974): 188–211, 189.

70 Richard Koszarski, *An Evening's Entertainment: The Age of the Silent Feature Picture, 1915–1928*, vol. 3 of *History of the American Cinema* (New York: Charles Scribner's Sons, 1990), 100.

71 The *Los Angeles Times* estimated CSU membership at six to ten thousand. IATSE membership was generally acknowledged to be about sixteen thousand.

See "Unions Order Major Film Strike Today—Fight over Designers Threatens Production in Every Studio," *Los Angeles Times*, March 12, 1945, p. 1; *Variety*, February 6, 1946, p. 3 and February 13, 1946, p. 3; "Sorrell Group Asks Rise of 50 Per Cent," *Los Angeles Times*, February 12, 1946, p. 1; and "Sorrell May Postpone Film Strike Deadline," *Los Angeles Times*, February 16, 1946, pp. 1, 4.

72 "AFL Unions' Fight Paralyzes Studios," *Los Angeles Times*, March 13, 1945, p. 2.

73 "New Row Adds 100 Workers to Studio Strikers," *Los Angeles Times*, August 29, 1945, p. A2.

74 "Dozens Injured in Melee at Warners' Entrance: Union Leader Arrested," *Los Angeles Times*, October 6, 1945, p. 1.

75 "Sorrell Faces Court Action," *Los Angeles Times*, October 23, 1945, pp. 1–2. The particular propensity of LA employers and police to use injunctions to circumscribe movement and assembly in public places is documented in Benjamin Aaron and William Levin, "Labor Injunctions in Action: A Five-Year Survey in Los Angeles County," *California Law Review* 39.1 (March 1951): 42–67.

76 "Scores Hurt in New Studio Riots," *Los Angeles Times*, October 24, 1945, pp. 1, 12.

77 "10,000 May Picket Film Studio Today," *Los Angeles Times*, October 11, 1945, pp. 1–2.

78 "700 Film Strike Pickets Arrested," *Los Angeles Times*, November 16, 1946, pp. 1, 3.

79 Table 17, "Families and Dwellings in Selected Cities, 1930, data compiled from US Bureau of the Census, Fifteenth Census of the United States, 1930," in Robert M. Fogelson, *The Fragmented Metropolis: Los Angeles, 1850–1930* (1967; Berkeley: University of California Press, 1993), 146.

80 Sam Boal, "Los Angeles Has It, But What Is It?" *New York Times* magazine, September 4, 1949, p. 37. See also Richard Longstreth, *City Center to Regional Mall: Architecture, the Automobile, and Retailing in Los Angeles, 1920–1950* (Cambridge, MA: MIT Press, 1998).

81 Dana Cuff, *The Provisional City: Los Angeles Stories of Architecture and Urbanism* (Cambridge, MA: MIT Press, 2000), 61–117.

82 Paul Buhle, "The Hollywood Left: Aesthetics and Politics," *New Left Review* I/212 (July–August 1995): 101–19; Paul Buhle and Dave Wagner, *Radical Hollywood: The Untold Story behind America's Movies* (New York: The New Press, 2002).

Chapter 5

■

Oh No, There Goes Tokyo

Recreational Apocalypse and the City in Postwar Japanese Popular Culture

WILLIAM M. TSUTSUI

In his book *Ecology of Fear*, Mike Davis seeks to establish Los Angeles's reputation as the "disaster capital of the universe," a "Book of the Apocalypse
theme park," and, quite simply, "Doom City." Davis chronicles the rich profu-
sion of novels and films that have "managed to destroy Los Angeles in a remarkable, even riotous, miscellany of ways," listing 138 literary and cinematic
Armageddons between 1909 and 1996. "The City of Angels," Davis assures us,
"is unique, not simply in the frequency of its fictional destruction, but in the
pleasure that such apocalypses provide to readers and movie audiences. The
entire world seems to be rooting for Los Angeles to slide into the Pacific or
be swallowed by the San Andreas fault." And although New York City can
also claim more than its fair share of imaginary annihilations and plentiful
moviegoers eager to cheer its demise, Davis confidently concludes of LA that
"No other city seems to excite such dark rapture."[1]

But Mike Davis, it seems, has been spending too much time in Southern
California and not enough watching Japanese movies, television series, and
animation. There can be little doubt that, in the years since World War II,
fictional apocalypse has been visited upon Tokyo more frequently (and often
with much greater thoroughness) than any other location on the globe. In
what one observer has called the "doom-laden dreams" of Japanese popular
culture,[2] Tokyo has fallen victim to earthquakes, tidal waves, fires, floods, cy-
clonic winds, volcanoes, alien invasions, supernatural curses, viruses, toxic
pollution, all nature of giant monsters, robots, and blobs, and, needless to
say, every imaginable form of nuclear explosion. Domestic and worldwide
audiences have been exposed to "innumerable replications of Tokyo being
stomped and burned to destruction" in a staggering variety of media and
genres,[3] from silent movies depicting the Great Kantō Earthquake of 1923 to
cold war–era science fiction and special effects films, from live-action chil-

dren's TV shows to animated television series and movies, from blockbuster disaster and action pictures to comic books and video games. Through most of the postwar period, and certainly since the mid-1960s, Japanese media consumers could take in the fictionalized obliteration of their capital city on television or at a nearby movie theater at least every week, and sometimes every day.

The regularity of annihilation fantasies in popular culture has mirrored Tokyo's historical vulnerability to catastrophic events of natural and man-made origin. As Donald Richie has observed, albeit somewhat reductively, "The Japanese, in moments of stress if not habitually, regard life as the period of complete insecurity that it is; and the truth of this observation is graphically illustrated in a land yearly ravaged by typhoons, a country where the very earth quakes daily."[4] Tokyo, in its relatively short history of just five-and-a-half centuries, may well have been destroyed and reconstructed more than any other major world city. In the Tokugawa period (1600–1868), the crowded, wood-built Edo (as it was then known) was regularly devastated by major conflagrations: the dense downtown area of the city suffered ruinous fires on at least thirty-one occasions from the seventeenth to the nineteenth centuries, with Edo Castle burning eight times and the landmark Nihonbashi Bridge ten over the same span of time. The great Meireki fire of 1657 claimed almost 50,000 homes and 108,000 lives; the Gyōninzaka blaze of 1772 left more than thirty square miles of the central city scorched.[5] Fire took its toll on the modern city as well, as the Great Kantō Earthquake and subsequent firestorm killed up to 140,000 and left almost two million homeless, while the firebombings of 1945 reduced wide expanses of the metropolis to burnt-over wastelands. In the single attack of March 9–10, now known as the Great Tokyo Air Raid, almost seventeen square miles of the city were set aflame and 80,000 people died. Other Japanese cities have suffered substantial catastrophes—a tsunami that devastated Osaka in 1934, major fires in Hakodate in 1935 and Shizuoka in 1940, the Great Hanshin-Awaji Earthquake that struck Kobe in 1995, and the wartime bombings of sixty-six urban areas, including Hiroshima and Nagasaki—but Tokyo's record of repeated, all-encompassing cataclysms is unmatched.

Despite this history of real-life disasters, the apocalyptic imagination in Japanese popular culture since World War II has generally been understood as reflecting the lingering trauma of Hiroshima and Nagasaki. "Of course," Susan Napier assures us, "the atomic bombings . . . are the most obvious catalyst to apocalyptic thought," a notion long assumed by commentators on Japanese mass entertainments.[6] Although some have suggested that guilt and remorse over the war have led Japanese filmmakers to rehearse Armageddon so compulsively on both the big and small screens, far more observers tend to point to unresolved tensions, fears, and feelings of vulnerability, as well as lingering animosities from the bombings, defeat, and the ensuing cold war. Akira Mizuta Lippit, for one, has argued that "the destruction of visual order by the atomic light and force has haunted Japanese visual culture," inspiring an ongoing search for ways to address the invisible scars of war and the "unrepresentable nature of the atomic bombings."[7] Such views have been articulated most consistently (and insistently) in recent years by the successful pop artist Murakami Takashi, who has argued vigorously for the formative influence of Hiroshima and Nagasaki—and postwar society's inability to deal with these horrors—on the creativity of Japanese popular culture. To Murakami, it fell to the makers of fantasy worlds—animators, comic book artists, science fiction writers, film and television producers—to reflect on the shared history of trauma that could not be discussed in mainstream society, the suppressed memories of the "twofold violence Japan experienced [in World War II] as both victimizer and victimized, as well as its fear of the Cold War."[8] Thus, the creators of Japan's "doom-laden" pop culture have

> re-imagined Japan's gravely distorted history, which the nation chose to embrace at the very beginning of its postwar life by repressing memories of violence and averting its eyes from reality. Granted, [Japan] is seemingly suspended in a historical amnesia, having little sense of the past and withdrawing from reality. Yet [we continue] to mine the ancient narrative strata of the Pacific War and recast the reality of the Cold War into another form. How many times have [we] burned Tokyo to cinders, tirelessly fended off invaders, and persevered through radioactive contamination in order to chip away at the imaginary reality that forced [us] into self-withdrawal?[9]

While Murakami thus interprets the compulsive fictionalized annihilation of Tokyo as a legitimate, even sincere means of addressing deep-seated anxieties and unsettled legacies in postwar Japan, other commentators have seen the mushroom clouds of cinema and cartoons as a cynical trivialization of the horrors of the nuclear age. Critics have frequently chided the filmmakers of Hollywood and Japan for favoring the apocalyptic spectacle of a city in flames over reasoned engagement with "the serious ethical implications of atomic use and development."[10] Indeed, as Richard Hodgens has written, "A twelve-ton, woman-eating cockroach does not say anything about the bomb simply because it, too, is radioactive, or crawls out of a test site, and the filmmakers have simply attempted to make their monster more frightening by associating it with something serious."[11] To Jonathan Lake Crane, cinematic bugaboos like Godzilla and Mothra were "pathetic claptrap" that sought to "answer the most significant question of the 20th century with tacky special effects, papier-mâché sets, and idiotic plots. How can lumbering dinosaurs spewing atomic fire, giant carnivorous plants, and implacable mutant insects approach the fiery chaos that engulfed Japan?"[12] A few authors have been even more skeptical, dismissing radioactive mutation and nuclear holocaust, the favored means of delivering Armageddon in both American and Japanese films since World War II, as nothing more than expedient plot devices. Bill Warren observed,

> In the 1930s the equivalent gimmick was electricity; in the 1920s, it was surgery and often gland operations. In the 1950s, it was radiation that got the monster going. The 1930s didn't suffer from fear of electrical annihilation; although the 1950s did tend to be worried about atomic warfare, radiation in science fiction films wasn't a means of expressing this fear, probably not even unconsciously. It was just a way of originating an unusual or interesting menace. . . . Radiation was used to explain many wonderful things, from giant insects to walking trees to resurrecting the dead. This was not a form of nuclear paranoia, merely cheap and simple plotting.[13]

As one American critic reflected on his childhood of watching giant monster movies and alien invasion pictures, "The end of the world? No big deal. By the time I was ten, I'd been through it dozens of times. . . . If the planet is spared in one film, it is quite grimly written off in the next."[14]

Perhaps the most time-honored interpretation of postwar science fiction films, especially those of an apocalyptic nuclear bent, was that offered by Susan Sontag in her influential 1965 essay "The Imagination of Disaster." Sontag's analysis lay somewhere between the extremes of Murakami's vision of Japanese pop as traumatized self-reflection and the jaundiced view of celluloid Armageddons as mere gimmicks. To her, the appeal of postwar sci-fi cinema was its charming "intersection between a naïve and largely debased commercial art product and the most profound dilemmas of the contemporary situation," particularly regarding the nuclear threat.[15] Thus a film like *Rodan* (*Radon* [1956]), in which giant pteranodons obliterate the Japanese city of Fukuoka, nods to the "mass trauma [that] exists over the use of nuclear weapons and the possibility of future nuclear wars" while also reveling in "the aesthetics of destruction . . . the peculiar beauties to be found in wreaking havoc, in making a mess."[16] Urban obliteration in postwar science fiction, Sontag goes on to argue, serves a complex psychological function for the anxious moviegoing masses, at once distracting us from and numbing us to the ever-present possibility of nuclear tragedy. "Ours is indeed an age of extremity," Sontag wrote,

> For we live under continual threat of two equally fearful, but seemingly opposed, destinies: unremitting banality and inconceivable

terror. It is fantasy, served out in large rations by the popular arts, which allows most people to cope with these twin specters. For one job that fantasy can do is to lift us out of the unbearably humdrum and to distract us from terrors—real or anticipated—by an escape into exotic, dangerous situations which have last-minute happy endings. But another of the things that fantasy can do is to normalize what is psychologically unbearable, thereby inuring us to it. In one case, fantasy beautifies the world, in the other, it neutralizes it. The fantasy in science fiction films does both jobs. The films reflect world-wide anxieties, and they serve to allay them.[17]

Scholars following in Sontag's interpretive footsteps have generally stressed the darkness and pessimism in the apocalyptic imagination of postwar Japanese popular culture. Given the ubiquity of "repetitious scenarios of sublimated nuclear cataclysm"—and, above all, the destruction of Tokyo—in Japanese animation, television, and sci-fi cinema, such a conclusion is hardly surprising.[18] Susan Napier, who has written extensively on Japan's "imagination of disaster," thus stresses "the utter bleakness of the worlds delineated" in Japanese science fiction, contrasting the nihilistic tone and profound pessimism of Japanese apocalyptic fantasies with the less gloomy visions served up by Hollywood and other Western purveyors of mass entertainment.[19] Although Napier, like Murakami, stresses the importance of the shadows cast by Hiroshima and Nagasaki, she notes that Japanese pop culture is notably darker today than it was in the immediate postwar decades, when forms like *kaijū eiga* (giant monster movies) had a less somber spin on Armageddon. As Napier argues, the "secure horror" of earlier decades, wherein the audience could be assured that the monster would be vanquished and the survival of the Japanese collectivity affirmed by the end of a film's final reel, has now given way to "open-ended nihilism," a profound and perhaps hopeless dystopian consciousness particularly prevalent in recent manga and anime.[20] At best, such dire visions of the end (frequently depicted as the end of Tokyo) are seen as providing a cathartic release for the unresolved postwar tensions stressed by Murakami as well as a new host of concerns raised by Japan's systemic social and economic crises of the past twenty years.

But if postwar Japanese popular culture is indeed so nihilistic and haunted by the specters of Hiroshima, defeat, and cold war vulnerability, why then have so many of the Armageddons visited upon Tokyo by Japanese animators and filmmakers been so exuberant, exhilarating, humorous, and even downright joyful? For all the darkness of Japanese sci-fi fantasies, I would argue that there is a strand of optimism woven tightly into the apocalyptic imagination of Godzilla movies, futuristic TV series, and end-of-the world anime. There is also a celebration of the visual spectacle of devastation, of Sontag's "beauties to be found in wreaking havoc" and the "primitive fascination with scenes of destruction."[21] What's more, pop culture depictions of mushroom clouds rising over Tokyo and burned-out urban ruins have, at times, expressed the subversive visions and liberating fantasies of postwar Japan, challenging taboos and exploring alternatives to business-as-usual. And strikingly, many of the fantasies rooted in this cultural embrace of disaster have been conservative, even reactionary ones: the apocalyptic nightmares conjured in Japan over the past half century have often been exercises in nostalgia, not the "nostalgia for the present" that Fredric Jameson sees characterizing science fiction in general[22] but a nostalgia for the kind of systemic destruction (and the social and political consensus that it can galvanize) last seen in Japan in 1945. Thus, as I will explore in this essay, the theme of urban catastrophe in Japanese popular culture may be less about exorcizing the demons of Hiroshima and less a reflection of a profound and consuming nihilism than an unruly form of recreational fantasy, the expression of a kind of pop millenarianism, and the ultimate gimmick in the imaginative quivers of postwar Japan's sci-fi dreamers.

Susan Napier argues that there have been cycles of apocalypse in postwar Japanese popular culture, distinct clusters of films and anime that imagine urban catastrophe, spaced at roughly twenty-year intervals, tracking the ups and downs of perceived social, economic, and political anxieties in Japan. The idea is appealing, not least because disaster and end-of-the-world movies have been said to trace a similar periodicity in Hollywood, with celluloid Armageddons proliferating in the 1950s, 1970s, and 1990s.[23] But however neat and tidy historically it would have been for fictionalized visions of Tokyo's doom to have followed directly on the real-life ordeals of Hiroshima, the "oil shocks" of the early 1970s, and the "Great Recession" of the 1990s, the actual situation was hardly so simple. In fact, the depiction of apocalypse has been a constant in postwar movies, television, and animation, with the destruction of Tokyo a commonplace and remarkably consistent feature of Japan's visual culture across the decades from the 1950s to the present.

That being said, the experiences of Hiroshima and Nagasaki did figure prominently in Japanese cinema during the decade and a half after World War II, especially in the years following the departure of the American occupation in 1952. The postwar "A-bomb" films did include some somber musings on war and the lingering nuclear threat, like Kurosawa Akira's acclaimed *Record of a Living Being* (*Ikimono no kiroku* [1955]), as well as a number of documentaries, some more melodramatic and sensationalistic pictures, and a handful of overtly political treatments of the atomic attacks. Perhaps surprisingly, satire was also an option, as in Kinoshita Keisuke's *Carmen's Pure Love* (*Karumen junjōsu* [1952]), which featured an elderly character who had lost a son in Hiroshima and subsequently blamed all the bad luck in her life, including an election loss by a political candidate she supported, on the effects of the atomic bombs.[24] The most famous (and enduring) treatment of Japan's atomic legacies, however, was *Gojira* (1954), the movie that launched the postwar genre of *kaijū eiga* and established the master narrative of giant irradiated monsters attacking and devastating the Japanese capital city.

Gojira was a brooding and dark film that drew on memories of Hiroshima and the firebombing of Tokyo in a visually arresting, emotional style.[25] The story of a Jurassic survivor rendered huge and radioactive by U.S. hydrogen bomb testing in the South Pacific, *Gojira* traces the monster's attacks on Tokyo—rendering the city a smoldering, flattened wasteland, much as it had been in 1945—and the creature's ultimate destruction by a new super-weapon devised by a Japanese scientist. The film was intended by its makers as a strong antiwar and antinuclear statement aimed at an adult audience; "Believe it or not," director Honda Ishirō once remarked, "we naively hoped that the end of Godzilla was going to coincide with the end of nuclear testing."[26] As a number of commentators have observed, however, *Gojira* was, for all the scenes of Tokyo in flames, the images of irradiated infants, and its often funereal tone, a fundamentally optimistic movie. For despite all of Godzilla's destructive fury, the monster is eventually defeated and the Japanese nation, even if wounded by this latest radioactive menace from across the seas, survives intact at the end. Above all, the film shows a tremendous faith in science and progress—as the creature, spawned by American science gone wrong, is finally vanquished by the yet more powerful creations of Japanese science—and a profound trust in the Japanese establishment (the state, the military, the intellectual elites) as dependable, benevolent, and competent.

Moreover, while *Gojira* mourns, from a safe imaginative distance, the losses of Hiroshima, Nagasaki, and the bombing of Tokyo, the film also casts an unexpectedly positive light on the experience of catastrophe and suggests a kind of perverse nostalgia for the salutary impact of systemic crisis on society, politics, and interpersonal relations. For most of *Gojira*, up until Godzilla's devastating nighttime raids on Tokyo, a palpable atmosphere of debate, division, and discord hangs over the movie: scientists argue with government officials over whether the monster should be studied as a specimen or destroyed as a threat; in a famous scene in the Japanese Diet, parliamentarians clash (first with words and eventually with their fists) over whether information on Godzilla should be made public or suppressed; and even at the family level, contention is rife, as a love triangle divides loyalties and strains relationships among the film's major characters. But the attacks of Godzilla and the spectacle of Tokyo in shambles bring a sudden end to the disagreements and the pervasive sense of division in society. Faced with their capital city in ruins, the characters in *Gojira* put aside their differences and rally together in unified resistance to the radioactive enemy: the decision to kill the monster is embraced by all, political squabbles become moot, and even individual strife fades away, as the climactic suicide of the scientist who created the super-weapon solves the troublesome love triangle.

In the closing scenes of *Gojira*, as the creature's demise is confirmed, the assembled throngs erupt in spontaneous cries of "What exhilaration! What jubilation! We have won!" As some scholars have suggested, this ending might constitute a therapeutic restaging of the conclusion of World War II, with Japan coming out on top this time around; yet the scene also seems to celebrate the spiritual unification of the Japanese collectivity, ultimately drawn together in harmony and strength (out of the political divides, social schisms, and individual animosities that marked Japan in the 1950s) by a common foe and a brief glimpse into Armageddon. Even the destruction of Tokyo by a huge, fire-breathing lizard can have its bright spots for the Japanese people, or at least so *Gojira* bids us to conclude.

The period from the late 1950s to the early 1970s was the high tide of growth and optimism in "miracle economy" Japan. As the historian Yoshikuni Igarashi has observed, the "darkness that had prevailed [in the early 1950s] had vanished from the screen and Japanese society,"[27] and in its place came a new confidence, a fresh expansiveness, and an unprecedented faith in economic progress, both for individual Japanese and for the nation as a whole. Yet despite the surging GNP statistics and the celebration of major landmarks in Japan's return to global "great power" status—the 1964 Tokyo Olympics, Expo '70 in Osaka—the years of "high-speed growth" were the very time that images of apocalypse, especially the fictionalized devastation of Tokyo, fully suffused Japanese popular culture, and above all those forms of it aimed at Japanese youth.

Gojira was Japan's first giant monster picture, a genre that flourished from the mid-1950s and virtually came to define Japanese mass culture to global consumers, at least up until the 1970s. The Godzilla franchise would emerge as the leading brand in *kaijū eiga*, with twenty-eight films produced by Tōhō Studios in the half century after 1954, making it the world's longest continuous film series. But Godzilla was hardly the only gargantuan, mutant creature to appear in postwar Japanese theaters: Tōhō developed a range of other cinematic monsters before settling on Godzilla as the studio's leading man. Thus Japanese cities faced attack from a huge reptilian flying squirrel in *Varan the Unbelievable* (*Daikaijū baran* [1958]), the pteranodons in *Rodan*, and a colorful irradiated moth goddess in *Mothra* (*Mosura* [1961]), to name just a few. Other Japanese movie companies were quick to enter the genre as well, notably

Daiei, whose featured property was Gamera, a giant, tusked turtle that could fly and breathe fire, and that had an inexplicable soft spot for Japanese children. Gamera starred in seven films between 1965 and 1971, bringing a fiery holocaust to Tokyo more than once, and would return in the 1990s for a new series of apocalyptic adventures. Giant, destructive monsters even turned up in period pieces, as with the 1966 *Daimajin* trilogy (that involved a mammoth stone warrior bringing justice to samurai society), and in a range of futuristic sci-fi films, including the charming *Warning from Space* (*Uchūjin Tokyo ni arawaru* [1956]) featuring aliens shaped like huge starfish seeing the sights in central Tokyo.

The typical plot of Japanese monster movies of the postwar "golden age" was entirely predictable: a giant creature attacks Japan, usually cutting a swath of destruction through Tokyo and managing to knock down a landmark or two in the process. The construction of Tokyo Tower, which was completed in 1958, was a boon for the special-effects crews, and just about every monster took a swing at this symbolic new addition to the city's skyline (a larval Mothra, for instance, bent the tower in half and spun a huge cocoon there). The authorities rally to stop the monstrous threat, but despite deploying every sort of military hardware, they always prove impotent in stopping the attack. Ultimately, however, the monster is vanquished and Japan is saved by some lucky twist of fate (such as a convenient volcanic eruption), a fortuitous scientific discovery, or an expedient plot device credible only to a juvenile audience. From the early 1960s, the pattern of the Godzilla films was for the star of the series, usually depicted in a heroic light, to defend Japan from enormous invading creatures in hand-to-hand (or claw-to-claw) combat. Even in these scenarios, urban annihilation—the destruction of miniature mock-ups of Tokyo flattened, burned, and detonated by actors wrestling in latex monster suits—was part of the standard formula.

A striking feature of *kaijū eiga* was the regularity with which Tokyo was destroyed, only to be reconstructed before the next monster lumbered through town and the movie cameras rolled again. Tokyo thus took on a fantastical "self-healing" quality, as the presumed multiple rebuildings of the city were apparently accomplished without any human agency: in none of the monster films from the 1960s or 1970s do we see machinery removing debris, workers repairing buildings, or civil leaders charting the redevelopment of their ravaged capital. This offscreen spontaneous regeneration of the urban fabric was particularly impressive (and expeditious) in the live-action television series *Ultra Q* (*Urutora Q* [1966]) and its more famous successor, *Ultraman* (*Urutoraman* [1966–67]). Both of these very popular weekly shows aimed at youth audiences were produced by Tsuburaya Eiji, the special-effects master behind the Godzilla franchise and Tōhō "suitmation," and featured an attack on Japan (and usually on Tokyo) by a new giant monster in each episode. In *Ultraman*, Japan is protected by the elite "Science Patrol" and is ultimately saved in each installment by the titular character, a kind of cosmic cop, a red and silver giant alien from Nebula M-78 who is committed to defending the Earth from all foes, domestic and intergalactic. As the Japanese critic Tatsumi Takayuki has perceptively observed, "in the mid-1960s, the weekly Japanese TV series *Ultra Q* [and *Ultraman*], featuring a variety of post-Godzilla monsters, accelerated the alternation between destruction and reconstruction. However fatally Tokyo gets destroyed by brand-new monsters, you will find the very same city reconstructed quickly and beautifully next week. Armageddon happens once a week, Resurrection the following week. This is the two-beat jazz that Japan was dancing in its high-growth period."[28]

Such a "two-beat jazz" was enacted across a wide range of Japanese popular culture, even well into the 1970s. The television series *Zone Fighter* (*Ryūsei ningen zōn* [1973]), for example, featured a family of transforming superheroes who battled a stream of giant baddies from space, blithely obliterating Tokyo neighborhoods with nary a thought for casualties or the work of rebuilding. Animation was naturally suited to this apocalyptic aesthetic, and one of the most celebrated early examples was a series called *Time Bokan* (*Taimu bokan*) that first aired in 1975–76. Extremely popular with children, *Time Bokan* revolved around comically futuristic "mecha-battles" between squeaky-clean superheroes and a ragtag trio of bumbling villains. Each episode ends with the inept bad guys consumed by a towering mushroom cloud that swirls into the shape of a human skull, lest any of the show's young viewers miss the obvious symbolism. As Murakami Takashi has noted, "Although each episode of the series concludes with the villains' demise, symbolized by a skull-shaped mushroom cloud, these enemies are wholly restored to their fiendish selves in the following installment."[29] Thus, even nuclear annihilation could lead to immediate resurrection in the fantastical and endlessly hopeful realm of popular culture in Japan's high-growth decades.

One critic has suggested that "The more complicated a civilization becomes, the more fun it is to imagine the whole works going up in flames."[30] And in high-growth-era Japan, it seems, nothing beat the exhilarating fun of seeing Tokyo Tower toppled or the forces of darkness thwarted (at least until the next commercial break) by a little nuclear blast. But for all the scenes of ruin, from the Tōhō creature features of the late 1950s to the anime of the 1970s, Japan's fictionalized urban apocalypses were generally painless, self-correcting, and thoroughly optimistic spectacles. The repeated destruction of Tokyo was "cheap and cheerful,"[31] colorful and exciting, a kind of visual condiment to accompany the main event of giant monsters wrestling to the death. The speed with which the metropolis recovered, bouncing back essentially unchanged on a weekly basis, was a reflection not just of the utterly fantastic nature of these pop culture depictions but also of a profound and cheery confidence in progress, born perhaps of Japan's unprecedented economic advance and of the real-life thoroughness with which Japanese cities were being demolished, redeveloped, and transformed at this time.[32] It is probably no coincidence that video games like Space Invaders, where destruction—"game over"—could be erased and the fantasy completely reset with the simple insertion of another coin, were also being developed in these years of abundance and change. Susan Napier has contended that this apocalyptic temperament in the postwar Japanese imagination constituted a "subversion of modernity," a rejection of notions of progress that always seemed redolent of their Western origins.[33] Yet in *kaijū eiga*, *Ultraman*, and their pop culture progeny, with their endlessly and automatically regenerating urban landscapes, we may actually have seen the ultimate celebration of modernity and expression of faith in the sure hand of progress and the resilience of the Japanese nation.

From the early 1970s through the late 1980s, a period bookended by the unsettling impact of the "oil shocks" (that brought to a close the "miracle economy") and the exuberant (and perhaps even more unsettling) excesses of the go-go "bubble economy," the apocalyptic imagination remained firmly rooted in Japanese popular culture. The buoyancy and lightheartedness of previous years' depictions of disaster were less in evidence, however, and the end of the world (or at least of Tokyo) took on a decidedly darker cast. Yet for all the new and more starkly dystopian visions that appeared in films, on television, and in animated features, an enduring optimism and a pervading confidence in redemptive, spontaneous, and inevitable recovery from annihilation continued to characterize mainstream mass entertainments in Japan. The smoldering wreckage of Tokyo remained an image that more often evoked hope than despair.

Academic commentators usually stress the "bleak urban imagery" and the sense of "social and psychological collapse" in the apocalyptic pop culture of Japan in the wake of the "oil shocks."[34] For example, the landmark animated television series of the 1970s, *Space Battleship Yamato* (*Uchū senkan Yamato* [1974–75]), pivots on the grim vision of a coming Armageddon. In the year 2199, the Earth has been reduced to a radioactive wasteland by an endless barrage of nuclear bombs from the distant planet Gamilus. Humans, unable to stop the alien attacks, have retreated ever deeper underground to avoid the seeping radioactivity. Just as it seems that all life is about to be annihilated, a message is received from the planet Iscandar, promising a device that will scrub the toxins from the Earth's surface (called Cosmo-Cleaner D) and providing instructions on how to construct an advanced intergalactic vessel. The

new spacecraft is built, curiously enough, from the wreckage of the Battleship Yamato, the pride of the Imperial Japanese Navy, sunk on a suicide run
to Okinawa in 1945. The resurrected ship and its crew face almost countless
hazards on the way to Iscandar but are eventually successful in their mission,
retrieving the Cosmo-Cleaner and returning victoriously to regenerate the
Earth. Strikingly, despite the opening scenes of a cratered and lifeless Japan,
still arguably the most moving image of Armageddon ever rendered in anime, the *Space Battleship Yamato* series remained well within the confines
of "secure horror," ending with humanity's salvation and the affirmation of
existing structures of authority. Moreover, the series seems to suggest, even
nuclear holocaust is reversible, albeit through mysterious and purely fantastical means, just as the urban destruction inflicted by Godzilla and the creatures on *Ultraman* could always be remedied, out of sight and beyond rational
analysis.

The vision of the Earth scoured by radiation and then spontaneously reborn recurred frequently in Japan's animated imaginary in the 1980s. An influential example was the *Daicon IV Opening Animation,* a five-minute short
created by a group of amateur artists for a national science fiction fan convention in 1983. The film, whose creative team went on to form the leading anime
studio Gainax, combined a rapid-fire series of tributes to other subculture
favorites (from *Godzilla* to *Ultraman* to *Space Battleship Yamato*) with stunning imagery, high technical values, and narrative innovation. At the climax
of the story, "The energetic flight through the sky of a girl in a bunny costume
is followed by the explosion of what could only be described as an atomic
bomb, which destroys everything. In a pink-hued blast, petals of cherry blos-
soms—Japan's national flower—spread over the city, which is then burned
to ashes, as trees die on the mountains and the earth is turned into a barren
landscape."[35] After the apocalypse, where the animators pay homage to the
familiar (to the point of being trite) stock footage of nuclear blasts originally
produced by the U.S. Atomic Energy Commission, the world is magically
regenerated by a beam from an orbiting spaceship, trees bursting fully grown
from the scarred ground and a carpet of green racing around the planet. In
the end, as Murakami Takashi puts it, "The world is revived, becoming a place
of life where people joyously gather together"; Earth's new beginning is bright
and promising.[36]

An even more significant case is *Akira*, possibly the most important animated movie ever made in Japan, created by Ōtomo Katsuhiro (and based on
a two-thousand-page manga epic he also penned) in 1988. The film begins
with a blinding light, symbolizing the destruction of Tokyo in World War III,
before the action begins in 2019 in Neo Tokyo, a new city rapidly constructed
next to the dark, gaping crater of "Old Tokyo." As Susan Napier notes, Neo

Tokyo is "a place of overwhelming aesthetic and social alienation, a decaying cityscape that is physically fragmenting."[37] This dystopian vision of the Japanese city's future—with riots in the streets, a venal authoritarian state, millenarian cults, terrorist movements, biker gangs, and a peculiar government program for developing psychic mutants—has led critics to brand *Akira* a virtual celebration of nihilism, a grindingly pessimistic yet exhilarating and even cathartic cinematic experience. *Akira*, according to Napier, was "disaster for the fun of it" or, as another commentator put it, "the post nuclear sublime," a reflection of the mounting alienation and increasingly obvious disfunctionality of Japanese society in the 1980s.[38] The movie closes with Neo Tokyo being consumed by a vast psychic holocaust, not visually dissimilar to an atomic blast, that leaves the city in ruins. Yet in the manga version of *Akira*, which enjoyed the same spectacular popularity in Japan as the anime, the ending is significantly different and considerably more optimistic, recalling *Space Battleship Yamato* and the hopeful finale of *Daicon IV*: as a gang of young bikers ride out of the ruins of Neo Tokyo, "the city reconstitutes itself, the rubble seeming to rise up and re-form in front of the reader's eyes."[39]

The disaster film genre has also been generally interpreted as reflecting Japan's dark and troubled imagination in a time of unsettling economic, social, and demographic transitions. Although disaster films rose to prominence in Hollywood in the 1970s (with blockbusters like *The Poseidon Adventure* and *The Towering Inferno*), Japanese filmmakers took catastrophe as their theme more consistently through the postwar period and commonly portrayed disaster on a citywide, nationwide, or even planetary scale. Thus, the world fell victim to nuclear war in both *The Final War* (*Dai-sanji sekai taisen* [1960]) and *The Last War* (*Sekai daisensō* [1961]); Tokyo was ripped apart by winds in *Fūsoku 75* (1963); the apocalyptic prophesies of Nostradamus were visited on Japan in *The Last Days of Planet Earth* (*Nostradamus no dai yogen* [1974]); Tokyo Bay burst into flames in *Tokyo-wan enjō* (1975); and *Deathquake* (*Jishin rettō* [1980]) brought the Japanese capital tumbling down. The mother of all disaster films, however, was undoubtedly *Japan Sinks* (*Nihon chinbotsu*) which was the highest-grossing domestic release in Japan in 1974. The movie was based on the best-selling 1973 novel of the same name by leading sci-fi author Komatsu Sakyō and depicted "a series of catastrophic fires, tidal waves, volcanoes, and soap opera histrionics before climaxing with the entire nation itself plunging into the drink."[40] The film (like the novel) was presented with thoroughly sober, pseudo-scientific solemnity, leading Napier to describe it as "an elegy to a lost Japan," "a freeze frame of the Japanese citizenry . . . with their sense of an eroding identity and an ambivalent attitude toward power and success."[41] Watching not just Tokyo and other Japanese cities crumble and fall but indeed the whole Japanese archipelago slip seismically beneath the waves prompted another commentator to conclude that, in the Japanese apocalyptic imagination, "Progress was to be inseparable from pessimism. As Japan grew in postwar affluence, so did the need to drown it."[42]

Japan Sinks the novel, even more so than the movie, described the death throes of the islands in a distinctive manner, combining allusions to the atomic attacks and the firebombing of Tokyo with a highly aestheticized, almost erotic portrayal of the nation's submersion. Thus, as that paramount symbol of Japan erupts, Komatsu writes, "The window did not have a direct view of Mount Fuji, but a huge gray mushroom-shaped cloud was rapidly rising and spreading over the clear, pale blue March sky." And as Japan begins its final slide, Komatsu depicts it as a living creature, almost a monster: "The dragon was stricken. A fatal illness was eating at him, destroying his very marrow. Racked with fever, his vast bulk covered with bleeding wounds, he thrashed about, vainly struggling against the fate that was tearing at him. The encroaching blue sliding over him was like the shadow of death."[43] But, in the end, the message of the novel is hardly entirely dark: the Japanese homeland is lost, but a majority of the Japanese people are saved, relocated to other lands through immense effort and (as Komatsu details it) immense resistance from other nations. Tatsumi Takayuki reads this as a metaphor for the globalization of Japanese business, which was proceeding briskly at the time and drawing many of Japan's corporate managers (and their families) to assignments abroad.[44] Strikingly, Komatsu's novel ends not with despair or elegiac regret for the loss of the physical space of Japan but with the hopeful notion that misfortune will challenge the Japanese people and push them to ever greater heights (as, one might suggest, the previous devastation of 1945 had done): "This, then, will be a test for the Japanese. Their bridges have been burned behind them. They have no choice but to go forward. Whether they wish it or not, the chance to achieve adulthood is being forced upon them."[45]

The Godzilla series was revived in the 1980s after going on hiatus in 1975 due to slipping box office returns. The reborn King of the Monsters was intended to be darker, more adult-oriented, and inflected with a new moral valence. Godzilla still brought cinematic destruction to Japanese cities, especially Tokyo, but the creature—no longer compelling as radiation-made-flesh or as a metaphor for wartime suffering—was transformed into a conscience for Japan, an uncontrollable natural force that was meant to remind the nation of its vulnerability and pop the bubble of Japan's inflated pride. Longtime producer Tanaka Tomoyuki was insistent that Godzilla trample the ostentatious landmarks of Japan's fin-de-siècle prosperity: the skyscrapers of Shinjuku, the glittering waterfront developments around Tokyo Bay, "the vain symbols of these abundant days." "Japan is rich and people can buy whatever they want," Tanaka explained. "But what is behind that wealth? Nothing very spiritual. Everyone's so concerned with the material, and then Godzilla comes and rips it all apart. I suspect that is good for us to see."[46] Whether audiences perceived the message of the new films in this way is uncertain, as Tokyo continued to heal itself spontaneously between the almost annual new releases and, although Godzilla kept coming back movie after movie, Japanese society invariably held firm in the face of monstrous onslaughts and the films never seemed to challenge seriously the desirability of modern life or the inevitability of progress. Moreover, in the scenes of urban devastation, now enhanced with improved special effects, exhilaration, an air of festival, and occasional humor—Sontag's hoary "aesthetics of destruction"—banished any real sense of sorrow, anxiety, despair, or cosmic retribution for material excess from the screen. Godzilla may have walked through Tokyo with a scowl on his face, but Japanese audiences still seemed to greet his urban perambulations with a laugh and a smile.

As Japan traversed the millennium, apocalypse remained a prominent feature of the pop imaginary. Visions of Armageddon were assumed by commentators to be a natural response to the ills that beset Japanese society in the years after the collapse of the "bubble economy" in 1989. In the "Great Recession," or the "lost decade," as the darkest years of this economic downturn came to be known, not only did the fortunes of Japanese industry and finance suffer but the nation's political and administrative elites splintered and proved themselves impotent, while Japan's core social institutions—the family, schools—also appeared to fracture and fail. But despite what one scholar has termed a "profound sense of rupture and uncertainty,"[47] Japanese audiences did not wallow in somber and nihilistic visions of a dystopian future. Fictionalized apocalypses may still have referenced the now distant memories of Hiroshima and the Tokyo bombings, but those traumas seemed not so much raw wounds as deep sediments in the popular imagination. Instead, many mass entertainments of the 1990s and early twenty-first century looked backward to wartime and high-growth-era Japan with overt nostalgia, and urban devastation was often perceived with a kind of millenarian edge, wide-scale destruction being imagined as just the kind of systemic reset that was needed to galvanize a more cohesive and coherent society in a Japan locked in a "postwar without end."[48] And, at century's close, two real-world instances of catastrophe demonstrated just how intertwined fact and fantasy have become in Japan's contemporary apocalyptic imagination.

Two events in 1995 demonstrated chillingly how fictionalized visions of Armageddon could provide templates for real acts of violence and structure popular responses to actual disasters. On March 20, 1995, five members of the religious cult Aum Shinrikyō released sarin gas on subway lines in Tokyo, killing twelve, injuring thousands, and profoundly disrupting the transportation network and the daily lives of millions of city residents. Aum, founded in 1984 by Asahara Shōkō, has often been described as a "doomsday cult" which, drawing on Buddhist, Hindu, and Daoist traditions, as well as a rich history of millenarianism in Japan, embraced a profound "desire for destruction" and a "consuming hunger for Armageddon."[49] Aum's millenarian vision—that the destruction of the current, debased world, beginning with Tokyo, would lead to the birth of a new paradisial civilization—was derived in large part from the apocalyptic images that suffused Japanese postwar popular culture. Thus, as has been widely reported, in addition to being fixated on Nostradamus, Hiroshima, and the American post-nuclear miniseries *The Day After*, Aum's charismatic leader Asahara was a compulsive reader of the manga *Nausicaä of the Valley of the Wind* (*Kaze no tani no Naushika*), set in a dystopian, post-apocalyptic future, and his prophecies of Japan's fate, with the archipelago becoming a nuclear wasteland and being consumed by the seas, resonated with works like *Space Battleship Yamato* and *Japan Sinks*.[50] Indeed, Aum workers even borrowed the term "Cosmo-Cleaner" from *Yamato* to describe an air purification and filtration system that they were working on for the cult's headquarters. Interviews with Aum members after the sarin attacks revealed that many of the core "renunciates" were, in fact, dedicated science fiction fans, often with idealistic yearnings for the simple verities of pop culture (good guy defeats bad guy) and an attraction to the aesthetics, technology, and liberating possibilities of apocalypse. Not surprisingly, Aum made extensive use of manga as a means of attracting converts.[51] As one observer suggested, the Aum disciples who naively sought salvation for themselves and redemption for Japanese society in the gassing of unsuspecting Tokyo commuters were, in the end, the "children of Godzilla."[52]

Not long before the Aum attacks, on January 17, 1995, the city of Kobe in western Japan was shaken by the Great Hanshin-Awaji Earthquake, which measured 7.2 on the Richter scale. The disaster, unprecedented in its scale since World War II, killed more than five thousand people, destroyed over one hundred thousand buildings, left a fifth of the city's residents homeless, and caused a total of at least $200 billion in property damage. To some commentators, the sight of Kobe in ruins brought to mind wartime devastation; Akira Mizuta Lippit, for example, called the earthquake an "avisual echo of World War II . . . a return of the repressed atomic bombing" and argued that "the displaced or deferred spectacles forced the nation to revisit the primal scene of postwar Japan. The Kobe earthquake . . . reintroduced long-dormant images of wartime Japan."[53] Not all—or perhaps not even most—spectators saw the prostration of Kobe through these same historical lenses, many instead comprehending the catastrophe through more proximate and familiar experiences of fictionalized apocalypse. "More than a few survivors compared the experience to being an extra in a giant monster movie," one observer recounted.[54] For Miyawaki Shūichi, the president of the toy manufacturer Kaiyōdō, the sight of the destruction immediately inspired comparisons to *kaijū eiga*: "I know it's insensitive to say this [after such a terrible disaster], but I think *Gamera* got it wrong." The journalist Okada Toshio concurred.

> At the time of the earthquake, I raced to Kobe from Osaka, hopping on whatever trains were still running, taking lots of pictures. I agree, *Gamera* got it wrong. To create a realistic effect of destruction, you need to drape thin, gray noodles over a set of rubble. Otherwise, you can't even approach the reality of twisted, buckled steel frames. It was like, "If you call yourself a monster-filmmaker, get here now!" When Mt. Mihara erupted in 1986, the production team of the 1984 *Godzilla* film went there to see it. They *were* true filmmakers.[55]

Perhaps not surprisingly, Aum's Asahara Shōkō interpreted the Kobe quake as part of a vast conspiracy by the United States government and imagined the plot playing out very much like a science fiction blockbuster, as America's "mysterious Great Power . . . set off the earthquake either with a small, distant nuclear explosion or by 'radiating high voltage microwaves' into the ground near the fault line."[56]

Even many observers (and victims) of the Kobe earthquake not associated with a "doomsday cult" were inclined to read the experience of disaster in millenarian terms. Apocalypse, as many movies, television series, and anime had been suggesting for decades, did indeed promise a kind of vital regeneration, a reaffirmation of human ties and the forging of a shared commitment to the process of rebuilding. This may have been best captured by the architectural critic Suzuki Akira, who reflected on the ruins of Kobe and the energized potential created by destruction.

> I stood in the city as it was then—an environment demolished, warped, burned—and shuddered to think that nothing remained to protect me. . . .
>
> All the networks of production and activity that converge in the city were lost, together with the hitherto unnoticed niceties of daily life. And yet the city managed to maintain an uncanny vitality. (Pessimism was overcome as residents, volunteers, and government workers set to work on their own initiative.)
>
> No doubt the wasteland will soon be replaced with a city to rival the one that was there before. Tokyo, where I live, has done this many times over. But once that new city is built and all of its activities are resumed, it will lose the strange vigor of the wasteland. Indeed, once a city is built, its past as open ground is inevitably forgotten.

The loss of a city creates a void. A void in which people move with a strange animation. But inevitably we suppress the memory of the void and its vitality by covering it over with yet another modern city.[57]

In this light, then, the imagination of apocalypse seems less a reflection of pessimism and nihilism than a potential cure for it, a kind of pop millenarian vision of hope and communal striving. As Michael Barkun has argued, "Disasters paradoxically inflict deprivations but also confer benefits. In the midst of disaster, its victims frequently experience moments of intense warmth, community, comradeship, and fellow feeling absent from their workaday lives. How frequently they say, 'If only people could always be like this!'"[58]

According to Murakami Takashi, the real-world experiences of Kobe and, above all, the Aum subway attacks "thoroughly shattered the post-apocalyptic . . . dream of creating a new world" among Japanese pop culture consumers weaned on fictional Armageddons.[59] But the kind of millenarian urge that infused Aum and that also ended up shaping some responses to the Kobe disaster continued to be expressed broadly in Japanese films and animation at the turn of the twenty-first century. Nostalgia for the war and for the experience of postwar recovery, both times of social solidarity driven by shared catastrophe, has been a major theme in recent years in Japanese popular cinema, with films like *Always* (*San-chome no yūhi* [2005]) harkening back to the years of economic striving in 1950s Tokyo and *Yamato* (*Bokutachi no Yamato* [2005]) restaging the war in a spiritually uplifting, disaster film mode. In *Yamato*, for example, one officer declares, on the eve of the battleship's final sortie, "Defeat brings understanding. That's the only way Japan can be helped. Achieve understanding today and Japan will be saved. We are pioneers in the rebirth of our nation. Isn't that all our hearts' desire?" Other works similarly celebrated annihilation as a valuable reset for society, implicitly (and sometimes explicitly) espousing disaster as a means of forging consensus, bringing out the best in the Japanese people, and imagining a new beginning. In Kon Satoshi's anime series *Paranoia Agent* (*Mōsō dairinin* [2004]), for instance, Tokyo is consumed by a giant dark blob, the manifestation of mass hysteria and personal anxieties. "This is just like right after the war," one older character remarks after the blob withdraws, leaving the city in shambles. Yet apocalypse clears the air, dispelling personal and social demons, it elicits wistful memories of the halcyon days of the 1950s, and, predictably enough, it leads to the rebuilding of Tokyo in a magically quick two years.

Japan's apocalyptic imagination at the millennium has remained insistently optimistic, even more so in some ways than in previous decades, and faith in the establishment, particularly the military and the state, has been usually overt. In the 2006 remake of *Japan Sinks*, repackaged as a sleek action/adventure picture with glossy special effects and little of the elegiac air of the first film or the original novel, Japan is miraculously rescued from submersion at the eleventh hour by some credulity-defying science and the extraordinarily brave, dedicated, and selfless service of Japanese civil servants. We are left at fade-out with the archipelago a little soggier but the state revealed as eminently trustworthy and firm, the Japanese family resolute in a time of uncertainty, and the Japanese spirit indomitable. The Godzilla films of the early twenty-first century send a similar message: though Tokyo never escapes ruin, the end of the world always seems to be averted, at least in large part, thanks to the professionalism, resolve, and effectiveness of the Japanese Self-Defense Forces. Thus, even in the wake of Aum's terrorism and the Kobe earthquake, "secure horror" remained the norm in depictions of disaster in Japanese popular culture and, remarkably enough, a certain playfulness continued to sneak into cinematic visions of the apocalypse. In the satiric *The World Sinks, Except Japan* (*Nihon igai zenbu chinbotsu* [2007]), a delightfully cheesy comedy that pokes fun at Japan's global aspirations, debates over immigration policy, and the disaster movie genre, the story breezily ends with Japan, riven by ethnic tensions and economic ills, joining the rest of the world under the waves. Trauma and the lingering shadows of Hiroshima and Nagasaki are nowhere to be seen at the end of *The World Sinks, Except Japan*; Armageddon is just good for one final laugh before the credits roll.

Tatsumi Takayuki has observed that "While nuclear disaster began as an essential tragedy in the mid twentieth century, it has gradually transformed itself into a kind of literary motivation for black comedy."[60] One might well conclude that even in Japan with its unique history of nuclear trauma, cinematic and animated apocalypse has become a gimmick, an expedient plot device, or a kind of visual spectacle that neither the creators of popular culture nor its consumers have yet to tire of thoroughly. Armageddon—particularly the destruction of Tokyo, always convenient as a stand-in for Japan as a whole or as a symbol of state authority and all the urban excesses an audience might imagine—has thus been a constant in the postwar Japanese imagination, an image as common as heart-pounding car chases in action films or dreamy sunsets in romances. But if catastrophe was always close at hand in the creations of Japanese pop culture, its meanings were far from monolithic, changing over time to reflect the Zeitgeist, artistic trends, market demands, and audience expectations. To read Japan's "doom-laden dreams" as pervasively freighted with darkness and trauma is to overestimate the psychic legacies of Hiroshima and Nagasaki and to minimize the recreational quality of the "aesthetics of destruction." It is also to misunderstand the postwar apocalyptic imagination as, above all, a commemoration of loss and a kind of therapeutic arena for addressing unresolved tensions. Those fictional mushroom clouds and firestorms that have engulfed Tokyo for the past sixty years have, more often than not, affirmed progress, science, and the status quo and, at times, have even expressed nostalgic, reactionary yearnings for the return to an elusive (and illusive) past of collective unity and common purpose.

In the realms of Japanese popular culture, the city was not a dystopian space, nor was it by any means a thoroughly utopian one; instead it functioned as a plastic imagined landscape upon which to act out fantasies of graphically exhilarating annihilation and make manifest a thoroughly mainstream faith in the modern and the enduring presence of the nation. At least in the apocalyptic pop of monster movies, disaster films, and end-of-the-world anime, the city was not perceived as a place of lived experience, though the cityscapes and skylines of animated and celluloid Tokyo mirrored the quotidian reality of everyday life, but the urban became a kind of visual and ideological shorthand for the historical fragility of the Japanese city and the postwar inevitability of growth and change, what Stephen Barber has aptly called the "contradictory charge of desolation and elation."[61] Oh no, there goes Tokyo . . . but it will be back, and it may be even better than before.

Notes

1 Mike Davis, *Ecology of Fear: Los Angeles and the Imagination of Disaster* (New York: Vintage Books, 1998), 7, 276, 278, 281. On visions of the destruction of New York City, see Max Page, *The City's End: Two Centuries of Fantasies, Fears, and Premonitions of New York's Destruction* (New Haven: Yale University Press, 2008). Page asserts that "No city has been more often destroyed on paper, film, or canvas, and no city's destruction has been more often watched and read about than New York's" (14).

2 Patrick Macias, *TokyoScope* (San Francisco: Cadence Books, 2001), 198.

3 James Orr, *The Victim as Hero: Ideologies of Peace and National Identity in Postwar Japan* (Honolulu: University of Hawaii Press, 2001), 63. See also Ken Hollings, "Tokyo Must Be Destroyed: Dreams of Tall Buildings and Monsters, Images of Cities and Monuments," *CTheory* (1995), http://www.ctheory.net/articles .aspx?id=69 (accessed December 20, 2008). The imaginary obliteration of Tokyo was, as Max Page has described the vision of New York's destruction, "a common narrative, inscribed in all popular forms of communication and culture," and not the province of either elite art forms or mass entertainment alone. Page, *The City's End*, 4.

4 Donald Richie, "'Mono no Aware': Hiroshima in Film," in *Film: Book 2, Films of War and Peace*, ed. Robert Hughes (New York: Grove Press, 1962), 68.

5 William Kelly, "Incendiary Actions: Fires and Firefighting in the Shogun's Capital and the People's City," in *Edo and Paris: Urban Life and the State in the Early Modern Era*, ed. James McClain, John Merriman, and Ugawa Kaoru (Ithaca: Cornell University Press, 1994), 310–13.

6 Susan Napier, *Anime: From* Akira *to* Princess Mononoke (New York: Palgrave, 2000), 197; see also Susan Sontag, "The Imagination of Disaster," in *Against Interpretation and Other Essays* (New York: Farrar, Straus & Giroux, 1966), 218.

7 Akira Mizuta Lippit, *Atomic Light (Shadow Optics)* (Minneapolis: University of Minnesota Press, 2005), 4, 120.

8 Murakami Takashi, *Little Boy: The Arts of Japan's Exploding Subculture* (New York: Japan Society, 2005), 205. Murakami has been memorably described by journalist Ian Buruma as "a painter of cartoon images, both childlike and sinister, a highly successful designer (of Louis Vuitton bags, among other things), a maker of mildly pornographic dolls, an artistic entrepreneur, a theorist, and a guru, with a studio of protégés that is a cross between a traditional Japanese workshop and Andy Warhol's Factory." Ian Buruma, "Virtual Violence," *New York Review of Books* 52.22 (June 23, 2005), http://www.nybooks.com/articles/18072 (accessed December 20, 2008).

9 Murakami, *Little Boy*, 204–5.

10 Joyce A. Evans, *Celluloid Mushroom Clouds: Hollywood and the Atomic Bomb* (Boulder, CO: Westview Press, 1998), 77.

11 Quoted in Vivian Sobchack, *Screening Space: The American Science Fiction Film*, 2nd ed. (New York: Ungar, 1987), 49.

12 Jonathan Lake Crane, *Terror and Everyday Life* (Thousand Oaks, CA: Sage, 1994), 102.

13 Bill Warren, *Keep Watching the Skies! American Science Fiction Movies of the Fifties*, vol. 1, *1950–1957* (Jefferson, NC: McFarland, 1982), xiii.

14 David J. Schow, foreword to Kim Newman, *Apocalypse Movies: End of the World Cinema* (New York: St Martin's Griffin, 2000), 10.

15 Sontag, "Imagination," 224.

16 Ibid., 218, 213.

17 Ibid., 224–25.

18 Mick Broderick, *Nuclear Movies* (Jefferson, NC: McFarland, 1991), 19.

19 Susan Napier, *The Fantastic in Modern Japanese Literature* (London: Routledge, 1996), 184; Susan Napier, "Panic Sites: The Japanese Imagination of Disaster from *Godzilla* to *Akira*," *Journal of Japanese Studies* 19.2 (Summer 1993): 330.

20 See Napier, "Panic Sites," esp. p. 350.

21 Stuart Galbraith IV, *Monsters Are Attacking Tokyo!* (Venice, CA: Feral House, 1998), 11.

22 Fredric Jameson, *Postmodernism, or, The Cultural Logic of Late Capitalism* (Durham: Duke University Press, 1991), 279.

23 Napier, *Anime*, 199; Stephen Keane, *Disaster Movies: The Cinema of Catastrophe* (London: Wallflower, 2001), 6.

24 See Richie, " 'Mono no Aware.' "

25 For an overview of *Gojira* and an elaboration of some of the points raised here, see William M. Tsutsui, *Godzilla on My Mind: Fifty Years of the King of Monsters* (New York: Palgrave Macmillan, 2004), esp. chapter 1.

26 Quoted in Galbraith, *Monsters*, 49.

27 Yoshikuni Igarashi, *Bodies of Memory: Narratives of War in Postwar Japanese Culture, 1945–1970* (Princeton: Princeton University Press, 2000), 121.

28 Tatsumi Takayuki, *Full Metal Apache: Transactions between Cyberpunk Japan and Avant-Pop America* (Durham: Duke University Press, 2006), 13. In these obser-

vations, Tatsumi draws on (but does not cite) the influential arguments of No-
bel laureate Ōe Kenzaburō in a 1973 essay decrying the effects of *kaijū eiga* on
Japanese children. Notably, Ōe muses on the effect the constant cycles of urban
destruction and regeneration in *Ultraman* and similar series may have on the
ability of Japanese youth to apprehend the reality of devastation and rebuilding.
Ōe Kenzaburō, "Hakaisha Urutoraman," *Sekai* (May 1973): 154–62.

29 Murakami, *Little Boy*, 12.

30 Newman, *Apocalypse Movies*, 18.

31 Keane, *Disaster Movies*, 12.

32 The apparently endless remaking of Tokyo after World War II, both in bricks-
and-mortar reality and in imaginary works of apocalyptic entertainment, might
also be seen as reflecting the "creative destruction" Joseph Schumpeter described
as "the essential fact about capitalism." That pop culture visions of urban devastation and regeneration should reflect a widespread faith in capitalism—as in progress, modernity, the strength of the nation, and the ultimate promise of science
and technology—should not be surprising in the context of "miracle economy"
Japan. Schumpeter, *Capitalism, Socialism, and Democracy* (New York: Harper
and Row, 1942), 82–83. See also Page, *The City's End*, 15, 27–28.

33 Napier, *Fantastic*, 227.

34 Ibid., 3, 184.

35 Murakami, *Little Boy*, 10.

36 Ibid.

37 Napier, "Panic Sites," 336.

38 Ibid., 347; Freda Freiberg, "*Akira* and the Postnuclear Sublime," in *Hibakusha
Cinema*, ed. Mick Broderick (London: Kegan Paul, 1996).

39 Napier, *Fantastic*, 217.

40 Macias, *TokyoScope*, 200.

41 Napier, "Panic Sites," 335.

42 Macias, *TokyoScope*, 199.

43 Komatsu Sakyō, *Japan Sinks*, trans. Michael Gallagher (Tokyo: Kodansha, 1995),
184, 209–10.

44 Tatsumi, *Full Metal Apache*, 166.

45 Komatsu, *Japan Sinks*, 231.

46 Tsutsui, *Godzilla*, 72–73.

47 Tomiko Yoda, "A Roadmap to Millennial Japan," in *Japan after Japan: Social and
Cultural Life from the Recessionary 1990s to the Present*, ed. Tomiko Yoda and
Harry Harootunian (Durham: Duke University Press, 2006), 49.

48 Harry Harootunian, "Japan's Long Postwar: The Trick of Memory and the Ruse
of History," in *Japan after Japan*, ed. Yoda and Harootunian, 99.

49 Robert Jay Lifton, *Destroying the World to Save It: Aum Shinrikyō, Apocalyptic
Violence, and the New Global Terrorism* (New York: Henry Holt, 1999), 58, 83. On
the heritage of millenarian movements in Japan, see Gregory Smits, "Shaking Up
Japan: Edo Society and the 1855 Catfish Picture Prints," *Journal of Social History*
39.4 (Summer 2006): 1045–77. Smits describes how catastrophe—particularly the
destruction in Edo wrought by the 1855 Ansei Earthquake—stoked millenarian
movements and contributed to a sense of "proto-nationalist" solidarity among
Japanese commoners in an era of political and social tension.

50 See, for instance, Lifton, *Destroying*, 197; Napier, *Anime*, 195.

51 See Frederik Schodt, *Dreamland Japan: Writings on Modern Manga* (Berkeley: Stone Bridge Press, 1996), 228ff.; and Daniel Metraux, *Aum Shinrikyō's Impact on Japanese Society* (Lewiston, NY: Edwin Mellen, 2000), 66–68.

52 Lifton, *Destroying*, 258.

53 Lippit, *Atomic Light*, 102.

54 Macias, *TokyoScope*, 202.

55 Quoted in Murakami, *Little Boy*, 166.

56 Murray Sayle, "Nerve Gas and the Four Noble Truths," *New Yorker*, April 1, 1996, p. 68.

57 Suzuki Akira, *Do Android Crows Fly over the Skies of an Electronic Tokyo? The Interactive Urban Landscape of Japan* (London: Architectural Association, 2001), 56–57. Similar sentiments were expressed in Hiroshima in 1945. Immediately following the atomic bombing, the ruins of the city were covered with a verdant green carpet of plant growth that made the devastation look surprisingly vibrant and optimistic to many observers. With the rapid reconstruction of the city, however, the new plant life quickly disappeared, to the regret of some commentators with a similar respect for the "void." See William M. Tsutsui, "Landscapes in the Dark Valley: Toward an Environmental History of Wartime Japan," *Environmental History* 8.3 (April 2003): 294–311.

58 Michael Barkun, *Disaster and the Millennium* (New Haven: Yale University Press, 1974), 7–8. See also Rebecca Solnit, *A Paradise Built in Hell: The Extraordinary Communities That Arise in Disaster* (New York: Viking, 2009).

59 Murakami, *Little Boy*, 176.

60 Tatsumi, *Full Metal Apache*, 178.

61 Stephen Barber, *Projected Cities: Cinema and Urban Space* (London: Reaktion Books, 1995), 124.

Chapter 6

■

Postsocialist Urban Dystopia?

LI ZHANG

China's transition to a market economy and its entry into the orbit of global capitalism have been elements in a highly uneven and disorienting process. By retaining a remarkable economic growth, the Chinese state is a successful example of how socialism can transform itself to adapt to the globalizing world through reforms (rather than revolution). But such fast capital accumulation and large-scale privatization have intensified social inequality and dislocation in recent years. This troubling trend is reflected in the rising popular discontent, resistance, and civic unrest that have spread from the city to the countryside (see Lee 2007; O'Brien and Li 2006; Zhang 2004). There has emerged a sense of profound confusion, anxiety, and spiritual emptiness among some social groups as they have faced the challenges brought by this transformation. As socialist ethics, morality, and values are fading away, market forces and mass consumerism are taking a tight grip on everyday life in Chinese society.

The city is at the heart of these breathless changes and ruptures. Cityscape has become the very subject of transformation, a key site of social struggle, and a source of popular imaginary regarding the trajectory of a society in the remaking. Yet, not all Chinese cities have the same fate and opportunity in this process. While some are becoming wealthier and gaining prominence on the national and global stages, others are declining, marginalized, and even forgotten. In the meta-narrative of development and growth, large metropolises (such as Beijing, Shanghai, Guangzhou, Shenzhen) have come to stand for prosperity, progress, glory, and hope, thus receiving most of the public and global attention. They are regarded as the concrete realization of the New China dream, a negation of the Maoist utopia and a triumph of consumer paradise. But this sanguine, one-dimensional view tends to mask other shades of the city and troubled urban experiences that are painful and disorienting.

This essay addresses the following questions: How have the images of dark urbanism surfaced in contemporary Chinese popular culture and popular social imaginary? What are the social conditions that have generated such representations? What are the distinct characteristics of these images and how are they different from the Euro-American form? What is the critical potential of urban dystopia in the specific Chinese historical and cultural context? My essay consists of two parts: First, I will investigate the Other Chinese city that has become relatively invisible and silent in the tale of China's miracle economic success by reading two recent Chinese films that were produced outside the mainstream system.[1] Both provide a powerful social commentary on the society in transition, yet the images they invoke are distinctly different. I argue that if we can call this form of dark representation "postsocialist urban dystopia," it must be historicized. I will therefore contextualize the textual analysis of films by incorporating my ethnographic research on migration, housing, consumerism, and spatial politics in Chinese cities.[2] As I will show, this form of critique is created at a time when the Maoist utopia has gone wrong and lost attraction, while a new neoliberal fantasy of economic boom in the age of global capital is also losing credibility among certain disfranchised and marginalized social groups.[3] Further, the representation takes a distinct neorealist form that focuses on the present and everyday life rather than technological overkill. Urban dystopia, which grew out of the Euro-American experience, thus should not be simply taken as a universal cultural form.

Second, I will further explore the condition under which the particular form of urban critique, as manifested in the documentary and cinematic forms, is gaining ground in contemporary China. To do so, I will provide a brief history of critical forms by tracing the decline of socialist forms of critique and the rise of several new forms in the milieu of recent neoliberal turns. Finally, I will briefly comment on a strategic move by the current regime to "build a harmonious society" in order to appease rising societal tension, critique, and potential opposition.

Twice Disenchanted

Dystopia, the antithesis of utopia, or utopia that has gone wrong, is a distinct, popular genre of literature and film in modern Western societies. It is often manifested in an imagined or future society completely controlled by an oppressive and corrupt government, or by forces of technologies beyond the original intention of human designers (such as in *Dark City* and *Blade Runner*). Sometimes, it is set in the contemporary world we live in and magnifies the vices of capitalist urbanity in the form of lust, greed, crime, and violence (such as in *LA Confidential*). The city often figures centrally in the literary and cinematic representations of noir, a nightmarish kind of life that constantly haunts people in post-industrial societies.[4] As a form of ideology, the images of urban dystopia are usually deployed as a critique of social conditions produced under different historical and cultural circumstances. In his analysis of *Blade Runner*, Williams argues that "the genre as a whole clearly reflects the exhaustion of contemporary ideologies and their inability to escape, in Henry Hermes's apt phrase, from the 'imagination of disaster' that has dominated so much of our century" (1988: 384).

Such noir depiction was rarely invoked and recognized as a distinct genre of representation in socialist China, partly due to the fact that the mainstream media and cultural production were heavily controlled by the party-state. The Maoist state preferred a brighter portrayal of society by promoting "revolutionary romanticism" and "socialist realism." The post-Mao era witnessed a much more complex cinematic production of multiple styles (Lu and Yeh 2005). Yet, probing the "dark" aspects of social life in media representation is still viewed by authorities as potentially subversive and thus largely filtered out by official censorship.[5] One cannot help but wonder whether the notion of "dystopia" can serve as a meaningful tool in delineating and commenting on the contemporary Chinese social terrains. When I first started to do research for this essay, I was highly skeptical about the relevance of this Euro-American cultural form to contemporary China. After I watched several films of the Sixth-Generation and the "new documentaries," my view began to change. These new filmmakers have certainly drawn inspiration from the style of noir in producing their own versions of dystopic images of Chinese cities, but it is also important to note that their works perform a very different kind of critique and take a distinct form of neorealism.

The Sixth-Generation is also called "the urban generation" because "the setting and tales of urban experience are the signature marks of independent films" (Cui 2005: 99). It began to emerge in the early 1990s and consists of younger, independent filmmakers who engage in "experimental practices outside the official production system and its ideological censorship" (Cui 2005: 96). These new filmmakers are responsible for raising their own capital for production through joint ventures with international investment. Because of their independent status, the Sixth-Generation filmmakers are more daring and edgy in exploring new form and content. The city is undeniably the focal point of this new urban generation. Their films pay closer attention to the life and struggle of "insignificant" people drifting in the shadow of metropolitan high-rises and present a more individualistic, melancholy picture of a disorienting and alienating urban world.

The other trend is the New Documentary Movement, which began in the early 1990s and reached its peak in 2003, made possible by the availability of inexpensive handheld camcorders. "The 'movement' revolved around questions of how to use documentary film to grasp at truths both big and social, small and personal, contradictory and contested" (Chang 2005). A group of young, bold filmmakers set out to reveal the untold story of what Chang calls "the raw and the real" (2005) of human experience and spirit, particularly that of people struggling in the midst of China's economic restructuring and social transformation. Since the products of both the Sixth-Generation and the New Documentary Movement are deemed by authorities as overly critical in exposing social problems, they are largely inaccessible to the audience in mainland China but have found their way through international channels.

The images of urban social landscape provided by these films form a sharp contrast with two prominent visions of utopia: a socialist utopia upheld by the Maoist regime and a late socialist utopia promoted by the reform regime. The former depicts an ideal society of absolute egalitarianism and absence of private property and crime, in which material wealth is abundant and people work for the sake of self-fulfillment rather than necessity. Chinese people were assured by their leaders that this perfect world was not a fantasy but would come true in the near future. However, the road to the Maoist utopia turned out to be disastrous, as evidenced by endless political movements such as the Great Leap Forward and the Cultural Revolution, which brought a great deal of turmoil, human suffering, and death (see Friedman et al. 1991; Potter and Potter 1990). After this utopianism was rejected in the late 1970s, another form of visionary society, crystallized in the new reform leader Deng Xiaoping's notion of *xiaokang shehui* ("modestly comfortable society"), became popular. This new vision was presented as part of the preliminary stage of socialism, one that was sensible and accessible. In such a society, everyone would enjoy a decent standard of living and a measure of comfort. In the early years of the economic reform, this vision was highly appealing to Chinese people who were fatigued by endless revolutionary struggles. It became a powerful source of inspiration for the nation to put its energy into economic development and capital accumulation. While the discourse on *xiaokang shehui* promised that all citizens would eventually arrive at this comfortable and prosperous society, it also avowed that the path to it was not necessarily an even one and that some people could get ahead before others. Slogans such as "to be rich is glorious" (*fuyu guangrong*) encouraged individuals to accumulate private wealth ahead of others. Two decades later, this uneven path has led to soaring socioeconomic disparity, dividing the country into what I would call "Two Chinas." While some Chinese have surpassed the dream of *xiaokang* and become members of the new affluent class, living in their private paradise—newly constructed, gated commodity housing compounds—others have fallen behind. The new, successful China is inhabited by only a relatively small privileged social class. For the ordinary people struggling on the bottom of society (those labeled as *ruoshi qunti* ["the weak and disadvantaged social groups"]), the vision of *xiaokang* remains distant. A sense of betrayal is fermenting as they become increasingly disillusioned by the reform regime's promise of new prosperity. The emergence of the Sixth-Generation films and the New Documentaries is a response to the double disenchantment of Mao's utopia and Deng's reform utopia, and an effort to grapple with the bewildering experiences of new urban life.

The films I focus on here offer two very different visions of urban noir in an emerging postsocialist milieu. Before engaging in a detailed analysis of the films' content, I would like to draw out some distinct, contrasting features of dystopia portrayed by them.

West of the Tracks (*Tie Xi Qu* [2003]), directed by Wang Bing, is a nine-hour epic of the decline and rusting away of an industrial city, Shenyang, in northeastern China, and a commentary on the dismal condition of the blue-collar working class struggling on the brink of dying, state-owned enterprises. This documentary film provides a powerful account of what the dramatic transition to market liberalization brings to Chinese factory workers caught between the old and new systems. Focusing on their everyday life, work, and leisure during the deindustrialization period, the documentary tells a tale of pain, loss, and hopelessness as the workers saw their factories shutting down and their neighborhoods being demolished to give way to new commercial developments. Using the style of naturalism, this documentary offers no plot or narration. It is a straightforward testimony of the social marginalization and dislocation of the working class in what is known as the "rustbelt."

Suzhou River (*Suzhou He* [2000]), directed by Lou Ye, a member of the Sixth-Generation of Chinese filmmakers, is a twisted love story. It is set in the industrial districts of Shanghai along the heavily polluted Suzhou River that runs through the city. Although Shanghai has been hailed as a window into the new China of fantastic growth and an emerging metropolis of global finance, trade, and real estate, there exists another world inside it that is rarely seen by people from the outside. Against the official and mainstream representation of Shanghai as a newfound paradise, what is unfolding in this film is a gloomy, decayed, and lawless society dominated by money, greed, and pleasure-seeking. There is virtually no trace of socialism here; it is a world run by gangsters and driven by consumer desires.

If *Suzhou River* can be read as a commentary on a society afflicted by capitalist vices, the kind of dystopia depicted in *West of the Tracks* is a critique both of socialism frozen in time and of encroaching capitalism that ruthlessly sweeps anything in its way. But the former evokes more imaginative work and drama in the storytelling, while the latter strives to stay close to the raw and the real. Both films, however, shift our gaze from the glamour and visibility of thriving metropolises so frequently covered in the story of China's economic miracle to the invisible world of "insignificant" people and the painful decline and deterioration of once powerful regions.

Living through the Death of Socialism

Even though China has undergone market reforms for more than twenty years, socialist institutions, practices, and ways of life did not vanish at once. The death of socialism has been a long, slow, and sometime agonizing process for those who live in the middle of it. The crisis of state-owned enterprises began to surface in the early 1990s. By the late 1990s, it had reached the point where many enterprises were forced to close down, privatize, or cut back their workforces in order to become competitive. By 2000, millions of state workers were laid off (*xiagang*), struggling to survive on the margins of a highly commercialized society.[6] As Solinger characterizes this unexpected downturn, "those very individuals who were themselves once enshrined in the former regime" found themselves betrayed and discarded "in a most heartless, Darwinian struggle of the fittest" (1999: 2). *West of the Tracks* is an "ordinary epic" (Chang 2005) of how Chinese factory workers and their families in the city of Shenyang lived through this slow death of a socialist economy. Under high socialism industrial workers were the core of a privileged social class— the proletariats whose well-being was the basis of state legitimation (Walder 1984). They enjoyed the urban welfare system that gave them virtually free housing, food, schooling, health care, and so forth (Whyte and Parish 1984). The heavy industry developed in the cities in the northeast had once stood for the might of a rising socialist China. But now the very livelihood of these industrial workers is threatened by massive unemployment; what faces them is a stark reality brought by failing state enterprises in an extremely competitive market economy. In short, the socialist industrial powerhouse has now become the "rustbelt" of economic stagnation.

This three-hundred-minute film is cut from over three hundred hours of footage and consists of three parts: Rust, Remnants, and Rails. It opens with a scene of an endless railway track and lifeless factories covered by snow, shot from the point of view of a slowly moving train. The light is dim, the air is cold, and occasional snowflakes cover the camera lens, making the vision fuzzy. This traveling gaze appears again and again to bear witness to the agonizing demise of an old system. The head engine of the train, which still carries the old trademark, Dong Fang Hong (Red Eastern Horizon), a popular name used in Mao's years, represents the time train of socialism, out of sync with the rapidly changing economy and social world. The entire story is told by workers themselves as they live the routines of work, leisure, and social life. There is no striking protest or extraordinary social movement; instead most of the scenes are made up of silent shots of workers' mundane activities (such as working in the smelting factories and cleaning up after work) or their conversations during break time.

The story of Rust is set in an industrial complex of several smelting factories specializing in copper, zinc, lead, and other sheet metal production. In its heyday in the 1980s, this community had over one million people and enjoyed a high degree of job security and socialist benefits. But the enterprises began to falter in the 1990s and closed down one by one. The story begins on the eve of the final shutdown when the demise of this state industry was clearly felt in the freezing cold air. Many workers (especially women) had already been laid off; the remaining workers were offered only a minimum wage of 200 yuan per month and had not been paid for a year. There is no single protagonist in the story; rather, it unfolds around a group of workers who are watching their factory going down like a sinking ship, helplessly waiting to be submerged in the water. Feeling betrayed by the socialist state's promise of an "iron rice bowl" or "a job for life," these workers are stranded between a dying socialist planned economy and expanding market capitalism.

The break room—dark, dilapidated, lit up by a few bare light bulbs—becomes a center stage where these workers narrate their understandings of fate, political corruption, social tensions, and their struggle to make a living in face of the upcoming factory shutdown. Because of the reduced production, workers are given little work and have ample free time. They spend most of the time chatting and smoking in the break room, unmotivated to compete or improve production efficiency. "Slacking off" becomes the norm and reinforces the stereotype of socialist workers as lazy and unmotivated. Workers become idle bodies, stuck in an old, dying planned economy. Meanwhile, the surrounding world is transforming rapidly into a commodity economy. The break room becomes a metaphor for their social world, one that is out of sync with a society now dominated by market competition. Boredom and anxiety coexist here. The radio they listen to is the only tangible linkage to the outside world. The content of the broadcasting, usually information about the stock market, high-tech development, state policies, consumer advertisements, popular music, and so on, appears irrelevant in the world the factory workers live in. They listen to it only to pass the time. The contrast between the slow, suffocating death of socialist enterprises and the thriving market economy is also presented through the factory loudspeakers. The existence of loudspeakers is a sign of socialist legacies, yet the content of the broadcasting has changed somehow. Against the bleak reality of deserted factories comes the upbeat music and lyrics that celebrate China's new future and prosperity.

Figure 6.1. A bleak scene of lifeless factories covered by snow in *West of the Tracks*.

Figure 6.2. Abandoned factories seen from a slow-moving train in *West of the Tracks*.

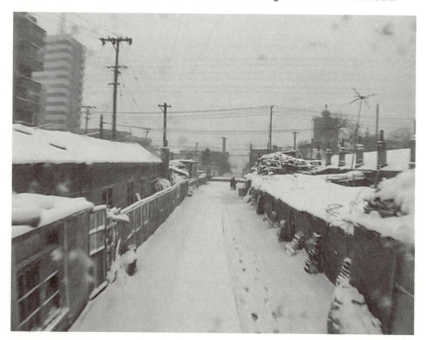

The future is in our hands.
Let us tell a tale of spring,
Reform, opening up, and great prosperity.
Hold the banner high, here begins the future
Onward to a magnificent new epoch.

Anyone who is familiar with the songs of the Maoist era can easily recognize the trace of socialist romanticism. Like many revolutionary songs, the words used here are quite familiar—"future," "spring," "banner," and "epoch"—and intend to portray a bright, overly optimistic picture of the society. But this one signifies a very different kind of utopia, one of wealth and economic success rather than revolution and class struggle. The symbolism of weather is important here and throughout the film. The three northeastern provinces are known for their extremely long, cold winters. But the particular winter portrayed in the film appears eternal, serving as the chilly backdrop against which the tale of the laid-off workers is told. For the workers left on the ruins of failed state factories, this new epoch of prosperity does not belong to them. They are simply discarded as unproductive bodies in an everlasting winter.

Remnants shifts the focus from the factory to the neighborhood. It traces a forced relocation and demolition of a working-class community, known as Rainbow Row, due to a pending commercial project. This is a typical story of "accumulation by dispossession" (Harvey 2003) unfolding in many Chinese cities today. Local governments and developers form alliances to advocate for urban redevelopment as a strategy of fast capital accumulation (see Zhang 2006; Hsing 2006). Although Rainbow Row resembles a slum—poorly constructed housing erratically placed along narrow mud roads, trash piling up on the streets, idle youth roaming around—this is a close-knit community and its residents have lived there for decades. But by 2000, most residents not only had lost jobs but also faced the loss of their community. They were waiting to be relocated to far suburbs. Although state agents are hardly present in this story and government policies are spread mostly via the radio and public announcement posters, the power of the developmental state is palpable. A year later, this community had become a site of ruins.

Forced relocation for urban development is becoming a highly contested issue in China. It often involves violent physical destruction and generates intense social conflicts between developers and residents. Elsewhere, I have given a detailed account of urban relocation–related conflicts in other Chinese cities and analyzed the key forces at work (Zhang 2006). What is depicted in this film echoes the general trend and popular sentiment I have found in my own research. The focal point of such conflict is compensation, but the rhetoric of property rights is often invoked by citizens in their struggle. There are three major players involved: local governments, developers/demolition companies, and homeowners. Most homeowners are not organized in confronting corporate and government power and thus must defend their rights on an individual basis. The families that refuse to leave their homes long after the surrounding houses have been demolished are labeled "nail households." Some even make suicide threats—a "weapon of the weak" (Scott 1985)—to demand better compensation. To maximize their profit margin, developers and demolition companies often arbitrarily reduce or hold back compensation money for displaced families. Sometimes they threaten and physically force reluctant residents out of their homes. A casual conversation between two workers in the film reveals that a man who refused to abandon his home was beaten to death by thugs hired by the developers. Several families featured in the film refuse to leave their home in order to bargain for a better compensation, but eventually they do leave after the water and electricity supplies are cut off and they find it very difficult to survive in the harsh winter.

In 2008 a striking picture of a "nail household" on a vulnerable island of mud in the middle of a huge construction site in the city of Chongqing began to be circulated on the Internet and in international media. The owners who lived and operated a restaurant there had engaged in two years of negotiation with the developer for fair compensation.[7] A week after the report was initially released, partially as a result of intense media pressure, a deal that gave the owners satisfactory compensation was reached and the house was demolished. While this story had a relatively happy ending, the vast majority of ordinary people forced to make way for urban redevelopment face nightmarish experiences.[8] As local government officials form extensive clientelist ties with developers, it is increasingly difficult to disentangle corporate interests from bureaucratic power, leaving individual homeowners little room to seek justice.

The most moving account of the distress of the industrial workers is in Rails, the last segment of this documentary, which focuses on the dire situation of one family living as scavengers. Old Du and his seventeen-year-old son are both unemployed and live in a small shabby hut near the railroad. Due to poor nutrition, his half-starved son is gaunt and frail. They make a living by collecting and reselling coal and metal objects brought by the through trains. Their activities are considered illegitimate but are nonetheless ignored by authorities. One day Old Du is suddenly arrested by railway security and accused of stealing coal. His son, who depends on his father for survival, is completely lost and anxious about his father's fate. As he sits alone in the dark, unheated home looking through old family photos, he begins to weep uncontrollably. Eventually Old Du is released, but their future remains tenuous. What the camera seeks to convey here is more than just sorrow and helplessness; it also reveals the courage and "the resilience of the human spirit as people struggle to triumph over adversity and make places for themselves in a world that dizzies with the speed of its transformation" (Chang 2005).

While capturing the "raw and the real" experiences of workers, *West of the Tracks* offers a subtle yet powerful critique of the postsocialist state and its neoliberal turn. What is so striking in the story told here is the lack of government help and the indifference of society toward workers' dilemmas. The critique is expressed through silent, gloomy images of abandonment. These images speak for themselves and are a form of powerful social commentary on the plight of workers. What is even more striking is to see how a neoliberal way of thinking about the self, responsibility, and success/failure is increasingly penetrating the popular mind-set, including that of the workers. Failure, in the environment of fierce market competition, is largely seen as a merely personal problem—the inability of an individual to manage his/her own life or to turn the self into an enterprising body. As one worker puts it in a conversation with his friends, "We are in this state of being because we are not capable [*mei nengnai*], further we have no money to start any business." In a new emerging economy, it is another kind of self-reliant and self-enterprising individual that is promoted in the official and popular discourses.[9] Blaming the self for one's lack of ability and/or capital becomes a common way of interpreting failure. This way of thinking, I believe, has in part contributed to the absence of large-scale, organized labor protests among China's laid-off workers, a situation that has puzzled many Western observers.

It is important to note that the neoliberal way of thinking has not completely engulfed social critique. For example, the discourse on corruption continues to serve as a popular way of explicating growing income disparity and the fall of state-owned enterprises in China. Workers in some areas have engaged in spontaneous, cellular-like activism to demand basic compensation or livelihood allowances from local officials while calling into question the legitimacy of their local governments (see Lee 2007). In their daily conversations in the break room, smelting workers frequently talk about how the managers and cadres of the factories steal public money to line their own pockets by taking kickbacks at the expense of the enterprise. The management and bosses rarely appear in the film. The longest presence is a banquet gathering at a local restaurant where factory managers and cadres talked about the imminent total privatization. They are well dressed in leather and wool coats with fur collars. They make a few empty promises to provide more work and pay to workers and are not worried about their own livelihoods since they have benefited and continue to gain from the privatization by transferring large amounts of state assets into their hands. The banquet eventually leads to karaoke, a scene in sharp contrast with the dire struggle of workers to make ends meet.

Divulging a Murky World

Suzhou River, a fictional film, tells a very different noir story that takes place in the grimy industrial districts of Shanghai. It unfolds around four characters and is told from the view of an unseen, lonely videographer. He falls in love with a mysterious showgirl, Mei Mei, who performs as a mermaid in a small aquarium at a nightclub. At the same time, he runs into a motorbike courier, Mardar, who tells a heartbreaking story about his lost love. The film flashes back to what has happened. Mardar is a hardworking motorcycle messenger in the city. A well-to-do business man hires him to escort Mudan, his sixteen-year-old daughter, to her aunt's house whenever he has a date with a woman. But a client of Mardar persuades him to participate in a kidnaping plan by using Mudan as a hostage to demand ransom from her father. Over time, he and the innocent girl fall for each other. As they become more deeply involved, Mardar wants to pull out of the kidnaping but is forced to finish the job. He keeps Mudan in a room for several days until the ransom is paid by her father. When the woman who orchestrates the kidnaping embraces her accomplice with cheer and a bag of cash in hand on the riverbank, he stabs her to death and escapes with the money. Meanwhile, Mudan is shattered as she cannot understand how Mardar could have betrayed her. Heartbroken, she jumps into the Suzhou River in front of him as revenge and claims that she will return as a mermaid someday. The police never recover her body from the river, and Mardar believes that Mudan is still alive and is determined to find her after his release from prison some years later. As he meets a beautiful showgirl named Mei Mei (who is played by the same actress as Mudan) who looks strikingly like Mudan, he is convinced that Mei Mei is the changed Mudan. He becomes obsessed with her and begins to visit her daily and tell her his story. Mei Mei is cold in the beginning but gradually grows to be touched by Mardar's love story and his devotion to the (dead) girlfriend. She wants to test the love of her videographer boyfriend, asking him several times: "If I disappear someday, would you look for me like Mardar?" "Yes," answers the unseen man in a monotone. "You are lying!" She responds. Realizing how flimsy this relationship is, Mei Mei vanishes without a trace one day. Are Mei Mei and Mudan one and the same? Viewers can never be sure, and the film keeps the mystery alive until the end.

Unlike mainstream Chinese films, *Suzhou River* uses a set of new techniques to give viewers a simultaneously real and dreamlike feeling. As one reviewer nicely put it, "the movie dances nimbly between two stylistic opposites: neorealism, a quasi-documentary technique that employs straightforward, unembellished stories and nonprofessional actors; and poetic surrealism, in which life is seen as a waking dream" (Howe 2001). What I am particularly interested is how the city and urban life are represented, what kinds of images are made available, and what these images say to us. I start with the physicality of the city space. Rather than portraying Shanghai as a magnificent metropolis of global and national trade and finance, the world that appears in this film is grim and decaying. It is made up of erratically constructed rundown houses and dark alleyways. There are no modern high-rises, shopping plazas, luxury hotels, or freeways. The river that runs through it is full of sewage and industrial waste. This part of the city, chosen as the background for the story, is one often eclipsed by new urban developments and forgotten in the meta-narrative of modernity and progress (see Zhang 2006). But it is precisely this kind of place that the majority of ordinary people inhabit. The lighting used in the film is dim. Bare lightbulbs appear again and again, signifying an impoverished, noir living environment. Director Lou Ye successfully uses images of the murky river water and the torrential rains to create a dampened cosmopolitan atmosphere, the opposite of a bright utopia of sunshine and spring.

Another aspect of this film I want to highlight is a distinct social and cultural milieu that has emerged after socialism. The society represented here is one in which lower-class people struggle to make a living in the service sector and casual jobs. Moneymaking, market exchange, and pleasure-seeking are the dominant forces of everyday life. For example, the power of money erodes Mardar's blossoming love for Mudan and eventually destroys her, the symbol of innocent, unpolluted love. Human greediness corrupts souls and drives violent acts such as kidnaping and murder. The state is barely present in the story; instead the underworld becomes part of everyday life. Gangsters can be easily hired to beat people up; private security guards are mobilized for business and individual protection. The nightclub where Mei Mei works, Happy Tavern, is emblematic of a pleasure-oriented consumer society. Colorful neon lights flash in the night to lure men and women to come and have fun—eating, drinking, singing, and playing. They watch as the exotic mermaid swims in the water tank and once in a while displays a big, sweet smile. But the smile is simply part of the job she has to perform every day for her customers. Back in the makeup room, we see a cold and sad face without expression.

Even though we should not take Lou Ye's filmic representation of ordinary city life as a straightforward documentation of reality, the film speaks to a number of important changes in many postsocialist Chinese cities. During market liberalization, Chinese society has irrevocably changed into a mass consumer society in which money increasingly controls people's lives and determines their lifestyles. Sociologist Deborah Davis has termed this profound shift to domestic consumption and the valorization of a consumer ideology "the consumer revolution" in China (Davis 2000). While some researchers have highlighted the positive effects of the rising mass consumption—as a means of creating a new, relatively open space for democratic social interaction and personal freedom outside the direct purview of the state (Davis 2000; Erwin 2000; Yan 2000)—others have pointed out that material consumption is a highly uneven domain and can become oppressive to those in marginal social and economic locations (see Pun 2003). Yet little research has been done on the transformative and disorienting impact of mass consumer culture on the spiritual and moral world.[10] What happens when socialist morality is replaced by a capitalist mentality of profit calculation, money worship, sexual desires, and private pleasure? This sense of confusion and spiritual emptiness is nicely captured by the new independent films. *Suzhou River*, for instance, conveys a sense of profound aimlessness shared by the younger generation Chinese. Mei Mei, Mardar, and the videographer are all ordinary folks drifting in society and making a living by doing casual jobs that lead to no grand destinations. Even though the videographer never physically appears in the film, his voice carries a distinct tone that can be characterized as careless and indifferent. Mardar is cold and lacks purpose in life until he falls in love with Mudan and later becomes obsessed by his mission of redemption through the search for his lost love. The sensualized scene of Mei Mei as the mermaid in the water tank epitomizes an emerging consumer culture that caters to hedonistic desires and commodity worship. Entertainment for pleasure becomes one of the most lucrative industries while industrial production becomes all but invisible.

Finally, violent crimes (such as robbery, kidnaping, murder), which were relatively rare under Mao's regime, are reemerging and have created fear and anxiety among Chinese urbanites.[11] As a result of such heightened fear, private security and new technologies of surveillance are growing rapidly and are assuming the pivotal role of ensuring safety and maintaining order for organizations and gated residential communities. This trend of privatization of power and security, which is widely manifested in other transitional postsocialist societies, is a response to the increased sense of insecurity "when the visible hand of the state is being replaced by the invisible hand of the market," as Verdery suggests (1996: 219). In Eastern Europe and Russia, mafialike entities have emerged, controlling a large portion of the national and local economy and social life. But more important, as Verdery suggests, we need to read the public obsession with the mafia as a symbol that speaks to considerable anxiety about what a market-dominated society might bring. Similarly, the lawless society that accommodates gangsters and illicit activities as portrayed in Lou Ye's film can be read as a projection of the fear about what Chinese society might become when the market takes over.

Shifting Critical Forms

How do we make sense of these documentary and cinematic representations of Chinese cities? What do these images and the forms they deploy tell us about the large transformations within the history of critical forms in China?

To begin, let me clarify that the two forms I have focused on—documentary and cinema—are certainly not the only forms of critique deployed in contemporary China. There are other forms of critical reflection on society, government policies, and everyday life, including most noticeably the New Left intellectual discourses and the fragmented voices of disfranchised farmers, migrant workers, laid-off factory workers, and displaced homeowners. Overall, we can identify a significant shift in both the content and form of social critique from the high socialist period to the recent years of neoliberal restructuring that foregrounds the mass media.

During the first three decades of the socialist rule (1950s–1970s), the Communist party-state maintained tight control over society, especially urban society. Its power penetrated deeply into the social fabric and worked through the heart of society (see Yang 1988). The party-state was able to mobilize the masses to engage in endless state-orchestrated political movements. As Dutton (2005) has convincingly argued, through a vital trope of the friend-enemy divide the Maoist regime was able to engender and harness constant political passion and commitment to ideological struggles, which defined Chinese revolutionary politics. In this era, social and cultural critique was carefully directed and monitored by the state. There was the rise of socialist propaganda that relied on political pamphlets, big-characters posters (*dazibao*), loud-speaker broadcasting in public space, revolutionary films, and party-organized political parades. The media, mainly in the form of radio broadcasting and the press, was brought under tight control by the authorities. Its mission was to serve the state and act as the "tongue" of the party.[12] Propaganda work became the primary channel through which to express the ideas of the party and to highlight the socialist utopia. A special government branch designated to take charge of propaganda work was established from the top ministry level to the grassroots level. The act of "criticism and self-criticism" played a central role in socialist political life, and such criticism had to be directed at the people's enemies as defined by the party at a given time, at wrongdoing by others and self, or at shortcomings in the party's work rather than at the leadership or the party itself. It was dangerous to voice oppositional views that questioned or criticized the party-state's ideological standing and the socialist principles. Intellectuals during this period suffered greatly as they were more likely than others to express critical reflection and dissatisfaction with leftist politics.

The death of Mao and the rise of Deng Xiaoping created a new political climate. During the early 1980s, there was a flood of social critique primarily directed at the Cultural Revolution and the extreme leftist politics that devastated Chinese society. One of the most powerful forms was the "scar literature" (*shanghen wenxue*) that portrayed and critically reflected on the tragic experience of intellectuals and youth during the Cultural Revolution. A large number of novels, poems, and films created in this genre sought to rewrite recent socialist history by exposing social suffering and trauma inflicted by the Gang of Four, which resonated well with the Chinese public in general. Although some of the images produced in these fictions were dark and depressive, they took the form of socialist realism rather than the image of dystopia. Under Deng's new principle of "seeking truth from facts," social science writings also began to appear and the space of critical and independent thinking began to expand. Overall, social and cultural critique during the early years of the reform was largely oriented toward the recent past. There was a great deal of enthusiasm and optimism about the new reform regime and the future.

From the mid- to late 1980s, an enormous tide of cultural discussion known as the Cultural Fever engulfed Chinese cities. Although this movement was led primarily by intellectuals, its scope went far beyond cultural issues. It involved critical debates on several important issues concerning social and political changes facing Chinese society and was appealed to a large, enthusiastic public audience. Driven by the larger historical transformation of the reform, this movement offered critical reflections on how to best grapple with the complex relationship between tradition and modernity, science and future, China and the West, social transformation and new subjectivities.[13]

The 1989 student movement and the subsequent crackdown in Tiananmen Square marked a turning point in Chinese politics and the possibility of social critique. When students took the issues of anti-corruption and freedom of speech to the street, their collective action eventually invoked a strong, conservative response from the government. As political space was shrinking, cultural climate became chilly during the two to three years following the tragic event. But from the mid-1990s onward, the new Jiang Zemin leadership (1989–2002) embarked on a journey to deepen its market reform through a number of neoliberal-influenced moves—privatizing state-owned enterprises, allowing market forces to take over many state responsibilities of social welfare, privatizing public housing, enshrining private property ownership, and so on. The public's desire for political debates and action was dwindling or directed to a fervent mass consumer culture, especially among the younger generation. China seemed to be determined to embrace a liberal market and adopt neoliberal economic policies but at the same time seemed to have no intention of altering the authoritarian political rule.

During this period, the most influential social critique came from the "Chinese New Left" intellectuals. Led by its foremost thinker, Wang Hui, New Leftism is a critical response to a host of problems brought by encroaching capitalism and the neoliberal tendency in China today. New Left intellectuals claim that they are not against reforms but want to call for a social alternative to the neoliberal market economy to curtail market excesses, reduce the gap between the rich and the poor, and protect workers' rights and the environment. In an interview with Global Viewpoint in 2005, Wang Hui explained his position as such: "Today China is caught between the two extremes of misguided socialism and crony capitalism, and suffering from the worst of both systems. We have to find an alternative way. This is the great mission of our generation. I am generally in favor of orienting the country toward market reforms, but China's development must be more equal, more balanced. We must not give total priority to GDP growth to the exclusion of worker's rights and the environment."[14] Although highly critical about emerging social problems, New Left members (who prefer to call themselves "critical intellectuals") do not position themselves as dissidents against the regime; instead they see the current Hu Jingtao leadership as a likely force of change. They praise the new leadership for taking equality, corruption, and the welfare of the working class more seriously than have previous leaders. Thus, the New Left critique is primarily directed at liberal intellectuals (mostly economists) and the like who want more market and see the existing problems as a necessary stage of development. The New Left hopes to maintain a critical yet compromised position vis-à-vis the state and the market—that is, to accommodate marketization while correcting the social problems it entails through the intervention of government policies.

The rise of the Sixth-Generation films and, more broadly speaking, what Zhang (1997) calls the "New Entertainment" films speaks to the post-Tiananmen social condition. It is part of the larger tendency of Chinese society to retreat from direct ideological debates and political concerns and turn to a more attentive entertainment of the mass audience. What they confront is a new neoliberal milieu in which entertainment has become the focal point of the popular cultural industry and the ability to entertain has become the ultimate source of profits. In this context, experimental films like *Suzhou River* seem to face a dilemma as they strive toward two incompatible goals: to entertain a mass audience and to make a social critique. They do so by turning their attention to everyday urban experiences shaped by an intensified consumer market, but this effort in my view is not so successful. By contrast, the New Documentaries are more courageous in that they simply subdue the temptation to entertain and focus on the mission of social critique through a naturalist form of documentation. But for the same reason, they have lost market potential for mass consumption within China.

The Harmony Talk

While social critique from the media-centered popular culture remains weak, other forms of critical action (such as staged protests, appeals, and legal action) are gaining momentum. The stunning speed of capital accumulation is a double-edged sword in postsocialist China. Although the party-state has gained political capital and credibility from the fantastic GDP rates, escalating social disparity and the ruthless dispossession of certain social groups have led to new waves of labor unrest, farmers' protests, and middle-class activism. It is at this pivotal moment of heightened instability and insecurity generated by the neoliberal restructuring that the party-state turns to a new vision of society in the idiom of socialist harmony.[15]

In October 2006, the government formally announced its objective "to build a socialist harmonious society" (rather than just promoting economy growth) over the next ten years. President Hu Jingtao described several basic features of socialist harmony: democracy and the rule of law, equality and justice, trust and love, a society that is vibrant yet stable and orderly, and harmonious coexistence with nature. He further explained that a harmonious society (*hexie shehui*) should be able to allow the existence of socioeconomic difference, yet the difference must be kept at a tolerable level. More important, it is a society that accommodates social discord but seeks solutions in a peaceful, lawful manner. "Harmony" has become a ubiquitous catchword in the official media and local politics. In a sense, the fixation on creating a harmonious society is an expression of a new utopian world envisioned by the current reform regime against the possibility of a postsocialist dystopic order that has surfaced in some other regions. Yet, the party knows well that the key to maintaining harmony and stability is to grapple with the soaring inequality and unjust distribution of wealth. Premier Wen and President Hu repeatedly assured the public of their commitment to improve welfare and the livelihood of the poor and ordinary people, as well as curbing income polarization. But there is a great deal of resistance from local government officials and powerful business groups in the effort to shift resources and protect the rights of ordinary citizens. The rhetoric of harmony is conveniently deployed by authorities to deflect societal tensions and stifle serious social critique. In this context, any creative works that accentuate the dark aspects of social life or even allude to the idea of dystopia become especially discordant.

Beyond Mass Entertainment

The kind of dark images produced by contemporary Chinese independent films are quite different from what Western science fiction films offer. The depiction of an imagined, futuristic society or a technological nightmare has little purchase in China; instead the Chinese representations largely stay within the realm of realism or neorealism by focusing on the dismal elements of everyday life produced by a market-driven society that appears ruthless and disorienting. They rely on a mode of cinematic representation that reclaims the real and the raw while accentuating the bleak, disheartening, and unpleasant grains of postsocialist urban space and life, which mainstream filmmakers tend to shy away from. The two films I have examined, however, do not employ the same technique of representation and social critique. *West of the Tracks* explicitly relies on a "naturalistic" depiction to create an epic-like social document so as to excavate the quandary of Chinese industrial workers caught in the transition from a socialist planned economy to marketization. The images provided by this film are dark yet unmistakably Chinese. The city that appears in it is a site of the slow, painful death of socialism and a zone of social abandonment in a heartless atmosphere of market competition. By contrast, *Suzhou River* deploys more imaginative elements in its representation of a troubled cosmopolitan life that cannot be easily fixed in time and space. It is a relatively conscious exercise of certain noir techniques that invoke such themes as violence, crime, moral decay, betrayal, and tragic death. It conveys a strong sense of disillusionment with what a free market and mass consumerism bestow on Chinese society.

The kind of urban representation I have analyzed here can be seen as a form of what I call "post-ideological works," by which I do not mean to suggest that they are independent of ideology or exist completely outside the ideological realm. Rather, I mean that they do not advocate for either socialism or capitalism, the two competing tropes in recent Chinese history; instead they bring to light the deep predicament of a postsocialist world brought about by the exhaustion of the prevailing ideologies familiar to Chinese viewers. If fraught socialist institutions are bound to die, what capitalism brings to China is also troubling in a different way. This predicament has given rise to a deep sense of loss, disorientation, and highly fragmented urban experiences by ordinary city dwellers and migrants. Other Sixth-Generation films, such as Jia Zhangke's *Unknown Pleasure* (2002), *Xiao Wu* (1997), *The World* (2004), and Wang Xiaoshuai's *Beijing Bicycle* (2001), also encapsulate such feelings and experiences in cinematic form. With the intensification of social polarization, the newly rich and the marginalized underclass, paradise and hell, and pleasure and suffering will coexist in the same urban space. "Every city, like every person, wears different masks. Who is to say which one is the real one?"[16] Which urban experience is more real and representative, of course, depends on one's socioeconomic position within the city.

Why has the classic dystopic form not emerged as a prominent mode of cinematic representation in contemporary China? Two factors are pertinent here. First, there is still strong state censorship of media and the cultural industry. Overtly dystopian works run the risk of being simply suppressed or marginalized in the distribution process because they are not in line with the image of a glorious and harmonious society the party intends to cast. The films I have discussed are considered "experimental" in that they attempt to engage the Chinese audience in a new critical way, and they are not intentionally made for foreign audiences only. However, because of the "dark" representation of contemporary Chinese city life, most of the Sixth-Generation films and the New Documentaries have not been allowed to be screened publicly in mainland Chinese cinemas. They are able to find their way through various international venues and have thus gained reputations outside the mainland. However, pirated DVDs are also available on the Chinese market.[17] Ironically, when some of these films capture major awards at international film festivals, the state's news agencies do not hesitate to report such "good" news.[18] The second factor has to do with reception. The majority of Chinese viewers (perhaps with the exception of the younger generation born during the reform years) do not find the cinematic genre based on futuristic and sci-fi images of dystopia appealing, perhaps because of the absence of such a literary tradition. The term "dystopia" has been translated into Chinese as *fan wutuobang* and has a limited circulation, mostly among intellectuals and artists; it has never gained popularity in Chinese cinema, television, or literature.

To what extent can the experimental films impact contemporary Chinese society and urban life? How can the images they produced exercise broader transformative power in Chinese cultural politics? Can the images produced from the margins become an effective form of social critique? My research suggests that the influence of such cinematic representations has so far been limited to certain social and cultural strata (for example, urban intellectuals and cultural elites), yet they signify a promising possibility that the new film industry can engage in critical reflections on the marginalized experiences and the predicament of Chinese society beyond mere entertainment.

Notes

This essay was originally prepared for the conference "Urban Dystopias" held at the Shelby Cullom Davis Center for Historical Studies, Princeton University, May 18–19, 2007. I would like to thank Sara Friedman, Andrew Jones, Sheldon Lu, Leah Wiste, the participants at the conference, and the two anonymous reviewers for their thoughtful comments and critique. I am particularly grateful to Gyan Prakash for his insights and sound suggestions that helped me sharpen and broaden the argument during revision. My thanks also go to Chris Tong and Phyllis Davis, who helped me with the image used here.

   1 I adapt Liztinger's use of "Other Chinas" (2000) to "Other city" here to refer to the aspects of urban life that are marginalized, less glamorous, and thus have

not made headline news. This is not to deny the striking economic progress the country has made so far, nor is it to indulge in the "dark" side of the socialist state in order to entertain a Western audience. Rather, I want to bring out the very different shades of urban experiences and reflect on their large social significance.

2 My research over the past decade is primarily based on Beijing and Kunming and covers migrants' urban experiences, spatial politics, laid-off factory workers, the real estate industry, and middle-class homeowners.

3 See Ong and Zhang (2008) for a more detailed analysis of how we conceptualize postsocialism. Rather than viewing postsocialism in China as the end of socialism altogether, we argue that it is "a re-animation of state socialism realized through a strategy of ruling from afar. Citizens gain more latitude to pursue self-interests that are at the same time variously regulated or controlled by the party-state."

4 See Mike Davis's brilliant analysis of Los Angeles through the lens of noir literature and film (1992).

5 I do not suggest that the Chinese state has not changed or that the practice of censorship has not loosened in the reform years. To be sure, the state has allowed much more space for writers, filmmakers, artists, and social scientists to explore various aspects of society and social problems. Yet, such expressions are always ultimately kept within the range deemed acceptable by the authorities. Anything that is considered too dark or critical can be easily banned.

6 The numbers of laid-off workers vary by source. According to the *People's Daily*, there were about 6.8 million such workers in 2000, but this official number is likely conservative and thus smaller than the actual figure.

7 See "Woman Defies Chinese Developers," BBC News, http://news.bbc.co.uk/2/hi/6483997.stm.

8 The Chinese People's Congress passed a new property law (*wuquan fa*) in 2007 that sanctions and protects private property, but there is still widespread injustice in practice.

9 See Ong and Zhang (2008) for detailed analysis of this new way of neoliberal-influenced thinking in contemporary China.

10 For a few exceptions, see Smyer Yu's work on the growing number of netizens who seek spiritual guidance and comfort from digital Buddhas (2008).

11 The fears about crime are not limited to urban society; they are also a salient issue for rural residents. However, what is so striking in the city is the way such fears are visibly projected onto urban architectural designs (such as the widespread use of walls, gates, and metal bars), new surveillance technologies, and private security forces.

12 See Andrew Nathan's detailed analysis of the rise of propaganda and the role of the media and its relationship with the party-state in socialist China (1985).

13 See Xudong Zhang's in-depth account of the social origins, trends, and motifs of the Cultural Fever (1997).

14 "Global Viewpoint," *New Perspectives Quarterly* 24.3 (March 7, 2005).

15 In a very different cultural context, Nader (1990) argues that the use of harmony is political and harmony ideology can serve as a powerful tool in colonial and religious political orders.

16 This quote is from a review of *Suzhou River* at http://www.filmfestivals.com/paris_oo/film_suzhou.htm.

17 Due to the low cost and the availability of DVD players, more and more urbanites in China today watch films at home rather than going to movie theaters.
18 Special thanks go to Sheldon Lu, an expert on contemporary Chinese films, for
   discussing the Sixth-Generation films with me.

Works Cited

Chang, He. 2005. "The Raw and the Reel." *City Weekend Guide*, August 1.
Cui, Shuqin. 2005. "Working from the Margins: Urban Cinema and Independent
   Directors in Contemporary China." In *Chinese-Language Film: Historiography,
   Poetics, Politics*, ed. Sheldon Lu and Emilie Yueh-Yu Yeh, 96–119. Honolulu: Uni-
   versity of Hawaii Press.
Davis, Deborah. 2000. "Introduction: A Revolution in Consumption." In *The Con-
   sumer Revolution in Urban China*, 1–22. Berkeley: University of California Press.
Davis, Mike. 1992. *City of Quartz: Excavating the Future in Los Angeles*. New York:
   Vintage Books.
Dutton, Michael. 2005. *Policing Chinese Politics: A History*. Durham: Duke University
   Press.
Erwin, Kathleen. 2000. "Heart-to-Heart, Phone-to-Phone: Family Values, Sexuality,
   and the Politics of Shanghai's Advice Hotline." In *The Consumer Revolution in Ur-
   ban China*, ed. Deborah Davis, 145–70. Berkeley: University of California Press.
Friedman, Edward, et al. 1991. *Chinese Village, Socialist State*. New Haven: Yale Uni-
   versity Press.
Harvey, David. 2003. *The New Imperialism*. Oxford: Oxford University Press.
Howe, Desson. 2001. "Take Me to the 'River.'" *Washington Post*, April 6.
Hsing, You Tien. 2006. "Land and Territorial Politics in Urban China." *China Quar-
   terly* 187 (September 2006): 1–18.
Lee, C. K. 2007. *Against the Law: Labor Protests in China's Rustbelt and Sunbelt*. Berke-
   ley: University of California Press.
Litzinger, Ralph A. 2000. *Other Chinas: The Yao and the Politics of National Belonging*.
   Durham: Duke University Press.
Lu, Sheldon, and Emilie Yueh-Yu Yeh. 2005. "Introduction: Mapping the Field of
   Chinese-Language Cinema." In *Chinese-Language Film: Historiography, Poetics,
   Politics*, ed. Sheldon Lu and Emilie Yueh-Yu Yeh, 1–24. Honolulu: University of
   Hawaii Press.
Nader, Laura. 1990. *Harmony Ideology: Justice & Control in a Zapotec Mountain Vil-
   lage*. Stanford: Stanford University Press.
Nathan, Andrew J. 1985. *Chinese Democracy*. Berkeley: University of California
   Press.
O'Brien, Kevin, and Lianjiang Li. 2006. *Rightful Resistance in Rural China*. Cambridge:
   Cambridge University Press.
Ong, Aihwa, and Li Zhang. 2008. "Introduction: Privatizing China: Powers of the Self,
   Socialism from Afar." In *Privatizing China, Socialism from Afar*, ed. Li Zhang and
   Aihwa Ong. Ithaca: Cornell University Press.
Potter, Sulamith Heins, and Jack M. Potter. 1990. *China's Peasants: The Anthropology
   of A Revolution*. Cambridge University Press.

Pun, Ngai. 2003. "Subsumption or Consumption? The Phantom Consumer Revolution in 'Globalizing' China." *Cultural Anthropology* 18.4: 469–92.

Scott, James C. 1985. *Weapons of the Weak: Everyday Forms of Peasant Resistance*. New Haven: Yale University Press.

Smyer Yu, Dan. 2008. "Living Buddhas, Netizens, and the Price of Religious Freedom." In *Privatizing China, Socialism from Afar*, ed. Li Zhang and Aihwa Ong. Ithaca: Cornell University Press.

Solinger, Dorothy. 1999. "Laid-Offs in Limbo: Unemployment, Reemployment, and Survival in Wuhan, Summer 1999." Paper prepared for the conference "Wealth and Labour in China: Cross-Cutting Approaches of Present Developments," Centre d'Etudes et de Recherches Internationales, Paris, December 6–7.

Verdery, Katherine. 1996. *What Was Socialism, and What Comes Next?* Princeton: Princeton University Press.

Walder, Andrew G. 1984. "The Remaking of the Chinese Working Class, 1949–1981." *Modern China* 10.1: 3–48.

Whyte, Martin King, and William L. Parish. 1984. *Urban Life in Contemporary China*. Chicago: University of Chicago Press.

Williams, Douglas E. 1988. "Ideology as Dystopia: An Interpretation of Blade Runner." *International Political Science Review* 9.4: 381–94.

Yan, Yunxiang. 2000. "Of Hamburger and Social Space: Consuming McDonald's in Beijing." In *The Consumer Revolution in Urban China*, ed. Deborah Davis, 201–25. Berkeley: University of California Press.

Yang, Mayfair. 1988. "The Modernity of Power in the Chinese Socialist Order." *Cultural Anthropology* 3.4: 408–27.

Zhang, Li. 2004. "Forced from Home: Property Rights, Civic Activism, and the Politics of Relocation in China." *Urban Anthropology* 33.2–4: 247–81.

———. 2006. "Contesting Spatial Modernity in Late Socialist China" (with commentaries and reply). *Current Anthropology* 47.3: 461–84.

Zhang, Xudong. 1997. *Chinese Modernism in the Era of Reforms*. Durham: Duke University Press.

Chapter 7

■

Friction, Collision, and the Grotesque

The Dystopic Fragments of Bombay Cinema

RANJANI MAZUMDAR

The twentieth-century legacy of wars, conflicts, and accelerating violence has given birth to imagined worlds where ethical imperatives and moral stability appear to have collapsed. Philosophers, writers, and artists have typically addressed this legacy by forging an estrangement with the present, creating an archive of dystopian thought. While the philosophical and literary tradition has proven itself as an important site for dystopian commentary, it is the technological impetus of cinema, television, and photography that has fundamentally expanded and altered the dystopian archive. The genres of science fiction and horror with their mindscapes, images of technological rationalization, violence and the crisis of the soul, are perhaps the most obvious in their articulation of dystopian imagery. The other significant site of the dystopian is found in the world of the city films. The city as a site of darkness was seen in the expressionist films of the Weimar period and in the noir form of postwar Hollywood. In recent years, post-colonial urban crisis combined with contemporary technological modernity has provided significantly new resources for the dystopian in cinema. While contemporary films from Asia and Latin America have drawn on a neo-noir style to depict the city, in India, the topography of urban decay has significantly entered the world of Bombay cinema through a conscious subversion of its popular cinematic form. Existing on the margins of Bombay's mainstream cinema, these films offer inventive journeys into the nature of contemporary urban life, as well as its unpredictable and unstable future.

This essay explores the landscape of dystopia in three films that have self-consciously asserted their distance from the tropes of Bombay's popular melodrama. The films are Nishikant Kamat's *Dombivli Fast* (2005), Homi Adjania's *Being Cyrus* (2006), and Anurag Kashyap's *No Smoking* (2007). At the core of the three films lies India's most well-known multilingual city: Bombay. This is a city of two worlds where the rich and poor live cheek by jowl. The dense crowd and the entry of migrants everyday exert tremendous pressure on a space that is rapidly crumbling from within. Suketu Mehta's book *Maximum City* tries to articulate the experience of Bombay by combining detail with a distinctive stylized sensationalism of urban life. Bombay, in Mehta's description, is imagistic, excessive, adventurous, cruel, and desirable, but with vices that can be overcome redemptively. Bombay is a "real" metropolis whose modernity must be acknowledged in the city's cosmopolitanism and in its ability to house regional differences and economic disparity.[1] Such clichéd narratives of Bombay coexist with other narratives of nostalgic lament for a world that is lost, a city that was once charming but is now spinning out of control.[2] For many residents of the city, the traffic, the commuter train, and the acceleration in construction are part of a daily urban nightmare. Having been through a series of bomb blasts, Bombay lives increasingly with the fear of terrorist attacks, just as it lives with the crisis of water and housing shortages, daily toil, and the explosive heat generated in the city. Despite the overwhelming visual culture and urban transformation identified with globalization, civic crisis, chaos, and urban decay are expressed overwhelmingly as the dominant perception of the city. India's "maximum city" is imploding like many others in the world, but it is also facing a crisis of representation, particularly in its cinematic form.[3]

For most Western viewers, popular Bombay cinema immediately conjures the melodramatic and the excessive—a riot of color, romance, music, and dance. This has been the overwhelming signature of Indian cinema's place in the world, a perception that circulates widely. In an attempt to capture the uniqueness of Hindi film, the *Encyclopaedia of Hindi Cinema* says the following:

> There is nothing in the world quite like Hindi cinema. It is a unique, inimitable brand of cinema that, at its most typical, is a fictional and seductive universe peopled by handsome and righteous heroes, ethereally pretty and virtuous heroines, and venal and vile villains, besides an elaborate support cast of mother figures, patriarchs, siblings, friends, henchmen, bumbling fools and the like. These characters exist in a never-never land marked by sharp extremes. They break into song, dance, and laughter, just as they easily weep, howl and pour their hearts out. They express anger and resort to violence no less frequently than they spout gems of moral wisdom and hold forth on the virtues of peace and human solidarity. They are gripped as much by paroxysms of insanity and emotional excess as they are driven by the single minded pursuit of love and passion.[4]

While Hindi cinema has traveled to the Middle East and Africa through out the twentieth century, its expansion and increasing popularity in Europe and

America after globalization, both with the Indian diaspora and others, is more recent. It is the global circulation of Hindi cinema and its survival despite Hollywood's expansion in the world that made people take notice of this cinema's emotional reservoir, its complicated relationship to modernity, its universe of character types, and its utopian urges. Crucial to this engagement was the question of melodrama and how popular cinema developed its unique properties, formal conventions, and philosophical underpinnings in relation to melodrama's powerful twentieth-century cinematic imagination.

Broadly defined, melodrama in the Indian context is a powerful form that draws the social world into the realm of the family to present heart-rending conflicts through extremes of emotion, nightmarish conditions, and tragedy. Placing the individual as a figure in a harsh modern world, melodrama attempts to resolve the injustices of the world by creating oppositions between different sets of moralities and then have these conflicts redeemed through the power of poetic justice. It is a form that expresses the insecurities of modernity and then seeks to resolve the chaos and crisis of the world through some kind of utopian myth. That which is not always possible in real life is played out as an emotionally saturated performance of excess.[5] In Bombay's melodrama, tragedy and loss play a significant role, but the darkness of unbridled primordial energies is usually contained or worked out through ethical conflicts. The overwhelming presence of melodrama constitutes a habitual relationship between the spectator and the popular film narrative. The cinematic apparatus repetitively projects the performative language of acting, song picturization, ethical wordplay (dialogues) and the mise-en-scène associated with melodrama, which over a period of time has generated a catalogue of well-known tropes that the audience is familiar with.[6] There are figures, relationships, and spaces that acquire significance over time. From the point of view of film spectatorship, the accumulation of melodrama's visual codes creates an optical regime that is structured by habit. In this situation how do we look at or engage with cinematic interventions where the codes of melodrama break down? Would such a breakdown create an alternative spectatorial engagement?

Maintaining a distance from melodrama, the films discussed here take the melodramatic form as their referent, only to subvert its established logic. What emerges thus is a new, melancholic, sometimes sinister imagination where the city of Bombay is explored and slowly rendered strange for the spectator. A critic for the *Indian Express*, a major English-language daily, labeled these films "India's off mainstream urban cinema." All the films use the crime narrative to invoke a cynical worldview and an entirely different perceptual entry into the city. We see a complete absence of tradition and a gradual destruction or absence of romance. Urban life is draped in an architectural mise-en-scène that is marked by friction and collision.

Made by filmmakers with a particular sensibility of Bombay, the three films mediate the biographical, the regional, and the psychological. For director Nishikant Kamat, the experience of living in a Marathi-speaking suburb and the hardships of commuting long distances found a voice in his debut film, *Dombivli Fast*, which is also the name of a Bombay suburban train. In *Being Cyrus*, director Homi Adjania foregrounds the world of the Parsee community that he belongs to. Anurag Kashyap's early years of struggle when he first arrived in Bombay made him see the world from a very different perspective. The film industry's inability to experiment with new ideas and his battles with the censor board and the courts over his earlier films (*Paanch* [2003] and *Black Friday* [2004]) shaped the psychological landscape of *No Smoking*. *Dombivli Fast* is a Marathi film, *Being Cyrus* is an English film, and *No Smoking* is a Hindi-language film. The films occupy three different but overlapping linguistic worlds, all of which are present in Bombay. *Dombivli* is seen from the point of view of a middle-class Marathi resident, *Being Cyrus* is Adjania's attempt to show the dysfunctional world of the Parsee community in Bombay, and *No Smoking* is the world seen from the point of view of the outsider to the city.

Globalization and the Urban Fringe

The experience of globalization since the 1990s brought about many shifts in the nature of the relationship between cinema and the urban experience. Globalization grew rapidly, transforming daily life through the circulation of delirious signs of prosperity, lifestyle images, commodities, and new forms of visual culture. Prosperity stories are imaged in shopping cultures, video arcades, cafés, fast food joints, coffee shops, and bookstores. The language of urban renewal, shop signage, branding, and the power of light has created an intoxicating sensorium. A plethora of surfaces in the city are covered with brand advertising and overproduced electrically generated images of film stars and models. The navigation of these spaces generates an optical regime of magic and presence. This new changed landscape also feeds off the powerful presence of "Bollywood mania," now a part of international events, Indian diplomacy, special investment pages of financial papers, theme restaurants, and corporate branding in South Asia and the world.[7] As we will see in the following pages, films like *Dombivli Fast*, *Being Cyrus*, and *No Smoking* introduce formal innovations that actively disturb and haunt globalization's visual culture of brightness to sculpt an alternative language of space that is dark, melancholic, and dystopic. This is a cinema that exists on the periphery of Bombay's cinematic excess where the "blindness" generated by habitual cultures of seeing is rearranged to make the spectator see what has not been seen before. The ordinary and extraordinary worlds of the films forge an aesthetic in sharp contrast to that of melodrama. While there are no ready explanations for how and why these films have appeared on the horizon, a contemporary map of the transformations affecting the circuits of cinema can provide us with some tentative insights.

The first major development is the transformation of the media landscape with the expansion and popularization of television. Until the 1990s television viewers in India had to deal with the programming decisions of the state-run channel (Doordarshan). Most of this was pedagogical and entertainment was never a priority. After the expansion of cable TV, television changed from a two-channel system to one with more than fifty channels by 1996. New programming emerged to cater to this sudden boom.[8] Television became the convergence point for talent from the film industry, advertising, and journalism. Today Indian television is cluttered with soap operas and has become the site for the reinvention of Indian melodrama's fascination for the family.[9] Television shows churned out every night deal with issues of marriage, adultery, betrayal, and religious rituals. In the last fifteen years television has acquired a centrality in the world of entertainment in ways that it did not have earlier. The director Karan Johar admitted that after the release of his last film, *Kabhie Alvida Na Kehena* (2006), the classic family melodrama of Hindi cinema was in some crisis because no one wanted to pay for something they would easily have access to on television.[10]

The second major development has been the rise of multiplexes in the last ten years. India is seeing the accelerated conversion of older, single-screen theaters into multiscreen multiplexes and the construction of new multiplexes linked to retail and mall culture. Single-screen theaters do not seem profitable in the way they did before globalization. The segmentation of the audiences into different spaces within a single complex has triggered an interesting phenomenon where a mix of genres, art cinemas, mainstream fare, Hollywood, and regional cinemas coexist. The Indian multiplex, says Aparna Sharma, "has come to position itself, not so much by identifying with particular kinds of films, as by being a theatre for accessing the 'latest' from a wide spread of cinematic fare—mainstream or fringe—in comfortable, colorful and inviting surroundings."[11] The multiplex phenomenon is negotiated by the film industry in different ways—terms like the multiplex hit, the multiplex film, multiplex audiences, and the multiplex era are now part of daily discourse in the film industry, but there seems to be little consensus on what this actually means. While some see the multiplex audience as an urban elite interested in lifestyle stories, very similar to the demands of the overseas market of the Indian diaspora, others see the multiplex audience as a more refined audience that gives filmmakers a chance to experiment with new ideas.[12]

Still others feel the multiplex allows some of the offbeat experimental films the possibility of a theatrical release.[13] It seems no particular form or style can really dominate the screen time of the multiplexes. This is something that was clear right from the beginning of the multiplex boom in India. The discourse on the multiplex phenomenon cuts across the world of the industry, critics, and audiences today, generating a popular assumption that at the multiplex, the *unusual* is finally possible.

The third area of change can be seen in the widespread circulation of a belief within the film industry that the offbeat new kind of cinema does not experience financial loss. In the speculative boom of the current juncture, there is a perception that films made with small budgets are no longer losing money. With film producers getting a multiplex release and signing television, music, and DVD rights, the production money appears to be recouped. This new network for the circulation of cinema has suddenly changed the economics of production as many smaller-budget films are now being produced on non-mainstream themes. The fiction of "no loss" is part of everyday discourse, creating a space for the entry of a new breed of directors who can deliver a high-production value film within a small budget.

Finally, we need to recognize that since the year 2000 the accelerated circulation of international cinema through DVDs has led to a resurgence of cinephile culture. DVDs are now available through rental networks managed by scores of small DVD shops that have emerged in the neighborhoods of all big cities in India.[14] Added to this is a fairly powerful culture of downloading films, something that has become popular after the entry of high-speed Internet connectivity that provides greater bandwidth to download films. Downloaded films are also circulating within a community of cinephiles. There is also the pirate market where European art cinemas, Hollywood films, and contemporary Asian cinema are all available for sale. Information about these films also circulates informally. The proliferation of DVD culture has led to the resurgence of film clubs, short film appreciation courses, and regular screenings and discussions of films at universities, research institutions and other prominent venues. In cities like Delhi, Calcutta, and Bombay a growing presence of cinephile culture is now quite evident. The decreasing cost of LCDs and DVD players has enabled the creation of film clubs and discussion forums.

These transformations in the circuits of cinema after globalization have led to speculations about a new, imaginary spectator who can handle a different kind of cinema. It is this contemporary context that has given rise to a cinema on the margins of the popular, which we can provisionally call the Fringe. Thus the Urban Fringe emerges from the periphery of the industry, struggling against prevailing forms to create a new cinematic language.

Largely made by young directors, the Fringe has made its entry within a network of information, technological, and financial flows. This is an anti-genealogical, rhizomatic formation that is not easy to categorize but constantly surprises us with innovation and experimentation.[15] For Gilles Deleuze and Félix Guattari, the rhizome constitutes a formation that is diverse, unpredictable, and in constant movement. It is the opposite of the genealogical form of the tree. The rhizome is characterized by heterogeneity; it is a form that has neither a beginning nor an end. It is a countermodel formation with no unity or hierarchy. The rhizome is in a constant state of flux—capitalism's networks of production, distribution, and consumption do not operate like closed circuits but move in unpredictable and multiple pathways. The circuits through which the Urban Fringe travels today has a rhizomatic form where it is hard to privilege any single circuit over the others. Rather, the Fringe formation emerges as an assemblage at the intersection of all the circuits, one that can ceaselessly change and reinvent itself. This is precisely why it is difficult to classify the Fringe as a closed genre; we should see it more like a formation in motion. Some of the international directors whose influences are openly acknowledged by Fringe directors are Martin Scorsese, David Fincher, and David Lynch from the United States, Wong-Karwai from Hong Kong, and Park Chan-Wook from South Korea. The films do not speak the language of counterculture or realism associated at one time with the Indian art cinema movement of the 1970s.[16] Nor do the films adhere to the dark stories crafted in gangster films made in the recent past by such filmmakers as Ramgopal Varma.[17] In the Urban Fringe, the epic scale of melodrama becomes small, the cavities are made starkly visible, friction is overwhelming, and characters no longer need to be redeemed. Like a virus, the Fringe exists alongside the delirium of globalization today, portraying space as bad object. Experimenting with the morphology of vision, the Fringe pushes the possibilities of "seeing" through narrative and spatial journeys that appear unfamiliar in relation to the melodramatic form of popular cinema. In a context where "Bollywood" has emerged as a chapter in Indian diplomacy and advertisement for India's global rise, these films suggest a very different world.

Perception and Vigilante Action in Nishikant Kamat's *Dombivli Fast*

Dombivli Fast narrates the story of Marathi-speaking bank clerk Madhav Apte, who spends hours traveling by train everyday to work. The routinization and repetitiveness of his life is established right at the beginning through a montage that conveys shortage of time. One day things go wrong and the protagonist goes berserk when his inner world snaps and takes over. Inspired by Joel Schumacher's *Falling Down* (1993) and Martin Scorsese's *Taxi Driver* (1976), *Dombivli* presents the protagonist as a vigilante figure who proceeds to fight the corruption in the city by taking the law into his own hands. The vigilante film is an international genre that has had substantial circulation in India, popularized significantly in the 1970s when the angry hero took action against the system that denied him justice. Amitabh Bachchan played the role of the angry man in several films (*Zanjeer* [1973], *Andha Kanoon* [1983]) and was followed by actors playing similar roles in other films (*Ghayal*, 1990).[18] *Dombivli* in a sense works with the idea that the contained vigilante figure of Bombay cinema is unable to respond to the horrifying landscape of the contemporary city. Rewriting the older narrative, Nishikant Kamat pushes the vigilante figure to its limit using the philosophical apparatus of films like *Falling Down* and *Taxi Driver*.[19]

Dombivli Fast's opening train sequence is preceded by scenes of Apte and his family—his wife and two children—at home. The sound of the alarm clock, the pressure cooker, the milk boiling over, cooking, the cramped nature of the apartment, the wife's nagging, and water shortage are all carefully identified in the sequence. Apte travels to the heart of the city everyday for work. On the train he listens to the chatter of the commuters and occasionally reads. He works at a bank, operating a cash-counting machine and a computer, eats his lunch alone, and then walks to Churchgate station to take the train back home. The catalogue of itineraries is mundane. The body is consumed by this suburban pace and rhythm, with absolutely no time for anything else. Nishikant Kamat builds the train sequence cinematically to show Apte's almost mechanical movement shaped by visual impressions of jostling crowds, the blur of the cityscape, and a noisy soundscape of train sound, cash machines, and the din of the city. The obligatory nature of daily travel generates a listless drift; the only change in Apte's facial expression occurs when he sees the yellow signs announcing the departure or arrival of the train. This daily rhythm overwhelms the protagonist and the spectator. Kamat repeats the movement to work and back several times during the opening montage, constantly accelerating the pace of the editing. The montage ends with a blur of snapshots dissolving to the opening title. The train as a central feature of daily experience is established with great force.[20]

People spend several hours traveling by the Bombay suburban train. The increase in the population living far away from central Bombay led to a reevaluation of travel networks to ensure people from a distance could commute to the heart of the city. The expansion of train tracks resulted in an increase in the time of travel, which produced a dehumanized alienation. Commuters soon became conscious of a transport apparatus that eventually trapped everyday life into the space of work, sleep, and the train.[21] Rapid transit and public conveyances brought bodies in close contact. This was the congregation of a crowd in motion whose shared travel time generated sweat, fatigue, nervous eccentricities, and anger. The daily experience of travel instilled an exhaustive rhythm and melancholia. In *Dombivli Fast*, Kamat narrates the breakdown of this daily rhythm when a man in the traveling crowd snaps and revolts against the city.

Madhav Apte does not go back home for three days after he explodes. Armed with a cricket bat, Apte acquires a menacing persona as he moves through a city that is almost fated to collapse because of corruption, inequality, and indifference. In his journey across Bombay's deadly streets, Madhav becomes an active figure whose rage makes him see the city with a heightened perception. This perceptual entry into the city does not generate urban images through modes of distraction (*flanerie*) but through sustained vigilante action.[22] The figure of the vigilante is an imaginative urban figure, whose defiance of the law produces a different order of urban mobility. As against the aimless loitering associated with many urban figures, Madhav Apte's purposeful mobility creates a heightened order of perception. This vigilante vision operates like a counter-flaneur imagination that is not made of surfaces but of dystopic "excavations." Kamat carefully narrates the links between crisis and corruption through urban impressions that make connections between power, the state, and the repercussions in the lives of ordinary people. The mundaneness of everyday life is the subterranean landscape that explodes in the protagonist's mind, leading to vigilante action. In an interview the director said, "I am a Bombay boy and familiar with the problems of the city—water, garbage on the roads, traffic indiscipline like parking in a no-parking zone, corruption and the like. The script grew from these irritations. In the movie, the protagonist also exhibits a lot of angst about the city's problems . . . very basic problems."[23] This autobiographical reference to an experience of the city is evident in *Dombivli*'s Bombay as a space of heightened irritations. Another journalist responded to the film saying, "*Dombivli Fast* is a story of the fateful collision between ideals and reality and how one man tries to resolve this disquieting dissonance." As Madhav Apte snaps, his inability to handle indifference and corruption makes him move purposefully, striking out at everyone in his way. Less violent than *Falling Down*, *Dombivli*'s vigilante action displays a series of urban sites—the police station, the heroin factory, long lines of residents waiting to buy water from a municipal tanker, and the trains themselves. The inability of the legal system to contain the problems of the city leads to Apte's action. Unlike earlier vigilante films, most notably those starring Amitabh Bachchan (*Zanjeer, Aakhri Raasta* [1986], *Andha Kanoon*), *Dombivli* shows how Madhav Apte's actions are directed against the general breakdown of the city and are not a personal vendetta. He views the city as a diseased space articulated quite literally in the last shot of the film when we see insects eating away at a dead animal. Though declared a hero by many in the city, Madhav Apte is killed by a police officer on the Dombivli Fast train, when he is finally returning home to his family.

Dombivli draws the spectator into its landscape of civic crisis, whether at the police station, in the hospital, near a water tank, or at the inauguration of a swimming pool. The experience of disenchantment is amplified by the film's structure, which rapidly moves through spaces of decline. The narrative appears almost like a series of newspaper reports on the city woven together into the journey of a single figure, that of Madhav Apte, who then seeks revenge on the numbing activity of daily news by making the city turn its eyes on him. Apte is a misfit, unable to exist in either familial or public space. As a man of the crowd, he represents the plight of the millions who travel by train everyday. The pressure on the city's fabric combined with corruption fractures Apte's internal existence, leading to an explosive and violent engagement with the city. The resultant perceptual journey violently tears away at the mask of everyday life. The routine and the mundane become the site of uncontrolled rage. Urban rhythm is restructured to produce a counter-flanerie perception that is also counter-travelogue in style.

Figure 7.1. Sequence of stills from Nishikant Kamat's *Dombivli Fast*.

Madhav Apte's vigilante action shocks the urban spectator to see life differently but also turns Apte into a media event. This is vividly presented towards the end of the film when Apte explodes in a hospital where he is made to wait endlessly with a homeless boy who is injured. The callousness of the officials and the endless discussion about the hospital's modern gadgetry anger Apte, who points his gun at a doctor's head to make sure the injured boy is admitted. Following this, Apte becomes news—television cameras swoop down to the hospital, reporting the excitement around the event. This results in a frenzied television loop where a number of people express their opinion through sound bites. Nishikant Kamat mobilizes two strands here—the voice of apathy identified with those who see Apte as a crazy figure, and the voice of wonder and rage of people who admire Apte's action. The consolidation of these voices by the director reveals his desire to enter the crowd's mental landscape through shock treatment and spectatorial adventure.

Bombay in *Dombivli* is not just a backdrop but the heart and subject of the film. Apte's walk is not that of a wandering pedestrian but of a reactive force, unveiling the city through a serious encounter with locations. At one level *Dombivli* can be called a "city exposé" film where the daytime and nocturnal journeys of a man of the crowd introduce a range of perspectives. City

Figure 7.2. Sequence of stills from *Dombivli Fast.*

space is, however, projected as a counter-tourist sign of marginality and alienation that evokes a fundamental sense of loss in the city. The breakdown of interior life and the disheartened relationship to public space leads to a vigilante action narrative where the protagonist's mobility pushes the boundaries and possibilities of perception. The dystopic in *Dombivli* is related to a crisis of perception. The habitual world of seeing is dismantled and recast to generate a concentrated attention on the problems of the city. Thus counter-flaneur in its form, vigilante action is one of the powerful ways in which distraction is transformed into an intensity of perception. The inability to see and the need to see are two sides of the same question that *Dombivli* poses in relation to the cityscape. You see everyday and yet you do not see anything. The perceptual entry into the city is the point of blindness. The full play of the dystopic imagination through a novel perceptual entry is the first step toward seeing. All the narrative strategies deployed in the film address this question of seeing.

Society, says the philosopher Zygmut Bauman, is like a thin film of order that functions like a cover-up operation to deny and suppress the chaos beneath. For Bauman, chaos is a terrifying experience for those gripped by the "routine of the given." Chaos is like a "break in, 'the given', an irruption, a crevice in the otherwise solid rock of normality, a hole in the smoothly flowing routine of being."[24] *Dombivli* generates this clash between perceived states of "normalcy" and chaos, using the point of view of the vigilante figure to unravel the muck of the city. Chaos is the subjective force of the city that takes center stage in *Dombivli* to map both the utopian desire of a man of the crowd and the dystopian present that shapes such a desire.

The Grotesque Imagination in Homi Adjania's *Being Cyrus*

If *Dombivli* rewrites the vigilante story, then *Being Cyrus* grapples with the brother-sister relationship—another major trope of Bombay's popular melodrama. The brother-sister bond was always seen as sacrosanct, with the brother usually emerging as the protector of his sister's honor. The power of this relationship in post-independence cinema seemed to address the persistent memory of rape and abduction that haunted many who had lived through the Partition of India into India and Pakistan.[25] The brother as the protective armor who would fight to save his sister's honor (*izzat*) seemed to stage, in literature and cinema, the trauma of rape during the Partition riots without ever referring to it directly. The recurring play of this sibling bond is twisted in *Being Cyrus* through the imaginative rendering of the Parsee community.[26] If *Dombivli* mediated Bombay through a Maharashtran identity, then *Being Cyrus* relies on the Parsee community's internal, dysfunctional world to enter the city of Bombay. Director Homi Adjania says, "Real life has an underbelly that is stark, humourless and somber. It is sinister and threatening. Often cinema tries to capture it for what it is. It pulls no punches. Ugliness and beauty, darkness and light, morbid and funny are two sides of the same coin. Cinema has the capacity of flipping that coin and making it land on its edge, capturing flashes of both sides as it slowly spins to a stop. We have attempted this approach in the writing of 'Being Cyrus.'"[27] One critic described the film as "a black comedy that takes you through the bizarre experience of life."[28]

As a story, *Being Cyrus* narrates the encounter between Cyrus (Saif Ali Khan), the protagonist, and a dysfunctional Parsee family. Cyrus is introduced as a friendly and helpful character who comes to live with a sculptor, Dinshaw Wacha Sethna (Naseeruddin Shah), and his wife, Katy Sethna (Dimple Kapadia), who live in Panchgani, a resort close to Bombay. Dinshaw and Katy have a strange marriage that moves from bantering to verbal abuse to high degrees of hysteria. The crisis of their relationship is evocatively staged through the mise-en-scène of the interior—a huge rambling house that appears messy and decaying with old Parsee furniture strewn all over. The phone does not work properly, the kitchen is full of unwashed dishes, the walls are decrepit, and time has its own logic. Adjania dissects the Panchgani home with great flourish to showcase the lack of maintenance inside the house. The tranquil atmosphere of Panchgani is certainly not the highlight of Dinshaw and Katy's household. Dinshaw is a man of poetry and philosophy, a dreamer who dopes most of the time, unable to have any connection with everyday life. Katy is younger, voluptuous, and crazy; she flirts with Cyrus and dreams of all the things she could have been. Life for her is stifling. Through Cyrus's first-person narration, the spectator is introduced to the Dinshaw household. The initial introduction to the couple ends with the camera pulling out, highlighting the beauty of the architecture that shapes the driveway of the house. The sunlit, leafy, and tranquil entranceway belies the force of what will unfold from the recesses of the house.

The film proceeds to reveal Cyrus's plan with Katy to kill her elderly father-in-law, Fardounjee Sethna (Honey Chaya), in Bombay. Katy is involved with her brother-in-law Farokh Sethna (Boman Irani), who lives with his wife, Tina Sethna (Simone Singh), and his father, Fardounjee. As a person with a deceptive mask, Cyrus is the quintessential urban stranger with many layers to his personality. While Katy has motive, Cyrus's plan is not clear to the spectator. As the plot unfolds to its climax, we learn that Cyrus is manipulated to kill by his elder sister Tina (Katy and Dinshaw's sister-in-law). The siblings grew up as orphans in different homes, but during the course of the film we are unaware that Tina is actually Cyrus's sister. We learn this only at the end of the film when the twistedness of the relationship is revealed.

Figure 7.3. The dysfunctional marriage of Katy (Dimple Kapadia) and Dinshaw (Naseeruddin Shah) in Homi Adjania's *Being Cyrus*.

Figure 7.4. Katy (Dimple Kapadia) flirting with Cyrus (Saif Ai Khan) in *Being Cyrus*.

As Cyrus kills Fardounjee in cold blood after befriending him, he wipes away all evidence of his being there, leaving fingerprints to implicate Dinshaw and Katy instead. The prehistory to the use of fingerprints is elaborately staged in the film w".en Cyrus is shown working with fingerprints under a microscope in Panchgani. The camera pans over Dinshaw's sculptures placed on two shelves of the room, which appear like masks with features that evoke the non-human. The association of this imagery in the room where Cyrus is planning his actions is the first experience of the uncanny in the narrative. Dark thoughts and dark imagery are played out together, not in an attempt to explain or show causality but to evoke a sense of dread and mystery, all of which spirals into a shocking climax. The film's twistedness is its force as we enter the city of Bombay from Cyrus's point of view. Decaying Parsee buildings and rooms, old furniture, ancient elevators, rotten food, old pictures on the wall, and melancholic music are foregrounded to present a sinister world where the protagonist's actions create a menacing atmosphere. "The incomprehensible has become routine," says Zygmut Bauman.[29]

One striking quality of *Being Cyrus* is its play with interior space. Instead of spending screen time on the public spaces of the city, Adjania constructs Parsee identity through inner landscapes. Public space is depicted only through long shots of Bombay placed intermittently in the narrative. The relationship between the exterior and interior warrants some close attention. In his book *Non-places: Introduction to an Anthropology of Supermodernity*, Marc Auge explores the experiential realm of what he refers to as the "supermodernity" of the contemporary. The "acceleration of history" in this moment leads to an overabundance of events and an abundance of space.[30] Thus we see the explosion of non-places like malls, airports, generic restaurant designs, and hotel architectures as a sign of the contemporary. "If a place can be defined as relational, historical and concerned with identity, then a space which cannot be defined as relational, or historical, or concerned with identity will be a non-place."[31] Therefore non-places have a generic form; they are divorced from local context.

Others have drawn on Auge's argument to suggest that "as non-places multiply, the images of disappearing places must be advertised and semioticized to be perceived at all."[32] Disappearing spaces are contoured in the historical imagination by quotation, making references to signs that are not easily retrievable.[33] Disappearing places are contrasted with non-places, which lack historical specificity. I have argued elsewhere that the family film genre (focusing on family dramas) has responded to the desire for new surfaces through the creation of vast architectural interiors of opulent wealth.[34] Reminiscent of the Hollywood musicals of the 1930s, the panoramic sets of the family films place wealthy families in what can only be described as virtual non-places. Just as the musical shied away from engaging with the signs of America's economic depression in the 1930s, the panoramic interiors of the family films appear as "non-places," expressing an anxiety about Bombay's physical locations (place). If Auge's non-place is the negation of place, then the interior of *Being Cyrus* is a negation of the non-place mise-en-scène of the panoramic interior. The interior of *Being Cyrus* addresses the anxiety around the disappearance of Parsee identity. The interior functions as a cultural landscape that plays with Parsee furniture, eccentric personalities, food, antiques, and photographs. But rather than use the interior to express a nostalgic or utopian desire for retrieval, *Being Cyrus*'s interior emerges as the site of dystopia, negating the principles of design that make up the panoramic "non-places" of so many of Bombay's recent family films. What we see in the film is a crumbling world where, in contrast to the family film's desire for transcendence from the street, the interior becomes ominous and sinister, shadowing the proliferation of non-places with the expressive force of dark space.

The imagination of the interior as cloistered space, undisturbed by the public activity of the street, remains a powerful fantasy that coincides with developments in literature, design forms, and architecture. The interior as a place of privilege, comfort, and protection from the uncertainty of the world outside emerged as an important site for the construction of a modern, individual identity. The interior has had a wide-ranging place, evident in the literary genres that appeared in different parts of the world. It is in this world that the nineteenth-century figure of the detective makes his entry to traverse both interior and exterior space in his search for clues to solve the criminal act of murder. In an insightful essay, Tom Gunning suggests that in detective fiction we see an "optical exchange between interior and exterior."[35] Drawing on Benjamin's dynamic play of the interior and exterior as central to the modern experience, Gunning suggests a conjoining of architectural and optical play that constitutes the detective's mode of investigation. Thus the passageways, the stables, the nooks and crannies, the window, and the footprints moving from room to room, combined with the routines of the household and its relationship to the world outside, come together in detective fiction. The uncanny enters the dialectical play of the optical; the interior becomes unstable as the exterior expresses through the interior.[36] In the landscape of cinema, the detective form takes on a special force as we are made to "see" the scene of crime along with the characters, the world of objects and architecture, all of which is on display. *Being Cyrus* operates largely as a detective film. But what is striking in the film is the way the killer has control over clues, the scene of the crime, and the unraveling of the plan for the spectator. All this is presented through a Parsee world where the interior acquires a special significance in relation to the city of Bombay. The murderer comes from outside and enters a strange world of the interior.

One of the interesting devices deployed in the film is the use of the family photograph as the receptacle of a dark and uncanny story. After the initial introduction, Cyrus uses a wedding photograph to introduce the spectator to Dinshaw Wacha's extended family. The camera first pans across a gray wall with framed black-and-white pictures to finally rest on a typical wedding photograph of the extended family. Cyrus's voice on the soundtrack says, "Leo Tolstoy once said, all happy families resemble one another, each unhappy family is unhappy in its own way. This is about the Sethna family." The camera then dissects the wedding photograph, zooming into close-ups for the audience to understand all the connections Cyrus is making as he says, "This is my side of the story." The photograph is shot like a formal studio portrait of the entire family placed in two rows. Katy, Dinshaw, and Fardounjee are standing in one line with Farokh and Tina, dressed in marriage attire, sitting in front on two chairs. The photograph is used performatively as a trace of a world that needs to be deciphered like a puzzle. "At the end of the twentieth century," says Marianne Hirsch, "the family photograph, widely available as a medium of familial self-presentation in many cultures and subcultures, can reduce the strains of family life by sustaining an imaginary cohesion, even as it exacerbates them by creating images that real families cannot uphold."[37] In *Being Cyrus*, the cohesion of the "happy family" of the photograph is dissected through events that go way back into Cyrus's own family history, revealed only at the end of the film. But this journey is presented in the form of a web-like narrative, not as a simple tale that can explain the present from the standpoint of the past.

Cyrus's first meeting with Fardounjee in Bombay is evocatively introduced, highlighting the peeling walls of the apartment corridor and dim lighting. Adjania's desire to use the classic features of film noir is evident here. Fardounjee has a conversation with Cyrus at the door; he does not allow Cyrus entry into the house the first day, but on the second day Cyrus makes his entry. Fardounjee's helplessness, vulnerability, and ill treatment at the hands of his son makes Cyrus connect with him. At least this is what it appears to be, but *Being Cyrus* is about the deceptive world of appearances.

The back room where Fardounjee is housed is cluttered with old objects, photographs, and a loud television set. In this mise-en-scène of decrepit decay, Fardounjee recounts his daily experience with his son, presented in the film through images of hunger and humiliation unfolding over his voice. The old man is a burden to his son. The dusty, stale appearance of the room, the clutter of objects, and photographs on the wall suggest a familial history that is familiar and yet not easy to decipher. The evocative and stylized use of the photograph as a formal device to enter the peculiar world of the Sethna family creates an interesting narrative enigma.

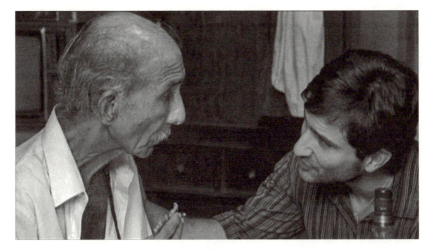

Figure 7.5. Cyrus (Saif Ali Khan) chatting with Fardounjee Sethna (Honey Chaya) in *Being Cyrus*.

The photograph exists as a memory text that triggers Cyrus's engagement with his own past. In her work on the family photograph, Annette Kuhn argues that memory stories are usually haunted by secrets.[38] In *Being Cyrus* the secret points to a sinister world beyond comprehension whose key connection lies in the photograph. The family functions as an "idea," a sign to be unraveled with the engaging work of a voyeuristic eye. But such a journey must also create preparedness for the unexpected, which is a significant quality of *Being Cyrus*, developed through the use of subconscious imagery. The use of nightmare sequences charts a psychic world that appears incomprehensible. This is the nature of memory that makes the past fragile, always in the process of slipping away. All one is left with are traces that do not fall into place. Cyrus's surreal nightmares are intersections of twisted memories and fragmented voices that unfurl to allude to the force of manipulation and catastrophic change. Cyrus's experience of homelessness haunts his psychic world. Interestingly, Cyrus's nightmare is located in an abandoned factory that is stylized to the point where its gestural and spatial world only conjures the unexplainable. A schizophrenic identity is hinted at, but characters flow in and out of this cosmos with no attempt toward explanation or coherence.

The combination of narrative devices, surprises, and performances present the spectator with a strangely unnerving world of the Parsees. When placed with the more prominent melodramatic imagination of Hindi cinema, *Being Cyrus* appears cruel, bizarre, and unpredictable. At one level the film stages a crime narrative with a mysterious twist in the tale. At another level the film plays with traditional expectations only to subvert them. Challenging assumptions and conventional identifications of the popular film narrative, *Being Cyrus* in effect generates an interesting engagement with the possibilities of the grotesque.

The grotesque is generally viewed as an aesthetic category that involves a stylized disruption and distortion of serialized and canonical assumptions. As against the ethical force of melodrama, the grotesque imagination surprises us with its sudden intrusions and projection of situations that are saturated with ominous tension. The bizarre, the unreal, ugliness, and the excessive appear in the realm of the grotesque through strategies where the visual field is reconstituted to disrupt habitual viewing practices. The form of the grotesque generates terror because our lived world seems unreliable, strange, and unstable. This instills a fear of life rather than death where humanity's restless soul finds relief in negation.[39] In *Being Cyrus* Adjania works with this sense of ominous force that exists within our daily life experience. Consciously moving against the codes of melodrama, Adjania casts a grotesque shadow and mood in the film. The film's most horrific moment is the chilling murder of Fardounjee.

Cyrus arrives at the apartment with food and alcohol for Fardounjee. They drink and chat, and Fardounjee enjoys his meal. Cyrus is both irritated by and affectionate with Fardounjee. At some point during the conversation, Cyrus gently places a glinting knife in the middle of the table with all the food. Fardounjee looks worried, but Cyrus reassures him, walks around the room, comes back, and asks for the key to the adjoining door. When Fardounjee does not respond, Cyrus bends down, picks up the knife, and stabs him. This

Figure 7.6. Cyrus stabs Fardounjee in *Being Cyrus*.

Figure 7.7. Cyrus as the quintessential stranger in *Being Cyrus*.

clinically staged murder is followed by Cyrus calmly removing his fingerprints from the room. He calls Katy and has a strangely disgusting conversation with her about the mess in the house with Katy's nervous laughter ringing
in the room. Cyrus's first-person narrative reveals Katy's desire for property,
which caused her to plan the murder. Cyrus refers to Katy as a "lucky bitch."
It is obvious that the next stage of the plan includes the murder of Tina, who
now stands in Katy's way. Katy urges Cyrus to be ready for Tina. Cyrus calmly
relaxes, his feet up on the arms of the chair that holds Fardounjee's murdered
body. Cyrus looks at Fardounjee and starts eating. We wait for Cyrus's next
move, assuming that his target will now be Tina. The spectator is in for a
surprise, however. Cyrus not only kills the son, Farokh Sethna, who arrives
unexpectedly but makes sure that Dinshaw and Katy get implicated in the
murder. At this point in the film neither Katy nor the audience knows that
Tina is Cyrus's sister. The murders of Fardounjee and Farokh are moments
that stage some of the classic motifs of the grotesque imagination.

As a concept the grotesque is usually deployed to articulate or express
psychic currents that exist beneath the surface of life. These currents could be
catalogued as unnamed fears, complexes, nightmares, and anxiety.[40] Excitement, perversion, and the ludicrous coexist in the grotesque imagination.[41]
Thus in *Being Cyrus* Adjania plays with spectatorial anticipation and then

suddenly produces a series of grotesque surprises. After Fardounjee's murder Dinshaw and Katy go to jail and Tina inherits Fardounjee's property. The audience realizes that Tina and Cyrus are siblings and witnesses the former's psychic control over Cyrus. The film ends with Cyrus leaving Tina when he realizes that his sister intends to make a move with another Parsee family. The grotesque raises its head to shock us and dismantle the very ordinary world in which the sacrosanct bond of the brother-sister relationship is usually orchestrated. Murder, decay, and psychic dislocations produce an urban world that is at once familiar and estranged, shocking us out of our habitual relationship to popular images.

The Kafkaesque Imagination of Anurag Kashyap's *No Smoking*

Anurag Kashyap's *No Smoking* is the story of an arrogant upper-class corporate executive who is referred to as K (John Abraham) in the film.[42] In terms of its dialogue with Hindi cinema, *No Smoking* subverts both the romance narrative and the revenge plot commonly associated with popular melodrama. A chain-smoker, K lives with his wife, Anjali (Ayesha Takia), in a modernist penthouse in Bombay. Anjali and K's dysfunctional relationship is particularly affected by K's smoking. An unnamed anxiety envelops K's personality, which often results in nightmarish journeys when he is in his bathtub—a recurring feature in the film. Sick of K's smoking habit, Anjali decides to leave him. This prompts K to take the advice of friends to visit Baba Bengali (Paresh Rawal) and his rehabilitation center, Prayogshala, which is set in a carpet factory in Dharavi (Asia's biggest slum). At the Prayogshala, K is virtually forced to enter into a bizarre contract with Baba Bengali's world of restrictions and rules. If Baba's rehabilitation program instructions are not adhered to then the body of the client suffers in stages. In the first stage hearing is impaired, in the second stage fingers are chopped off, and in the third stage relatives and friends disappear and die. K's arrogance creates in him a great desire to violate the rules of the rehabilitation program, taking him and the spectator through a hallucinatory experience where reality, fantasy, dream, and nightmare overlap in a surreal landscape. The synoptic description of the film provided here is at one level the surface story of *No Smoking*. But the film is only metaphorically using smoking as its stepping-stone to embark on an allegorical journey where a world of strangers, dwarfs, fanatics, minority women, and crazies emerge—a Kafkaesque imagination that draws the spectator into a journey of mental and physical collisions. In this journey, K's ability to collate evidence, little events, and memories gets jumbled up in a nightmarish collapse of identity and vision.

Figure 7.8. K (John Abraham) smoking in his bathroom in Anurag Kashyap's *No Smoking*.

Figure 7.9. Baba Bengali (Paresh Rawal) in his rehabilitation center in *No Smoking*.

The world of *No Smoking* is the world of instrumental reason. Baba Bengali represents the power associated with rule-bound bureaucratic structures. Thus any contract signed with his Prayogshala is binding, placing the client in a vulnerable position. The film playfully depicts the signing of the contract. A larger-than-life, bizarrely giant book of rules is shown to K who says it's too thick for him to read it. At this point Baba Bengali offers him a pocket edition. Then the contract is shown to K—a close-up reveals a legal document that K must sign. When he refuses, he is beaten, coerced, and put into a magic box, finally forced to sign not only the contract but also a blank check made out to Prayogshala. Baba then explains the steps needed to quit smoking. Rewinding and fast-forwarding a videotape recorder, K is shown the horrors that he will experience if he breaks the rules. Vignettes of his friends and their losses are presented in black-and-white television imagery, a technique repeated often in the film. This rule-bound society is shown as fascistic, one person holding all authority and making his own rules. Baba Bengali's persona is structured to make references to a host of powerful figures—Kashyap himself acknowledges that Baba could be the chief minister of Gujarat, Narendra Modi, implicated in the Gujarat riot of 2002, or the health minister, Mr. Ramados, who was responsible for the ban on smoking in film. Baba could be a politician, a powerful film producer, or anyone from the Indian censor board. Clients who come for help are forced to submit to Baba's terrifying demands and then, to save their own skin, must send others into the same world of terror. Only then can they get back what they have lost. In the film there is a special focus on the smoking fingers that are cut off if the rules of the Prayogshala are not followed. But if the victim sends a new client to Baba for rehabilitation after he has lost his fingers, the fingers come back in a little box and can be screwed back on with the help of a ring. Thus instrumental reason as the mode of control is established as a fundamental principle in the film. Kashyap says, "You can only survive if you join the system, not if you desire to be independent of it."[43] What is significant in the film is the way the narrative plays with formal devices to evoke bleakness and complete paralysis.

Anurag Kashyap's personal admiration for Franz Kafka's *The Trial* has been openly acknowledged by the director.[44] The desire to intertextually dialogue with Kafka's world was evident in the use of K as the protagonist's name. Kashyap had two motives in the film: to challenge authority, which he does through the story, and to destabilize the spectator's desire for predictable narratives. But Kashyap wasn't interested in either a logical resolution or any sense of hope. Rather it was his explicit aim to sharply go against the language of coherence and force the film's defeatist imagination to take center stage. Kashyap's critique of authority and film culture was embedded in his form

Figure 7.10. K's first meeting with Baba Bengali in *No Smoking*.

and for this he drew on Kafka's experimental narrative imagination. Kafka's fiction usually contains a simultaneous rendering of realistic and dreamlike situations. The reader experiences uneasiness when two different and irreconcilable interpretations of reality are presented. There is a desire to find clues that will mark unreal events as fictive, but such a dichotomy is never provided in Kafka's fiction. The reader experiences shock when the unreal emerges as a new concept of reality. Through repeated use of objects of familiarity, the different interpretive orders of reality get blurred. The piling up of disturbing details instills greater anxiousness in the reader when there is realization that the unfolding events are not taking place in a dream.[45] It is this desire for a Kafkaesque world that inspired Kashyap to use several interesting narrative devices in the film.

No Smoking opens with a landscape image of the Siberian snowscape, pierced by the sound of the phone. The outdoor image cuts to K drowsily talking on the phone to his wife in a makeshift, shed-like structure. K is in Siberia; Anjali is perched at the window with Bombay's distant streets visible from her high-altitude position. K hears the sound of the military singing a popular Russian song and we see them walking across the snow. K's eyes dart between the TV screen in the room, which shows a bathtub placed in the middle of the snow, and a Russian commentator. Suddenly we see K looking at the snow through a wide glass window. A man with a camera is standing facing the spectator. We then move back to the conversation between K and Anjali and this time K himself is on TV for a flashing moment. Then we are back to the Russian commentator, who says "vodka" as if responding to Anjali's reference to vodka on the phone. K puts his coat on, has no idea where he is, and goes out to ask the guard for a cigarette. Suddenly we hear the sound of a gunshot. K breaks the glass window in the room and runs out into the snow toward a bathtub, which appears again as a black-and-white image on TV. An armed guard runs after K as he lunges for a packet of cigarettes sitting prominently on the snow. He turns around with two cigarettes in his mouth and an impish smile to face the guard. A shot is fired by the guard and the sequence transitions to K in his bathtub at their penthouse home with Anjali knocking on the door. The repeated use of the bathtub accelerates the state of confusion; as a familiar object the bathtub's fluid placement in different orders of reality enhances the protagonist's anxiety in the film.

Both at the level of the image and at the level of the soundtrack, the philosophical approach of the film is inscribed in the opening sequence. Technologies of vision (television), images of terror (Siberia), the desire to smoke, the confusion between dream and reality, the medley of languages, the conflict of spaces, and the desire to break free engage the spectator in a strangely mesmerizing experience. The bathtub plays a significant role in the film since it is the only reference point for the imaginary journeys made by K. The loop between televisual imagery and the real collapses, a technique deployed throughout the film. The events are experienced in a state in which K cannot keep track of what is going on; his own comprehension cannot keep pace with the speed of the unfolding events. A series of discordant images surround him and space becomes both deceptive and suffocating. Though Kashyap uses a ripple effect in several sequences to perhaps suggest an imaginary dream world, the technique only enhances the confusion and plays with the spectator's anticipation.

In a sense, the world of *No Smoking* is a world of absolute entrapment where the filmmaker tries to exceed the limits of social control through K's

Figure 7.11. K in Siberia in *No Smoking.*

Figure 7.12. K with his friend Abbas Tyrewala (Ranbir Shorey) smoking in the bathroom in *No Smoking*.

journey. This approach is structured in the film through a carefully crafted tussle posed between power and desire. Plagued by doubt and uncertainty, the protagonist faces a rigidly circumscribed world where the security of habit (smoking) is being challenged. The tussle unfolds into a paranoid nightmare where the real collapses into a landscape of simulations and media technologies generate tremendous anxiety. Thus the entire narrative is punctuated by television and film images. Baba Bengali himself owns a giant video library that contains information on all his clients. Nostalgia and the past are inscribed in the film through sepia tone cinematic images when K and his friend, Abbas Tyrewala (Ranbir Shorey), reminisce about the time when they were caught smoking in the bathroom. This sequence is played out as a film within a film with canned laughter and the sound of the projector mixed with the dialogue on the soundtrack. The sequence ends with the image playing on TV in a nightclub where K is sitting with Abbas.

Earlier Anjali is shown watching *Schindler's List* on TV. Even the future is depicted by Baba Bengali using television images. Reality in *No Smoking* constantly slips away in a manner akin to Jean Baudrillard's world of the hyperreal where the assumed connection between the real and the imagined, between representation and reality, becomes unstable. What we experience in the hyperreal is the simulacrum that is a copy without an original; it is its own pure simulation.[46] Reality has been replaced by the simulations of the real, and knowledge of material life and spatial boundaries suffer dislocation.

The narrative bleakness of the film is profoundly enhanced through its play with architecture and death. Many theorists have noted the shift from the notion of architecture as solid mass to modern architecture's overwhelming focus on planes and surfaces. This shift generated a different aesthetic imagination where space became a product of planes. Thus says Mark Wigley, "Modern architecture is the new architecture of the surface, the surface liberated from structural mass."[47] This play with surfaces brought architecture into a unique relationship with cinema, most effectively articulated in the field of art direction.[48] The architectural plan for *No Smoking* was a very important concern for Anurag Kashyap right from the inception of the film.[49] Through surrealist sequences combined with a plethora of electronic, glass, and steel surfaces, *No Smoking* foregrounds the two most important spaces of the film. The first is K's penthouse designed to evoke a cold modernist aesthetic. The second is the world of Baba Bengali, a "primitive" world of the underground set in the Dharavi slums of Bombay. Kashyap has often said the film approached Bombay through its surfaces. The narrative needed a language where characterization would be subservient to surface and conflict would result through the collision of surfaces.[50] The film's art director, Wasiq Khan, used his skills to give fruition to Kashyap's imagination.

K's home was a set constructed on the top floor of a high-rise building in Bombay's Worli district. Wasiq Khan used glass, white walls, and a minimalist décor to evoke a sanitized coldness.[51] The house lacked warmth, which in many ways expressed the state of K's marriage and his own personality. K is made to move a lot in the apartment, which allowed the cameraman to visually sculpt and navigate the interiors. The coldness of the white walls is contrasted to Baba Bengali's Prayogshala—where textured walls with figurines are cast in a brownish hue. Characters of various religions, ethnicities, shapes, and sizes occupy this place. The white walls clash with the brown walls, not in the form of a binary opposition between good and evil but to highlight the different psychic regimes of the film. The most striking play with architecture is presented when K first goes to Baba Bengali's Prayogshala. The sequence begins with K talking to Anjali on the phone standing near his apartment window. Bombay appears through the window as a dim background. This privileged high-rise occupancy is then contrasted with a spatial descent—K's travel to Dharavi. A combination of camera angles reveals the vastness of Dharavi and its density. As K walks through the slum to his destination, we encounter faces, people at work, boxes piled up, waste, wire work, welding, and so on. This is a little township where people are engaged in a range of activities. K arrives at his destination—the carpet factory where he is sent down through a pothole to Baba Bengali's den. K meets several women sitting on the stairs who direct him to continuously go down. After a while we are not sure how many floors he has gone down. The spatial configuration of the high-rise view of the penthouse with its white walls and even lighting appears very different from the architectural layout of Baba Bengali's den, which is at least several feet under the ground. Kashyap has often spoken about how *No Smoking* is a film about K's descent into morality. Morality here is the coercive apparatus of the system that makes people conform. In giving this vision a particularly spatial expression through art direction, Kashyap and Wasiq Khan foreground the expressive landscape of surfaces as a central feature of the film. *No Smoking*'s protagonist is not a rounded personality, but someone we know only superficially. The same is true for the other characters. Bodies are also approached in the film like the solid surfaces of the city. Surfaces overwhelm the narrative in a manner where the boundaries between reality, dream, and nightmare intermingle.

To the landscape of built surfaces is added the electronic surface of television, which as I have already suggested plays a crucial role in fracturing the ability to maintain separate boundaries of comprehension. The repeated use of the television screen to show seamless movement between the "real" world of the film and its imaginary landscape also foregrounds the techniques of surveillance. Surveillance is everywhere. You cannot escape it. In an imaginative rendering of this experience, the film shows K arriving in Siberia after he has travelled half the world to escape the all-seeing eye of Baba. K is desperate for a cigarette. We see a succession of superimposed dissolves of maps, people, and spaces, a form used in documentaries dealing with territorial conflict, television news, instructional videos for the army, the secret service (seen in the James Bond series), and adventure films. This mode of showing travel enhances the power of surveillance as a management issue. K reaches the heart of the Siberian desert and hears the sound of the phone. The figurines of Baba's den are etched onto a pothole cover located right in the middle

Figure 7.13. K in Dharavi (Asia's biggest slum) in *No Smoking*.

Figure 7.14. K followed by telephone surveillance in *No Smoking*.

of the desert. A man emerges from the pothole holding a cell phone and hands it to K, who is informed that his brother is in hospital. In the next shot K is running back to Dharavi to appeal for his brother's life. The constant use of the figurines on walls, potholes, cards, and boxes accelerates the cognitive dissonance of the film. Like the bathtub, the figurines appear everywhere. But here as the emblematic sign of Baba's all-seeing eye, the figurines enter mental and physical space, shocking us with the power of surveillance in the film.

No Smoking is structured to evoke a series of oppositional elements not for resolution but to enhance the irreconcilability of the conflicts. The theme of body and soul is alluded to but takes full expression in a climactic and powerful moment in the film. Having refused to follow Baba's instructions blindly, K's soul is separated from the body and is about to disappear in a simulated gas chamber. The soul is depicted as K's double in the film. The references to Nazism and the gas chamber begin in K's home when Anjali is first shown watching *Schindler's List* on TV. Moving through various states of mind, K finally finds himself in the Prayogshala's gas chamber after his wife's death, which occurs when K violates the rehabilitation instructions a second time. Although this is the stage when the fingers are supposed to be chopped off, Baba takes Anjali away, ghoulishly dissecting then stitching her up on a table dripping with blood. In a popular melodramatic form, K would seek revenge for what Baba has done to him and his wife. Here, however, the descent into darkness is relentless. At the Prayogshala gas chamber designed by Wasiq Khan, K is joined by several other inmates, each with his own story.[52]

The surreal quality of the sequence is highlighted through lighting and special effects. The bathtub appears again in the gas chamber. A woman is making announcements from a protected booth, getting everyone to stand in line for a bath. Everyone is in uniform. The poet Gulzar's evocative lyrics play on the soundtrack, referring to an ashtray filling up. The gas chamber stands in for the ashtray as we see the souls of all those who defied Baba's rehabilitation program lining up on two sides of a wide pit. The screen is suddenly overcast with the glow of fire in the pit and soon all the inmates (souls) disappear into nothingness.

Just before the main action at the chamber of death, K's soul sees his body across shiny transparent glass. The body is unaware that the soul is trapped in the gas chamber. The body survives in the world, but the soul disappears once the body submits to the apparatus of Baba's rule-bound system. The human soul as the bearer of truth, independence, and freedom is now unhinged and unacceptable to the system. The soul is the threat that must be extinguished. Thus the evocation of holocaust imagery generates a disturbing world. Body and soul are separated; the system continues to thrive in the absence of the soul. In an interesting response to the film soon after its release, Gyan Prakash notes,

> The distinction between dream and reality is deliberately blurred and narrative logic is distorted in order to draw our attention to the dystopic space of the city. So intent is the film on extracting bleak images from spaces that it ceases to matter that the story is set in Mumbai. You can identify Dharavi and Worli, but the film's look and its international citations make particular identities immaterial. *No Smoking* suggests that we need surreal images and distorted logic, not tightly plotted narratives to make sense of the over rationalized

Figure 7.15. K lining up with inmates at the gas chamber in *No Smoking*.

and all powerful system that stalks our lives. The cinematic city has turned as dark as the night.[53]

The surreal imagery and distorted logic of the film finds it's most spectacular and climactic moment when K wakes up early in the morning almost at the end of the film to find Anjali sleeping next to him. He walks to the bathroom and the audience heaves a sigh of relief with the hope and knowledge that the nightmare is finally over and K is back from his bathtub hallucinations. But this is not the logic Kashyap wants to follow. As in Kafka's fiction, for Kashyap, the "real" is worse than the nightmare and so K washes and raises his right hand to the mirror to see two of his fingers missing. We are provided no resolution to this narrative moment as the credits of the film start rolling. This is intercut with a brief sequence where K is shown at his office desk, trying to persuade a friend on the phone to visit Baba Bengali. His fingers are back and he is now part of the system. The spectator is unable to separate or integrate the two worlds of the film. The "real" is perpetually experienced as a nightmare.

Postscript

To conclude a journey through the intense mental and spatial landscapes of three significant films made in the period that we identify with globalization is virtually impossible. Given the non-genealogical formation of the Urban Fringe, it would be hard to provide a closure to this journey. All we can do is offer a few thoughts on the future and hope for more surprises and unpredictable forms. The mythology of the "eternal present" that globalization has unleashed will then be forced to confront alternative cartographies of urban space. The current bubble of globalization is based on a frenzy of land and financial speculation that seems to be sweeping South Asian cities today. This speculative cycle of expansion may unintentionally have opened its doors for a disruptive aesthetic, which also seems to speak a global language. This is a cinema that embodies the crisis of the human and produces the family as an unstable category, defying the moral universe of melodrama. While melodrama as a form has had a rich history in India, giving shape to several critical narratives, the current crisis clearly needs a different kind of engagement. For any archaeological excavation of the cinematic archive of the contemporary, twenty years from now the films about Bombay discussed in this essay will appear as traces that bear witness to a charged and conflictual landscape of the city at the turn of the twenty-first century. Coexisting with a plethora of other images, films like *Dombivli Fast*, *Being Cyrus*, and *No Smoking* will continue to remind us that we need to keep digging and looking for discontented images that fleetingly point to subterranean geographies of the city, images that perpetually interrogate and question the meaning of life.

Notes

I would like to thank Anurag Kashyap and Homi Adjania for providing the images used in this essay. Thanks are due to Nishikant Kamat for providing the DVD of his film. Debashree Mukherjee and Nupur Jain helped me with some newspaper and online sources. Finally, I must thank Ravi Sundaram, Shaswati Mazumdar, Gyan Prakash, and Shohini Ghosh for their comments and suggestions.

1 Suketu Mehta, *Maximum City: Bombay's Lost and Found* (New York: Knopf, 2003).
2 Gerson Dacunha, "Decline of a Great City," *Seminar*, no. 528 (August 2003).
3 See the introduction to my book *Bombay Cinema: An Archive of the City* (Minneapolis: University of Minnesota Press, 2007) for an extended discussion of globalization and the delirium of the present. Popular Bombay cinema in India today not only exists within this all-pervasive urban delirium but is also fundamentally a part of the delirium.
4 Saibal Chatterjee, "Hindi Cinema through the Decades," in *Encyclopaedia of Hindi Cinema* (New Delhi: Encyclopedia Britannica, 2003), 3.
5 For different approaches to melodrama, see Christine Gledhill, ed., *Home Is Where the Heart Is: Studies in Melodrama and the Woman's Film* (London: British Film Institute, 1987); Ben Singer, *Melodrama & Modernity* (New York: Columbia University Press, 2001); and Peter Brooks, *The Melodramatic Imagination: Balzac, Henry James, Melodrama, and the Mode of Excess* (New York: Columbia University Press, 1985).
6 See Rosie Thomas, "Melodrama and the Negotiation of Morality in Mainstream Hindi Films," in *Consuming Modernity: Public Culture in a South Asian World*, ed. Carol Brekenridge (Minneapolis: University of Minnesota Press, 1995), 157–82. For an account of the popular tropes of Hindi cinema or what has been referred to as a "circuit of communication" in the 1950s, see Ravi Vasudevan, "The Melodramatic Mode and the Commercial Hindi Cinema: Notes on Film History, Narrative and Performance in the 1950's," *Screen* 30.3 (1989): 29–50, and his introduction to the edited book *Making Meaning in Indian Cinema* (New Delhi: Oxford University Press, 2000). Also see Lalitha Gopalan, *Cinema of Interruptions: Action Genres in Contemporary Indian Cinema* (London: BFI Publishing, 2002); and Madhava Prasad, *The Ideology of Hindi Cinema: A Historical Construction* (Delhi: Oxford University Press, 1998).
7 For a discussion of the current circuits of Bombay cinema, see Ashish Rajadhyaksha, "The 'Bollywoodization' of the Indian Cinema: Cultural Nationalism in a Global Arena," *Inter Asia Cultural Studies* 4.1 (2003): 25–39.
8 See Christiane Brosius and Melissa Butcher, eds., *Image Journeys: Audio Visual Media and Cultural Change in India* (Thousand Oaks, CA: Sage, 1999).
9 See Shohini Ghosh, "Married to the Family: Cultural Apprehensions in the Narratives of Film and TV," *Indian Horizons* 55.1 (January–March 2008): 54–62.
10 Karan Johar, interview by the author, Bombay, November 2002.
11 Aparna Sharma, "India's Experience with the Multiplex," *Seminar*, no. 524 (2003): 43.

12 Komal Nahata, editor of the trade journal *Film Information*, interview by the author, Bombay, January 2005.

13 Rajat Kapoor, director of *Raghu Romeo, Mixed Doubles*, and *Mithya*, interview by the author, New Delhi, July 2006.

14 For a vivid account of contemporary DVD circulation and piracy, see Ravi Sundaram, "Uncanny Networks," *Economic and Political Weekly* 39.1 (January 3–9, 2004): 64–71.

15 For a full discussion of the rhizome, see Gilles Deleuze and Félix Guattari, *A Thousand Plateaus: Capitalism and Schizophrenia* (London: Athlone Press, 1988), 2–25.

16 The New Wave of the 1970s included among other things a strong desire for realism and realist strategies of representation. While experimental cinemas were also produced during this wave, the realist aesthetic dominated the form of the majority of the New Wave films. The Urban Fringe is marked by its anti-realist form. The filmmakers do not want to be identified with any art cinema movement. Their form appears different from both the realist New Wave films and popular melodramas. What we see here is an entirely different cinematic language. For an introduction to the key filmmakers of the New Wave, see John Hood, *The Essential Mystery: Major Filmmakers of Indian Art Cinema* (Hyderabad, India: Orient Longman, 2000).

17 For a discussion on the gangster films of Ramgopal Varma, see chapter 5 of my *Bombay Cinema*.

18 For a discussion of the Bachchan phenomenon, see Madhava Prasad, *Ideology of the Hindi Film: A Historical Construction* (Delhi: Oxford University Press, 1998), 138–57. Also see "Rage on Screen," in my *Bombay Cinema*.

19 Nishikant Kamat, interview by the author, New Delhi, June 2006.

20 *Variety* commented specifically on the opening montage and Kamat's deft editing of the sequence. See *Variety*, August 4, 2006.

21 For an interesting account of the Bombay suburban train compartment as a place where bodies jostle and exist within a culture of suspicion, see Radhika Subramaniam, "Culture of Suspicion: Riots and Rumor in Bombay, 1992–1993," *Transforming Anthropology* 8.1–2 (1999): 97–110. For a different account of the train in a European context, see Marc Auge, *In the Metro* (Minneapolis: University of Minnesota Press, 2002). Though Auge's account of train travel in Paris is somewhat romantic, it does articulate a world of unsaid stories.

22 For Walter Benjamin, the flaneur was a "panoramically situated" spectator who observed and absorbed through random selection the visual impressions generated by the new commodity space of industrial modernity. The flaneur's gaze was fragmented and adventurous as he/she confronted the magical world of the commodity displayed in shop windows of city streets. As a perceptual mode *flanerie* depends on distraction and a free movement of subjectivity where the gaze is organized according to a "spontaneous, unmitigated and seemingly unsystematic turn of attention towards the surface phenomena of the exterior world." Encke Gleber, *The Art of Taking a Walk: Flanerie, Literature and Film in Weimar Culture* (Princeton: Princeton University Press, 1998), 26.

23 "In Conversation: Nishikant Kamat," posted on http://passionforcinema.com/, March 30, 2007.

24 Zygmut Bauman, *Life in Fragments: Essays in Postmodern Morality* (Cambridge, MA: Blackwell, 1995), 14–15.

25 The Partition of India is one of the most catastrophic events in the history of the country; the violence lasted for fifteen months, starting on August 16, 1946. More than half a million people were affected as Hindus, Sikhs, and Muslims killed each other in the most inhuman way. As a frenzy of killing spread over large parts of the country, violence, destruction, rape, and looting left two emergent nations scarred with the despair and trauma of tortured memories. In the world of cinema, there is an overwhelming silence where the trauma of the event surfaces not through realistic narratives but through allegorical journeys. For a discussion of films that deal with the traumatic discourse of the Partition, see Ira Bhaskar, "The Persistence of Memory: Historical Trauma and Imagining the Community in Hindi Cinema" (Ph.D. diss., New York University, 2005). Also see Rebecca Brown, "Partition and the Uses of History in Waqt/Time," *Screen* 48 (2007): 161–77.

26 These were descendants of Persian Zoroastrians who emigrated to the subcontinent of India during the eighth century.

27 Homi Adjania, interview in *The Hindu*, February 26, 2006.

28 Although quite different from Spike Jonze's *Being John Malkovich* (1999), the title of the film, the bizarre dreamscapes, and the film's warped sensibility are reminders of Jonze's film.

29 Zygmut Bauman, *Liquid Fear* (Cambridge: Polity Press, 2006).

30 Marc Auge, *Non-Places: Introduction to an Anthropology of Supermodernity* (New York: Verso, 1992), 26–31.

31 Ibid., 77–78.

32 Joan Ramon Resina and Dieter Ingenschay, eds., *After-Images of the City* (Ithaca: Cornell University Press, 2003), 22.

33 Ibid., 22.

34 For a fuller discussion of the panoramic interiors of the family films, see chapter 4 of my *Bombay Cinema*.

35 Tom Gunning, "The Exterior as Interior: Benjamin's Optical Detective," *boundary 2* 30.1 (2003): 110.

36 Ibid. The entire essay develops the relationship between interior and exterior.

37 Marianne Hirsch, *Family Frames: Photography, Narrative and Postmemory* (Cambridge, MA: Harvard University Press, 1997), 7.

38 For a discussion of the family photograph and its uncanny secret life, see Annette Kuhn, *Family Secrets: Acts of Memory and Imagination* (New York: Verso, 1995).

39 Geoffrey Haphram, "The Grotesque: First Principles," *Journal of Aesthetics and Art Criticism* 34.4 (Summer 1976): 461–68. A version of the grotesque imagination in the Indian context can be described as *Bibhatsa*, which is one of the nine Rasas mentioned in the *Natyashastra*, a text on dramatic theory. *Bibhatsa* evokes the same state of disgust and shock as does the idea of the grotesque. *Bibhatsa* has been an influence on Indian art, and its gestural language can be seen in many Indian classical dances. In popular cultural forms like cinema, we see different ways of portraying *Bibhatsa*, but given film technology and its global circuits, the influences on the form have been worldwide. In particular, the anti-genealogical formation of the Fringe shows a diversity of influences that are far too complex to retrace. I have therefore deliberately deployed a broad understanding of the idea of the grotesque.

40 Peter Fingesten, "Delimiting the Concept of the Grotesque," *Journal of Aesthetics and Art Criticism* 42.4 (Summer 1984): 419–26.

41 Ibid., 422.

42 The desire to explore and excavate the darker side of the contemporary both psychologically and spatially is a characteristic feature of Anurag Kashyap's cinema. He has often been described as a rebel figure, an underground filmmaker, and a director with a fascination for quirkiness, the bizarre, and the absurd who is committed to finding a cinematic language not plagued by the pressures of industry, tradition, or acceptability. Kashyap displays a disdain for moral and social explanations. Instead, he chooses to provocatively inhabit the world of despair in all its brutality. Drawing on diverse cultural sources—from English and Hindi literature to graphic novels, comics and pulp literature, from Italian neo-realism to Hollywood's film noir—we see the emergence of a distinctly different kind of cinematic imagination in Kashyap's work.

43 Anurag Kashyap, interview by the author, February 2008.

44 Ibid.

45 Christine W. Sizemore, "Anxiety in Kafka: A Function of Cognitive Dissonance," *Journal of Modern Literature* 6.3, Franz Kafka Special (September 1977): 380–88. Also see Frederick R. Karl, "Space, Time, and Enclosure in 'The Trial' and 'The Castle,'" *Journal of Modern Literature* 6.3, Franz Kafka Special (September 1977): 424–36; and Stéphane Moses and Ora Wiskind-Elper, "Gershom Scholem's Reading of Kafka: Literary Criticism and Kabbalah," *New German Critique*, no. 77, special issue on German-Jewish religious thought (Spring–Summer 1999): 149–67.

46 Jean Baudrillard, *Simulacra and Simulation* (Ann Arbor: University of Michigan Press, 1994), 2, 6.

47 Mark Wigley, *White Walls, Designer Dresses: The Fashioning of Modern Architecture* (Cambridge, MA: MIT Press, 2001), 349.

48 For elaborate discussions on the relationship between cinema and architecture, see Giuliana Bruno, *Atlas of Emotion: Journeys in Art, Architecture and Film* (New York: Verso, 2002); and Dietrich Neumann, ed., *Film Architecture: From* Metropolis *to* Blade Runner (New York: Prestel, 1999).

49 Anurag Kashyap, interview by the author, Bombay (during the shooting of the film), December 2006.

50 Ibid.

51 Wasiq Khan planned the interiors on the basis of design catalogs and images he had seen on the Internet. He was keen to create a modern interior that could be an apartment in any part of the world. The rooms in K's apartment did not have a personal touch or any sense of cultural identity. Wasiq Khan, interview by the author, December 2006 (during the shooting of the gas chamber sequence).

52 For the gas chamber design, Khan drew on expressionist iconography. He was also very influenced by the set design of Fritz Lang's *Metropolis* (1927) and Robert Wiene's *Cabinet of Dr. Calligary* (1920). He was also fascinated by woodcuts, which led to the design of the figurines in all the places associated with Baba Bengali. Khan interview.

53 See Gyan Prakash, "Mumbai City: Injurious to Health," Sunday special article in the *Times of India*, November 4, 2007.

Imaging Urban Crisis

Chapter 8

■

Topographies of Distress

Tokyo, c. 1930

DAVID R. AMBARAS

In March 1930, nearly seven years after a massive earthquake destroyed three-fourths of the city's buildings and killed roughly one hundred thousand people, Tokyo officially celebrated its reconstruction as, in the words of Mayor Horikiri Zenjirō, "the seat of our empire, the axis of our nation's political and economic life, . . . and the fountainhead of our national culture."[1] In the same month, perhaps not coincidentally, the satire and comic art magazine *Tōkyō pakku* (Tokyo Puck) featured on its back cover a painting by Miura Shun titled *Tokai* (Metropolis), which depicted a far more disconcerting version of urban modernity. Whereas the reconstruction celebrations and commemorative publications foregrounded the imperial family, the imperial palace, and symbols of Japanese success such as the Marunouchi business district, Miura filled the center of his vista with two very different figures: a light-skinned "modern girl" sporting a Western-style bobbed haircut and a transparent dress that reveals her genitalia, with lips, cheeks, and breasts highlighted in red; and a contrastingly dark, corpulent man with animal-like features who looms over her, his walking stick handle approaching her genitals like a snake. This metropolis is, first and foremost, a hypersexualized space of women, as well as a threat to women. It is also a place of human sacrifice. Behind the couple, on the right, workers crush against each other as they proceed toward the entrance to a factory that glows red like the mouth of an oven into which they are being fed. Above the factories, cranes tower like hulking gallows. In the center, a crowd of men in Western suits and hats, no doubt office workers, also pushes forward toward a less distinct destination. Behind this crowd, one male figure lies on the ground (whether he has collapsed or is sleeping is not clear), and a black dog approaches him. Other black, four-legged figures emerge from the fringes of the cityscape, beneath its high-rise buildings. The sky, in red and black, appears to be on fire.

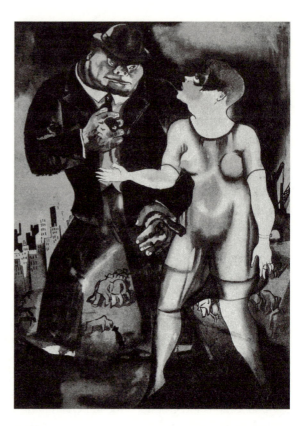

Figure 8.1. Miura Shun,
Metropolis (Tokai).
Tōkyō pakku 9.3 (March
1930): rear cover.

Miura's painting offers a striking representation of the matrix of sensations and anxieties that infused Japanese urban life, most acutely symbolized
by Tokyo, in a period of rapid transformation. Driven by Japan's industrialization, the population of Tokyo's city wards and five surrounding districts rose
from 2 million at the turn of the century to 3.7 million in 1920 to 5.4 million
in 1930. The post-quake reconstruction boom also produced a redesigned
central cityscape, replete with regularized blocks, new concrete and glass
office buildings, tree-lined boulevards, renovated parks, modernist bridges,
rationalized waterways, and suburban middle-class "culture houses" within
carefully planned "culture villages" or Ebenezer Howard–inspired "garden
cities."[2] The spread of cinemas, cafés, department stores, and dance halls, and
the changing styles they displayed, further underscored the impression that
modern urban life was an experience of speed, sensation, and the streets that
delivered emancipation from the bonds of the past.

Yet despite this ebullience, to many contemporaries, urban modernity
signaled the destruction of Japanese social values by Western materialism
and individualistic hedonism, of which the modern girl served as the prime

example. With her Western clothes, hairstyles, and outlandishly direct attitudes toward men, this figure was more cinematic fantasy than sociological
reality: for example, in novelist Junichiro Tanizaki's *Chijin no ai*, her power
came from her ability to be mistaken for Mary Pickford or one of Mack
Sennett's "bathing beauties." But such images powered an agitated discourse
that, on the one hand, heralded the modern girl's arrival as a harbinger of
necessary social revolution and, on the other, gave voice to, in Harry Harootunian's words, "the growing sense that the processes guaranteeing cultural
reproduction (not to forget biological reproduction) were in danger of disappearing altogether."[3]

Modern life also created pervasive anxiety in the mass of urbanites who
struggled to keep their footing in an everyday realm destabilized by persistent economic crises, from the postwar bust to the 1927 financial panic to
the depression triggered by the 1929 Wall Street crash and compounded by
the Minseitō government's poorly timed retrenchment policies. By the end
of the decade, workers and labor unions in both large factories and small
plants confronted management over the increasing implementation of industrial rationalization programs, job reductions, and other cost-cutting measures.[4] The struggles of the lower classes also attracted widespread attention;
the word *donzoko*, meaning the lower depths, gained widespread currency
as shorthand for their plight, while the word *runpen* (short for the Japanese
transliteration of lumpenproletariat) came into its own as a signifier of the
growing number of homeless people in shelters or living on the streets. The
white-collar middle classes also struggled to secure their status and lifestyles,
providing the motif for films such as Ozu Yasujirō's "Daigaku wa deta keredo"
("I Finished College, But . . ." [1929]), in which a young man tries to conceal
his unemployment from his mother and fiancée, only to see the latter take
work as a café waitress to support the family. But while Ozu could turn the
subject into a lighthearted piece of entertainment (the young man winds up
gainfully employed), others could not, particularly in an intellectual environment in which Marxist writers, drawing on the work of Eugen Varga and
others, wrote assuredly of the impending collapse of capitalist society, and in
particular of what cultural critic Ōya Sōichi called the "accelerated decline of
the intelligentsia."[5]

Like these other representations of modern life, Miura's *Tokai* encom-
passed far more than specific developments in Japan. With its allusions to the
work of George Grosz and Otto Dix in Germany, Miura's painting highlights
the fact that images of the urban condition drew not only on individuals' immediate experiences or particular national categories but, just as important,
on the categories and constructs made available through the operations of an
increasingly globalized circuitry of modernity. As Yoshimi Shunya and others
have noted, an awareness of the cosmopolitan simultaneity of "the modern"

decisively shaped the identities and strategies of Japanese culture producers and consumers during the interwar years, thus underscoring James Donald's argument that people create for themselves an image of "the city" that is only partly based on the features of their particular physical location. "This traffic between urban fabric, representation and imagination fuzzies up the epistemological and ontological distinctions," notes Donald, "and, in doing so, produces the city between, the imagined city where we actually live."[6]

Hence, as Donald and other students of the subject have observed, the role of the media in teaching people how to experience the city cannot be separated from the city itself. Writing on late Wilhelmine Berlin, for example, Peter Fritzsche explains,

> Both the aesthetics of modernism and the culture of consumption distorted the city by embellishing its most fantastic characteristics.... Coffee-house poets, peep-show exhibitors, vaudeville artists, and police-beat reporters sensationalized the city and also recast it in their image. The terms of mediation cannot be separated from the metropolitan experience; the falsification of the city, its people, and its history has become a permanent part of the city. . . . The word city, at least since the turn of the century, is not just a fabrication that overlaid, sensationalized, and falsified the actual city; to a large extent it came to be part of it, through the industries of sensationalism. As the boundaries between the real and the imagined become blurred, the potential to fabricate the city has in fact made the city more fugitive.[7]

In modern Japan, as elsewhere, the forms of urban representation and the ends to which they were applied multiplied rapidly. Government reports and commemorative albums, geographical gazettes, urban plans, social surveys, professional bulletins, parliamentary debates, cultural criticism, general-interest books and magazines, popular guides and how-to manuals, movies, photography, art, songs, and above all the daily press provided urbanites (as well as rural consumers) with mental maps for navigating the city, either in its ostensible totality or in a more fragmented mode. In this essay, I would like to consider how the media worked to construct one particular version of modern urban life that both reflected and fueled contemporary fears that the city was a showcase not of progress but of insecurity and inexpressible horror, with its darkest essence in a place connected to but not articulated in the disturbing metropolis of Miura's depiction. This topography could be perceived in a series of cases, which appeared with disturbing regularity in the press during the 1920s and early 1930s, that involved the murders or suspicious deaths of infants, most of them illegitimate, taken in for a fee by a variety of receivers, sometimes acting alone and sometimes in connection with networks of brokers. Many cases involved a single infant, but many involved larger numbers, sometimes in the dozens. The death of infants due to these illicit transactions was itself not a new phenomenon; part of a longer history of dealing with unwanted children throughout Japan, such cases had figured in the popular press from its inception in the Meiji era. These problems appeared in their most concentrated, virtually quotidian form in cities, with the most sensational occurring in Tokyo; and the agitated reporting on them traced the circulation of marginal infants and adults across a gendered and classed cityscape that connected slums, flophouses, factories, cafés, upper-class homes, midwives' clinics, the streets, and newspapers themselves (where infants for adoption were often advertised).

Reports of these cases can certainly be placed within a broader governmental project to elucidate dark spaces and transgressive figures and subject them to disciplinary surveillance or pedagogic protection. But they also circulated as commodities within a marketplace of images of the city and potentially provided consumers (and the topographers who produced them) with not simply moral messages but also sensory stimulation, the experience of what Edgar Allan Poe called "pleasurable pain," or opportunities to confront the uncanny aspects of urban life. As *faits divers*, such episodes may also have performed, in Deborah S. Reisinger's words, "a function through which the public may vicariously live out its desires or fantasies, which are prohibited by society." Indeed, an examination of this topography is a necessary step to, again drawing on Donald, "make sense of the individual in the metropolis not only in terms of identity, community, and civic association, but also in terms of a dramaturgy of desire, fascination, and terror."[8]

In the remainder of this essay, I will treat these issues by focusing on the representation of Iwanosaka, a slum neighborhood where, in the spring of 1930, the police arrested several beggars, scrap collectors, and day laborers in connection with the suspicious deaths of at least three dozen infants. Of the many large-scale cases of infant deaths, that of Iwanosaka attracted the most sustained attention, providing investigators and critics with not only a steady stream of readily sensationalized news stories but also a specific place in which to conduct fieldwork and on which to base their arguments about conditions in the metropolis and in Japan more broadly. As one contemporary noted, "This case was not just about hard times, or about the kinds of foster child murders that were so commonplace (*arifureta*); because it told of a dire (*shinkoku*) aspect, it led to the general mobilization of journalism. The actions of the printed words surprised social researchers, or rather, the truth of the incident led to astonishment at the reality of this group of collective murderers and their ongoing crimes."[9] In examining the Iwanosaka archive, then, my intention is not to uncover the "reality" at its core but to show how various forms of representation—the "general mobilization of journalism," "the actions of the printed words" (and images), and the combination of journalistic, literary, and social scientific modes—instituted this "reality" in people's perceptions of the metropolis. At the same time, rather than see accounts of Iwanosaka and related materials as simply sensationalist or simply governmental, I would like to consider the instability of the authors and readers themselves in order to emphasize the unsettling attractiveness that accrued to such apparently repulsive images, and to suggest that in a moment of wrenching socioeconomic crisis, "Iwanosaka" appeared as a grotesque reflection of the anxieties of Japan's petty bourgeoisie.

Death in the Village of Devils: The Iwanosaka Case

Iwanosaka was a slum neighborhood in Itabashi, on the northern edge of Tokyo, bordering Saitama Prefecture. Situated along the Nakasendō road, this area had been the site of a thriving post town (*shukuba machi*) during the late Tokugawa and early Meiji years, with ample work for entertainers and in the sex trade; but it was marginalized in the mid-Meiji years when the construction of the Ueno-Takasaki rail line diverted passengers and business to the east. Nonetheless, the area's population grew as both slum clearance in the older city wards drove inhabitants to the fringes and urban growth provided a new pool of immigrants; by the 1920s, Iwanosaka was a complex of cheap flophouses and tenements with some two thousand inhabitants, most in the lowest class of casual laborers, beggars, and entertainers.[10]

    This case began on April 13, 1930, with the death of one-month-old Ogawa Kikujirō. Kikujirō was the adopted son of Ogawa Kiku, a thirty-five-year-old shaven-headed "Amida Buddha worshiper" (*nenbutsu gyōja*)—actually a beggar—who lived with her common-law husband, Ogura Kōjirō, also a beggar, in an Iwanosaka flophouse. Kikujirō was the fifth child of Murai Ogijirō, an office building watchman, and his wife, Kō. Kō had delivered the baby at the clinic of Ishizuka Teru, a licensed midwife in Itabashi; there, she had encountered Deya Koyono, an Iwanosaka resident and the common-law wife of an unemployed brick vendor, and in conversation indicated that she would like to give up the child for adoption. In exchange for Koyono's promise to find an upstanding adoptive family, Kō gave her the baby, along with eighteen yen cash and a supply of clothing. Koyono then approached Fukuda Hatsu, a forty-year-old female day laborer (*yoitomake*) from Iwanosaka; Hatsu in turn gave the baby and ten yen to Ogawa Kiku, who entered him into her household register as her own son. A few days later, Kiku's husband, Kōjirō, woke to find the baby cold and bleeding from the nose; he called Hatsu, and they took the baby to the nearby clinic of Dr. Nagai. Hatsu told Nagai that Kiku, who had a bad arm, had accidentally suffocated the baby while nursing him. Nagai, suspecting foul play, contacted the police, who raided the neighborhood. Kiku, it turned out, had since the preceding year caused the deaths of five infants in her care; just one month earlier, she had fatally injured an adopted baby by "accidentally dropping" him in the public bath. Over the next few days, officers arrested not only the persons involved in Kikujirō's death but also four other common-law couples, all of them casual laborers, who were associated with the deaths of several other infants in their charge.

The police soon released Fukuda Hatsu, the day laborer, for lack of concrete evidence. On April 18, however, she appeared at the local charity clinic with the emaciated corpse of an infant girl, claimed that it was her own daughter who had died of natural illness, and, in what appeared to be a common practice, intimidated the doctor on duty into issuing a death certificate to that effect. The doctor then informed the police, who again arrested Hatsu. Hatsu was known in the neighborhood as a broker of unwanted babies; this baby was reported to have been delivered to her three days after its birth by a garbage collector from neighboring Saitama Prefecture. Hatsu had taken six infants into her own care, all of whom died suspicious deaths (they were reportedly fed heavily watered-down milk), and had placed several others with women such as Kiku. Of the infants known to have passed through Hatsu's hands since 1926, the *Tōkyō Asahi shimbun* reported, only two were still alive, and they were in the charge of local beggars who used them to evoke sympathy and increase their earnings. Police reported that approximately seventy beggars residing in Iwanosaka used children in their trades and that all of these were received children. In June and July of that year, a third round of arrests centered on scrap collector Yoshida Hikohachi (age thirty-five) and his common-law wife, Sue (age twenty-eight), who had killed or let die five children they had received, some of them from Hatsu. In addition to these cases, the police and the press connected a number of other incidents to the Iwanosaka affair: for example, several infant corpses discovered along the nearby Arakawa River were considered to have been abandoned by individuals tied to the network who panicked when it was exposed.

The total number of infant deaths in the Iwanosaka case is hard to verify, and newspapers varied in their figures. The *Tōkyō Asahi* claimed thirty such deaths per year; the *Tōkyō Nichinichi shimbun* reported fifty-two deaths in the preceding few years; while the *Yomiuri shimbun* put the total at seventy-three. In an internal report later published in the April 1931 issue of the magazine *Fujin saron* (Women's Salon), Inspector Takatomo Masakatsu of the Itabashi Police Precinct limited his discussion of the affair to roughly three dozen infants, all of whom died within a few months of entering the neighborhood.[11] Similarly, no solid evidence exists to determine the actual number of infants placed in or through Iwanosaka. But observers agreed that the worsening economic slump had led to a marked increase from seventeen to eighteen infants a year in the early 1920s to perhaps thirty to forty per year at the end of the decade.

Few of these cases appear to have been prosecuted. Infanticide was extremely hard to prove, although reports that Fukuda Hatsu's biological children were all in good health while her adopted children starved would appear to be quite damning.[12] The police were aware of problems in the area but were powerless to do anything for some time prior to Ogawa Kiku's arrest. When officers finally did raid the neighborhood, inhabitants were overheard muttering, "They've looked the other way until now."[13] Yet authorities were able to bring to trial only Ogawa Kiku and to convict her only of the murder of Kikujirō. Kiku confessed to having deliberately smothered Kikujirō because he cried all the time; the fact that Kikujirō's birth mother had been identified and was available to testify was also a decisive element in prosecutors' ability to obtain a conviction. (News reports referred to the mothers of the infants as mainly factory girls, elite widows, daughters from good homes, and schoolteachers, the latter a symbol of the new professional working woman.) But while Kiku admitted to having taken in five infants for money, she claimed that all the other deaths were due to the infants' inherent weakness or illness. Kiku may have been adhering to an established script for such cases, but Tokyo district attorneys failed to obtain evidence of murder in these and the other cases they investigated and were forced to treat them as deaths due to malnutrition and similar causes.[14]

Newspaper allegations that the women of Iwanosaka had used their earnings to hold raucous drinking parties served to heighten the public's perception of gruesome perversity, but police officials, social workers, and other observers did in fact acknowledge that, as Itabashi precinct police chief Harada told the *Tōkyō Nichinichi* newspaper, many infant deaths were not the result of deliberate starvation but rather the consequence of "ignorant love."[15] In an article titled "An Exploration of Iwanosaka, the Murderers' Village," Fuyuki Reinosuke, a contributor to the elite journal *Fujin kōron* (Women's Review), stated that foster parents in the neighborhood could be quite affectionate toward their newly acquired infants; hence, the issue was not necessarily one of child abuse but rather of the realities of slum life.[16] All agreed, moreover, that these problems extended beyond Iwanosaka to the entire urban lower class.

News reports of infant murders or deaths in Iwanosaka, including another incident involving a child in Fukuda Hatsu's care, continued until December 1932, as far as I have been able to ascertain. The public outrage over these cases contributed to the passage in 1933 of a new Law for the Prevention of Cruelty to Children (Jidō gyakutai bōshi hō), which granted the state new powers of intervention into (lower-class) families and other at-risk areas; meanwhile, Iwanosaka came to be identified with the atmosphere of "erotic grotesque nonsense" that marked the depression years.[17]

Iwanosaka, the Daily Newspaper, and the Cityscape of Dead and Abused Children

The Iwanosaka case entered the consciousness of the Japanese populace principally through the daily press, and, despite its particularly horrific dimensions, it presented readers with an amalgam of readily recognizable elements. Beginning in the 1870s, metropolitan newspapers, as Narita Ryūichi has written, used stories of people's inability to restrain their emotions or discipline their bodies as signs of the semicolonial barbarism from which Japan had to escape, and identified crime- and cholera-infested slums as a dark, savage realm beyond the pale of the community of national subject/readers (a view that would be modified in subsequent decades).[18] But while the press disseminated this new pedagogy of civilization (and while Japan transformed itself into a colonial empire), its persistent depiction of various examples of violence, filth, disease, and crime, and its mapping them on the urban landscape, also induced readers to see these as "normal" features of modern city life. As a perusal of the Tokyo daily press in the Meiji era and beyond reveals, reports of the discovery of infant corpses in the city's waterways, gutters, garbage dumps, and temple grounds, of abandoned or abused infants and children, and of infants killed by their mothers at birth appeared with sufficient frequency to constitute a readily recognizable aspect of this evolving urban space. In the period preceding the Iwanosaka case, for example, readers had learned of the crimes of Kimura Tōichi, a street vendor in the Asakusa entertainment district who in 1927 took in five illegitimate infants, strangled them, and buried their corpses in the hills near his hometown in neighboring Chiba Prefecture. Readers also knew about Takakura Sei, the wife of a snack vendor who in 1928 was convicted and sentenced to death for the murder of eleven infants in her charge. In the months immediately following the first Iwanosaka reports, they would read about, among other cases, a midwife who had killed fifteen infants in her charge and the discovery of seven infant corpses in two pieces of luggage at Shinjuku Station.[19]

From their earliest incarnations, Japan's popular newspapers also presented reports of urban deviance as spectacles, curiosities, or tales for readers whose tastes bore the imprint of Tokugawa-era popular cultural practices. Readers' desires may have been informed by the widely disseminated texts and images of late-Tokugawa kabuki theater, which was marked, according to Samuel Leiter and James Brandon, by "cold-blooded and ferocious violence, realism pushed into fantasy and grotesquery, novelty for novelty's sake, sexual aggressiveness, and assertion of female will."[20] Just as important, in his work on Meiji-era popular newspapers, literary historian Yamada Shunji has emphasized the fictitious aspects of reporting and the organization of narratives to accommodate readers' desire for entertaining tales (*monogatari*), with which they were most familiar from their reading of popular Edo-era literary forms known as *gesaku*. Among the motifs that gained popularity in this literature/news space was that of the abuse of children by stepmothers or foster mothers; and as Yamada suggests, some readers may have appreciated the detailed accounts of physical cruelty for the vicarious sadistic pleasure they offered.[21] While reading habits and writing styles evolved over the following decades, the public's desire for *monogatari* continued to influence the organization of the news, in which the motif of child murder, along with related narratives of hardship, remained prominent. For example, one article, "Yo wa mujō! Kanojo ga eiji o korosu made" (The world is heartless! Until she killed her infant—A story that cannot be read without shedding tears), which appeared in the *Yomiuri shimbun* on January 22, 1930, contained a number of tropes—a young girl's dream of the city and rupture with the countryside, people not being who they seem, cafés as sites of entrapment and degradation, the isolation of the unattached woman leading inexorably to crime, and the body of a dead infant—whose ubiquity guaranteed that they would inform the reading of the Iwanosaka case and others like it.[22]

Rapidly expanding literacy since the turn of the century had fueled an explosive demand for newspapers, and rapid technological change enabled the press to meet this demand and cultivate even more readers. By the 1920s, Tokyo's commuters were able to peruse one paper on their morning trajectories to work and another evening edition on their return, as well as the special editions (*gōgai*) that followed important events. In 1930, Tokyo's leading papers, including the *Tōkyō Asahi*, the *Yomiuri*, the *Tōkyō Nichinichi*, the *Hōchi*, and the *Miyako*, boasted a combined circulation of roughly 1.7 million (including regional editions).[23] Needless to say, the competition for readers was intense, sensationalism was a powerful tool in this struggle, and crime was a crucial element of sensationalism. As Unno Hiroshi argues, "In the 1920s, crime came to be read as the sign of the city. Not only did newspapers sensationalize crimes, but crime magazines such as *Hanzai kagaku* (Crime Science), *Hanzai kōron* (Crime Forum), and *Tantei shōsetsu* (Detective Novels) came into being, and the genre of crime journalism was established. In other words, urbanites wanted to read articles and novels about crime. The city did not simply breed crime; it offered it to its inhabitants as words and images, thereby satisfying their curiosity."[24] The repeated accounts of the Iwanosaka case, each offering the discovery of new details or additional crimes, also aligned this case with the forms of the detective novel, which, as James Donald notes, "stages the city as enigma: a dangerous but fascinating network of often subterranean relationships in need of decipherment" and permits readers the vicarious experience of getting at this concealed reality.[25]

Evolving print technology and design concepts both satisfied the demands of sensationalist competition and generated even greater possibilities for sensationalist constructions of the city. The early Meiji years had seen the emergence of newspapers that utilized multicolored woodblock prints (*nishiki-e*), a popular Edo-period art form, to illustrate stories, but by the mid-Meiji years the standard form of the daily press was pages of single rows of text with nominal headlines (or simply black or white dots indicating each item) and occasional drawings. Over the following decades, the layout evolved to include more photographs and large-font headlines and subheads (often three or four of different sizes) that traversed several rows of text. For example, the first three of the *Tōkyō Asahi*'s reports on the Iwanosaka case carried the following headlines:

Hearing this makes one's flesh and hair stand on end / The village of murdering devils in Tokyo's Itabashi / Beggars, laborers, and others plot together / Murdering foster children is a habit / The strange death of thirty in a year / All of the villagers to be arrested (April 14, 1930, morning edition, p. 7)

Even more bizarre: the dark side of the murderous devils' hamlet / The chief of Itabashi precinct himself takes the lead / A decisive major action under way / Receiving a foster child makes the villagers feel like the nouveau riche / Two thousand people leading lives of despair and self-destruction / Upper-class women's illegitimate children among those sacrificed (April 15 1930, evening edition, p. 2)

The suspicious religious practitioner in the village of killers / Confesses her cruel crimes / Cleaning up the frightful foster child murders / Itabashi police precinct officers in a major action / Four hundred children adopted/ Wives bearing three babies a year / The stunning public morals of the hamlet (April 15, 1930, morning edition, p. 7)

Photographs of Iwanosaka's dilapidated tenements (*nagaya*), with junk strewn across the unpaved alleyway, doorless entries leading to darkened spaces, and hunched-over inhabitants peering awkwardly at the camera, also grabbed the reader's attention and reinforced the air of grotesquerie surrounding the events.[26] Greater use of boldfaced paragraph headings, as well as the highlighting of key phrases within the body of the story, generated effects like those noted by Fritzsche in Berlin's dailies: "[They] caught the reader's eye again and again as it wandered down the column . . . [and] provided fresh sensations at rapid intervals. They were at once compelling and distracting, inducing readers to stop and look and also driving them onward."[27]

Yet even as Iwanosaka jumped out from the page as a bizarre aberration from normal life, newspaper layouts could also reinforce the perception of these events as just another part of the curious jumble of the city. For example, in the morning edition of the *Yomiuri shimbun* (page 7) on June 15, 1930, a report of on-site investigations of Iwanosaka and debates over new laws to protect children from abuse appeared next to articles on the struggles of the taxi industry, the crisis of the movie industry, and violent clashes at Nihon University, as well as petty crimes. But this page also featured the latest installment in the story "The girl and Mister Tokyo," subtitled "Only till I made it happen—Yankee girl is free—an outdoor drama," which featured illustrations of a woman's high-heeled foot stepping on that of a Western-clothed man and of a man in a straw boater following a couple down a dark street at night. The lower portion of the page, meanwhile, contained advertisements for birth control methods ("regulating pregnancies for a bright life"); for the latest issue of *Hanzai kagaku* (Crime Science), with descriptions of the novelty and strangeness of its contents and the warning "Hurry! Hurry! Before it sells out!" accompanied by a drawing of a masked woman smoking a cigarette; as well as for men's hats, women's breast bands, girls' underwear, miso paste, a kimono clothier's sale, health remedies, summer courses for students, and Ribbon Citron drink. In the reader's eye, then, Iwanosaka could be connected to other stories of economic turmoil and social strife, to sexual intrigue and urban play, to birth control, to the fad for the bizarre or grotesque, as well as to clothing, food, and education. And in the daily press, the Tokyo of Iwanosaka was also the Tokyo of such upbeat spectacles as the Shōchiku Musical Revue's *Tokyo Dance*—advertised as "a new special attraction of the reconstructed capital."[28]

What may have given Iwanosaka its potency, in addition to the scale of the incident, was the fact that many Tokyoites readily recognized its characters—the beggars, "Buddhist practitioners," blind musicians, and motley entertainers (*chindonya*)—from their meanderings in the city's modern play spaces, train stations, and media spaces. For example, a George Grosz–like cartoon in the July 1928 issue of *Tōkyō pakku*, titled "Kanraku no kage: Ginza shoken" (In the Shadow of Pleasure: A Ginza Sighting), depicted a grotesque "family" of three—a blind female shamisen player with blotchy face and patched robe being led by the sleeve by an emaciated boy with an oversized shaved head (her own child or a rented begging prop) and followed closely by an adult male with a dull-witted expression, disheveled hair, and a tattered hat—standing against a backdrop of modern high-rise buildings. Yet rather than simply linger in the shadows, as the cartoon's title would have it, in this image the massive woman and her entourage occupied the city center. The children in such images struck a particular chord of concern. Reacting to news of the Iwanosaka case, a contributor to the April 16, 1930 edition of the *Tōkyō Asahi* noted, "It pains the heart to still see, on the streets of the imperial capital, the figures of small children prostrating themselves (*dogeza*) [to beg]. Driven off like stray dogs by café waitresses and waiters, little children cling tenaciously to customers, trying to sell them fortunes or tissue paper. Doll or flower peddlers also call out from the streets." In late 1927, the Tokyo City Social Bureau had conducted a survey of children accompanying adult beggars and found that the largest number came from Iwanosaka.[29] The flood of Iwanosaka reports may thus have jarred urban readers into reflecting on the possibility that simply by enjoying or traversing the city, they had come closer to its horrors than they could have imagined.

Figure 8.2. Yazaki Shigeshi, "In the Shadow of Pleasure: A Ginza Sighting." *Tōkyō pakku* 17.1 (July 1928): 18.

Iwanosaka and Slum Discourse

Readers also recognized the Iwanosaka figures because they appeared in the context of four decades of reports and social scientific surveys of slums in Tokyo and other cities. The "discovery" of the slums had been prompted in the 1870s and 1880s by outbreaks of contagious disease such as cholera, which were found to have spread from areas with high crime rates. As literary scholar Maeda Ai has observed, "The stagnant, filthy atmosphere associated with the backstreets of the city [Tokyo] would come to be dreaded as a hor- rifying symbol of evil, not only from the standpoint of medical science but in the realm of morality." Leading newspapers began publishing reports on slum life, while the magazine *Kokumin no tomo* (The Nation's Friend) intro- duced readers to Western texts on slums such as George Sim's *How the Poor Live and Horrible London*, Charles Booth's *Life and Labour of the People in London*, and William Booth's *Darkest England and the Way Out*. These devel- opments set the stage for the appearance of books such as Matsubara Iwagorō's *Saiankoku no Tōkyō* (Darkest Tokyo [1893]), which, appropriating the trope of darkness that marked both William Booth's writing and H. M. Stanley's *In Darkest Africa*, depicted the slums as an agglomeration of monstrosities that constituted the antithesis of Tokyo as a center of modern civilization.[30] Over the following years, new-middle-class journalists, social workers, and other professionals, eager to establish their own position as the vanguard of moder- nity and custodians of national welfare, would publish multiple accounts of conditions in urban lower-class districts, with varying degrees of sympathy for their inhabitants. As Christopher Hill has recently noted, slum exposés constituted, along with naturalism, criminology, and Social Darwinism, part of the transnational "spread of a broader social imaginary" that "found its expression in the observation of social others, the 'scientific' analysis of their instincts and drives, and the creation of narratives that presented such in- dividuals as both aberrant (because of the extreme circumstances of their existence) and exemplary (because science showed that their basest desires were universally human)."[31]

But slums also came to constitute part of the encyclopedia of "manners and customs" of Japan's cities, with widely read magazines such as *Fūzoku gahō* (Illustrated Manners and Customs) offering various images of the al- legedly indolent or actually decrepit poor both within their dwellings or ab- jecting themselves on the city streets (for example, begging by adults and children was featured as one item in a 1909 photographic series on "ways of going through life in Tokyo").[32] Meanwhile, the turn-of-the-century jour- nalistic fashion of inserting "reporters in disguise" into the concealed, mys- terious spaces of the city led to numerous articles about slums and poverty in prominent magazines such as *Chūō kōron* (Central Review), *Shin kōron*

(New Review), *Bōken sekai* (Adventure World), and *Jogaku sekai* (Girl Students' World), as well as to various book-length compilations such as Harada Tōfū's 1903 *Kichinyado* (Flophouses) and Murakami Sukesaburō's 1912 *Tokyo ankoku ki* (Chronicle of Tokyo Darkness).[33] The reportage blended easily into the guidebook, teaching both urbanites and those attracted to the metropolis about its multiple hazards. Kawakami Gazan's 1902 *Makutsu no Tōkyō* (Tokyo of Devils' Lairs), for example, placed the slums and beggars into a cityscape also occupied by fraudulent advertisers, shady brokers and kidnapers, gamblers, entertainers, and of course unlicensed sex workers and their bosses. The slums and their psychologically unstable inhabitants also served as the final chapter and symbolic endpoint of Ishikawa Tengai's 1909 *Tōkyō gaku* (Tokyo-ology), which Miriam Silverberg has described as "a key to the cultural codes" of the late Meiji era and "one long illustration of Georg Simmel's theory of the transformation of social relationships and cultural life in a developed money economy." Ishikawa depicted the capital as a battlefield, not for the faint of constitution, and offered readers several hundred pages of advice on how to negotiate its social relationships, opportunities, and dangers. "Because the poor are the losers of Tokyo life," he noted, "they provide some reference, as well as an admonition, for people actually living in Tokyo or about to do so."[34]

Government officials and new urban social scientists, often drawing on data from Europe and the United States, also decisively shaped the public's imagination of the slums, just as they contributed to a broader discourse on Tokyo or "the city" as a site of baleful elements portending disease and degeneration if not properly administered.[35] By 1911, the Home Ministry had begun conducting surveys of the living conditions of the poor in Tokyo and throughout the country. After World War I, when many slum dwellers had been dispersed to the outer districts or to smaller pockets within more ordinary neighborhoods, newly established government social bureaus and private research agencies sought to render the poor visible and legible according to a matrix of quantifiable values, such as household size, income, and expenditures, that were based on (and prescribed) the standards of living to which "normal" Japanese should be assimilated. Thus, by 1930, surveys and maps produced by the Tokyo City Social Bureau and Tokyo Prefecture Social Section represented the capital's inner wards and surrounding districts in terms of the distribution of "households in need of protection" (*yōhogosha setai*), while areas of concentrated poverty were identified primarily by their architectural and infrastructural shortcomings as "inadequate residential areas" (*furyō jūtakuchi*).[36]

Nonetheless, the slum reportage, in article or book form, continued to capture the imagination of the Japanese public. Perhaps the most important of these texts to appear in the post–World War I years was *Shisen o koete*

(Across the Death-Line [1920]), the lightly fictionalized account by Protestant social reformer Kagawa Toyohiko of his upbringing and decade of life and work among the poor in Kobe's Shinkawa slum. Kagawa's story was an immense success, selling over one hundred thousand copies in its first three months, going through dozens of printings in its first few years, and being reissued numerous times throughout the decade. While Kagawa's literary style was justly criticized as amateurish, he presented some extremely powerful images that may well have come to the minds of many readers when they later encountered news reports of Iwanosaka or other cases. For example:

> Marui and his family of six persons lived in a room nine feet by six in Azuma-dori. The other room in the house, of six feet square, was occupied by his sister and her two children. The adopted child that had died was only three months old and, of course, was not yet weaned. They had no money to buy milk, however, and as they had to feed it on rice-gruel and rice-water it had died. The body was laid on a dirty, hired quilt and was covered with the soiled woollen kimono that had been given with the baby. Eiichi [the Kagawa character] lifted the kimono and looked at the baby's face. The sight of it gave him an inexpressible horror. Its eyes were sunk in its head and bloodshot, its cheeks fallen in, and its hands dried up like leaves on a withered bough. Eiichi inquired into the circumstances and learnt that the man's sister had been dazzled by the offer of five yen if she would adopt the baby, and had taken the money, since she was very poor, although she knew it meant the murder of the child.

In another passage, Kagawa described a slum dweller who, in addition to acting as a pimp for his wife, "adopts a child and kills it, adopts a child and kills it, and then each time he moves 'cause he's too ashamed to stop in the neighbourhood." He also offered readers the image of Tsuta, "an ugly woman who got her living chiefly by going out begging every day with two babies hanging around her, one in front and one behind"; one of these babies was borrowed from the neighborhood, and the other, which died, had been adopted for a fee. In general, the people of this slum were seen to "live on adopted children."[37]

A large number of Kagawa's readers appear to have been women, many of whom were from the middle class or aspired to membership in this social stratum and who in the interwar years often conceived of their reading practices as a form of self-cultivation (shūyō) designed to prepare them for married life.[38] Evidently, vicariously experiencing Kagawa's repeated shocks and traumas constituted a welcome element in training the sensibilities of respectable Japanese women. Women's mass-circulation magazines also published information on the Iwanosaka case that other outlets did not: in particular, *Fujin saron* (a new magazine fighting for a share of the market) offered not only graphic details on the death of baby Kikujirō but also Ogawa Kiku's own account of her upbringing, sale into prostitution, turn toward drift and mendicancy, debilitation from venereal disease, descent into the slums, and involvement in the practice of baby farming.[39] It was also in women's magazines that one found statements such as Ōhara Makoto's claim that what marked the Iwanosaka case was the fact that "women who as village housewives controlled their kitchens" were committing murder on the side. The attempt to fit female day laborers and beggars into the recently invented category of housewife, and their tenement and flophouse living arrangements into cultural forms centered around the kitchen, may itself appear somewhat awkward, but it highlights the ways in which this case was constructed as a conspiracy against the norms of modern womanhood and family life to which readers of these magazines were expected to conform.[40]

Hence, by the end of the 1920s, as the reconstruction of the imperial capital approached its triumphal conclusion, the slums of Tokyo (like the slums of other Japanese cities) had been not eradicated but displaced toward the ever-expanding periphery and, like the sentiments of revulsion and curiosity that they produced, rendered indispensable to the discursive mapping of the modern urban experience. As both *Shinpan Dai Tōkyō annai* (The New Guide to Great Tokyo [1929]), a mass-circulation compendium edited by the reputed "modernologist" Kon Wajirō, and the volume on Great Tokyo in the more academic or quasi-official *Nihon chiri taikei* (Outline of Japanese Geography [1930]) demonstrate, readers seeking to understand the capital in its totality would have been considered unable to do so without at least some exposure to the photographs, tables, graphs, lists of sundry occupations, and narrative accounts that constituted the slums and their inhabitants.[41] And in the latter volume, published, coincidentally, only days after the death of baby Kikujirō was reported, Iwanosaka itself appeared as one of the most important slums of the day.

Slum Topographers and the Petty Bourgeois Uncanny

The mapping of Iwanosaka took place in the midst of what one official called the "murderous depression" that affected the general Tokyo population during the late 1920s and early 1930s. Although no reliable statistics exist, scholars estimate that urban unemployment nationwide exceeded 20 percent and may have risen as high as 30 percent during the depression years. Surveys conducted in 1929 and 1930 by Tokyo authorities indicate that Iwanosaka was in one of the hardest-hit parts of the capital: it was located in Kita Toyoshima, within a district known as Itabashi-chō; here, more than 18 percent of the roughly 45,000 inhabitants were identified as in need of assistance.[42]

Those involved in the exploration of Iwanosaka were themselves highly sensitive to the pervasive instabilities of everyday life. To Mori Jirō, writing in the July 1930 issue of the magazine of the Japanese settler community in Korea, slum dwellers in Iwanosaka were so desperate that they debated with themselves "whether to do something to get themselves thrown in prison, or to commit suicide, or to 'rise up in the world' and become a beggar"; under these conditions, the appeal of taking in an infant for ten yen became, understandably, irresistible and the consequences equally foreseeable. To Mori, Iwanosaka was above all a space of death. A local physician informed him that two hundred children had died of various causes since 1926 and that three hundred children currently in the neighborhood had been received from elsewhere: "Young children are playing without a care in the world in the alleys by the sinister tenements. Predictably, the six- or seven-year-olds have nursing infants strapped to their backs. It is a tragedy beyond words to witness this scene of carefree play by those who were lucky enough, one in ten, to reach the age of six or seven and those who are fated to be smothered to death in their infancy." The future was far from promising for those who survived the early years, he continued, as they would soon learn—from their parents—to be beggars' helpers or criminals, and then be sold off into slave-like mining gangs in Hokkaidō (for boys) or into silk mills and then again into unlicensed brothels (for girls). Contrasting Iwanosaka with the thriving theaters and department stores of the metropolis, Mori noted that he had seen "two Tokyos that are too far apart," and posed the same question that Iwanosaka's denizens posed: What in the world will happen? "Of course, I didn't know what would happen. But incredibly, whereas a couple of years ago I would have imagined that the problem would somehow take care of itself, now that thought did not occur to me. This was because now, before my eyes, I felt I could see a frightful, oppressive future on the verge of exploding."[43]

While Mori appears to have maintained some psychological and material distance from the scenes he observed (for example, he reported giving a small gift of money to one desperate family), other investigators may well have seen in this neighborhood an uncanny reflection of their own personal anxieties. As Anthony Vidler has suggested, the uncanny is "a frame of reference that confronts the desire for a home and the struggle for domestic security with its apparent opposite, intellectual and actual homelessness."[44] Clearly, this operation is apparent in the impressions recorded in the June 1930 issue of *Shakai fukuri* (Social Welfare) by Kurosawa Takenari, who had been hired by the Tokyo Prefecture Social Section to survey the neighborhood the preceding March, shortly before the child murder cases reached the public's attention (readers of his report, however, would have been fully aware of the case). As part of a series of articles titled "Jissai tanpō: Fukeiki fudoki" (Actual Explorations: Topographies of Hard Times), Kurosawa recounted his unsettling journey through a maze of ramshackle tenements and flophouses where "parents and children, old and young cling together, simply prolonging their existence."[45] In one four-and-a-half mat tenement flat with a broken glass door and an entry crammed with bits of rubber for repairing footwear, a man with long, unkempt hair complained to the reporter about his difficulties finding work and feeding his family, while his wife picked lice off their daughter's clothes and put them into her mouth; whether she was eating them or spitting them out was not clear, but "she showed no sign of stopping." Next door, an out-of-work bamboo craftsman with a bad leg and his wife related their struggle to survive and feed their child by peddling roasted beans, while Kurosawa noted that "from the adjoining flat I could hear the sounds of a baby wailing as if on fire while its mother struck it with the flat of her hand; and from just outside a foul stench arose from the toilet shared by the residents of these twelve flats." Many of the inhabitants had worked in trades rendered obsolete by new technologies—"tubmakers oppressed by metal washbasins, rickshaw pullers losing out to taxis and buses, and pallbearers made unemployed by automobiles." Other able-bodied workers, devastated by a lack of jobs, sought livelihoods as scrap collectors; but because the scrap business itself had stagnated, the rapid increase in collectors in Iwanosaka (more than one hundred, according to a local wholesaler) led to a dangerous drop in income for each.

Kurosawa's exploration led him deeper into the world of beggars: a back-alley tenement known as Tarō nagaya, where able-bodied men all pretended to have jobs, but "I have never seen anyone actually go to work." Progressing further into the darkness, he peered into the smoke-filled, filthy room of an "Amida worshiper" beggar (like Ogawa Kiku)—"a man with hair grown long like wild grass on his head, and a seven-year-old boy making a fire over a dirty portable stove"—who had settled in the slum after several years of drift in the countryside. "The room was in an unspeakable condition." Going even further through the "tunnel" tenement to its rear, he found, in a "deformed" (*hentaiteki*) section, a group of beggars known as *kenta*, whose occupation involved striking their heads on the ground and wailing pitifully. These beggars' livelihoods depended on their ability to flaunt either a physical disability or a pitiable child, which they rented from a pool of children raised for this purpose. In the case of one family he visited, the forty-six-year-old father put his son out to beg and denied him food or the chance to go to school if he did not earn enough. This father, who was sufficiently well-off to have purchased new bedding and mulberry tea cabinets for their rather spacious flat, argued without remorse (and "with a trace of alcohol on his breath") that an adult male could not earn enough to support his family: "If I let my old lady and the kids do it, they'll make [two or three times what I could.]" Of the family's five children, the oldest, a girl of fifteen, had already been sold into a geisha house (brothel) in Nagano Prefecture.

Like Mori or the cartoonist Yazaki, Kurosawa contrasted the plight of Iwanosaka's denizens, and the victims of economic dislocations more broadly, with the spectacular consumerism that filled the showcases of the modern metropolis: "Citizens are inebriated with joy as the imperial capital has been reconstructed after the earthquake conflagration. But while the great department stores, theaters, and splendidly arrayed avenues take in and disgorge tens of thousands of men and women throughout the day, behind them the flames of unemployment are rising. With flames flying here and there, a sea of fire has already spread." Kurosawa's concerns were far from disinterested, however: in fact, he was one of several hundred unemployed "low-income salaried workers" hired by Tokyo government agencies as part of their program of relief for the educated classes.[46] In this light, Kurosawa's meditation on street entertainers practicing their *nagauta* songs in an Iwanosaka tenement is quite revealing: "This is how these people prepare to pursue the new occupation to which they have been led after failing to secure a sacred livelihood in a sacred land. When reflecting on this, one cannot simply write it off it as an example to be avoided." Equally suggestive is Kurosawa's account of his having followed one beggar out of the neighborhood. This man left his lodgings neatly dressed in a kimono and *haori* jacket, took a bus to a stop near the grounds of a popular temple, and walked to the cemetery, where he changed into rags, reemerged into the crowd, and began pressing his forehead against the ground to attract almsgivers. At sixty-seven, this man was one of Iwanosaka's most skilled beggars, and he now lived "an easy life, heedless of the depression." Having confronted the ghastly misery from which he feared he was barely separated, Kurosawa may now have seen in this beggar a distorted or mocking version of the commuting salaryman—whose own everyday existence, as depicted in countless stories, involved kowtowing for a living—who lived free of the worries that people like him faced. (Indeed, in *Shinpan Dai Tōkyō annai*, one contributor had written that "In Shimura, on the northern edge of Itabashi-chō, there is a famous hamlet of beggars, whose boss leads a life of luxury that the petty bourgeoisie could never even hope to approach.")[47]

Some of Kurosawa's colleagues wrote more bluntly about their positions. In an article in the same journal, Hyōdō Fumitomo recalled walking the city's streets "like a stray dog" looking for work before finally being hired by the Prefecture Social Section: "How ironic that I, who am at present in a condition that should be inscribed onto [social survey] cards, could be rescued by means of [conducting] a survey of the card class [i.e., the lower classes]!"[48]

Confronted by the ambiguity of their positions on this social map, some investigators endeavored rhetorically to situate themselves more firmly on the side of orthodox morality, while others looked to Marxism and the awakening of the oppressed classes in the slums (although perhaps not the most lumpen elements) as the solution to their own problems.[49] In either case, their experiences resonated far beyond the social work community. Indeed, in April 1930, the popular economics and current affairs magazine *Sarariiman* (Salaryman) published a fictionalized reportage, in the style of proletarian literature, about one such white-collar recipient of unemployment assistance (the article was dedicated to Tokyo mayor Horikiri). The protagonist, Nakamura Shōsuke, lost his job because he took time off to attend the funeral of a prominent left-wing politician who had been assassinated by rightists. He has five children, his rent is in arrears, he has to pawn his children's clothes to get his own Western suit out of hock, and his wife is unable to nurse their youngest child due to lack of nourishment. He lacks money for lunch each day and, although it is winter, he has no overcoat. Assigned to survey households in need of assistance, he inscribes the first card with the details of his own family. Later assigned to work late at a settlement house (writing New Year's greeting cards for a local politician), he misses the last train home and must spend the night as a virtual vagrant, seeking shelter from the icy rain. Shōsuke's efforts to organize his peers to press for systematic unemployment relief also fail, leading to his further disillusionment and dismissal. At the story's end, "There was no rice in his kitchen, and of course there was no money. Behind him, Shōsuke's wife and five children were on the verge of starvation."[50] What Kurosawa described as a world where "parents and children . . . cling together, simply prolonging their existence," could not be contained within the space of the slum but stood for a more generalized experience or fear of hardship and social demise—Vidler's "intellectual and actual homelessness"—which may have struck the petty bourgeoisie with particular psychological force in the depression era.

Containing and Imagining Transgression

The media image of the poor salaryman, burdened by several children, reminds us that the Tokyo/Japan in which this case and others like it unfolded was one in which the pro-natalist state had criminalized abortion and sought with increasing vigor to limit access to birth control in the name of national strength and public morality, as well as a perceived need to safeguard women's bodies.[51] Awareness of this context is crucial to any consideration of the desires that may have run through people's minds as they perused accounts of Iwanosaka or other cases of this nature. For example, in his 1928 novella "Aru jisatsu kaikyūsha" (A Member of the Suicide Class), the modernist writer Asahara Rokurō (himself an erstwhile salaryman) offered the following conversation between two office workers:

> K. suddenly exploded in a long, off-key laugh: "Ah ha ha ha ha...
> "You know, my wife is pregnant again. This is my turning corner. Please don't laugh."
> "Is that so? That's . . ."
> "Exactly. 'Is that so? That's . . ?' But nobody knows how to complete the sentence. . . ."
> I couldn't bear K's self-ridicule (*jichō*) worming its way into my emotions.[52]

K's despair over the hopelessness of salaryman existence is compounded by his wife's repeated pregnancies and ultimately drives him to suicide. But for other members of the city's struggling middle and working classes, the possibility of giving away one's unwanted infant, even if doing so meant tacit complicity in its death, may have been a preferable alternative. (Baby Kikujirō, as noted earlier, was the fifth child of an unemployed office building watchman and his wife; while their class position might be debated, their actual living conditions would most likely have differed little from those of an unemployed, low-level, white-collar worker's family.) And reading about a place in the city or on its fringes to which unwanted children could be dispatched, about midwives as intermediaries, about communication through newspaper ads, and about other aspects of these cases may have allowed men and women to imagine it as an impersonal transaction, with the consequences unquestioned and identities and consciences protected by the anonymity of the metropolis.

The police and the media worked hard to block these avenues and impose social and moral sanctions on transgressors. For example, while some midwives may have helped their clients give away their infants out of actual concern for their hardships, the daily press treated all of them as evil parasites who, like abortionists, used innuendo-filled newspaper ads to attract vulnerable women and to profit handsomely from their misfortune. The Metropolitan Police Department, meanwhile, launched an investigation of birthing clinics in Tokyo in July 1930, stripping the licenses of thirty-seven that were deemed "inappropriate."[53] And while news stories like the above-mentioned "Yo wa mujō" (The World Is Heartless) emphasized the pitiful plight of single mothers of illegitimate infants, and social work agencies stepped up their efforts to protect these women, other texts served to sanction those who strayed from their prescribed paths. Kikujirō's birth mother, Murai Kō, first appeared in the press accounts as a woman devastated by the death of her child, weeping over the corpse and saying, "I believed he was with a good family; when I see his face and that of the devil nun [Ogawa Kiku], I feel as if I have been killed as well." Yet according to an account in *Fujin kōron*, when asked to take home the baby's remains, Kō apparently demurred, stating that since the baby had been given to someone else, that party should be responsible for the burial. Kō was thus transformed in the media's eyes from an aggrieved mother to a "heartless" (*mujō*) one—now described, for example, as dressed and made up like a mistress at a house of assignation. News reports of the trial of Ogawa Kiku also emphasized that Kō had given up her baby "as one would give away a dog or cat." Meanwhile, editorialists for the conservative magazine *Nihon oyobi Nihonjin* (Japan and the Japanese) used the infant deaths at Iwanosaka and in other cases, along with reports of illegal abortions, to decry the utter degradation of sexual morality among Japan's middle and upper classes.[54]

Yet while media sanctions may have generated a certain disciplinary effect, a very different type of response to the reporting on these and other *faits divers* was also possible. "The hearer of a *fait divers*," writes literary scholar Sophie Beaulé, "becomes aware of a chasm at the edge of the normal, the chasm of the abnormal. . . . Crucially important, moreover, is that the hearer finds that he himself, psychologically or emotionally, is at the edge of this chasm, poised to fall in. . . . [H]e realizes that he too could just as easily be consumed by the chasm he confronts. The *fait divers* is told in the news in such a way as to heighten these emotions of fear and anxiety." Drawing on the work of Georges Auclair, Beaulé observes that the *fait divers* nurtures fear of the violence repressed within us, "our instinct for death, murder, and destruction." Moreover, "The virulence of our aggressivity is reinforced, in contemporary society, by the constant oscillation between the mythology of happiness, along with its stereotyped individual realization, and the fact or fear of violence, disorder, and death."[55] Could female readers of the Iwanosaka stories have seen in Ogawa Kiku or Fukuda Hatsu distorted versions of themselves, which they risked or feared becoming? Could they have imagined a transgressive pleasure in the act of killing infants, who played such an important symbolic role in discourses on personal and national health and happiness? And, going beyond the Iwanosaka case, how might male readers have responded to the front-page story of Nakajima Ihachirō, who was arrested in June 1930 following the discovery of seven infant corpses he had placed in two pieces of luggage deposited at Shinjuku Station? A college graduate and former colonial policeman, Nakajima had moved to Tokyo and, posing as a gentleman seeking to adopt a child, gained access to midwives and parents from whom he received child support money along with his victims.[56] The petty-bourgeois failure turned drifter, Nakajima was also a warped version of the striving entrepreneur, another topic of contemporary salaryman fiction and white-collar media discourse more broadly. If the detective and the criminal were separated by only a hair's breadth, as the crime novelist Edogawa Ranpo observed, what of the consumer of crime stories and the criminal? The *fait divers*, so central to the representation of urban experience in the modern era, could permit readers to envision themselves as transgressors, to enjoy scenes of others' misfortune, or to skirt the world of misery, while maintaining a safe "distance between them and the event itself."[57]

In 1936, veteran social worker Kusama Yasoo published *Donzoko no hito-tachi* (People of the Lower Depths), in which he described the inhabitants of Iwanosaka in terms of their hunger and lack of sexual vitality. He noted that in Iwanosaka, unlike other lower-class neighborhoods, unlicensed street prostitutes did not ply their trade because while the local men might be driven to anxiety by their digestive systems, they lacked the instinctive energy required to arouse their sexual organs. They were, to Kusama, "like sloughed off skins" (*nukegara*).[58] In the same year, the Itabashi Ward Office published a study titled *Tokushoku aru hinmin buraku Itabashi-ku Iwanosaka* (Iwanosaka: A Slum Neighborhood with Particular Characteristics), which, in an effort to mitigate the area's notoriety, argued that the slum residents "lead a surprisingly peaceful, charming social life," relatively free from the problems of itinerancy, crime, and suicide. Describing the residents as "good workers living lives of utter defeat as the lowest class of society without any dissatisfaction or resentment," the author suggested that Iwanosaka revealed the warm human feelings of the sort one would find in communities in the provinces.[59] Despite their strikingly different nuances, both texts emphasized the character of Iwanosaka as a place of sedimentation, where the detritus of modern society found its final abode. And these texts constitute the general endpoint of the representation of Iwanosaka within contemporary discourses on the modern metropolis. Long before this time, the daily press and popular magazines had moved on to other *faits divers* and sensational stories, of which the city provided an endless supply. And beyond this point, with the outbreak of war against China in 1937, social work programs and discourse would shift away from the destitute and decrepit toward an emphasis on promoting the health of the "human resources" who could serve the nation as factory workers, soldiers, or mothers of the next generation of Japanese subjects.

These various forms of representation, as this essay has suggested, had combined to produce in the Iwanosaka case a set of images that both shocked the sensibilities of readers and investigators and were necessary to their understanding of themselves as part of a modern metropolitan social formation. They reinforced the sense, common to many interpretations of the modern condition, that modernity was best apprehended through contrasts—between, for example, utopian promise and dystopian reality—or in terms of dark mysteries concealed beneath the surface of social relationships, and that the modern (urban) subject was compelled to navigate anxiously between these two positions, ever unsure as to which was the "truth" or in which direction he/she was being led. Yet while it is possible to analyze the sources discussed in this essay in terms of a history of representations (or psychology), the point remains that many participants in the discourse on Iwanosaka and related matters sought to expose and ameliorate what they perceived to be real, intolerable social conditions; from this perspective, their interventions provide crucial material for a social history of the tangible experiences of inequality and oppression that indeed characterized the everyday life of Tokyo and, more broadly, imperial Japan. (Nonetheless, because they were produced primarily by middle-class authors for middle-class audiences, these texts offer little if any opportunity to hear the unmediated voices of those under investigation—the inhabitants of Iwanosaka, for example—to whom the metropolis no doubt looked and felt remarkably different.)[60] The two approaches cannot, of course, be disentangled, nor can the tension between them necessarily be reconciled. And perhaps unease with these tensions, with the "traffic between urban fabric, representation and imagination," is as fundamental to the study of urban modernity as the above-noted contrasts were to its contemporary manifestations.

In the decades following the Iwanosaka case, mobilization for total war, the destruction by bombardment of Tokyo (and sixty-five other cities), and the reconstruction and rapid economic growth that eventually ensued all contributed to a radical reconstitution of metropolitan space, the urban population, and the experiences of urban life for a Japan that was increasingly standardized in its living patterns. Yet throughout these decades, the "general mobilization of journalism" and "the actions of the printed word," along with those of ever proliferating technologies of communication and representation, continued to encourage urbanites to imagine their environment in terms of a rapid succession of sensations and of contrasts between normalized ideals of happiness and episodes of indescribable horror, presented in the most lurid terms (which may nonetheless exercise a disturbing attraction). Iwanosaka, as a physical location, faded from the map of Tokyo in the course of the wartime and immediate postwar years; in subsequent decades it survived mainly in a handful of "true crime" histories or as a reference point on timelines of the depression era.[61] Yet as Japan's postwar social contracts have come under increasing stress in recent years, as governments confront anew the problem of how to deal with unwanted infants (despite the legality of abortion), and as the specter of unemployment and homelessness again hovers on the edges of salaryman consciousness, one may find the city, "real" or imagined, becoming home to tales of darkness that reverberate with the history of Iwanosaka.

Notes

I would like to thank Gyan Prakash, David Gilmartin, Steven Vincent, and the participants in the Urban Dystopias conference for their helpful comments on various versions of this paper.

1 Horikiri Zenjirō, "Teito fukkōsai o mukaete," in *Nihon chiri taikei*, vol. 3, *Dai Tōkyō hen*, ed. Yamamoto Mitsuo et al. (Tokyo: Kaizōsha, 1930), 465.

2 Population figures from Tōyō Keizai Shinpōsha, ed., *Meiji Taishō kokusei sōran* (Tokyo: Tōyō Keizai Shinpōsha, 1975), 637; Tōyō Keizai Shinpōsha, ed., *Kanketsu Shōwa kokusei sōran* (Tokyo: Tōyō Keizai Shinpōsha, 1991), 1:33–35. On urban growth and architectural developments before and in the wake of the earthquake, see Jordan Sand, *House and Home in Modern Japan: Architecture, Domestic Space, and Bourgeois Culture, 1880–1930* (Cambridge, MA: Harvard University Asia Center, 2003); and Koshizawa Akira, *Tōkyō no toshi keikaku* (Tokyo: Iwanami Shoten, 1991). For general histories of Tokyo in this period, see Edward Seidensticker, *Low City, High City: Tokyo from Edo to the Earthquake* (New York: Knopf, 1983) and *Tokyo Rising: The City since the Great Earthquake* (New York: Knopf, 1990); and Ishizuka Hiromichi and Narita Ryūichi, *Tokyo-to no hyakunen* (Tokyo: Yamakawa Shuppansha, 1986).

3 Harry Harootunian, *Overcome by Modernity: History, Culture, and Community in Interwar Japan* (Princeton: Princeton University Press, 2000), 13. Tanizaki's novel *Chijin no ai* appears in English as Junichiro Tanizaki, *Naomi*, trans. Anthony Chambers (New York: Vintage International, 2001); the reference to Pickford and Sennett appears on p. 28. On the modern girl, see also Barbara Sato, *The New Japanese Woman: Modernity, Media, and Women in Interwar Japan* (Durham: Duke University Press, 2003); and Miriam Silverberg, "The Modern Girl as Militant," in *Recreating Japanese Women, 1600–1945*, ed. Gail Bernstein (Berkeley: University of California Press, 1991), 239–66. Historian Narita Ryūichi has referred to the 1920s as an era of the "overflourishing of sexuality" in Japan. Narita Ryūichi, "Sei no chōryō: 1920 nendai no sekushuariti," in *Jendā no Nihonshi*, vol. 1, *Shūkyō to minzoku, shintai to seiai*, ed. Wakita Haruko and S. B. Hanley (Tokyo: Tokyo Daigaku Shuppankai, 1994), esp. 541–60.

4 See, for example, Andrew Gordon, *Labor and Imperial Democracy in Prewar Japan* (Berkeley: University of California Press, 1991).

5 Ōya Sōichi, "Shūshokunan to chishiki kaikyū no kōsokuteki botsuraku," *Chūō kōron*, March 1929. See also Aono Suekichi, *Sarariiman kyōfu jidai* (Tokyo: Senshinsha, 1930); this text is discussed in Harootunian, *Overcome by Modernity*, chapter 4.

6 James Donald, *Imagining the Modern City* (Minneapolis: University of Minnesota Press, 1999), 10. On simultaneity, see, among others, Yoshimi Shunya, "Sōsetsu: Teito Tōkyō to modanitii no bunka seiji," in *Kakudai suru modanitii*, vol. 6 of

Iwanami kōza kindai Nihon no bunkashi, ed. Yoshimi Shunya (Tokyo: Iwanami Shoten, 2002), esp. 47–57; Harootunian, *Overcome by Modernity*; Sand, *House and Home*; and Gennifer Weisenfeld, *MAVO: Japanese Artists and the Avant-Garde, 1905–1931* (Berkeley: University of California Press, 2001).

7   Peter Fritzsche, *Reading Berlin, 1900* (Cambridge, MA: Harvard University Press, 1996), 9–10.

8   Deborah S. Reisinger, "Murder and Banality in the Contemporary Fait Divers," *South Central Review* 17.4 (2000): 85; Donald, *Imagining the Modern City*, 71; Poe's "pleasurable pain" is quoted in James Hevia, "Leaving a Brand on China: Missionary Discourse in the Wake of the Boxer Movement," in *Formations of Colonial Modernity in East Asia*, ed. Tani E. Barlow (Durham: Duke University Press, 1997), 116. For a recent discussion of the relationship between the fashion of "hunting for the strange" (*ryōki*) and the transgressive aspects of urban life, see Jeffrey Angles, "Seeking the Strange: Ryōki and the Navigation of Normality in Interwar Japan," *Monumenta Nipponica* 63.1 (2008): 101–41. On the uncanny, see Nicholas Royle, *The Uncanny: An Introduction* (Manchester: Manchester University Press, 2003).

9   "Eijigoroshi no zangeki o hete ichinen: Iwanosaka buraku o ika ni subeki ka?" *Fujin saron* 3.4 (April 1931): 224.

10 The sources I am using to reconstruct this case are the following: various articles in the *Tōkyō Asahi shimbun* (hereafter TAS), the *Tōkyō Nichinichi shimbun*, and the *Yomiuri shimbun*; Ōhara Makoto, "Moraikogoroshi no shinsō," *Fujin saron* 2.6 (June 1930): 48–55; Fuyuki Reinosuke, "Iwanosaka satsujin buraku no tanpō," *Fujin kōron* 15.6 (June 1930): 147–50; and Takatomo Masakatsu, "Teito ankoku Iwanosaka no jissō," *Fujin saron* 3.4 (April 1931): 224–32.

11 TAS, April 14, 1930; *Tōkyō Nichinichi*, April 20, 1930, evening, p. 2; *Yomiuri shimbun*, June 9, 1930, evening, p. 2; and Takatomo, "Teito ankoku Iwanosaka no jissō."

12 For a discussion of the difficulties in proving infanticide in other countries, see, for example, Sherri Broder, "Child Care or Child Neglect?: Baby Farming in Late-Nineteenth-Century Philadelphia," *Gender and Society* 2.2 (June 1988): 129–48; and Shurlee Swain and Renate Howe, *Single Mothers and Their Children: Disposal, Punishment and Survival in Australia* (Cambridge: Cambridge University Press, 1995).

13 Ōhara, "Moraikogoroshi no shinsō," 50.

14 Several of those arrested were fined for filing false information on official documents. On cultural scripts in infanticide cases, see Swain and Howe, *Single Mothers and Their Children*.

15 *Tōkyo Nichinichi*, April 19, 1930, evening, p. 7.

16 Fuyuki, "Iwanosaka satsujin buraku no tanpō," 148.

17 On the Law for the Prevention of Cruelty to Children, see, for example, Yasuoka Norihiko, *Kindai Tōkyō no kasō shakai: Shakai jigyō no tenkai* (Tokyo: Akashi Shoten, 1999), 113–36. For a recent study of the erotic grotesque nonsense moment, see Miriam Silverberg, *Erotic Grotesque Nonsense: The Mass Culture of Japanese Modern Times* (Berkeley: University of California Press, 2007).

18 Narita Ryūichi, *Kindai toshi kūkan no bunka keiken* (Tokyo: Iwanami Shoten, 2003), esp. chapter 2. On newspapers and national communities, see Benedict

R. O'G. Anderson, *Imagined Communities: Reflections on the Origin and Spread of Nationalism* (New York: Verso, 1993). Fritzsche, *Reading Berlin*, discusses this process/effect specifically with regard to the creation of an urban public.

19   TAS, July 5, 1927, morning, p. 11; February 4, 1928, morning, p. 7; March 27, 1928, morning, p. 11; July 4, 1928, morning, p. 7; June 1–3, 1930; and July 3, 1930.

20   Samuel L. Leiter and James R. Brandon, introduction to *Kabuki Plays on Stage*, vol. 3, *Darkness and Desire, 1804–1864*, ed. Samuel L. Leiter and James R. Brandon (Honolulu: University of Hawaii Press, 2002), 1.

21   Yamada Shunji, *Taishū shinbun ga tsukuru Meiji no "Nihon"* (Tokyo: NHK Bukkusu, 2002), 172–84.

22   *Yomiuri shimbun*, January 22, 1930, p. 3.

23   This figure is drawn from the rough figures included in Yomiuri shimbun 100 nenshi Henshū Iinkai, ed., *Yomiuri shimbun 100 nenshi* (Tokyo: Yomiuri shimbun 100 nenshi Henshū Iinkai, 1976), 317–19, 331, 336, 342. The percentage of each paper's circulation comprised by regional editions is not clear. In the case of the *Yomiuri shimbun*, roughly one-third of the issues were distributed in the prefectures adjoining Tokyo (in the Kantō region and Shizuoka Prefecture).

24   Unno Hiroshi, *Modan toshi Tōkyō* (Tokyo: Chūō Kōronsha, 1983), 183.

25   Donald, *Imagining the Modern City*, 70. See also Harootunian, *Overcome by Modernity*, 116–18, which draws on the writing of Marxist critic Hirabayashi Hatsunosuke; and Unno, *Modan toshi Tōkyō*, 173–92, which analyzes the detective novelist Edogawa Ranpo in relation to the constitution of readership and urban space.

26   TAS, April 15, 1930, morning, p. 7.

27   Fritzsche, *Reading Berlin*, 135–37.

28   This advertisement appeared in TAS, April 17, 1930.

29   TAS, April 16, 1930, morning, p. 3. For the survey of children in the charge of beggars, see Tōkyō Shiyakusho, *Jidō renkō no kojiki ni kansuru chōsa* (Tokyo: Tōkyō Shiyakusho, 1929), reproduced in Isomura Eiichi, ed., *Toshi kasō minshū seikatsu jittai shiryō shūsei II: Kusama Yasoo 1927–1937 nen chōsa* (Tokyo: Akashi Shoten, 1993).

30   Maeda Ai, "Utopia of the Prisonhouse: A Reading of *In Darkest Tokyo*," trans. Seiji M. Lippit and James A. Fujii, in Maeda Ai, *Text and the City: Essays on Japanese Modernity*, ed. James A. Fujii (Durham: Duke University Press, 2004), 44–53, passage quoted on 44; see also Narita, *Kindai toshi kūkan no bunka keiken*, 10–12, 80–111. For Matsubara's text, see Matsubara Iwao, *Saiankoku no Tōkyō* (1893; Tokyo: Iwanami Shoten, 1992). For examples of early reportages, see Nakagawa Kiyoshi, ed., *Meiji Tōkyō kasō seikatsushi* (Tokyo: Iwanami Shoten, 1994).

31   Christopher Hill, "The Body in Naturalist Literature and Modern Social Imaginaries," in *Bi jiao shi ye zhong de chuan tong yu xian dai = Tradition and Modernity: Comparative Perspectives*, ed. Kang-i Sun Chang and Hua Meng (Beijing: Beijing University Press, 2007), 350. I have discussed the emergence of the new middle class and conceptions of society or the social in my book *Bad Youth: Juvenile Delinquency and the Politics of Everyday Life in Modern Japan* (Berkeley: University of California Press, 2006), and in "Social Knowledge, Cultural Capital, and the New Middle Class in Japan, 1895–1912," *Journal of Japanese Studies* 24.1 (Winter 1998): 1–33.

32 For the photographs: "Tōkyō shichū yowatarigusa, sono ni," *Fūzoku gahō* 395 (April 1909). By the 1890s, *Fūzoku gahō* boasted a circulation of over 135,000 and reached not only urbanites but also subscribers in distant rural villages. Nagamine Shigetoshi, *Zasshi to dokusha no kindai* (Tokyo: Nihon Editaa Sukuuru Shuppanbu, 1997), 118.

33 See Harada Tōfū, *Kichinyado*, vol. 1 of *Makutsu sōsho* (Tokyo: Daigakkan, 1903); and Murakami Sukesaburō, *Tōkyō no ankoku ki* (Tokyo: Kyōhokusha shuppan, 1912). Murakami's articles had first appeared in the magazines listed.

34 Kawakami Gazan, *Makutsu no Tōkyō* (Tokyo: Kokumin Hyōronsha, 1902); Ishikawa Tengai, *Tōkyō gaku* (Tokyo: Ikuseikai, 1909), esp. 510–41, passage quoted on 541. For Miriam Silverberg's observations, see her "Constructing a New Cultural History of Prewar Japan," in *Japan in the World*, ed. Masao Miyoshi and H. D. Harootunian (Durham: Duke University Press, 1993), passages quoted on 131 and 133. On this book, see also Henry D. Smith, "Tokyo as an Idea: An Exploration of Japanese Urban Thought until 1945," *Journal of Japanese Studies* 4.1 (Winter 1978): 59.

35 For one example of this mode of turn-of-the-century sociological writing, which incorporated Western orthographic symbolism into its title, see Miyake Iwao, *Toshi?* (Tokyo: Kyōkado, 1906). Henry Smith has described the main tendency in thinking about the city from 1895 to 1923 as "the city as problem," with some of its principle manifestations being anti-urbanism, municipal socialism, and bureaucratic reformism. Smith, "Tokyo as an Idea," 57–68.

36 Nakagawa Kiyoshi, "'Hinkon' e no kanshin ga motarashita mono: Kindai no shakai chōsa e no oboegaki," in *Senzen Nihon shakai jigyō chōsa shiryō shūsei*, ed. Shakai Fukushi Chōsa Kenkyūkai (Tokyo: Keisō Shobō, 1995), 3:39–62; Nakagawa Kiyoshi, *Nihon no toshi kasō* (Tokyo: Keisō Shobō, 1986); and Narita, *Kindai toshi kūkan no bunka keiken*, 19–22. On housing categories and surveys, see Iwata Masami, "Kaisetsu: Dai yon kan 'Furōsha, furyō jūtaku chiku' chōsa ni tsuite: Hinkon to 'kyojū' keitai," in *Senzen Nihon shakai jigyō chōsa shiryō shūsei*, 4:26–42, and the surveys reproduced in this volume.

37 Passages are quoted from Kagawa Toyohiko, *Across the Death-Line*, trans. I. Fukomoto and T. Satchell (Kobe: Japan Chronicle Office, 1922), 129–30. For the original, see Kagawa Toyohiko, *Shisen o koete* (Tokyo: Kaizōsha, 1920). On the background to the publication of *Shisen o koete*, see Ban Takezumi, "Kagawa Toyohiko o debyū saseta zasshi *Kaizō* de no rensai," *Yorozu banpō*, http://www.yorozubp.com/0305/030507.htm (accessed October 2, 2007).

38 On women's magazines, reading, and self-cultivation, see Barbara Sato, *The New Japanese Woman: Modernity, Media, and Women in Interwar Japan* (Durham: Duke University Press, 2003); and Maeda Ai, *Kindai dokusha no seiritsu* (Tokyo: Iwanami Shoten, 1993). For evidence of Kagawa's popularity among women readers, see Maeda, *Kindai dokusha no seiritsu*, 269–70, and Nagamine, *Zasshi to dokusha no kindai*, 196–97.

39 Ōhara, "Moraikogoroshi no shinsō," 48–55.

40 Ibid., 48. For a recent study of the development of these cultural norms and forms, see Sand, *House and Home*.

41 Kon Wajirō, ed., *Shinpan Dai Tōkyō annai*, 2 vols. (1929; Tokyo: Chikuma Shobō, 2001), esp. 2:227–57; Yamamoto Mitsuo et al., eds., *Nihon chiri taikei*, vol. 3, *Dai*

Tōkyō hen (Tokyo: Kaizōsha, 1930), 370–80. For a discussion of the experience of lower-class people being pushed into settlements in the most unhygienic parts of the expanding metropolitan area, see Arakawa Motoi, "Mikawashima saimingai no ni, san kei," *Shakai fukuri* 14.9 (September 1930): 88–92.

42 Tōkyō-fu Gakumubu Shakaika, *Yōhogosha ni kansuru chōsa: Tōkyō-fu gogun shakai chōsa* (Tokyo: Tōkyō-fu Gakumubu Shakaika, 1931), reprinted in *Senzen Nihon shakai jigyō chōsa shiryō shūsei*, vol. 2, ed. Shakai Fukushi Chōsa Kenkyūkai (Tokyo: Keisō Shobō, 1988), 121–44. Authorities recognized that the surveys were not exhaustive, due in part to the "migratory nature of classes subject to the survey" (123), as well as to deliberate misinformation provided by some subjects. For the phrase "murderous depression," see Takatomo, "Teito ankoku Iwanosaka no jissō," 225. On the depression, see Andrew Gordon, *A Modern History of Japan: From Tokugawa Times to the Present* (New York: Oxford University Press, 2003), estimate of urban unemployment on 184; also Jack Douglas Downard, "Tokyo: The Depression Years, 1927–1933" (Ph.D. diss., Indiana University, 1976).

43 Mori Jirō, "Iwanosaka buraku o miru: Moraikogoroshi to hinminkutsu," *Chōsen oyobi Manshū* 272 (July 1930): 102–6.

44 Anthony Vidler, *The Architectural Uncanny: Essays in the Modern Unhomely* (Cambridge, MA: MIT Press, 1992), 12. See also Ranjani Mazumdar, "Ruin and the Uncanny City: Memory, Despair, and Death in *Parinda*," in *Sarai Reader 02: The Cities of Everyday Life* (2002): 68–77, http://www.sarai.net/publications/readers/ 02-the-cities-of-everyday-life/05ruin_uncanny.pdf (accessed October 10, 2007).

45 Kurosawa Takenari, "Iwanosaka tanpōki," *Shakai fukuri* 14.6 (June 1930): 67–78. All quotations in the following discussion are from this source.

46 The Tokyo City Social Bureau employed 55 of these individuals to survey households in need of protection within the city wards, and the Tokyo Prefecture Social Section employed 143 to survey households in need of protection in the five districts beyond the city wards. Tōkyō-shi Shakaikyoku, *Tōkyō shinai yōhogosha ni kansuru chōsa* (Tokyo: Tōkyō-shi Shakaikyoku, 1930); and Tōkyō-fu Gakumubu Shakaika, *Yōhogosha ni kansuru chōsa: Tōkyō-fu gogun shakai chōsa* (Tokyo: Tōkyō-fu Gakumubu Shakaika, 1931), both reprinted in *Senzen Nihon shakai jigyō chōsa shiryō shūsei*, 2:107–44.

47 *Shinpan Dai Tokyo annai*, 2:256.

48 Hyōdō Fumitomo, "Ōshima-chō no chōsa o ryō shite," *Shakai fukuri* 14.6 (June 1930): 56–60.

49 For the emphasis on orthodox morality, see Hyōdō, "Ōshima-chō," 59–60; for an example of the Marxist turn, see Hasegawa Shū, "Dai sansōgai no hitobito to kataru," *Shakai fukuri* 14.6 (June 1930): 53–56. For concerns regarding the "irredeemable lumpen character" of day laborers, see Kishi Yamaji, "Tōkyō no iisuto saido," *Kaizō* 12.6 (June 1930): 77.

50 Furuya Kiyoshi, "'Hōkyū seikatsu shitsugyō tōrokusha' no shuki," *Sarariiman* 3.4 (April 1930): 84–87.

51 See, for example, William R. LaFleur, *Liquid Life: Abortion and Buddhism in Japan* (Princeton: Princeton University Press, 1992); Tiana Norgren, *Abortion before Birth Control: The Politics of Reproduction in Postwar Japan* (Princeton: Princeton University Press, 2001), 22–35; and Sabine Frühstück, *Colonizing Sex: Sexology and Social Control in Modern Japan* (Berkeley: University of California Press, 2004).

52 Asahara Rokurō, "Aru jisatsu kaikyūsha" (1928), in *Aru jisatsu kaikyūsha* (Tokyo: Tenjinsha, 1930), 27, reprinted in the series *Gendai bakuro bungaku senshū* (Tokyo: Hon no Tomo Sha, 2000). Along with his stories of the desolation of salarymen's lives, Asahara also wrote about salaryman entrepreneurialism, as well as stories of bourgeois flaneurs pursuing rumors of working women's sex clubs in the office buildings of nocturnal Tokyo. See other stories in *Jisatsu kaikyūsha*, as well as Asahara Rokurō, "Marunouchi no tenjō," in *Modan TOKIO Rondo* (Tokyo: Shunyōdō, 1930), reprinted in *Yoshiyuki Eisuke to sono jidai: Modan toshi no hikari to kage*, ed. Yoshiyuki Kazuko and Saitō Shinji (Tokyo: Tōkyō Shiki Shuppan, 1997), 141–51.

53 TAS, July 5, 1930.

54 On Murai Kō, see Ōhara, "Moraikogoroshi no shinsō," 53. On the trial, see TAS, January 22, 1931, evening, p. 2. For the conservative critique, see "Bakuro sareta sesō no ichi danmen," *Nihon oyobi Nihonjin* 204 (July 1930): 103–5.

55 Sophie Beaulé, "Function and Meaning of the *Fait Divers* in French Detective Fiction," in *Crime Scenes: Detective Narratives in European Culture since 1945*, ed. Anne Mullen and Emer O'Beirne (Amsterdam: Rodopi, 2000), 149–59, passages quoted on 151, 155.

56 TAS, June 1–3, 1930. For another example of this type of case: In 1933, police arrested Kawamata Hatsutarō, a self-proclaimed college graduate and former trading-company employee in Southeast Asia, for the murder of twenty-five infants whose corpses he buried near the grounds of an aristocrat's estate in suburban Meguro. Kawamata told investigators that he had planned to use the child support money he received with each infant to begin a new life in either Hokkaidō or Manchuria. TAS, various issues, March 11, 1933–April 2, 1933.

57 Beaulé, "Function and Meaning of the *Fait Divers* in French Detective Fiction," 155. Edogawa Ranpo is quoted in Unno, *Modan toshi Tōkyō*, 188. In this regard, see also Jeffrey Angles's discussion of the *Ryōki uta* poems (1928–35) of the mystery writer Yumeno Kyūsaku, some of which show "the bloody doppelganger emerging from the subconscious darkness of social repression, but the figure remain[ing] at a remove from the narrator; in the end, they are not one and the same person but two irreconcilable parts of a bifurcated whole." Angles, "Seeking the Strange," 124–25.

58 Kusama Yasoo, *Donzoko no hitotachi* (Tokyo: Genrinsha, 1936), 143, reprinted in Kusama Yasoo, *Kindai kasō minshū seikatsushi I: Hinmingai*, ed. Isomura Eiichi (Tokyo: Akashi Shoten, 1987).

59 Tōkyō-shi Itabashi Kuyakusho, *Tokushoku aru hinmin buraku Itabashi-ku Iwanosaka* (Tokyo: Tōkyō-shi Itabashi Kuyakusho, 1936), 2. In 1932, Tokyo City formally incorporated the five outlying districts as twenty newly configured wards, thereby becoming the world's second largest city in terms of population and fifth in terms of area.

60 For one memoir of a childhood in Iwanosaka, see Koitabashi Jirō, *Furusato wa suramu nariki* (Nagoya: Fūbaisha, 1993). The author was born in 1938.

61 See, for example, Kata Kōji, *Shōwa hanzai shi* (Tokyo: Gendai Shuppankai, 1974).

Chapter 9

■

Living in Dystopia

Past, Present, and Future in Contemporary African Cities

JENNIFER ROBINSON

Fictional dystopias generally portray imaginary places. And yet one of the common strategies of the genre is to create plausible futures, taking the reader from a more or less recognizable present into a future that might be. The principal dynamic for the production of a fictional dystopic "elsewhere," then, is a temporal shift drawing the present into the future.[1] In Western-based urban studies the recent deployment of dystopic narrative forms has merged with decades-old habits of projecting a host of unwanted (if not unimaginable) features of cities onto an "elsewhere," but an elsewhere that has been largely spatially rather than temporally defined. According to the founding fathers of urban studies, cities were to leave behind the folk cultures and practices of sociability and interaction that characterized life in agricultural or pre-industrial communities. These features were also to be found in the present, in "backward" cultures located in contemporaneous but geographically distant elsewheres, largely in poorer, colonized places and imaginatively strongly associated with Africa. Park, Simmel, Benjamin, and Wirth all built urban theory by casting features they declared to be non-urban into the realm of "tribes," "kraals," and "primitives," both spatially (over there) and temporally (back then) elsewhere.[2] For current-day dystopic urban writers, it is once again Africa that carries the burden of imaginative spatial and temporal projection. But now this involves casting (mostly African) poorer cities as the future of all cities. What this means is that according to some of the most prominent urbanists of our time, many millions of people are already living in dystopia.

This essay takes as its starting point this observation: that the deployment of a dystopic narrative structure in contemporary urban studies rests on the assumption that the urban condition in many places is already dystopic. Rather than dystopia being an imaginative place we might arrive at some day depending on the political choices we make, in this genre people are already living there. The essay considers the analytical and political consequences of this dystopic strand of writing about cities. First, I explore the affinities between this style of writing and the colonial practices that have shaped the field of urban studies. Are there some unexamined assumptions at work in this genre that mean some places are too easily cast as dystopic, whereas others become the unnamed standard for a desirable present/future that is in peril? Second, I assess the genre based on the observation that in these analyses dystopia is not an imaginative futuristic elsewhere but an immediate and present geographical elsewhere. In my view this raises a series of very practical and political concerns about the veracity and political effects of these representations of actually existing places. I ask whether the portrayal of certain cities as dystopic is accurate, or reasonable, at the very least because representations of the present shape assessments of possibilities for the future. And so I ask where the "spaces of hope,"[3] if any, are imagined to be located for these lived-in dystopias, and where one might identify lines of escape, alternatives to dystopic presents and futures.

The past, the present, and the future are all at stake, then, in these dystopic representations of our urban world. So I turn, finally, to consider some alternative ways to engage with the complex spatialities of past, present, and future in cities through the lens of the South African post-apartheid urban transition. I reflect on the writings of novelist and proto-urban theorist Ivan Vladislavić. His alternative form of futurism, which we might call an anti-dystopia, draws our attention to the intertwining of past, present, and future in the diverse spaces of the city. Instead of relying on the shock value of dystopias deeply implicated in longstanding negative representations of poorer and especially African cities, it places hopefulness for the future in the creative potential of cities that assemble difference, juxtapose temporalities, and draw connections with many different elsewheres.[4] It is my contention that it is the mundane and often immanent elsewheres of urban practice and the urban imagination that might chart some plausible political pathways from the present to desirable futures. Insofar as dystopic writings subsume these in the noir world of unwanted futures and abandoned presents, they fail to generate materially grounded political imaginations for urban futures.

Dystopia and the Intellectual Burdens of "Third World Cities"

Thus, the cities of the future, rather than being made out of glass and steel as envisioned by earlier generations of urbanists, are instead largely constructed out of crude brick, straw, recycled plastic, cement blocks and scrap wood. Instead of cities of light soaring towards heaven much of the twenty-first century urban world squats in squalor, surrounded by pollution, excrement and decay.[5]

Where are today's cities heading? Mike Davis's contemporary *Planet of Slums* takes a view of the urban future through the experience and likely future growth of what he calls slums. His intervention is important for a number of reasons—not the least of which is that a prominent Western-based urbanist sets out to take seriously the urban crisis facing most of the world[6] rather than being content to assess and predict urban futures based on the narrow experiences of wealthier and prominent cities. The urban future, he suggests, needs to be explored from the point of view of the world's poorest urban citizens, who are also the most rapidly growing segment of the global urban population. His is a critical and angry perspective, characteristic of his wider writing and politics. He sketches an extraordinarily dystopic view of the present state and likely future of the world's cities. Along with some other Western-based writers on cities, he argues that the trajectories of contemporary global capitalism, militarist imperialisms, and an architecture of neoliberal global governance set the parameters for increasing poverty and inequality in cities and render opaque the bases for opposition and potential transformation.

Following Tom Moylan, we could see Davis and others as showing affinity with a new genre of critical dystopian fiction he sees emerging in the 1990s, specifically in response to the resurgence of conservatism, capitalism, and militarism on the global stage.[7] These are dystopian narratives that retain close ties with a utopian impulse in that they are concerned to extend critiques of these developments, even as they seek to identify and imagine possible alternatives to the dominant order. By creating exaggerated, defamiliarizing or satirical but recognizable alternative worlds, *critical dystopias* stir readers to identify the injustices and power relations of the present. They open spaces of possibility for challenging these forms of power, now rendered more recognizable. However, dystopias that tend to pessimism or to closing off any sense of possible paths to an alternative future, Moylan suggests, have more affinity with the skepticism of anti-utopias than with the persistent utopianism that underwrites the narrative structure of critical dystopias.[8] In narrative terms, in an *anti-utopian* text there would be little or no hope of escape from dystopia. I will suggest that in their mobilization of the dystopian genre, new urban dystopian writers have tended toward an anti-utopian perspective. This could ultimately undermine the critical and political rationale for presenting their analyses in this form.

Another analytical lens to borrow from literary discussions of the dystopian genre is introduced by Varsam,[9] who identifies a subcategory of "concrete" dystopic narratives. These draw on specific empirical histories, such as slavery, or contemporary forms of violence and oppression to mark the potential for futures that might repeat or extend these historical episodes. For her, concrete utopias, following Ernst Bloch, draw on actual events in the present, which she sees as always full of latent possibilities for transformation, to portray possible utopian futures. *Concrete dystopias* on the other hand tend to connect the past with the future, building cautionary tales of future possibilities based on actual past experiences, commonly in relation to slavery. The concrete dystopias of contemporary urbanists, however, involve the forward projection of the worst features of the present urban condition, which then operate as a dystopic imaginary designed to provoke political change in the present.

A new genre of urban dystopian writing, hoping to mobilize political opposition to the inequalities and injustices seen in the poverty and living circumstances of many millions of urban (slum) dwellers around the world, is certainly to be welcomed—alongside the many other urgent interventions being proposed to address these issues.[10] The dystopic narrative strategy might well be an effective means to provoke critical responses and stimulate imaginative reactions to what is, by all accounts, a global emergency. However, it also functions to structure the description of the problem in particular ways and to shape, if not constrain, the form of possible responses. In the case of Davis and other contemporary urban dystopian writers, I will argue that the dystopian genre form itself (especially in its anti-utopian version) together with the legacy of dystopian imaginations in the field of urban studies work to circumscribe and potentially to diminish the political impact of these important interventions.

Dystopic readings of cities have been around a long time—they have formed the foundation for urban reform in cities for well over a century. In that sense Baeten is quite correct to argue that dystopic imaginations have frequently provoked utopian interventions in cities.[11] For nineteenth-century British reformers, as well as urban reformers in many different contexts around the world, the depiction of urban life as dystopic served to mobilize sentiment and resources for improvements, most notably for working-class, poor, and often racialized groups. Davis and other contemporary dystopians thus fall in a long line of urban visionaries. However, a significant common thread across these visions and interventions has been the ways in which the differential class and race burdens of urban decline have all too easily tied both dystopic visions and imagined solutions to racialized and hierarchical fantasies of danger and moral disorder.[12] Observers in the UK note how these racialized and class-based dystopias persist in contemporary assessments of urban problems.[13]

For poorer cities that have long been seen as not-quite-urban and certainly not-modern, the ease with which a dystopic fantasy comes to rest on the
features that mark out their differences from wealthier urban contexts is remarkable, if not surprising. Urban studies, after all, has generated a firm analytical narrative that places poorer cities in a different category from wealthier
cities, marked by many of the features of urban decline—economic failure,
rapid cultural change, physical decay, personal danger, environmental degradation—which figure strongly in dystopic urban imaginations. These traditions have their roots in racialized colonial assumptions and the West's self-
identification of its cities as the norm for determining what is modern and
urban. The new dystopic trend in urban studies resonates with these longstanding intellectual habits analytically dividing wealthier from poorer cities
and consequently assessing urbanism in poor contexts on a limited and narrow basis.

Certainly, in the new dystopic urbanism the time chart of urban theory is
flipped from setting urban experiences in places like Africa and South America into the West's past (as traditional, tribal, primitive, racialized) or from insisting that poorer cities' futures are portrayed in the present of wealthier cities. Instead, cities in poorer places now commonly configure anxieties about
the future of urbanization and urban living everywhere. Ironically, then, the
"lack" of development is transfigured from a marker of backwardness into
a vital indicator of the futures that cities everywhere might face. Depleted
infrastructure and "desperate resilience" in the face of economic crisis characterize this noir modernity.[14] As Koolhaas et al. observe in their reflections
on Lagos, "The fact that many of the trends of modern, Western cities can be
seen in hyberbolic guise in Lagos suggests that to write about the African city
is to write about the terminal condition of Chicago, London, or Los Angeles.
It is to examine the city elsewhere, in the developing world. It is to recon-
sider the modern city and to suggest a paradigm for its future."[15] Inverting the
spatialized temporalities associated with conventional ethnocentric views of
modernity casts the contemporary lived experience of urban Africa into the
future as a form of "concrete" dystopia.[16] However, it is not simply the temporal inversion that achieves this new placing of poorer cities in the zone of
a lived dystopia. The urban dystopia genre depends on recounting the characteristic (stereotypical) features of "Third World cities" as indicators of this
futuristic present—features such as extensive poverty, informality, economic
decline, infrastructural decay, and failures of collective provisioning. In assessing the politics of dystopic urbanism, in the following section, I want to
suggest that the temporal and spatial structure of the concrete dystopia genre,
as well as its dependence on a stereotypical representation of the Third World
city, substantially restricts the political potential of the genre.

The Politics of Urban Dystopia

Dystopic urbanisms project slightly different assessments of the politics of this future urban form. For Koolhaas and collaborators the noir character of African or Third World urbanism recedes as thinking through Lagos also stimulates an energy for new imaginations for the use of urban space, the recycling of infrastructure, and the potential of these new forms to encourage more efficient solutions to urban living. No-go areas, traffic congestion, and markets that take over railway lines and freeways become "destinations" for trading and constitute proof of collective resistance to the colonial planners and post-colonial regulators. The wasted land of flyovers and intersections is well used not only for markets but also for production and retail networks stretching to Dubai, Johannesburg, and Nairobi; traffic jams are also markets; rerouted traffic provides opportunities both for criminals and for those living in otherwise marginal places. Taking a closer look at dystopia, it turns out, is an excellent way to gather new ideas about how to draw, photograph, and perhaps plan cities. But there is no concern at all to identify or imagine paths out of dystopia for the people who live there. Whereas some external commentators rail against the colonial and neoliberal origins of urban catastrophe and call for action by the state and capital to address urban shortcomings,[17] Koolhaas et al.'s enthusiasm for the inventiveness of urban life in Lagos, for example, sees them suggest that the apparent problems of circulation or mobility do not need solving, as they have generated a new, exciting mode of urbanism alongside opportunities for markets, sociability, and production.

Mike Davis in contrast actively disavows any sense that the dominant informality of poorer cities or the inventiveness of their citizens holds any promise in the face of the formidable forces that lead, apparently inexorably, to deepening poverty. In his view, in the tracks of colonialism and global capitalism processes of segregation, inequality, exploitation, and neglectful or peremptory forms of rule are producing a planet of slums. Davis sketches a picture of poverty and inequality in poorer cities that is compelling and utterly disturbing, drawing on a body of literature about poorer cities—academic, policy, and popular writing—often ignored in the production of dominant academic understandings of cities. Not only is he popularizing the need for significant levels of action to address urban poverty, he has also insisted that mainstream urban scholarship needs to incorporate the experiences of poorer cities if the future of cities in general is to be understood. But the developmentalism that has kept much of the literature he cites on "Third World cities" separate from that concerned with wealthier and Western cities continues to frame his approach. In my view it also lies at the heart of the strategies he uses to produce what is ultimately a form of textual anti-utopia rather than a critical dystopia preserving a sense of political hopefulness. For the "Third World city" approach (perhaps itself a dystopian genre) tends to neglect the diversity of urban experiences that take place in all cities in favor of a relatively narrow focus on the features that define the development problematic. The poorest areas, most decayed infrastructures, and most extreme experiences of poverty come to stand in for the whole city—and in the dystopic urban genre for the future of all cities—substantially diminishing the opportunities for understanding the global urban condition.[18]

At best, the rest of the city is brought into focus through a dualistic lens. For Davis specifically, the distinctive heritage of colonialism frames cities of polarized extremes, with the very wealthy excluding themselves from city life in elite privatized zones or absorbing what state funding exists for infrastructure, thus abandoning the poor in vast zones with no services and with dire environmental and health consequences. These sketches of the experiences of the poor are not wrong (as far as the experts, scholars, and activists he cites know): the desperate circumstances he documents demand action, urgently, everywhere they are found. But his relentless representation of the urban condition in poor countries through the most extreme examples (and he explicitly seeks the extremes to highlight his argument) reproduces the "Third World city" stereotype. It also has the effect of creating a dystopic narrative. Indeed, the science fiction style of the text is deliberately cultivated by using references to, for example, *Blade Runner*, to describe "off world" lifestyles of the urban wealthy and middle classes in gated communities and security villages. Thus the extreme examples of the real phenomena he describes mount to create an exaggerated and defamiliarizing account of cities, one that challenges and provokes but which, by charting a particular path through the urban experience, creates a textual world that diverges from the complexity and diversity of city life across the globe.

As with fictional dystopias, the production of this dystopic elsewhere is in the interests of forcing the reader to look again and in a new light at phenomena otherwise ignored or taken for granted. In many ways it is a productive strategy. But there are some significant consequences to the choice of dystopic narrative form. In Davis's case the "existential ground zero" he maps out, culminating in his representation of poor cities as a form of "Kurtzian horror,"[19] shocks and might stir readers to action, but it comes with an analytical and political price. Rather than being thought of as part of the range of urban political and economic dynamics that shape many different cities around the world, and that can potentially be changed, the processes at work in shaping urban poverty seem extreme, extraordinary, and, ultimately, in this dystopic view, unmovable.

Poverty and inequality in these cities are interpreted as necessary outcomes of an overweening functionalist and instrumentalist urban system. Actors from states to NGOs, private landlords to global service firms, the World Bank to the middle classes, all seem to work relentlessly and inevitably to the poor's disadvantage. Certainly Davis demonstrates how the power relations of urban processes are severely and cruelly stacked against the poor. Much of the time he draws our attention to processes that are conventionally used to characterize "Third World cities"—corruption, authoritarianism, clientelism, cronyism, and rampant unregulated private investment. But in creating a dystopic environment in which both the causes and outcomes of urban processes are extraordinary and extreme, there is no way of understanding how and why even the best of intentions and interventions might fail to aid the urban poor. Thus Davis portrays a dystopic world where invincible powers foreclose on the very future his critique wants to provoke: there seems to be no identifiable path to the future, as even progressive urban agency is always negated.

In Mike Davis's version of urban dystopia, then, the potential paths toward alternative futures seem to be resolutely blocked. In the wasteland that is the violent showdown he imagines between the forces of empire and the scattered resistance of the urban poor (or whoever is resisting from the shelter of the informal neighborhoods of the urban poor), there really does seem to be no path to the future. He reaches out to the inspiration of past political achievements (organized resistances, revolution) as he hopes that his Marxist understanding of the historical collective agency of the working classes will be matched by that of the informalized urban poor—although he offers little evidence of this in his account. This remains hovering as the only potential source of hope—a question he promises to pursue in a future book. Most unsettling, though, is his argument that the informal sector and informal housing—the majority form of urbanism in most poor cities—offer no solutions to the plight of the urban poor. He presents a range of evidence to suggest that they are in fact actively harmful to survival. What he describes as the "semi-utopian" view of the informal sector is based, he insists, on false assumptions.[20] Rather than a hopeful site for self-employment, self-provisioning, or subsistence, he sees the sector as based on structural-adjustment-induced unemployment, profoundly oversubscribed, reliant on super-exploitation, abuse, life-threatening activities, and child labor, and characterized by pure survivalism, Hobbesian competition, and the destruction of any preexisting bonds of dependence.

The structure of Davis's narrative tends, then, to mirror the skepticism of an anti-utopian form, showing little evidence of the residual utopian impulse that drives the critical dystopian genre. While Koolhaas et al. seem unconcerned with the question of escape from dystopia—so long as it is generative of architectural innovation—Davis seems to foreclose on the possibility of change. The fact of the extraordinary damage caused to millions of people through the economic devastation he outlines is not something to contest.

However, if we are interested in exploring the potential to act toward a different future—indeed, if we want a different future—we need to move beyond Davis's analysis. Given that people live in this all too real (if not concrete) dystopia, it is imperative that we think more carefully about the politics of change.

Both Baeten and Merrifield remind us that the figuring of dystopic futures (and aligning these with particular places or people) can enable creative urban interventions. However, dystopias can also profoundly misrepresent the city, drawing it toward a unitary representation, a singular narrative of the future, and thus limit opportunities for imaginative interventions. In contrast MacLeod and Ward comment on the patchwork of dystopia and utopia shaping the contemporary urban landscape. In stylized form, gated suburban utopias exist alongside revanchist exclusions and enclosures of the urban poor. But even this dualistic imagination misses so much of the mundane diversity and social interaction of cities. Instead, I want to argue that it is the multiplicity and simultaneity of city life that should draw our attention as a resource for imagining alternative futures for cities, as well as the creative agency and imagination of urban dwellers.[21]

Here, the fact that social scientific urban dystopias and utopias reference actual places is important. In this sense, they are set apart from fictional dystopias—the nonrepresentational space of the novel—even when the subject matter of such fiction concerns concrete historical situations such as slavery.[22] In borrowing from dystopic literary conventions and imaginaries dystopic urbanists pull actual cities and city spaces into fantasies and imaginative representations that are often one-dimensional. In doing so, the transformations they effect have significant consequences in the realm of urban intervention. The outcomes of such representational tactics could well be positive and stimulate progressive change—a representation of apartheid as urban dystopia certainly focused efforts to transform the racially divided spaces of the apartheid city, for example. But since cities are more complicated than dystopias suggest, such representations can be quite problematic in terms of the choices they delimit and thereby legitimate. Even the perhaps obvious case of representing South African cities under apartheid as dystopic[23] can be called into question. Historiographies, for example, move on and introduce new themes: in the case of apartheid, a new awareness of the significance of interaction, mobility, and connectivity in apartheid cities contrasts with the earlier political imperative of identifying, explaining, and opposing segregation and division. One might even find in the history of the apartheid city positive resources for imagining the future. It has been suggested, for example, that the fragmented and divided apartheid city might well help support survivalist informal activities in the present, such that development planners may be reluctant to instigate too many changes in the inherited segregated city form.[24] Like any dystopia, "apartheid" does not exhaust the South African urban experience. The complexity of the city's past and the multiple demands of its current challenges disrupt dystopic tendencies in urban analysis.

In Davis's account (and many others), dystopia often comes to rest in a real place—it is frequently instantiated in Kinshasa, Zaire. Not a city of the dead, he suggests, but a dead city, simultaneously miracle (for surviving at all) and nightmare (in terms of the way it does so), its population alternately heroic in their ability to cope with urban disaster and demonic in the range of cultural practices that emerge in the process. These stylized and stark binaries offer little in the way of dynamism or analytical purchase on where the future might be coming from in cities overwhelmingly characterized by informality and limited and precarious opportunities for survival. Underlying Davis's analysis, then, and unlike that of Koolhaas et al., we find the common assumption that creativity and new directions are unlikely to be found in poorer cities. Kinshasa, it seems cannot offer us solutions to urban problems—it can only represent the nightmare of an urban future that seems out of control.

In Davis's dystopia, then, how does all this end? What does the future hold? The endgame seems to be a militarized face-down in urban slums, where hope for a better future resides in the "gods of chaos": "If the empire can deploy Orwellian technologies of repression, its outcasts have the gods of chaos on their side."[25] Urban reformers across the nineteenth and twentieth centuries would agree on the difficulty of knowing and governing urban slums, let alone fighting a war in them. But is chaos all that remains of hope? Science fiction literary commentators would be hard-pressed to identify in Davis the critical political project that might give them grounds to characterize his narrative as a critical dystopia, intended to promote political action for change in the present.[26] For social and political science readers concerned with actual city futures it is profoundly disabling (and I would suggest inaccurate) to be left with absolutely no sense of a possible path forward in relation to actually existing cities.

Spaces of Hope?

Escape from conditions of poverty is a project many urban dwellers work at, as they seek livelihoods beyond their immediate neighborhoods or social circles or beyond the city, or seek to migrate to wealthier contexts where they perceive more opportunities despite the evident dangers of the journey.[27] In all sorts of ways it may not matter very much that Mike Davis entrains a dystopian imagination in his engagement with poor cities. However, David

Harvey, in his book *Spaces of Hope*, adopts a very different tone in his assessment of the politics of urban transformation. While he is equally attentive to the astounding nature of inequality and poverty in the world's cities (and he identifies this as much in Baltimore, USA, as in the poorest countries of the world), he also holds onto a critical utopianism. He suggests that we look to an otherwise unlikely source for inspiration, the project of neoliberalism: "The revolutionary agenda of neoliberalism has accomplished a lot in the way of physical and institutional change these last twenty years (consider the dual impact of deindustrialization and the diminution of trade union powers in Britain and the United States, for example). So why, then, can we not envision equally dramatic changes (though pointing in a different direction) as we seek for alternatives?"[28] Harvey insists that a dialectical utopian imagination needs to pay attention to both spatial outcomes and social process in formulating future visions. And in order to gain political traction, utopian thinking also needs to contend with problems of "authority and closure." He labels these as "materialist" problems in line with his own Marxist insights, but they would feature equally well in a range of other social and political analyses, notably Weberian. He elaborates: "Closure (the making of something) of any sort contains its own authority because to materialize any one design, no matter how playfully constructed, is to foreclose, in some cases temporarily but in other instances relatively permanently, on the possibility of materializing others. We cannot evade such choices."[29] He is trying to steer a path between a playful postmodernism where everything is open and possible and predetermined visionary utopias usually ungrounded in the circumstedes of the present. For him the challenge is to locate plausible political pathways from the present, pointing toward alternative future trajectories. Harvey's engagement with the terrain of utopia (in which he focuses mostly on cities) is an immensely useful resource for an urban studies haunted for some decades now by dystopic narratives of the experiences of poor cities. He presents a challenge to urbanists—whether their ambitions are to theorize the planet or work determinedly for a better future in specific cities or countries—to identify and enable political practices that establish feasible and transformatory future trajectories.

In relation to what is often presented as the limit case of Kinshasa, a city that has experienced profound economic decline, long-term infrastructural neglect, fragmentation of kin-based associational life, vast population expansion, and an informalization of state capacity, anthropologist Filip de Boeck has explicitly considered where change might come from—what are Kinshasa's "spaces of hope," he asks?[30] Churches have played a large role in diminishing the interdependencies of extended kinship networks in favor of nuclear family ties and, in de Boeck's view, while these churches do offer a kind of reinvented kin grouping, this is on the basis of an "often problematic attitude towards wealth, consumption and accumulation."[31] He looks instead to the continuing salience of the extended family, despite the painful consequences of the wave of witchcraft accusations that reflect and have precipitated a crisis in what is the fundamental social unit in the region: "Even while in crisis, it is still the most important remaining unit to explore and redefine anew the rhythms of reciprocity, commensality, conjugality and gender relations in the urban context. . . . It is the household that forms the necessary complement of, and precondition for, any successful and lasting (social, political, economic) redefinition of the urban space as a gestational space." However, he notes, "its possibilities are becoming increasingly impossible."[32]

While he notes the utopian fantasies of some Kinois artists, eager to explore a radical elsewhere even if that means abandoning the current city, he brings the reader back to the potential inherent in the existing heterotopias of contemporary Kinshasa. It is in the impressive capacity of Kinshasa's popular culture for appreciating simultaneity and multiplicity that he suggests, following Foucault's use of the term "heterotopia," that the possibility of overcoming the ruptures and fragmentations of the present exists. But as his analysis demonstrates, the autochthonous cultural capacity to hold different worlds together—visible and invisible, obverse and reverse, day and night, heaven and hell—has itself been fractured by the crisis. The spread of witchcraft accusations, he suggests, reflects a de-doubling, a setting free of the "second" city of the invisible and nighttime from the visible, daytime world, and the important mediations of social institutions that had previously captured such doublings for cohesion and stability. Again, though, he looks to existing dynamics in the present city to chart possible ways forward: he sees Kinshasa as structured through words, rumor, the constant refashioning of self and meaning, following Simone in interpreting the city as an infrastructure of people rather than things. And it is here that he identifies the potential for a new beginning for the city, in the "words [that] generate the quotidian poetry and prose of the city and form the foundation for urban culture." He leaves it to a Kinois writer, Vincent Lombume Kalimasi, to suggest that "The city is a never ending construction. The city can never remain a passive victim. The city is, on the contrary, a place of possibility, the place that enables you to do and to act."[33]

Following this analysis, the potential for new urban futures lies at the very least in the city itself, as a site of assemblage, multiplicity, and social interaction that offers the potential for something different to emerge. Not necessarily utopian, with an indeterminate future and many troubling tendencies at play in contemporary urban life, but directing us to attend to present sources of hope and to lend support to potential future trajectories.

Utopian—and by extension critical dystopian—narrative strategies might be an important means to galvanize political concern and action about contemporary urban conditions.[34] But there are particular dangers or limits entailed in the genre of the concrete dystopia—bleeding sometimes too easily from critical analysis into political dead ends. The tactic of using stereotypical representations of the present experiences of some cities as indicators of dystopian urban futures can severely limit political visions of the future in these places and undermine efforts to find imaginative strategies for effective intervention. If urban scholarship is to enable political action toward better urban futures, we probably need to find some countercurrents to dystopian tendencies, perhaps even to refuse the genre, in the same way that anti-utopians challenged the value of utopian thinking. In the next section, therefore, I explore an example of a literary work that puts the strategies of utopian/dystopian fiction into question and does so in the context of the rapidly changing city of Johannesburg in the 1990s, facing its apartheid past and making its uncertain future in a turbulent present. Drawing on this I want to propose three criteria for writing the city in the spirit of anti-dystopia: first, a narrator whose viewpoint is contestable; second, inspired by the spatiality of the city itself, a present replete with complexity and multiplicity; and third, following Harvey's assessment, a politics of the future that encompasses both possibility and limits.

Anti-Dystopias of South Africa's Urban Transition

In order to establish the case for anti-dystopian urbanisms, I turn to a literary fantasy of Johannesburg in transition, a fantasy whose warp is the urban landscape of inner-city Johannesburg and whose weave is a constantly changing South African English. Ivan Vladislavić's *The Restless Supermarket* deploys dystopian and utopian fantasies in decidedly ambiguous ways.[35]

He is writing at a moment in South Africa when the potential for changing the city seemed enormous and when actual progress was dramatic (the late 1990s, following the election of the first post-apartheid government in 1994). Much of the South African–based anti-apartheid movement was organized around urban issues. At the heart of the United Democratic Front, a mass movement that emerged in the early 1980s to contest apartheid rule were the numerous urban social movements formed to contest apartheid urban government. The anti-apartheid movement called for one-city-one-tax-base to demand redistribution of central city income to address the urgent service needs of the marginalized black population. And there were high expectations that the form of the city itself, with far-flung dormitory townships for black residents, would be changed. A more compact city, with opportunity for dense urban living close to places of work, was widely anticipated. In practice this proved immensely difficult to achieve, and the resurgence of formal modes of spatial governance more closely associated with the apartheid era (including evictions, relocations, and distant township development) has proved controversial and disappointing. But in contrast the deracialization of many inner-city neighborhoods and the emergence of numerous squatter settlements in relatively well-located places speaks to more substantial informal changes in both the form and use of the city's spaces. Vladislavić's novel inserts itself into these debates just at the moment when the apartheid city seemed doomed and an alternative post-apartheid city future seemed entirely possible. He stages this novel in a former white neighborhood that had already undergone substantial deracialization by the early 1990s. For many in Johannesburg, the history of this area captures well the complex racialized trajectories of utopian hopefulness and dystopian despair, as it moved from an all-white neighborhood of high-rise modernism to a predominantly black neighborhood with declining infrastructure and poorly maintained apartment blocks.[36]

Initially Vladislavić builds a sense of the emergence of dystopia by recounting the slow incremental changes shaping the world of the protagonist—a common science fiction strategy to set dystopia in the near future. In this case, though, the emergence of dystopia is already completed in the present, certainly for the reader who knows something about Hillbrow. This formerly dense, high-rise, white, lower-income neighborhood in downtown Johannesburg, with many highly desirable modernist buildings, was now sublet and rack rented, with a decaying infrastructure and a reputation for violence and illegal activities. Its racial composition had changed, first through the 1980s by middle-class black South Africans finding a foothold in the city there, but increasingly from the mid-1990s by immigrants from other parts of Africa who have made this area their base in the city and the region. While the end point of this transition may be known, the enchantment for readers who are familiar with the neighborhood lies in tracing the emergence and meaning of what is now a profoundly challenging and perplexing part of the city, whose reputation for violence and unknowability both for government and for many South African citizens is iconic of certain aspects of the post-apartheid city.[37]

The representation of this transition as dystopian depends, of course, on your point of view. For many thousands of new residents these changes represented an exciting challenge to apartheid urban form, as well as various kinds of new personal opportunities. But through the lens of the novel's protagonist and narrator, Aubrey Tearle, a retired proofreader of telephone

directories (Vladislavić worked as a proofreader himself), we witness the social, racial, and spatial transformation of this iconic neighborhood in downtown Johannesburg as dystopic. This change is encountered linguistically, as
Tearle is obsessed with the English language and its uses and abuses in the
"melting pot" that is inner-city Johannesburg. The wild inventiveness evident
in the ways in which language is used here—the names of shops, advertisements, newspaper headlines, or lists of things and the exorbitant errors of
European immigrants', Afrikaners', and Africans' diverse encounters with
English—is contrasted with Tearle's almost frenzied use of various editions
of dictionaries to seek to correct improper usage of language. He seems to
delight, though, in working out how it is that particular slippages and creative
inventions emerge in the process.

Where other commentators have read Vladislavić's fiction through the
lens of postmodern literary criticism and linguistics, notably to attest to his
minoritization of South African English,[38] his critical engagement with the
temporality and spatiality of the city is, I think, central to the insights he
offers for understanding the post-apartheid moment in a determinedly anti-
utopian and anti-dystopian fashion.[39] For the purposes of this discussion I
want to trace how he pulls past, present, and future through this urban fantasy
without isolating heroism or hopelessness in any one of them. Thus the apartheid past is not consigned to dystopia, and neither is the present represented
as an unambiguous site of utopian or dystopian possibilities. As Warnes notes
of Vladislavić more generally, he is seeking to find "a language to address both
past and future" in relation to the present transition.[40]

In part he achieves this anti-dystopian and anti-utopian stance by keeping our identification with the narrator in play—it is hard to build a solid
identification with the woes befalling a sometimes racist, often isolated character whose Europhilic reference points set him apart from his context and
orient him to a fading past.[41] And yet the narrator draws us to see how the
transformations in the city are slowly destabilizing his personal world and
ultimately violently attacking his person, as in many conventional science
fiction plots. Neither the apartheid past nor the post-apartheid future offers
stable reference points for assessing the politics of this urban experience.

If our inability to readily identify with Tearle's conservative response
to the changes of the post-apartheid city destabilizes the representation of
present-day Johannesburg as dystopian, a lengthy fantasy (authored by Tearle)
inserted in the middle of the novel does the same for any simplistic rendering of the post-apartheid moment as utopian. Here the close links between
Tearle's Johannesburg, his fantastical representation of its spatial disorder and
decline, and Vladislavić's own experiences of Johannesburg suggest that the
novel is quite consciously engaging with the spatial politics of this city in
transformation. The detail of the landscape of Johannesburg that Vladislavić

has observed in his life there (see *Portrait with Keys*, his autobiographical encounter with the streets of Johannesburg)[42] has been attentively drawn into the novel, forming the basis for Tearle's observations and reflections on the city. Within the novel Tearle himself in turn draws these details and experiences of Johannesburg into a lengthy fantasy about a fictional place, Alibia, which occupies the middle section of the novel. The two cities (Johannesburg/Alibia) are quite clearly interwoven in Tearle's imagination. The fantasy, taking the form of "The Proofreaders' Derby," is ostensibly an exercise for a competition to test proofreading skills and is composed out of various corrigenda that he (Tearle/Vladislavić) had been collecting over many years. As the dystopia of post-apartheid urban change is unfolding in the main narrative, this "parabasis"—"an opportunity to speak otherwise within the novel's own boundaries"—explores this in exaggerated magical-realist fashion and exposes the fantasy of a post-apartheid utopia to the critical lens of satire.[43]

The Proofreaders' Derby posits a fantastic world in which spaces literally shift around. The narrator—a proofreader in a world where editing or altering texts and maps causes actual changes in the physical world—is alerted to this as he wakes one morning to see a lake pressing at the doorstep of his house. Someone is drowning, but efforts to rescue him fail. A body washes up onto his doorstep. He ignores it and makes great efforts to reach his newspaper despite the lapping waves and the body on the veranda. Both the banal violence and astonishing implausibility of these opening scenes in Tearle's fantasy are replicated in the opening pages of the novel itself where, in Tearle's (and Vladislavić's?) Johannesburg, a hilarious, chaotic street scene unfolds involving a pink elephant, partying middle-class men, a homeless woman, and a shop owner. But it is closely followed, disturbingly, by a brief paragraph about a dead body.

> One Sunday morning not too long ago, on an overgrown plot in Prospect Road, I saw a body in the weeds, under a shroud of pages from the *Sunday Times*. I saw it from the window of my own flat, where I stood with a carton of long-life milk in my hand, and I could almost smell the pungent smell of the kakiebos crushed by its fall. It lay among the rusted pipes, blackened bricks and outcrops of old foundations that mark every bit of empty land in this city, as if a reef of disorder lay just below the surface, or a civilization had gone to ruin before we ever arrived.
>
> What do I mean by "we"? Don't make me laugh.[44]

It is this "reef of disorder" presaging the demise of "civilization" as Tearle knew it—order, predictability, and accuracy but also apartheid and authoritarianism—that is imagined to literally upend the city in Tearle's fantasy. For Vladislavić the idea of space as changing (in meaning, use, form) has been one he has pressed at in several other places in his fictional writing, and also engaged theoretically.[45] The transliteration of this idea into physical form takes a magical realist turn in this novel, building on earlier attempts. For example, in a short story published in 1989, "Journal of a Wall," he uses the vertiginous feeling after drinking too much to set the walls of his house into motion; as bricks peel off, the ceiling drifts away, and the walls unravel he is left "floating on the raft of the floor."[46] This extravagant spatial literality plays out in Tearle's fantasy, the Proofreaders' Derby, where minor disorders in the urban fabric, initially physically patched up by repairmen, become generalized and are followed by wholesale relocations of lakes and settlements, flying buildings, as well as tears in the physical fabric of space. While he notes that the seeds of decline were "sown in mischief and trivialities" (206), they soon amounted to "a spectacular descent into chaos" (209).[47] Fluxman, the proofreader-protagonist of the fantasy, is disappointed when the city fathers refuse the offer of help from the Proofreaders' Society of Alibia. He withdraws, refusing to do anything at all.

It is not difficult to read the Derby as an interrogation of post-apartheid urban transitions. As urban decline sets in in the inner city, small transgressions slowly mount, urban governance is steadily undermined, and wholesale disorder (from certain perspectives) ensues. Withdrawing (behind bars and gates, into privatized suburban worlds of privilege) is clearly an option many have taken. For the Tearles of this world, retired white people on modest incomes living in the inner city, often this is not an option. While many of the single, elderly, and transient (often seen as "cosmopolitan," but predominantly white) residents of Hillbrow have slowly moved out to suburbs, townhouses, gated communities, and retirement villages, there are many, especially elderly white people, who must continue to make their lives in a neighborhood that is not only changing in racial composition and physical fabric but also in language and social uses, and which has more recently become a violent and often dangerous place. Withdrawal and engagement are certainly pressing alternatives in this context.

But this choice to withdraw is ultimately not satisfying for Fluxman, Tearle's fantasy alter-ego, who is above all else, Tearle suggests, a "strategist." In what is perhaps a satirical reference to the numerous policy initiatives that have emerged in relation to the decline of inner-city Johannesburg, Fluxman declares, "Some observations I've made lately have led me to believe that looking the other way might not be the answer . . . I thought I could manage well enough as Alibia declined, preserving my own little corner amidst the ruins. Unfortunately it isn't that simple." Suggesting that the proofreaders themselves are succumbing to "minor disorders," he insists, "We must come up with a strategy" (215–16). Wielding their pencils, the proofreaders finally restore order to the city with much effort and sleepless nights.

Some of the spatial changes that had upended Alibia reflect the breakdown of typical apartheid separations—a shantytown comes flying in to replace a commercial building in the heart of town; people end up living among those they had previously worked hard to avoid; conflict ensues. The solutions proffered to some extent reinstate the apartheid ordering at the same time as they are concerned with the general repairing of the city, removing shanties from buffer zones, ensuring the appropriate distance between the haves and the have-nots: "The city pulled itself together. Slowly, the recognizable outlines of Alibia reappeared, as street after street and block after block was knocked back into its familiar, ordinary shape" (226).

If the hints of a post-apartheid utopia in this fantasy would have excited many readers—shantytowns flying in to the city center, for example, might be one version of post-apartheid planning utopia (and experience)—the dangers of reinstating the old order under the guise of solving contemporary problems shades into a more dystopic vision of the city in transition. The narrative works here partly to alert us to the ways in which the desire for order and certain (European/Alibian) assumptions about how to achieve that through specific forms of documented governance, maps, title deeds, bylaws, and spatial planning in fact underpinned the apartheid city. This is mirrored in the main narrative in a topsy-turvy episode during the café's closing-down party when Tearle finds himself constantly reprimanded as racist by the (no longer generous) companions he has spent many months criticizing for their lapses in language, judgment, and decorum or belittling in various ways for their racial background or national origin. The scene builds toward an angry knife attack on Tearle, from which he is fortuitously saved by his (pocket) dictionary. He is shocked when people accuse him, with his European ways, love of order, and narrow linguistic fastidiousness, of being responsible for apartheid (although, strangely, the Derby he is meant to have authored explicitly establishes this connection, suggesting a rather more self-knowing protagonist).

A short interchange in the midst of the party disturbs his personal detachment from South Africa/apartheid—and in so doing undermines his alibi for culpability for apartheid's wrongs. At the heart of the narrative of the book is Tearle's identification with a mural in the Café Europa, the coffee shop in Hillbrow he had been frequenting since his retirement and where much of the novel is set. The mural depicts a place called (he calls?) "Alibia." Soon after he was informed about the impending closure of the café as the changing neighborhood and clientele undermined its viability, Tearle reflects on his experiences there, and comments, "My eye was drawn to the city on the wall, to the walled city of Alibia, where I had roamed so often in my imagination" (19). The scene for him is European, a waterfront replete with yachts, promenade, workmen and warehouses, canals and cafés. European immigrants found elements they recognized there, and he remarks that "It was a perfect alibi, a generous elsewhere in which the immigrant might find the landmarks he had left behind" (19). He then asks, as someone born in Johannesburg, "What did Alibia mean to me?" He describes how the shape of his head matches the hill in the picture—finding himself in the image. This alibi, his sense of distance and lack of responsibility for the South African condition, is what is called into question during the café's closing down party. A young man asks him,

> "What you call this spot again?"
> "Alibia."
> "Isn't that where old Gadafi hangs out?"
> "You're thinking of Libya, Floyd. This is A-libia."
> "Pull the other one, Mr T. I can check it's only Cape Town."
> "What an absurd idea."
> "Look. Here's Khayelitsha." (253)

At the same time as Tearle's alibi, his distance from the city, is slipping, this exchange also reminds us that external (European) forces were also responsible for shaping apartheid's spaces, like Tearle himself. These alibis (absolutions) for the form of the apartheid city are in fact deeply implicated in it and potentially continue to operate. Thus any effort to read the spatial transformation of Alibia as a critical post-apartheid triumphalism over the conservative (and foreign) ordering principles of the past must contend with the sense that the (new) city fathers also have to do something about the crippling disorder of the city. In a quandary quite prescient to the challenges of post-apartheid urban planning, the question arises as to whether they are going to use these old, perhaps unexamined tools (the proofreaders, the bylaws, the maps, the texts, the language of order, removals, and deletions) and risk reinstating aspects of apartheid in a new/old guise. Present, past, and future crash into one another in disorienting and undecidable ways in this fantasy and the surrounding novel; the temporality of the city is determinately multiple, the politics of past and future ambivalent and certainly complicated.

If the descent into the spatial (post-apartheid) dystopia of the Proofreaders' Derby ends with the restoration of a politically ambivalent order, Tearle's personal dystopic adventure culminates as the Café Europa's closing-down party descends into chaos and violence. The novel ends with a moving and intimate walk through the inner city, Tearle in the company of a young woman, probably of mixed race. They are returning together from the hospital after helping a man who had attempted to save Tearle from the angry mob at the café but who had ended up stabbing himself in the head. The walk through the night (itself a gentle recuperation of nighttime streets from the violence of contemporary Johannesburg), with the sun about to rise and a light mutuality of interaction, establishes the future as potentiality. Tearle seems to have learned a thing or two in the night, and the simple possibility of mundane meetings in the landscape shared across race and generation—Tearle and Sharlaine both know the same streets, establishments, and routes through the city—speaks of a fragile hopefulness emerging out of the experience of living in the city itself.

It is the city itself, then, that Vladislavić draws on as offering the potential for a complex interrelationship between past, present, and future and that exposes the limits of dystopian and utopian imaginations alike. The politics of order and disorder, for example, are distributed uncomfortably across the post-apartheid divide. The temporalities of transformation are frequently in question, as the past not only inhabits the present but is still in play as offering potential solutions for the future. In spatial terms for Vladislavić and others the past is a weighty presence, as the difficulties involved in actually changing physical spaces severely undermine the possibility of the emergence of a post-apartheid city.[48] Nonetheless, the creative play of language, and the everyday interactions on the streets of the city, walked with attentive affection by Vladislavić and Tearle alike, present possible paths toward (post-apartheid) futures.

Conclusion

Assessing the continuing place of utopian thinking in urban theory, Pinder argues that it provides an opportunity for the theorist to act as a "partisan of possibilities."[49] For a critical dystopia, following Moylan, it is the residual sense of possibilities for transformation that are crucial to its political ambitions. However, the deployment of the dystopian genre in contemporary urban studies necessarily takes the form of a concrete dystopia, with many attendant pitfalls.[50] Not the least of these are the stereotypical and one-dimensional representations of urban spaces that are drawn upon to generate a dystopian version of contemporary urban life in some cities and to prefigure future trends elsewhere. This has such unfortunate resonances with the compromised history of urban studies, exceptionalizing the experiences of poorer cities in contrast to the desirable norms of urban experiences in the wealthier global North, that it is, I suggest, counterproductive to the political ambitions of the authors. However, the dystopic narrative form is also profoundly disabling of the quest to identify real possibilities for future trajectories in particular cities, since the range of urban experiences as well as the local inventiveness and rich diversity of many city contexts are ignored in favor of a search for evidence to support the dystopic narrative. In contrast to dystopic urbanisms, and drawing on the resources of a fictional engagement with an actual urban transition in South Africa, I have suggested that we might do better to adopt an anti-dystopian stance. Here it is rather the city itself—with its multiplicity, complexity, and coexisting temporalities—that can provide the impetus toward a politics of possibility.

Notes

1 T. Moylan, *Scraps of the Untainted Sky: Science Fiction, Utopia, Dystopia* (Boulder, CO: Westview Press, 2000).

2 J. Robinson, *Ordinary Cities: Between Modernity and Development* (London: Routledge, 2006).

3 D. Harvey, *Spaces of Hope* (Edinburgh: Edinburgh University Press, 2000).

4 A. Mbembe and S. Nuttall, eds., "Johannesburg: The Elusive Metropolis," in *Public Culture* 44 (2004).

5 Mike Davis, *Planet of Slums* (New York: Verso, 2006), 19.

6 Partha Chatterjee, *The Politics of the Governed: Reflections on Popular Politics in Most of the World* (New York: Columbia University Press, 2006).

7 Moylan, *Scraps of the Untainted Sky*; for other examples of dystopic urbanism, see R. Koolhaas, S. Boeri, S. Kwinter, et al., eds., *Mutations* (Bordeaux: Actar, 2000); and N. Smith, "New Globalism, New Urbanism: Gentrification as Global Urban Strategy," *Antipode* 34.3 (2002): 427–50. For thoughtful reflections on the reemergence of dystopic thinking on cities, see G. Baeten, "Hypochondriac Geographies of the City and the New Urban Dystopia: Coming to Terms with the 'Other' City," *City* 6.1 (2002): 103–15, and G. McLeod and K. Ward, "Spaces of Utopia and Dystopia: Landscaping the Contemporary City," *Geografiska Annaler, B* 84.3–4 (2002): 153–70.

8 Moylan, *Scraps of the Untainted Sky*, 180–82.

9 M. Varsam, "Concrete Dystopia: Slavery and Its Others," in *Dark Horizons: Science Fiction and the Dystopian Imagination*, ed. R. Baccolini and T. Moylan (New York: Routledge, 2003), 203–24.

10 See, for example, UN-Habitat, *State of the World's Cities, 2006–7* (London: Earthscan, 2006).

11 Baeten, "Hypochondriac Geographies of the City and the New Urban Dystopia."

12 See, for example, B. Yeoh, *Contesting Space: Power Relations and the Urban Built Environment in Colonial Singapore* (Oxford: Oxford University Press, 1996).

13 See Baeten, "Hypochondriac Geographies of the City and the New Urban Dystopia"; and McLeod and Ward, "Spaces of Utopia and Dystopia."

14 The quote is from Smith, "New Globalism, New Urbanism," 436.

15 Koolhaas et al., *Mutations*, 653.

16 Varsam, "Concrete Dystopia."

17 For example, M. Gandy, "Learning from Lagos," *New Left Review* 32 (2005): 37–53.

18 See *Ordinary Cities*, in which I develop this analysis more fully.

19 Davis, *Planet of Slums*, 198.

20 Ibid., 179.

21 Baeten, "Hypochondriac Geographies of the City and the New Urban Dystopia"; and A. Merrifield, "The Dialectics of Dystopia: Disorder and Zero Tolerance in the City," *International Journal of Urban and Regional Research* 24.2 (2000): 473–89.

22 Varsam, "Concrete Dystopia."

23 Apartheid is the image that explicitly indicates dystopia for Davis—as a form of segregation and exclusion taken to the extreme. Davis, *Planet of Slums*, 51.

24 For some distinctive approaches to the post-apartheid city that depart from the analytic inherited from apartheid, see Mbembe and Nuttall, "Johannesburg"; and S. Nuttall, "City Forms and Writing the 'Now' in South Africa," *Journal of Southern African Studies* 30.4 (2005): 731–48. On the continuities between apartheid and post-apartheid urban forms, see my "Continuities and Discontinuities in Local Government," in *Consolidating Developmental Local Government: Lessons from the South African Experience*, ed. M. van Donk, M. Swilling, E. Piterse, and S. Parnell (Cape Town: UCT Press, 2008); and A. Todes, "Urban Spatial Policy," in *Democracy and Delivery: Urban Policy in South Africa*, ed. U. Pillay, R. Tomlinson, and J. du Toit (Cape Town: HSRC Press, 2006), 50–74.

25 Davis, *Planet of Slums*, 206.

26 Moylan, *Scraps of the Untainted Sky.*

27 A. Simone, *For the City Yet to Come* (Durham: Duke University Press, 2004).

28 Harvey, *Spaces of Hope*, 186.

29 Both quotes are from ibid., 196.

30 F. De Boeck and M.-F. Plissart, *Kinshasa: Tales of the Invisible City* (Ghent: Ludion Press, 2004), 244.

31 Ibid., 248.

32 Ibid., 249, 250.

33 Simone, *For the City Yet to Come*; De Boeck and Plissart, *Kinshasa*, 259.

34 D. Pinder, *Visions of the City* (Edinburgh: Edinburgh University Press, 2005).

35 I. Vladislavić, *The Restless Supermarket* (Cape Town: David Philip, 2001).

36 An excellent account of this changing neighborhood is provided by A. Morris, *Bleakness and Light: Inner-City Transition in Hillbrow, Johannesburg* (Johannesburg: University of Witwatersrand Press, 1999).

37 On some of the challenges of governance and informality in this area, see A. Simone, "Pirate Towns: Reworking Social and Symbolic Infrastructures in Johannesburg and Douala," *Urban Studies* 43.2 (2006): 357–70.

38 S. Helgesson, " 'Minor Disorders': Ivan Vladislavić and the Devolution of South African English," *Journal of Southern African Studies* 30.4 (2004): 777–87.

39 M. Popescu, "Translations: Lenin's Statues, Post-Communism, and Post-Apartheid," *Yale Journal of Criticism* 16.2 (2003): 406–23.

40 C. Warnes, "The Making and Unmaking of History in Ivan Vladislavić's *Propaganda by Monuments and Other Stories*," *Modern Fiction Studies* 46.1 (2000): 67–89.

41 M. Marais, "Visions of Excess: Closure, Irony, and the Thought of Community in Ivan Vladislavić's *The Restless Supermarket*," *English in Africa* 29.2 (2002): 101–17.

42 I. Vladislavić, *Portrait with Keys: Johannesburg Unlocked* (London: Portobello Books, 2006).

43 Helgesson, "Minor Disorders," 784.

44 Vladislavić, *The Restless Supermarket*, 6.

45 H. Judin and I. Vladislavić, eds., *blank_____: Architecture, Apartheid and After* (Rotterdam: Netherlands Architecture Institute, 1998); Vladislavić, *Portrait with Keys.*

46 I. Vladislavić, *Missing Persons* (Cape Town: David Philip, 1989), 25–26.

47 Unless otherwise indicated, quotations are from Vladislavić, *The Restless Supermarket.*

48 I. Vladislavić, "Interview with Ivan Vladislavić (by Christopher Warnes)," *Modern Fiction Studies* 46.1 (2000): 273–82.

49 Pinder, *Visions of the City*, 265.

50 Moylan, *Scraps of the Untainted Sky*; Varsam, "Concrete Dystopia."

Chapter 10

∎

Imaging Urban Breakdown

Delhi in the 1990s

RAVI SUNDARAM

At some point in the long years of the 1980s the city of Delhi[1] entered its own "very special delirium."[2] The ingredients of this delirium included a powerful mix of urban crisis and an expanding media sensorium that produced a feeling that was exhilarating but equally terrifying and violent. Delhi's experience is also comparable to that of other rapidly growing cities, including Mexico City, Karachi, and Lagos, all places that have begun to produce a range of dynamic responses and reflections—artwork, music, literature, essays. In the fast-moving landscape of global event theory, however, yet another genre has emerged that seeks to explain the turbulent expansion of cities in the global South. This is a genre that can be best called "urban crisis" writing.

The most recent incarnation is Mike Davis's *Planet of Slums*, which reads the urban crisis in the post-colonial world as heralding a new apocalyptic "slumming" of the world's cities.[3] In Davis's narrative, a fetid, violent urbanism in the periphery is the future of modern capitalism, with collapsing cities and open sewage, vast migratory populations, and the retreat of secular and state forms. To Davis's discomfort, welfare and self-help are now provided not by the state or radicals but by religious movements of popular Islam and Christianity. Davis's book recalls Victorian reformers' deployment of shock-exposé and horror to focus on congestion, disease, and poverty in mid-nineteenth-century cities. In the post-colonial world, a version of the *Planet of Slums* has also crowded urban discourse in the past decade. This is the classic landscape of planners, older reform elites. This discourse fills op-ed columns, widely publicized releases of status reports on the city, and media campaigns. For social liberalism and the inheritors of twentieth-century progressive urbanism, post-colonial urban catastrophes are signatures of weakened sovereignties, the rise of neo-liberal global urban expertise and private developers, and the failing dreams of a more equal way of urban life imagined by planners.

Others have taken an entirely different path. When flying over Lagos in a helicopter a few years ago as part of his research project, Rem Koolhaas suddenly realized that the city that seemed on the ground like a "smouldering, burning rubbish dump" was in fact a stunning post-plan metropolis. Koolhaas saw vast complementary coherences amid the apparent chaos of Lagos,[4] a self-organized rhythm of urban life: markets, traffic interfaces, and network innovations that rendered its very "dysfunctionality" productive. When the post-independence order fell away, suddenly in the vast interstices of the planned city a new rhythm emerged, without mega-designs, first parasitic then productive and dynamic, or perhaps all of them together. Koolhaas's text has the merit of cutting through the apocalyptic critiques of urbanism; in his explication the dramaturgy of Lagos is filled with possibilities that speak beyond classic narratives of survival and loss. As a dramaturgy that evokes a different possibility of urban life to Western readers (to whom it is aimed), Koolhaas's meditation on Lagos fails on one count: the productive city of the South seems to have enveloped the dead into the ever-flowing and ever-living. If Mike Davis's doomsday narrative is aimed at shocking Western policymakers and readers with his catalogue of Third World shantytown horrors, Koolhaas's text flows well with the current vitalist moment in social theory, where fluid, self-organizing forms of life are privileged over rationalist control models. Koolhaas's narrative is the chapter of a novella to be written, the middle reel of a movie that has no ending. The lecture on Lagos may work as an abstract lesson for Western architecture, but it fails to capture an emerging urban media technics that is simultaneously productive and phobic, dynamic, adaptive, and equally violent.

Crisis Ingredients: Decay, Proliferation, and the Media Sensorium

In the advanced metropolitan centers, a significant allegory of urban crisis has been of infrastructural decline: imaging empty peripheral landscapes of former industrial areas, empty spaces, and abandoned techno-parks of rusted factories—all tomb signatures to a now buried modernist era. Dead machines litter these spaces, which act as a hidden back end to the post-urban sprawl. In the first issue of the architectural journal *Grey Room*, Antoine Picon suggested that these landscapes of rust exposed a certain anxiety, which opened the possibility of a grim future.[5] Picon's dark urban morphology overlaps with that of Paul Virilio: the end of classic landscape as a consequence of media networks, the loss of the autonomy of both technical objects and human species, all of which are now captured in science fiction, popular cyberpunk, and contemporary television shows. Dystopian post-industrial landscapes in

Western cities are paralleled by new generic spaces networked by communication fiber and "junkspace" design, a term coined by Rem Koolhaas. Thus, "Junkspace is a domain of feigned, simulated order, a kingdom of morphing. Its specific configuration is as fortuitous as the geometry of a snowflake."[6] As Jameson argues dolefully in his commentary on Koolhaas, architecture and design have become an endless "empire of blur," a mutation without reference.[7] A clutter of non-places has emerged in airports, malls, and transit points. The old modernist models of the productive industrial city have long disappeared; their debris now clutters the landscapes of rust as dystopian afterlives.

Others like Anthony Vidler have argued that modern urbanism has always been haunted by Enlightenment fears of "dark space," which is seen as a repository of superstition, non-reason, and the breakdown of civility.[8] "Dark space" constantly invades "light space" through the fear of epidemics, urban panic, the homeless multitude, and criminal activity. For the best part of the twentieth century modern urban planning and architecture have sought to stake out the idea of transparent space free from superstition, disease, myth, and non-rational behavior. Modernism's use of glass and light, and the advocacy of the grid as a rational mapping of the city, went along with the establishment of governmental authority. The norms and forms of modern urban governance would separate the civic from the criminal, the public from the private, the human from the non-human, putting in place a model that would promise the visible and healthy interaction of humans and things.

This bipolar model of urban life problematized by Vidler has been integral to modern urban management. It has come apart rapidly in recent years in many post-colonial cities. By contrast, the post-colonial scenario over the past few decades could not be more different. Urban life has imploded: the new expansion of cities has made classic urban management models irrelevant or simply inoperative. Endless proliferation marks the new post-colonial urban. Home workshops, markets, hawkers, small factories, and small and large settlements of the working poor now spread all over the planned metropolis or in regions where it was impossible to do so. Productive, non-legal proliferation has emerged as a defining component of the new urban crisis in India and other parts of the post-colonial world. "Informality" has emerged as one of the main designations of proliferation in recent years, first by policy scholars and later in debates within urban studies.[9] The informality debates begun by the International Labour Organization (ILO) economists[10] had begun to anticipate the emerging shape of the post-colonial metropolis in the 1970s. Informal work and settlement lacked governmental sanction, rapidly drawing in the new migrant poor, street traders, small workshops, and neighborhood factories. What has emerged right from the outset is informality's

ambivalence about the law, both in terms of housing settlements and production sites, which worked through tenure rather than formal title. Both
Solomon Benjamin's work on East Delhi's industrial clusters[11] and Timothy
Mitchell's insights[12] on informal housing in Egypt suggest that it is precisely
this ambivalence about entering legal domains that accounted for informality's strength. As Mitchell's work on Egypt shows, urban populations identified as informal tended to stay away from legal regimes of property as the
latter potentially destroyed local knowledges and brought the informals into
the extractive monetary structures of urban regimes.[13] Egyptian urbanist Asef
Bayat called informality "a quiet encroachment of the ordinary,"[14] in contrast
to classic political urban movements. Informality's political stance ranged
from pragmatic to mercenary, working variously with local politicians and
state employees to get services, local land speculators, small crime syndicates
that provided protection, and religious self-help groups. Illegal lotteries called
chit funds were often used to finance low-cost construction.

Informality was probably less unstructured than the early debates made
it out to be; it also developed complex internal inequalities of work and gender. What is important for this discussion is that informality emerged from
academic and policy debates in the 1970s to become a form of urban life that
took center stage in the dramaturgy of urban crisis in India by the end of the
century. For state planners, neoliberal civic groups, orthodox Marxists, and
the old secular elites informality became a model of wild, lawless urbanism
that made a mockery of zoning. Lacking civic services,[15] these zones emerge
in civic reports as hellish sites of polluting industries, theft of civic services,
and political vote banks. Informality was urbanism out of joint, a frightening
entity outside the law of the city. A selective phenomenology of urban informality as proliferating life clearly marks both Mike Davis's and Koolhaas's
texts. For Davis informality marks a morbid negation of any urban vision
of collectivist solidarity, while for Koolhaas informality is *life itself*, with an
organic rhythm, emerging from the bowels of the post-colonial city.

This unhinged proliferation of urban life is enmeshed in a world of media urbanism. Post-colonial cities today are also *media cities*, a tag typically
reserved for the "global city." From the late 1970s various combinations of
media consumption, circulation, and production have rapidly expanded in
Asian, Latin American, and African cities. Cassette and television culture has
given way to digital media, with a cultural morphology that does not simply
replicate forms of corporate and state control as in the broadcast age.[16] An
increasing body of research from Mexico, Nigeria, and Asia has shown that
post-colonial cities are vibrant hubs for new media productions, spurred on
by a range of low-cost urban infrastructures: mobile telephony, video and
digital technologies, and parallel distribution circuits. This produces a media

experience that assumes constant breakdown, recycled assemblages, serial dispersal, and endless proliferation of multiple forms and sites. Breakdown and productive life are enmeshed in a dynamic constellation.

The new technologies of urban government have increasingly acknowledged the enmeshing of media and urban life. The management of urban affect is through new techniques that are central to the current discourse of power. Urban populations are equally complicit in a shifting media anthropology of the senses, in every way going beyond the classic predictions of critical media theory. In this sense, the classic dualism of plan and counterplan, public space versus privatization, order versus productive chaos, cannot capture the growing entanglements of media politics and urban life—which inaugurates a new kinesthetic of movement, creation, and death.[17] The classic language of the modernist city (planning, the social, and reform) and its Western avant-garde critics (*derive*, counterpublics) appear like political technologies of a fast-receding era.

Returning to Rem Koolhaas, he gets one thing right: the idea that the urban crisis has exposed new and old/new assemblages that mutate, incorporate, and displace populations, spaces, and things. The present becomes dramatically visible—in often disturbing ways. Urban crisis emerges as a borderless zone of a permanent overflow. It is this zone that forms the core of this essay, with Delhi as the central site.

Delhi

In his "Short Guide to Towns without a Past," Albert Camus called them places "without tenderness and abandon." They are, said Camus, "suited neither to wisdom or the delicacies of taste."[18] By the 1970s it was the fate of Delhi, that quintessential empire city almost a millennia old, that it was viewed by the rest of the country through the prism of a drab and cruel urbanism of planning and the rule of corrupt political and cultural elites. Other metropolitan elites regarded post-Partition Delhi's largely migrant population as lacking in cultural capital—here rootlessness and migration, that most cosmopolitan of Enlightenment virtues, was now turned against itself. The great melancholy lament of Delhi's poets—which began with the sack of the city by Nadir Shah in the eighteenth century, followed by the wholesale destruction by the English East India Company's armies in 1857–58 and the caesura of Partition—all came to end with the postwar Masterplan's urban vision, which simply bypassed the past. Haunted by the dead, imprisoned in the ruins of the old city/slum,[19] the New City suffered a representational paralysis. What was Delhi if not for politics and the plan? The more Delhi's inhabitants protested by showing the vitality of the new migrant neighborhoods and markets and the strength of its universities and intellectual discussion, the more the city seemed condemned to that derisive urbanist label of a capital—comparable to a Washington, D.C., or Canberra. The dream of a transparent city freed from congestion and health risks, which motivated the planners, may not have succeeded on the ground, but it set up a discursive terrain that seemed difficult to break.

To be sure, visitors to Delhi in the 1950s and the 1960s might have observed a city lacking a modern urban rhythm, at least in comparison to Bombay and Calcutta. Urban civic and cultural life was muted; a very small elite clustered around state cultural institutions could not intervene effectively in the public life of the city. Much of this took place in the Lutyens zone, which continued to be the site for institutional growth, cultural centers, embassies, conference sites, and hotels, all forming a model of abstract space that the original design had envisioned. This was at a time when migration was steady; the city expanded to 2.6 million by 1970. Urban planning bodies managed the city through zoning laws, housing schemes, and refugee resettlement. Housing construction was steady and colonies expanded rapidly in the southern and western parts of the city. The migrants from West Punjab reinvigorated commercial life in the city, markets expanded, and new networks of credit and circulation were built through family and kinship ties, all laying ground for the rapid commercial explosions of the 1980s. By the 1970s a significant working-class presence was recorded, concentrated around small industries and the new export/industrial zones of Okhla and Noida. These movements of working people to Delhi, along with the increase in small industry and commerce, gradually changed the urban morphology, with the three decades after 1971 showing the most dramatic shifts. During this period, not only did the population of Delhi increase from 4 million in 1971 to 13 million in 2001, by 1998 there were 1,080 squatter settlements, housing approximately 10 percent of the population; a further 24 percent of the population lived in "unauthorized colonies." In addition there were illegal markets, street vendors, weekly street bazaars, and a very dynamic small business culture revitalizing markets. The footprint of Delhi now covers the "National Capital Region," which had a population of 37 million in 2001. In short, Delhi had changed from the stasis of a political capital, dominated by bureaucratic elites, to becoming nearly a "mega-city."[20]

The Delhi Masterplan of 1962 design by Albert Mayer[21] and his colleagues saw the city as a productive organism; easy movement was integral to this imaginary. This involved a careful distinction between forms of labor and subjectivity that were seen as appropriate to modern urban life in India; those who did not fit this model could be open for displacement in the event of a failed assimilation into urbanism. The first Masterplan had presumed a small city with a reasonable balance between private and public transport. For the most part, until the internal Emergency in the mid-1970s, this model held together, albeit with strains. With modest industrialization in the initial years after the 1962 Masterplan, Delhi was almost moving toward the model of a "productive" city that Mayer and his colleagues had in mind. The Masterplan's model had presumed a largely administrative capital, and this began to come apart in the late 1970s. By the time of the Asian Games in Delhi in 1982, the population of the capital had swelled with new migrants.

By the 1990s a feeling of crisis and constant breakdown in the city exposed the inadequacies of the Masterplan's confident modernist vision for Delhi. Crisis points of the city were rapidly mapped onto different landscapes: the liberal environmentalists' demand to remove "polluting industries" from the city, chaotic public transportation, and the alarmingly high death rates as a result of car accidents on the city's roads. Paranoiac security discourses after the civil conflicts in Kashmir and Punjab overflowed in Delhi in the shape of terrorist incidents. In the event, constant urban crises prised open the existing "political" arrangements of the city. These had involved the grafting of political claims by local populations within the routine practices of urbanism, a phenomenon approximating Partha Chatterjee's description of "political society."[22] This arrangement had accommodated the great expansion of the non-legal city after 1977, often with the help of local politicians. Since the mid-1990s, this older "political" model of urban growth has been thrown into complete confusion. A significant cause of this has been a middle-class environmental civic campaign that petitioned sympathetic courts, portraying the city as a space on the brink of ecological collapse and transportation disaster. Crisis scenarios by the turn of the century were identified and dramatized on a daily basis. Perceived in middle-class civic campaigns as the only space protected from the "corruption" of the political elites, court intervention in the city was fundamental, woven in with media landscapes and narratives of urban catastrophe.

The courts had been shifting steadily toward liberal interventionism in the 1990s, using the public interest litigations (PILs) initiated by civic groups as a site to generate an urban drama that occupied public life for more than a decade. Paradoxically, the 1962 Masterplan acted as an imaginary reference in this new constellation.[23] In early 2006 the Supreme Court began a legal process that pronounced that all construction, settlement, and informal habitation that was in violation of the 1962 Masterplan had to be demolished by the city authorities. This brought to a climax a legal discourse that had emerged from the 1990s when the first petitions began to be heard.[24] While the court orders began as an ostensible critique of commercialization, they eventually touched every neighborhood, hundreds of squatter camps, and thousands of small shops, as well as simple additions and modifications to homes. The court order served as the master reference in the crisis with daily violence when demolition squads moved in. Public anxiety was reflected in screaming headlines and nonstop news coverage. This brought to a climax and political crisis a discourse that emerged from the mid-1990s, when court orders periodically declared forms of life to be out of conformity with law: polluting small industries, speeding public buses, all settlement on "public land," and squatter settlements. The court orders mobilized images of urban chaos, executive-style command, and a cinematic urgency of movement suggesting immediate action. Practices that were ordinarily part of the pastoral power of government were suddenly rendered visible through dramatic civic judgments. In doing so very publicly, the courts accelerated images of crisis already in circulation in the hyperstimulus of the city. Egged on by a sympathetic media and advocacy groups, courts appointed special committees spread over every aspect of civic life, causing terror and fear in the neighborhoods they visited.[25] A phantom civic subject emerged in this very public legal discourse, identifiably middle-class, post-political, and projected as the injured legatee of the urban body.

Like Koolhaas's almost revelatory description of Lagos, the court orders from the mid-1990s continuously dramatized a vast surface of a previously hidden city. These included new "unauthorized" neighborhoods, informal and non-legal settlements, working-class migrations, and a vast network of small markets, neighborhood factories, and small shops. Horizontal networks of production and circulation, new work patterns, and a dizzyingly complex world of infrastructure support, tenure, and occupation emerged: a dynamic, productively chaotic mix, all of which became ingredients of the crisis narrative mobilized in court cases in the 1990s. Beyond the legal language of the court, vast traffic, new smells of plastic garbage, industrial waste, food shops, and fumes from buses and auto rickshaws all transformed and inflamed the sense of everydayness and produced a hyperstimuli of urbanism.[26]

This hyperstimuli was predicated on a vastly expanded media: video, sound, digital print, telephony, and *things* of media—cassettes, televisions, screens, CDs, posters, phones, and flyers. These spread all over the city and became inseparable from the urban experience. This corporeal mix gave the urban experience a visceral, overimaged feel—it also dispersed the classic morphology of the planned city. A significant form of media expansion in the 1980s was through a pirate infrastructure of non-legal copies, dispersed production, and rapid imitation and transfigurations of the legal media commodity. In an earlier essay I termed this phenomenon a pirate or recycled modernity,[27] unconcerned with modernity's classic search for originality and a significant part of the urban experience. More pragmatic and viral than avant-garde/tactical culture, pirate culture allowed the entry of vast numbers of poorer urban residents in Indian cities into media culture.

A clearly different kind of city had emerged in the discourses of the 1990s from the one imagined by the Masterplan. Endless proliferation was the secret of this new metropolis. Proliferation slowly mixed with a media sensorium to create a dynamic urban loop that seemed to push the city to the brink in the 1990s.

Pirate Cities?

A memory of the 1980s in Delhi is a clutter of events: the spectacle of the Asian Games in 1982, the assassination of Mrs. Gandhi and the pogrom against the Sikhs in 1984, the Rajiv Gandhi era, the arrival of terrorism and counterterrorism, the anti-Mandal agitation by upper-caste students, and the rise of Hindu nationalism. Everything seemed to partly confirm Delhi's status as a shadow theater of national political acts, possessing no history outside that of the national state. Remarkably, by the end of the decade this entire image began spinning out of control after the destructive cycle of the anti-Mandal agitation in the city, quickly followed by the Hindu nationalist campaigns to demolish the Babri mosque in Ayodhya. Post Ayodhya, "local" politics in Delhi began slowly gaining prominence.

Only today we can retrospectively suggest that the 1980s contained a secret unfolding history of Delhi. New productive sites and crisscrossing networks emerged, along with a vast economy of small and minor practices. The latter opened up a discursive space away from classic political acts of occupation of space or older notions of resistance. I want to argue that minor practices in Indian cities and perhaps in other parts of the post-colonial world went beyond classic post-Enlightenment discussions on everyday lives. To understand this point more clearly, we need to revisit the discussion of minor practices in social theory, notably the work of Michel de Certeau, with whom the concept has been most closely associated. In his *Practice of Everyday Life*, de Certeau distinguished "minor" practices from dominant or "foregrounded procedures": "A society is . . . composed of certain foregrounded practices organizing its normative institutions *and* of innumerable other practices that remain 'minor,' always there but not organizing discourses and preserving the beginnings or remains of different (institutional, scientific) hypotheses for that society or for others."[28] For de Certeau minor practices are implicated in the *productive* power of the everyday. He approached the everyday less from the standpoint of popular culture but from a certain gesture to the

Other. Thus for de Certeau the everyday is the "cultural activity of the non-producers of culture, an activity that is unsigned, unreadable and unsymbol-ized."[29] It is this productive banality that appealed to Meaghan Morris when she called for adopting de Certeau's work: "This is the banality which speaks in Everyman, and in the late work of Freud—where the ordinary is no longer the object of analysis but the *place* from which discourse is produced."[30] The logic for practice is tactical: it operates in the context of the marginalization of a large section of the population. Practice is not systematic: it is a mul-tiple series of effects that non-producers of culture generate in the everyday, crucially through consumption. This alternative productivity is "character-ised by its ruses, fragmentation (the result of the circumstances), its poach-ing, its clandestine nature, its tireless but quiet activity, in short by its quasi-invisibility, since it shows itself not in its own products (where would it place them?) but in an art of using those imposed upon it."[31] There are no true and false needs, nor is de Certeau interested in the motives of the tactical; he sees interest only in an *operational* logic of practice. De Certeau uses a Clauswitz-ian distinction between strategies and tactics. A strategy is the project of colonization of a particular place, the project of political, scientific, and eco-nomic rationality. A tactic is defined both by placelessness and a reliance on time. Though de Certeau warned against a "hagiographic everydayness," his *Practice of Everyday Life* is dedicated to the "ordinary man a common hero, an ubiquitous character, walking in countless thousands on the streets."[32] It is the unrecognized producers, "trail blazers in the jungle of functionalist rationality," who make the everyday radical, even though it lacks the mean-ing of older politics. De Certeau's prose is comparable to the older language of Marxism, albeit without the old subject-object of history: in its place we have the "marginal" and the "ordinary." Though the *Practice of Everyday Life* is devoid of an explicit discourse of resistance that has often been read into de Certeau's work, the utopian and psychoanalytic moments certainly offer space for such a reading.

De Certeau's important intervention needs a post-colonial revision while retaining the critical thrust of his work. "Minor" practices in Delhi and in many comparable urbanisms of Africa, Asia, and Latin America tended to be post-utopian, even post-political in the traditional sense. When import-substitution regimes based on national geographies retreated under economic crisis in the 1970s and the 1980s, new forms of urban strategy were deployed with great effect by migrants, squatters, and homeless populations. In urban Africa, as regimes failed to sustain the definitional aspects of rule (division of jurisdiction, policies), urban infrastructures were subject to heretical uses, with multiplication of sites of non-legal production and innovative recombi-nations.[33] This was the "pirate city," where the older infrastructure was either poached upon or incrementally built up by urban populations long abandoned by urban planning. Globalization increases the possibilities of this pirate urbanism by allowing the growth of low-cost (non-legal) networks spread across regions and generally weakening national sovereignty.[34] Cities increasingly failed to apply normative boundaries as had been hoped for by planning, and multiple circulations of commodities and money through unofficial channels further weakened civic authority, opening new channels for migrants to flow into peripheral neighborhoods. This kind of pirate urbanism has been noticed in Latin America (*piratas*), Africa, and the Middle East. Asef Bayat provides a vivid description of a similar world in Egypt.

> Cairo contains well over 100 "spontaneous" communities, or *manatiq al-ashwa'yya*, housing over seven million people who have subdivided agricultural lands, putting up their shelters unlawfully. The rural migrants and slum dwellers, on the other hand, have quietly claimed cemeteries, roof tops and the state/public land on the outskirts of the city, creating largely autonomous communities. By their sheer perseverance, millions of slum dwellers force the authorities to extend living amenities to their neighborhoods by otherwise tapping them illegally.[35]

This is a different "politics," often missed by older radical writers who tended to look for "resistance," public politics, or, worse, that catchall phrase, "civil society." Pirate urbanism could not fit any classic shoe, liberal or Enlightenment radical. Playing a complex game with the police, local officials, and slumlords and resisting periodic brutal displacement by city authorities, the new urban encroachments actually vastly expanded post-colonial cities in the 1970s and the 1980s. In this sense, though with significant local differences, India's capital city was no different.

In post-Emergency Delhi "minor practices" bypassed the normative framework of the plan, for the most part ignoring it. Neighborhoods, small factories, financing networks, and new workplaces in homes, markets, and roofs spread all over the city, particularly in the Trans-Yamuna districts and parts of West and North Delhi. Almost all of these sites grew in non-planned or unauthorized parts of the city. This growth predated the Emergency itself, but Delhi's pirate urbanism accelerated after 1977. As the unauthorized city grew, new municipal elections in 1982 opened the route for regularization of some areas, a mixture of neighborhood political mobilization, populism, and demands for infrastructure.

At any rate the secret or pirate city threw up a dizzying complexity of production sites, tenure, work practices, and agglomeration.[36] Every rule set up by the Masterplan was violated or "infringed," paradoxically contributing to the boom period of 1980–96 when production and markets grew at a dizzying pace. Small, flexible sites of production and circulation contributed most to this new morphology, feeding into political patronage at the local level, raising demands for regularization and infrastructure. The boom period allowed the city to absorb the hundreds of thousands of workers who streamed into Delhi after the Asian Games construction and the Punjab crisis. By the time the counteroffensive came in court judgments of the 1990s, Delhi had unknowingly become a metropolis with its own catalog of urban crisis and conflict.

New investigations reveal the remarkable fluidity of people, land tenures, things, and technologies across the city in the 1980s and the 1990s, often hidden by the hyperpolitical montage of that time. After studying Viswas Nagar, an East Delhi neighborhood for a decade, researcher Solomon Benjamin discovered that the classic worker-entrepreneur binary became fuzzy in small production clusters that dominated much of the non-legal city in that decade.

> Tracing life histories shows that these labels are interchangeable. Workers move on in three to five years to become foremen and after that, link to a variety of trajectories to start off their own firms in the main line of production, or into capital machinery. Some move to be trading agents. At times, these identities switch. Entrepreneurs and factory owners, even those from the financially astute group of the Marwari and Bania (trading castes), need to operate the machines on the shop floor to keep in close contact with the technological options that open up, and to respond to complex and dynamic market demands. Much of small firm finance is driven by complex local mechanisms such as pooled funds linked to real estate markets. These financial systems draw in all—workers, factory owners, renters and land "owners"—even if in varied degrees. This intimate knowledge of financier circuits, even if power within these is unequally distributed, is critically important to make possible transitions between factory owners/workers/traders/innovators/artisans.[37]

It appears that the slow erosion of models of surveillance built along sovereignties of the city plan and the nation enabled not just fluidity of work but also considerable travel—within countries and across borders. Globalization radicalized this movement as states collapsed as a result of wars (Africa) or economic crisis (Latin America). Illegal movements of migrants from Africa into Europe, and Latin America into the United States, have been accompanied by significant movements of small traders transporting goods across frontiers to bypass national-import export regimes. Simone speaks of illicit journeys not just to Europe but also to China and Taiwan as a source of cheap commodities that could be transported back home. Journeys were also made to Dubai, Istanbul, and Mumbai for similar purposes.[38] These travel stories of small traders began surfacing in all my encounters with small businessmen in Delhi, an increasing number of whom began traveling to east and Southeast Asia from the 1980s. These did always not come from traditional trading communities, similar to Simone's story of African traders. Lacking proper infrastructure, these were the "suitcase entrepreneurs" of post-colonial cities from the 1980s, whose ambition was not just local and national but also international and regional. The traveling salesman was an old figure in modern capitalism; the 1990s proliferation of small enterprise in India's cities saw a whole new generation of sales agents networking between pirate factories. Solomon Benjamin's fieldwork in the East Delhi pirate-industrial neighborhood of Viswas Nagar in the 1990s led him to describe suitcase entrepreneurs as

> Marketing agents traveling with their suitcases filled with samples of shoes, plastic fittings, small electrical products. . . . They use a low cost but an extensive network of trains and buses to reach retail and wholesale markets in this wider territory. The *Suitcase Entrepreneurs* come from various backgrounds. They can be specialized marketing agents employed by the large traders in Delhi's wholesale market for electrical products, *Bhagirath Palace*. They can also be marketing agents visiting Delhi from other smaller towns and cities.[39]

The rapid scrambling of urban work practices and spaces that took place in the 1980s has continued to this day and may indicate a new threshold in the expansion of post-colonial cities. Some have mapped this phenomenon onto a broader context of a "splintering urbanism"[40] in the wake of post-Fordist urban planning, where recent privatization of urban services transforms the very nature of urban life against which much of twentieth-century city writing had measured itself. The post-colonial expansion lacks the context of Fordism and a widespread public realm and infrastructure.

Wild Zone: Proliferation and Information

By the late 1980s the volatile mix of urban expansion, random violence, media explosions, and accelerating consumption set up the experience of living in Delhi as a series of kinetic shocks. Speed, an experience more associated with the commercial capital of Bombay, had arrived in Delhi. The Hindi writer Uday Prakash captured this mood well in one of his stories: "All around the pace of change was incredibly fast. Delhi had become a kaleidoscope. It had hundreds of brands of soaps, thousands of different kinds of toothpastes, a million different watches, thousands of different kinds of cars, panties, creams, brassieres, . . . compact discs, rifles remotes, cosmetics, designer condoms, tranquilizers."[41] In the same story, the endless landscape of consumption exists in the background of vast suburban growth, terrorism, assassinations, and the loss of memory to a world of things. In Prakash's city commodities that were explicitly artificial were becoming preponderant in daily life. This experience of the contemporary for millions of people, of a life where "nature" referred to memories before migration or childhood dreams, is close to what Walter Benjamin had once called the actuality of the everyday. This is a life where most of the urban residents know no products or objects other than those that are industrial, along with a perception of the present that seems never-ending, often mediated through the visual representations of events. Memories of the real "past" blur with memories of and identification with media narratives and experiences: television shows, cricket matches, film releases. This conceptual confusion between real and virtual memory, between "newness" and an eternal present, between objects and humans, shows a kind of untimely compression: features commonly associated in the West with "modernism" and "postmodernism" seemed to blur in one decade of flux.

It was in this confused cultural landscape that a pirate "aesthetic" emerged. This was particularly so in the early years of analog audio and video, layering the commodity (audio or video cassette) with an overinformationalized collage: ads, phone numbers, scrolling text, fake and real addresses. This found its way into different assemblages of space and network: local television, street advertisements, auto rickshaw and bus advertising, lamppost stickers. This crowding of surfaces set up an information zone of active disorientation in the initial years, blending into and sharpening the developing urban crisis. With its ever-expanding sensory and mobile worlds, pirate culture intensified the confusions between technology and the body as millions came into contact with a machine culture; there was a sense of the city as a delirious, out-of-control landscape of effects. In the same story, Uday Prakash captured this well: "Governments were formed and fell. . . . Everyone's memory was like a video cassette on which new images and voices were recorded every day and erased every night. Each morning everyone awoke with no recollection whatsoever of anything that had happened the previous day."[42] This bipolar vision of the city as a hellish present of technics and erasure reflects the feelings of the old left literary generation aghast at the speed and turmoil of the 1990s. There is a sense of the 1990s as a post-colonial Fall, with warping of space, desires, and an endless present.

A crucial space in the information zone of crisis was the emergence of aggressive local reporting and the dynamic headline in all the major papers. This made the newspaper an active archive of the present. Focusing on infrastructural collapse, headline font size increased steadily over the decade, racing to keep pace with an expanding city. Papers reported road accidents caused by speeding buses, regular blackouts, and water shortages. This sense of a city out of control even affected international reporting from Delhi. In 1993 the *New York Times* reported, "For the first time, there is a feeling of collapse here, the sense that this capital city—once a way station for Mogul armies, later an exhibition of British town planning by Sir Edwin Lutyens—is finally being overwhelmed by people and traffic and the final crumbling of fragile and inadequate public services." The report went on to quote Malavika Singh, who was then editor of *Business India*. The city was breaking apart, said Singh. "It's tearing at the seams. There's no power and water. The phones don't work. The bus drivers are mauling human beings as they go by. It is grim."[43] The story set up a picture of power outages, neighborhood riots, and garbage everywhere.

The prominence of crisis stories reflected a new form of writing and reporting about the city that emerged in the 1990s. The *Indian Express, Hindustan Times*, and the *Pioneer* all developed strong city reporting; later entrants were *The Hindu* and the *Times of India*. The Hindi papers with quality city reporting included *Jansatta* and *Rashtriya Sahara*, as well as the evening paper *Sandhya Times*. By the late 1990s Hindi television began offering Delhi-specific channels, which provided instant coverage of accidents. In print, local news began to gradually move to the front pages by the end of the 1990s; by 2005 city news had the same weight as national news. This reflected the growing predominance of an urban discourse in the city. Here narratives of consumption and spectacle coexisted with stories of death and disorder, sharpening the sensory experience of the growing metropolis. The newspapers' political reporting coexisted with an increase in the number of stories about brutal murders of old couples and families, infrastructure breakdowns, and traffic chaos. The urban reporting also presented a deliberate archival strategy: careful detailing, character types (victims, heroes, and villains), and an effort to move through diverse viewpoints—perhaps a diminishing quality in national journalism. While the reporting technique was almost surgical, akin to what Benjamin called the effects of the early film camera, it created a heightening of sensations through its sharp headlines and allegories of a dark city. Perceptions of urban disorder and untimely deaths increased as millions came into contact with a rapidly changing city. The narratives of the 1990s operated within a rapid traffic of urban crisis, shock, and media forms that reenacted them. This traveled from the social world of the city to the media and back, creating a dynamic interface that reinvented the relationship between the material and the imaginary. Stories about disasters, pollution, crime, and accident statistics flowed between print headlines, roadside electronic boards, text messages to mobile phones, and television ticker headlines. By publicly mixing delirium with death, the information zone unintentionally drew attention to an injured public body of the city.

Agglomeration, Crowds, and Power

Twentieth-century movements of proliferation and urban circulation combine the movements of modern capitalist commodities, money, and media. When this dynamic arrangement of money and media exceeds established orders of management and individual adaptation during crisis, the effects are visceral and devastating. In Elias Canetti's book *Crowds and Power*, the massification of urban life through commodification and rationalization becomes a productive force: the loss of individual autonomy is paralleled by the growth of power when the person joins a crowd. This dialectic is rendered turbulent during the crisis of runaway inflation. Canetti writes: "An inflation cancels out distinctions between men which had seemed eternal and brings together in that same inflation people who would scarcely have nodded to each other in the street."[44] In Canetti's prescient phenomenology the dialectic of the crowd and power is suddenly reversed in crisis, expanding numerically and across classes while losing power materially as money devalues. Only that which is outside circulation like treasure or family gold becomes valuable because it is rare. As in Canetti's narrative, the Indian Supreme Court's judgments on the city produced a parallel technique of agglomeration and exposure: everyone and every space that had gone outside the law of the city set up in the plan now became a culprit. These ranged from slum dwellers to shopkeepers, roadside repair shops to large stores in "unauthorized" land, a vast army of culprits before the court. If in Canetti the abstract movement of falling money value is the motor behind the expanding crowd during inflation, the Supreme Court judgment uses the formal abstraction of law to constitute the many.

In marking the centrality of the crowd to power, Canetti draws on and comments on the vast archive of European modernism. Here the crowd regulates the relationship between the individual and the mass, the public and the bystander, revolution and counterrevolution, as well as the techniques of the observer, the flaneur, and the detective, the vast corpus of the modern architectural movements from Corbusier to Mies, modern management, and surveillance in general. This centrality of the crowd has declined in contemporary urban discourse as well as urban planning. There is simply no easy road back to the prewar urban archive of the crowd, with a specific European drama of modernism and its avant-garde critic.

Yet in Canetti's formulation there is the deep insight of how agglomeration produces potential powers that get exposed and deployed in crisis. It was this potential power of the crowd redeemed from the mass that drove Walter Benjamin to examine the electric relationship between commodities, crowds, and death in his explorations on Paris in a terrain that stretched from Baudelaire to Blanqui. Benjamin revisits nineteenth-century Paris as a vast archive of productive phantasmagorias and hallucinations, commodities and corpses, debris that has gone out of circulation. It is both a hallucinatory and terrifying primal history of the modern European city, containing within it the "secret history" of urbanism to be unlocked with constellations, optical devices, and new critiques. In this journey there are always potential overflows[45]—of commodities leaving circulation or signs escaping design, taking on an afterlife. It is this ascription of a radical potentiality in the corporeal encounter between things and humans that is the weak link between Benjamin's time and ours. In the very moment that Benjamin was drawn to the mythic power of the crowd through his exploration of Baudelaire and Blanqui, he opened a way beyond it.

Conclusion

The plan gave way to something that still does not have a name in Lagos and in Delhi. For practical reasons I will call it the bypass.[46] This bypass emerged as a pragmatic appropriation of the city, more *media res* than "marginal." For many the bypass *was* the city, as much as such a thing can have a body or a persona. The bypass does not fit classical representational political technologies: the resistant, the tactical, the marginal, the multitude, or the movement. The bypass provides us with a vast parallel archive of the present of sounds, images, and disturbing countermemories, of new publics and cultural worlds of subaltern populations that flowed into the city from the 1980s. The bypass took its power from productive proliferation acting with a viral force that spread everywhere, producing a crisis in urban management, legal theory, and neighborhood politics. A fast-changing assembly of practices, the bypass imaged both the productive and disturbed lives of Delhi in the long decade. As a form of life indifferent to the law of the plan, the bypass became for the elites an allegory of the decline of Delhi.[47] The bypass was equally the site of vast, everyday violent encounters between urban populations and collapsing infrastructures, exposing public displays of technological death in the media. In every sense this constellation recalled the mixture of death, commodity worlds, technology, and desire that formed part of Benjamin's primal history of the nineteenth century.

Notes

1 A fragment of this chapter also appears in my book *Pirate Modernity: Delhi's Media Urbanism* (New York: Routledge, 2009).

2 The reference is to a well-known interview by Gilles Deleuze and Félix Guattari, "Capitalism: A Very Special Delirium," http://www.generation-online.org/p/fpdeleuze7.htm. The "long" 1980s can be dated from the late 1970s to the beginning of this century: the years including and preceding the period commonly called globalization, which is formally dated in India from the early 1990s.

3 Mike Davis, *Planet of Slums* (New York: Verso, 2006).

4 See his essay in Okwui Enwezor, Carlos Basualdo, Ute Meta Bauer, Susanne Ghez, Sarat Maharaj, Mark Nash, and Octavio Zaya, eds., *Under Siege: Four African Cities, Freetown, Johannesburg, Kinshasa, Lagos, Documenta11_Platform4* (Ostfildern-Ruit: Hatje Kantz, 2003).

5 Antoine Picon, "Anxious Landscapes: From the Ruin to Rust," *Grey Room*, no. 1 (Fall 2000): 64–83.

6 Rem Koolhaas, "Junkspace," *October* 100 (Spring 2002): 175–90.

7 See Fredric Jameson, "Future City," *New Left Review* 21 (May–June 2003): 65–79.

8 Anthony Vidler, *The Architectural Uncanny: Essays in the Modern Unhomely* (Cambridge, MA: MIT Press, 1994).

9 See Ananya Roy and Nezar AlSayyad, *Urban Informality: Transnational Perspectives from the Middle East, Latin America, and South Asia* (Lanham, MD: Lexington Books, 2004).

10 In 1972 the ILO used the term "informality" in its report on Kenya; the economic anthropologist Keith Hart had pioneered the idea in 1971 at a conference in Sussex. Hart provides a concise summary in a recent reflection: "The 'formal sector' consisted of regulated economic activities and the 'informal sector' of all those, both legal and illegal, lying beyond the scope of regulation. I did not identify the informal economy with a place, a class, a type of business or even whole persons. Informal opportunities ranged from market gardening and brewing through every kind of trade to gambling, theft and political corruption. My analysis had its roots in what people generate out of the circumstances of their everyday lives. The laws and offices of state bureaucracy only made their search for self-preservation and improvement more difficult." See the archive of Hart's writings at http://www.thememorybank.co.uk/.

11 See Solomon Benjamin, *"Productive Slums": The Centrality of Urban Land in Shaping Employment and City Politics* (Cambridge, MA: Lincoln Institute of Land Policy, 2005).

12 Timothy Mitchell, "The Properties of Markets" (working paper no. 2, Cultural Political Economy Research Group, University of Lancaster, 2004).

13 Timothy Mitchell, *Rule of Experts: Egypt, Techno-politics, Modernity* (Berkeley: University of California Press, 2002).

14 See Asef Bayat, "From 'Dangerous Classes' to 'Quiet Rebels': Politics of the Urban Subaltern in the Global South," *International Sociology* 15.3 (2000): 533–57.

15 Mike Davis combines World Bank reports, planner documents, and Marxist writings to call these new areas "pirate urbanization" where slumlords, speculators, and other sundry elements encourage privatized squatting over fallow or unproductive zones. Peri-urban and pirate urbanization are part of the morphology of urban hell in Davis's image of the "slum."

16 See Faye Ginsburg, ed., with Lila Abu-Lughod and Brian Larkin, *Media Worlds: Anthropology on New Terrain* (Berkeley: University of California Press, 2002).

17 Given Koolhaas's use of cybernetic metaphors in his essay, it is remarkable that he ignores the presence of a vibrant urban media in Lagos. For a useful corrective, see Brian Larkin, "Degraded Images, Distorted Sounds: Nigerian Video and the Infrastructure of Piracy," *Public Culture* 16.2 (2004): 289–314.

18 Cited in Vidler, *The Architectural Uncanny*, 178.

19 The old Moghul capital area of Shahjehanabad was called slum-like in the new planning documents.

20 The statistics on Delhi are voluminous. For a useful introduction, see the *Delhi Human Development Report* (Delhi: Oxford University Press, 2006).

21 The Masterplan team was composed largely of U.S. urban planners invited by the Ford Foundation to Delhi in consultation with the Indian government. Mayer was involved in a number of projects and was well regarded by Nehru. Mayer and his team worked through the 1950s to produce various drafts of the Masterplan.

22 Partha Chatterjee, *The Politics of the Governed: Reflections on Popular Politics in Most of the World* (New York: Columbia University Press, 2004).

23 The process was not without cruel irony. The long-forgotten document was reprinted by pirate publishers and sold on Delhi's pavements, finding a ready market among anxious residents fearing "non-conformity."

24 The best known of these were those initiated by the environmental campaigner M. C. Mehta, which led to the first of the dramatic judgments in the 1990s on polluting industries in Delhi.

25 The process began on February 16, 2006. See http://www.hindu.com/2006/02/17/stories/2006021711930100.htm for the story. The special committees consisted of non-elected "experts" and judicial officials appointed by the court to advise it. The committees were appointed on March 24, 2006.

26 The new artificial-industrial smells could be contrasted to the old fragrances of flower trees, fruit seasons of mango and *jamun* (a local plum), bazaars, and sweetshops, regularly celebrated by Delhi's poets and writers.

27 Ravi Sundaram, "Recycling Pirate Modernity," *Third Text*, no. 47 (Summer 1999): 59–65.

28 Michel de Certeau, *The Practice of Everyday Life* (Berkeley: University of California Press, 2002), 48.

29 Ibid., xviii.

30 Meaghan Morris, "Banality in Cultural Studies," in *Logics of Television*, ed. P. Mellencamp (Bloomington: Indiana University Press, 1990), 35.

31 De Certeau, *The Practice of Everyday Life*, 31.

32 Ibid.

33 AbdouMaliq Simone, "Pirate Towns: Reworking Social and Symbolic Infrastructures in Johannesburg and Douala," *Urban Studies* 43.2 (2006): 357–70.

34 This view is seconded by Simone, "Pirate Towns," 357.

35 Asef Bayat, "Un-Civil Society: The Politics of the 'Informal People,'" *Third World Quarterly* 18.1 (1997): 54.

36 See *Delhi Human Development Report*, chapter 2, for useful statistics including informal patterns of work and industry.

37 Solomon Benjamin, "Touts, Pirates and Ghosts," in *Bare Acts*, Sarai Reader 5 (Delhi: CSDS, 1995).

38 Simone, "Pirate Towns."

39 Solomon Benjamin, "The Lifestyle Advertisement and the Marxist Manifesto as Trojan Horses in a City of Stealth" (unpublished paper, 2005).

40 Stephen Graham and Simon Marvin, *Splintering Urbanism, Networked Infrastructures, Technological Mobilities and the Urban Condition* (London: Routledge, 2001).

41 Uday Prakash, *Short Shorts Long Shorts* (Delhi: Katha, 2003), 166.

42 Ibid.

43 Edward Gargan, "New Delhi Journal; And Now, Killer Buses: It's Just Too, Too Much," *New York Times*, June 12, 1993.

44 Elias Canetti, *Crowds and Power* (New York: Viking, 1960), 187.

45 See in particular the "Space for Rent," in *One Way Street: Selected Works*, ed. Marcus Bullock and Michael W. Jennings (Cambridge, MA: Belknap Press, 1996), 1:476.

46 The Indian Supreme Court's own legal language would call it "non-conforming," i.e., that which does not conform to the plan.

47 By 2004 vast displacements of squatter camps were under way as a result of the Supreme Court's rulings. In 2006 this was expanded by the court to include all non-legal forms (home extensions, shops, and establishments) and resulted in a major crisis in the city. After a number of general strikes later, the government hurriedly rushed through a new Masterplan to try and accommodate most establishments save the largest. The fate of the migrant squatter camps (*bastis*) remains the same as before: violent displacement to the periphery of the city.

Contributors

∎

David R. Ambaras is associate professor of history at North Carolina State University. His current research examines the experiences of down-and-out Japanese, discourses of marginality and social failure, and representations of "spaces of distress" in modern Japan and in East Asia under Japanese imperialism. He is the author of *Bad Youth: Juvenile Delinquency and the Politics of Everyday Life in Modern Japan* (2006).

James Donald is professor of film studies and dean of the Faculty of Arts and Social Sciences at the University of New South Wales in Sydney, Australia. He is author of *Imagining the Modern City* (1999), *Sentimental Education: Schooling, Popular Culture and the Regulation of Liberty* (1992), and the *Penguin Atlas of Media and Information* (2001); his edited books include *Thresholds: Psychoanalysis and Cultural Theory* (1991), *"Race," Culture and Difference* (1992), and *Close Up, 1927–1933: Cinema and Modernism* (1998). His main research project at present is on the modernism of Josephine Baker and Paul Robeson, funded by an Australian Research Council Discovery Grant.

Rubén Gallo is the author of *Mexican Modernity: The Avant-Garde and the Technological Revolution* (2005). His most recent book is *Freud's Mexico: Into the Wilds of Psychoanalysis* (2010). He teaches at Princeton University, where he directs the Latin American Studies Program.

Anton Kaes is the Class of 1939 Professor of German and Film Studies at the University of California, Berkeley. He is the author of several books in English and German that deal with multidisciplinary and comparative aspects of film history and theory, including the recent *Shell Shock Cinema: Weimar Culture and the Wounds of War* (2009). Major awards include Fellowships of the Rockefeller Foundation in 1978 and the Humboldt Foundation in 1984/85, a Guggenheim Fellowship in 1990, and an NEH and UC President's Research Fellowship in 1995. He was also a Scholar in Residence at the Getty Center for Art History and the Humanities in 1989–90 and at Bellagio in 1998. In 2007 he was the recipient of the Humboldt Research Prize.

Ranjani Mazumdar is associate professor of cinema studies at the School of Arts and Aesthetics, Jawaharlal Nehru University in New Delhi, an independent filmmaker, and was a Fellow at the Shelby Cullom Davis Center at Princeton University in 2003–4. She is the author of *Bombay Cinema: An Archive of the City* (2007). Her documentaries include *Delhi Diary 2001* (2001) on violence, memory, and the city; and *The Power of the Image* (co-directed), a television series on Bombay cinema. Her current research focuses on cinema in the 1960s, globalization and film culture, and film and history.

Gyan Prakash is Dayton-Stockton Professor of History at Princeton, and served as the director of Shelby Cullom Davis Center at Princeton University during 2003–8. A historian of modern India, his research interests include urban modernity, the colonial genealogies of modernity, and problems of post-colonial thought and politics. He is the author of *Bonded Histories: Genealogies of Labor Servitude in Colonial India* (1990) and *Another Reason: Science and the Imagination of Modern India* (1999). He has also edited several volumes of essays, including *After Colonialism: Imperial Histories and Postcolonial Displacements* (1995). His current research interest centers on urban history, and his book *Mumbai Fables* will be published in 2010.

Jennifer Robinson is professor of urban geography at the Open University in the United Kingdom and Honorary Professor in the African Centre for Cities at the University of Cape Town. Her recent book, *Ordinary Cities: Between Modernity and Development* (2006), offers a post-colonial critique of urban studies, explaining and contesting urban theory's neglect of cities of the global South. She is currently working on regrounding comparative methods to support a more properly international urban studies, and is developing a comparative research project on the politics of city strategies.

Mark Shiel is senior lecturer in the Department of Film Studies at King's College London. He is the author of *The Real Los Angeles: Hollywood, Cinema, and the City of Angels* (2010) and *Italian Neorealism: Rebuilding the Cinematic City* (2005); he is the coeditor of *Screening the City* (2003) and *Cinema and the City* (2001). He was a Fellow at the Shelby Cullom Davis Center at Princeton University in 2006–7, and his research has been funded by the British Academy and the Leverhulme Trust.

Ravi Sundaram is a Fellow of the Centre for the Study of Developing Societies and was a Fellow at the Shelby Cullom Davis Center at Princeton University in 2007–8. He is the author of *Pirate Modernity: Delhi's Media*

Urbanism (2009). His work rests at the intersection of the city and contemporary media experiences, and he is one the initiators of Sarai, an alternative, nonprofit space for an imaginative reconstitution of urban public culture, new/old media practice and research, and critical cultural interventions. As a member of the editorial collective of the Sarai Reader series, he has coedited its critically acclaimed publications: *The Public Domain* (2001), *The Cities of Everyday Life* (2002), *Shaping Technologies* (2003), *Crisis Media* (2004), and *Turbulence* (2006).

William M. Tsutsui is professor of history and dean of Dedman College of Humanities and Sciences at Southern Methodist University. A specialist in the business, environmental, and cultural history of twentieth-century Japan, he holds degrees from Harvard, Oxford, and Princeton universities. He is the author or editor of seven books, including *Manufacturing Ideology: Scientific Management in Twentieth-Century Japan* (1998) and *Godzilla on My Mind: Fifty Years of the King of Monsters* (2004). He received the 2000 John Whitney Hall Prize of the Association for Asian Studies and the 2005 William Rockhill Nelson Award for Literary Excellence.

Li Zhang is professor of anthropology at the University of California, Davis. She is the author of *Strangers in the City: Reconfigurations of Space, Power, and Social Networks within China's Floating Population* (2001) and *In Search of Paradise: Middle-Class Living in a Chinese Metropolis* (2010). She is currently working on a new project that explores the rise of psychotherapy and self-care in reform China.

Index

Note: Page numbers in *italics* indicate photographs or illustrations.